Buckle Street

High where the valley's edge gave a line to the
Old road that bore Rome's rulers and warriors
   Along the wild hill-spine, and steered them
      Down to the plains and the ways of judgment,

There flows a stream now, bedded in rubble and
Unnaturally suspended above the banks
   Of ancient plunging woodlands, calmly
      Watering genial upland pastures.

So Grace, the invader, scornful of gravity,
Follows the traces left by our interdicts,
   Scoops out from hard-core legal strictures
      Runnels of kindly communication.

THE WAYS OF JUDGMENT

The Bampton Lectures, 2003

Oliver O'Donovan

WILLIAM B. EERDMANS PUBLISHING COMPANY
GRAND RAPIDS, MICHIGAN / CAMBRIDGE, U.K.

© 2005 Wm. B. Eerdmans Publishing Co.

All rights reserved

Wm. B. Eerdmans Publishing Co.
255 Jefferson Ave. S.E., Grand Rapids, Michigan 49503 /
P.O. Box 163, Cambridge CB3 9PU U.K.

Printed in the United States of America

10 09 08 07 06 05   7 6 5 4 3 2 1

Library of Congress Cataloging-in-Publication Data

O'Donovan, Oliver.
The ways of judgement / Oliver O'Donovan.
p.   cm.
Includes bibliographical references and index.
ISBN 0-8028-2920-1 (cloth: alk. paper)
1. Political ethics. I. Title.
JA79.036 2005

172 — dc22

2005045107

www.eerdmans.com

Contents

III. LIFE BEYOND JUDGMENT: COMMUNICATION

Acknowledgments

As well as acknowledging my obligation to the Bampton Trustees for the invitation to deliver the Bampton Lectures in 2003, I should thank those institutions which invited me to speak and gave me an opportunity to discuss the questions raised here at various stages in my preparation: the University of Erlangen-Nürmberg, Bavaria; the Institution of Religion and Public Life, New York, where I gave the Erasmus Lecture in 1998; the University of Tulsa, Oklahoma, where I gave the Snuggs Lecture in 1999; the Law and Religion Institute, Emory University, Atlanta, Georgia; the Christian Theological Research Fellowship, Boston (1999); Societas Ethica, meeting at Askov, Denmark, in 2000; the Università Gregoriana, Rome, where I gave the McCarthy Philosophy Lecture in 2001; Valparaiso University, Indiana; SKH Ming Hua Theological College and St. John's College, Hong Kong, where I gave the Cheung Siu Kwai Lectures in 2002, and the Dean and Canons of Westminster Abbey, where I gave the Gore Lecture in 2002.

Thanks are due to the publishers of the following articles which bear more than a chance connection to parts of this book: "Epikie," "Liberté(b)," "Peine," "Révolution," from *Dictionnaire Critique de Théologie*, ed. I.-Y. Lacoste (Paris: Presses Universitaires de France, 1998); "Gerechtigkeit und Urteil, übgstzt, Bernd Wannenwetsch," *Neue Zeitschrift für Systematische Theologie und Religionsphilosophie* 40, no. 1 (1998): 1-16; "Government as Judgment," *First Things* 92 (1999): 36-44; "Payback: Thinking about Retribution," *Books & Culture*, July-August 2000, pp. 16-21; "Deliberation, History and Reading: A Response to

vii

Schweiker and Wolterstorff," *Scottish Journal of Theology* 54, no. 1 (2001): 127-44; "Law, Moderation and Forgiveness," *Gregorianum* 82, no. 4 (2001): 625-36, also in *Church as Politeia: The Political Self-Understanding of Christianity,* ed. Christoph Stumpf and Holger Zaborowski (Berlin: de Gruyter, 2004), pp. 1-11.

Too many individuals have helped me in discussion to be named separately; but I must express my continual debt, now as always, to my wife, Dr. Joan Lockwood O'Donovan, and to my Oxford colleague, Dr. Bernd Wannenwetsch. I am grateful, not for the first time, to the staff at Eerdmans, and especially Jon Pott, Editor-in-Chief, for encouragement and help; and finally to James Mumford, to whose labors I owe the compilation of the index.

Introduction

In a work entitled *The Desire of the Nations,* published a decade ago, I outlined what I called a "political theology," the purpose of which was to show how the political concepts wrapped up in Jewish and Christian speech about God's redemption of the world still had political force, generating expectations for political life that found one type of expression, though not the only possible one, in the political ideals of "Christendom," the European civilization that bridged the gap from late antiquity to early modernity, from which our modern political ideals have sprung.[1] At the end of that book I anticipated a sequel, a "Christian political ethics," the agenda of which would be set by political rather than by theological questions.

This present essay, based on the Bampton Lectures delivered in 2003 in St. Mary's Church, Oxford, attempts to fulfill that hesitant promise. Yet like so many intellectual promises, made with a high mountain view of the terrain and then worked out on the valley floor, this one has changed shape in the keeping. I am more cautious now about the pseudo-disciplinary designations, "political theology" and "political ethics." They correspond in a rough way, it is true, to the two ways of ordering the discussion, theological questions uppermost in the one, political questions in the other. But the suggested contrast of theory and practice, "theology" and "ethics," is misleading. The mysterious relation between the reflective and the deliberative operations of moral

---

1. *The Desire of the Nations* (Cambridge: Cambridge University Press, 1996).

ix

thought does not allow that kind of subject-division between them. Practical deliberation has no subject matter of its own but what is given it by reflection, and reflection needs no practical supplement other than simply turning the attention to the demands of action. The contents of this book, then, are no less theoretical than those of the earlier one, the argument of the earlier book no less practical than that which appears here. The second continues the exploration that the first began, into how theological and political concepts correspond; but it approaches the correspondence more from the political side.

I think of the two books as two phases in a single extended train of thought, then, and even dare to dream of the occasional reader who may take them one after the other in succession. That reader, at least, will appreciate how the train of thought is, like all worthwhile intellectual explorations, circular in its structure, delivering us back in the final chapter of the second book to the point from which we set out in the introduction to the first. In other ways the two books have a certain parallelism, both beginning with an examination of the political act, the act of judgment, and only then proceeding to the institutions of judgment in the political community. The second section of this work explores the shape of these institutions, and the third section takes up, as a theme for which the groundwork was laid in the first book, the formal opposition between political institutions and the church.

The enterprise is superficially similar to, but very different in spirit from, a line of enquiry promoted under the title "political theology" in the second half of the twentieth century, which also argued for the correlation of theological and political concepts, but made the former depend on the latter. After showing how theologians of the past had been the stooges of the political forces that made use of them, political theology set out to reorder our theological concepts to the service of a suitably liberal political world-view. The proper political orientations were taken to be well understood, the shape of our theological beliefs indefinitely negotiable. I start from diametrically opposite assumptions. The Gospel proclamation I take to be, in its essential features, luminous, the political concepts needed to interpret the social and institutional realities around us obscure and elusive. The work of political theology is to shed light from the Christian faith upon the intricate challenge of thinking about living in late-modern Western society.

I make no claims for my train of thought other than the claim proper to every work of theology: here faith seeks understanding. It is enough, perhaps, that I have thought these thoughts in my attempt to think the Christian faith as a practical commitment in my time and circumstance. Let those who can think them with me know that I am glad of their company; let those who cannot, accept a cheerful salutation on parting. But it may help the waverers if I point out where I think the value of such an enterprise as this especially lies. It has, in the first place, pastoral importance: to give guidance to those who, believing the Christian faith or capable of suspending their unbelief, have to exercise political responsibilities. Nothing very specialized need be envisaged here; we need not confine political ethics to the mirror-for-princes mold, as a professional science of politicians or civil servants. The responsibilities are those which we all face, regardless of our views on political institutions and the propriety of taking a leading role in them. In offering guidance from within the discourse of the church there need be no prejudice in favor of an "established-church" as opposed to a "peace-church" ideal, no preference for the life of a politician over that of a hermit. Hermit and politician both have to make up their minds as to whether they can acknowledge the institutions that claim to serve them (democratic elections, civil courts, or whatever), and whether they can or cannot defend some policy enacted in the name of the community of which they are part (decriminalizing cannabis, or going to war). We all have many occasions to decide whether to approve or disapprove. Insignificant as they may seem, such decisions are not inconsequential for our moral and spiritual integrity.

Political thought is, in its broadest view, a train of practical reasoning about practical reason, a reflection on how, by whom, when, and in what order decisions are to be made by human beings on human action. It is a reflective train of thought, not oriented directly to the last, deliberative moment of practical reason, the "point of decision," but to the social setting from within which that final point may be approached. If it is to be approached intelligently, the institutions and practices that generated it must themselves be intelligible. Deliberative political questions presuppose descriptions of political forms and realities. But these descriptions are not value-neutral systemic analyses; for without a knowledge of the good which political practices serve, analysis can give no account of the way in which they serve it. Political description is helpful only if it makes the institutions morally intelligible.

Political thought is therefore caught in a characteristic middle position between the *de jure* and the *de facto:* on the one hand, critical of moral judgments when they are dissociated and out of touch with institutional realities; on the other, critical of institutions when they fail to realize the moral goals that they presuppose.

We may be tempted to think that those with practical questions to resolve may excuse themselves the analytical endeavor and leave it to others in the division of intellectual labor. But political theory is neither an exact nor a progressive science, such as would allow us merely to keep up with its results. There are great political thinkers from whom no other thinker can afford not to learn, but they are not "experts" and they publish no "findings." Political theory shares with all philosophy the character of having no findings other than the arguments that lead to them. If political deliberation is to learn from political reflection, it must first undertake that reflection. If it is to be Christian deliberation, it must undertake Christian reflection.

Christian political thought has also acquired a secondary value in the circumstances of our time, which may, however, be no less important: it has an *apologetic* force when addressed to a world where the intelligibility of political institutions and traditions is seriously threatened. Christian theology sheds light on institutions and traditions, to address a crisis that is more pressing on unbelievers than on believers; and so it also offers reasons to believe. In our days it is not religious believers that suffer a crisis of confidence. Believers *did* suffer a serious one two or three generations ago, and the results of that crisis in small church attendance and the de-Christianizing of institutions are still working themselves out around us. But that crisis was precipitated by the presence of a rival confidence, a massive cultural certainty that united natural science, democratic politics, technology, and colonialism. Today this civilizational ice-shelf has broken up, and though some of the icebergs floating around are huge — natural science and technology, especially, drift on as though nothing has happened — they are not joined together anymore, nor joined to the land. The four great facts of the twentieth century that broke the certainty in pieces were two world wars, the reversal of European colonization, the threat of the nuclear destruction of the human race, and, most recently, the evidence of long-term ecological crisis. The master-narrative that was to have delivered us the crown of civilization has delivered us insuperable dangers.

So Western civilization finds itself the heir of political institutions and traditions which it values without any clear idea why, or to what extent, it values them. Faced with decisions about their future development it has no way of telling what counts as improvement and what as subversion. It cannot tell where "straight ahead" lies, let alone whether it ought to keep on going there. The master-narrative has failed; and even its most recent revised edition, announced as "postmodern," which declares the collapse to be the glorious last chapter, and plurality to be the great unifying principle, merely stands to the failure as the angel in the famous Czech joke stands to his own constant failures of prediction: "It's all in the plan! Don't worry! It's all in the plan!"

Now, apologetics is not a distinct genre of religious thinking. There are no apologetic reasons and arguments that do not belong in the ordered exposition of Christian belief traditionally known as "doctrine." The only satisfactory reason *to* believe is the reason *of* belief. If I could think out for myself a total and rationally coherent account of all my beliefs, I would have found all the reasons I knew for anyone else to believe as I believed. If I were then to urge some *other* reason for believing, it would have to be a pseudo-reason that I did not myself believe, and I would be a charlatan. Apologetics is, on the other hand, a distinct genre of *exposition*. For dialogue's sake I may organize my account of my beliefs in relation to somebody else's doubts or counter-arguments. The rational equilibrium remains the same: a reason for an unbeliever not to be swayed by an argument against belief is at the same time a reason for a believer not to be swayed by it. Yet different trains of theological thought may acquire greater or lesser apologetic weight circumstantially, as the crises or doubts of the culture may dictate at any moment. One train of Christian thought that carries apologetic weight in our times is the capacity of faith to display the intelligibility of political institutions and traditions.

At the end of a long period in which apologetics has concentrated on a narrow range of questions of epistemology and coherence, it is useful to recall the essential provisions of the will of John Bampton, Canon of Salisbury (*ob.* 1751), which was formerly reproduced at the head of every set of Bampton Lectures. Eight "divinity lecture sermons" were to be preached "upon either of the following subjects: to confirm and establish the Christian Faith, and to confute all heretics and schismatics — upon the divine authority of the Holy Scriptures — upon the authority of the writings of the primitive Fathers, as to the Faith and Practice of the primitive Church — upon the Divinity of our Lord and Saviour Jesus Christ — upon the Divinity of the Holy Ghost — upon the Articles of the Christian Faith, as comprehended in the Apostles' and Nicene Creeds." The alternative posed by the phrase "either of the following subjects . . ." is that of positive or negative Christian teaching, dogmatics or apologetics. This alternative is then elaborated by a list of the subjects that struck the testator in the mid-eighteenth century as urgent, whether in positive or negative form. The curiosity is that all these subjects could commend themselves as themes of apologetics. In eighteenth-century England, however, the battle-lines with unbelief fell, as Bampton's contemporaries understood it, along the fault-line between natural and revealed theology, and between Unitarianism and Trinitarianism. The mention of "schismatics" reminds us that for them belief had immediately political implications, too, and that crown as well as church might be threatened by loss of faith in the doctrines of the Apostles' and Nicene Creeds. My contribution may justify itself in terms of Bampton's foundation as taking up the task of confuting schismatics. The political concerns are very different. It is not a particular régime we are concerned to defend, nor the order of "Christendom" in general, but the coherence of political conceptions as such.[2] The argument that follows is that this coherence depends in important and surprising ways upon the faith expressed in the creeds.

I do not intend what is dismissively called "legitimation." The Christian faith is not to be offered to the world as the only hope for democracy and human rights, though there may be occasional observations to be made along those lines *en passant.* The display I have in mind is more critical, and the intelligibility more ambivalent. Recovery of theological description enables us to understand not only what the goods of our institutions and traditions are, but why and how those goods are limited

2. The minor notoriety gained by *The Desire of the Nations* as a "defense of Christendom" was somewhat unexpected by its author. For this discussion see nuanced assessments by Stanley Hauerwas and James Fodor, "Remaining in Babylon," *Studies in Christian Ethics* 11, no. 2 (1998): 30-55; by William Schweiker, "Freedom and Authority in Political Theology," *Scottish Journal of Theology* 54, no. 1 (2001): 110-26; and by Colin J. D. Greene, "Revisiting Christendom," in *A Royal Priesthood?: The Use of the Bible Ethically and Politically,* ed. C. Bartholomew et al. (Carlisle: Paternoster Press, 2002), pp. 314-40. Each is accompanied by my own response.

and corruptible, and to what corresponding errors they have made us liable. It enables us, in other words, to understand the dilemmas that our tradition has generated. Some of these may be susceptible of practical resolution, some may be intractable; but coping even with the intractable ones requires us to understand what it is that is intractable about them. We need the reality of our own political experience disclosed to us, as the prevailing master-narratives cannot disclose them. Christian theology in these circumstances resumes its ancient role of educating a people in the practical reasonableness required for their political tasks.

We may perhaps extend this into a general claim about ethics and apologetics: the critical edge of the encounter between belief and unbelief often locates itself where faith displays an ability to comprehend the tasks of life. It was an evil day for Christian thought when prophecy became the fashionable category for political reflection in place of practical reasonableness. On the threshold of the 1848 revolutions Kierkegaard remarked ironically that "in this age in which so little is actually done, such an extraordinary amount occurs in the way of prophecies." A prophet has no need of ethics, for "he makes prophecies, nothing more . . . a prophet can do no more anyway."[3] But ethics has by its nature the force of an apologetic, not merely because the existence of a community reflecting systematically out of Christian belief upon the challenges of living in love is "attractive," as children playing an innocent game may be attractive, but because it is interpretative. It gives us reason to believe that our lives are not, after all, merely thrown together, but are susceptible of a coordinated social meaning, even a beauty, such as St. Paul called a *taxis*.

3. *A Literary Review,* trans. Alistair Hannay (Harmondsworth: Penguin Books, 2001), pp. 94-95.

PART I

The Political Act: Judgment

I

The Act of Judgment

The authority of secular government resides in the practice of judgment. That is the thesis that the argument of this book will sustain, and it summarizes a characteristic biblical approach to government which has had a decisive effect in shaping the Western political
tradition. It has deep roots in ancient Israel's political experience, where,
at an early point in history, the "judge" *(shophet)* was apparently the only
standing officer of the Twelve Tribes, there being no other central institution, so that even the provision of military leadership fell to the
judge's care, as on the notable occasion in the narrative of the book of
Judges when the judge was a woman. Under the monarchy the king was
conceived as a judge, separating the wicked from the righteous, as appears in the little Psalm 101, a royal oath that ends with the alarming
promise, "Morning by morning I will destroy all the wicked in the land"
— that is to say, the king will hold judicial assizes daily. In the anonymous exilic oracle against Moab at Isa. 16:5 the restoration of the throne
is spoken of in terms of "one who judges and seeks justice." And in the
First Servant-Song of Deutero-Isaiah, where the Servant is depicted as a
king, it is said that he will "bring judgment to the nations . . . in his law
the islands will put their hope" (Isa. 42:1, 4). Yet it would be an oversim-
plification to say that in ancient Israel judgment was the essential function of government. Not least, it would fail to account for the two great
figures on whom so much reflection is focussed, those of Moses and
David. The one, as deliverer and lawgiver, stands *behind* the judges of Israel; he is the source of their authority, not of their number. The other,

as the recipient of a personal covenant with YHWH, underpins the identity of the people as a whole.

For the proposition that the authority of government resides *essentially* in the act of judgment, we must turn to the New Testament, where St. Paul described the function of civil authority as to reward the just and punish the evil (Rom. 13:4). Such an interpretation of authority, though this has not often been recognized, is in fact an iconoclastic one. It self-consciously dispenses with other functions of political authority that must have suggested themselves to readers of the Hebrew Scriptures as well as observers of the Roman world; it strips down the role of government to the single task of judgment, and forbids human rule to pretend to sovereignty, the consummation of the community's identity in the power of its ruler. This is, of course, in part an acknowledgment of the purely secular character of government in the Christian era — "secular," that is, not by its own profession, which is irrelevant, but by its actual position in salvation history. Other tasks that governments *might* perform, and in ancient Israel *did* perform, such as determining the form that public worship must take, could have no interest in a world where God had conferred his sovereignty upon his Christ. The higher goods of mankind's social destiny have been looked after in the proclamation of Christ; only the lower goods of judgment need concern earthly princes. For Paul, no less than for John of Patmos, there is only one political society in the end, which is the new Jerusalem; sovereignty is to be found there and nowhere else. Israel's identity is complete there, and the identities of other nations are of no account except insofar as they are found in Israel's God and his Christ. This passing usefulness, however, the rulers of the nations still have, pending the final revelation of Christ's sovereignty: they maintain a distinction within their societies between the just and the unjust.

This new way of envisaging the political function I have described, in an expression doubtless capable of improvement, as the "re-authorizing" of government as judgment.[1] This does not intend to say that the whole operation of government is thinned down, as in some libertarian fantasy, to the operations of civil courts of justice; it means

---

1. *The Desire of the Nations* (Cambridge: Cambridge University Press, 1996), p. 148. For a demurral at this term, see Nicholas Wolterstorff, "A Discussion of Oliver O'Donovan's *The Desire of the Nations*," *Scottish Journal of Theology* 54, no. 1 (2001): 97-109.

that political authority in all its forms — lawmaking, war-making, welfare provision, education — is to be re-conceived within this matrix and subject to the discipline of enacting right against wrong. My expression intends to sum up two contrasted but complementary assertions characteristic of the Christian tradition. In the first place, the terms on which the bearers of political authority function in the wake of Christ's ascension are *new* terms. The triumph of God in Christ has not left these authorities just where they were, exercising the same right as before. It imposes the shape of salvation-history upon politics. The operations of the Holy Spirit in the world drive the political leaders back upon the tasks of justice, and so effect a transformation. This offers a distinctive perspective on the evolution of political forms in history. For the hero-warriors of Troy the ultimate test is the survival of the city, for the warrior-monarchs of *Beowulf* the survival of the tribe; but that is ground we can never re-occupy. Even were the same conditions as once prevailed in Magna Graecia or Scandinavia to prevail again, we could not return to that state of mind in innocence; for something about our human vocation has been shown to us: we are called to a final destiny in the life of the new Jerusalem, subject to the throne of God and the Lamb. Only of that throne can it be said that by its sheer prevailing it gives life. All other thrones need further justification; their role is subordinated to the task of preparing the way for that final one. This was the ground of the distinction that arose within a Christian view of history between secular and spiritual authority, this-worldly and ultimate rule.

In the second place, political leaders are not simply denied their authority, but are constituted, on these new terms, as a secondary theatre of witness to the appearing grace of God, attesting by their judicial service the coming reality of God's own act of judgment. In the light of Christ's ascension it is no longer possible to think of political authorities as sovereign; but neither is it possible to regard them as mere exhibitions of pride and lust for power. To the skeptical question, "What else, basically, are the courts of this world — together with all its prosecutors and lawyers — than the necessary institutions which have come from original distrust?"[2] we are bound to answer, "Much in every way!"

---

2. Eberhard Jüngel, *Justification: The Heart of the Christian Faith*, trans. Jeffrey F. Cayzer (Edinburgh: T&T Clark, 2001), p. 140.

The term "judgment" is what the grammarians call a *nomen actionis,* that is to say, the name for a type of act, the "act of justice," as St. Thomas describes it.[3] When we read the famous prophetic texts in which the Hebrew noun *mishpat* is employed, we must always bear in mind its active force: the king "judges *(shâphat)* and seeks *mishpat"* (Isa. 16:5), and the Servant "will bring *mishpat* to the nations" (Isa. 41:1). The immediate concern of these texts lies with courts and litigation, though the Servant-Song shows how the international sphere, too, could come to be construed as a great court of divine judgment. The famous word of Amos 5:24, which bids us "let *mishpat* roll down like waters," has in view a flood of judicial activity. Courts are to be held every day "in the gate," appellants are to be heard quickly and without the need for bribes, verdicts are to be clear-sighted, decisive, and enforced. The active sense of *mishpat* famously influenced St. Paul, whose use of the Greek word *dikaiosunê* carried over the force of the Hebrew noun: the *"dikaiosunê* that is by faith" is God's *act* which sets wrong right (Rom. 3:21f.).

"Judgment," then, is more sharply focussed than the abstract noun "justice." This latter term has been used in broadly three ways in the moral discourse of the West. In the first place, and most conformably to modern usage, it has been used to describe a state of affairs, a kind of moral equilibrium obtaining between two or many things, a state which it is morally requisite to bring about or morally prohibited to disturb. In the medieval Western tradition this sense is represented especially by the Roman-law term *ius,* "right." In the second place, and most characteristic of the classical philosophical discussion, "justice" is the name of a virtue, which resides in those who are disposed to "render each his due." This virtue is either one of many, "special justice," differentiated from the other virtues by its specific reference to what we owe others, or it is the sum of all virtues, "general" justice, a sense which hardly survives in English, though, when English vocabulary was still fed from the Authorized Version of the Bible, it was spoken of as "righteousness." In the third place "justice" has been used to describe

---

3. *Summa Theologiae* II-2.60.1. The single most important Christianizing transformation that St. Thomas introduced into Aristotle's virtue-theory of justice was his concentration on *iudicium* as the focal act of justice. In this he was followed by Hugo Grotius, *De imperio summarum potestatum circa sacra* 5.1ff.

effective performance, the act of "judgment," which sets wrong right. When people "demand justice," what they want is for somebody to do something. We may distinguish the three conceptions of justice by speaking of justice-as-right, justice-as-virtue, and justice-as-judgment.[4]

The Christian discussion of justice has been generated by the confluence of these three streams, in which justice-as-judgment, predominant in the Scriptures, has mingled with justice-as-right from Roman law and justice-as-virtue from Plato and Aristotle. Although all three of these notions have application to political life, only the performative notion represents an originally political reality. For Plato, the just man is *like* a just city, but can exist *without* a just city, for justice-as-virtue is an ordered disposition of the powers of the soul, not of relations *among* and *between* people. Justice-as-right supposes a society, on the other hand, but without reference to political organs, so that in this sense the phrase "original justice" may be used of the pre-political social harmony of the Garden of Eden.

Let us venture upon a working definition: judgment is *an act of moral discrimination that pronounces upon a preceding act or existing state of affairs to establish a new public context.* On this I shall make four comments.

(1) Judgment is an act of *moral discrimination,* dividing right from wrong. The pretension of judgment is to resolve moral ambiguity and to make the right and wrong in a given historical situation clear to our eyes. It "defines," as Grotius says, "between two parties." It is an intellectual act, implying the exercise of intellectual virtue. In the Hebrew Scriptures, indeed, judgment often appears as the supreme expression of "wisdom." The famous story of Solomon and the two women is intended to display how the wisdom conferred by God on princes resolves the obscurities of conflicting claims. The emphasis laid by idealist thinkers on the intellectual character of political action is not due solely to Plato's famous thesis about philosophers and kings; it derives also from the ancient Near-Eastern association of wisdom-ideals with government.

---

4. The association of these different concepts of justice with different cultures is, of course, a simplifying generalization: Plato was far from uninterested in just states and deeds of judgment. Yet the "paradigm" of the just city is effectively established only in the soul of the just man (*Republic* 592ab).

(2) Judgment *pronounces upon a preceding act,* or on an existing state of affairs brought about by action. It is by definition reactive, following what it pronounces on. It is not, and never can be, a forward-looking action, like "founding" a city, "striking" a blow, or "broaching" a question, but derives its rational conditions from a reflective reference, like "answering" a question, "defending" an encampment, "noticing" a sound, etc. To pronounce a judgment is always to speak about something that already is the case. This is especially important for the theory of punishment: "retribution," i.e., reacting to the past, cannot be recommended as a *virtue* of judgment; it is quite simply a condition for judging at all, as opposed to, let us say, taking an initiative. When we have said that punishment is retribution, we have, as yet, said nothing as to how we may punish *well;* we have only said that punishment is, as such, a species of judgment.

(3) Judgment *establishes a public context,* a practical context, that is, in which succeeding acts, private or public, may be performed. The fact that an act must be by definition retrospective does not mean that it must be undertaken without a prospective object of action, another point of importance for the theory of punishment. No human actions are ever undertaken without prospective objects; they differ, however, as to whether their objects are *purely* prospective — "setting out on a journey" — or incorporate a retrospective object, too. The prospective object of the act of judgment is the securing of a public moral context, the good order within which we may act and interact as members of a community.

An act of judgment may therefore be assessed by the success of its outcome, as well as by the truth of its pronouncement. "Execution is the life of the law."[5] It achieves its goal only if a public moral context is established by the judgment, and the public moral context is, in some respect, more just as a result. This may involve making a substantial change to the public context, as when a new law turns something that we have hitherto done with perfect innocence (let us say, hunting foxes) into an offense overnight, or something we have done furtively (say, smoking cannabis) suddenly becomes legitimate. And so we may think of a good judgment as "creative," in that it brings new possibilities of ac-

---

5. John Donne, *The Sermons of John Donne,* ed. George R. Potter and Evelyn M. Simpson, vol. 1 (Berkeley: University of California Press, 1953), sermon 2, p. 173.

tion into play. Yet creativity is a metaphor that needs some care. We should not be misled by it into an excessive admiration of radical judgments at the expense of conservative ones; for a judgment that simply vindicates the existing public order against some affront may have better results than a judgment that modifies it. This judgment, too, "founds" a secure and enduring context for future action. Furthermore, while it is not inappropriate to say that human beings can be creative, imitating and witnessing to the radical creativity of God simply by making something new out of what they have found, no human act can be *radically* creative in the sense of giving existence to things that had no existence before. Judgment, unlike a work of art, creates the new only by pronouncing upon the old. The strength of its results will depend upon the truth and conviction that its reflection on the old can command.

Judgment, then, both *pronounces retrospectively on,* and *clears space prospectively for,* actions that are performed within a community. Some acts performed by public authority are not acts of judgment since they make no reflective pronouncement: the government signs a contract with one company rather than another, the Prime Minister appoints this minister rather than that to a cabinet post, but there is no suggestion that the disappointed company or minister have done anything wrong. Some acts performed by public authority, on the other hand, are not acts of judgment since they constitute no new public space: the Secretary of State for Health issues warnings to the public about safe levels of drinking, but we have exactly the same discretion over how much we drink as we had before. The form of the political act lies in this double aspect, retrospective and prospective, as pronouncement and foundation. Initiative in action does not constitute judgment, and neither does simple protest.

This double aspect makes judgment subject to criteria of *truth,* on the one hand, and to criteria of *effectiveness* on the other. These criteria are not alternatives. Success on one front cannnot compensate for failure on the other. Nor do they relate to different *moments* of the judgment. The two sets of criteria apply at one and the same moment to one and the same act. A well-made judgment is a statement that is true, and *as such* a deed that is effective. To take the example of criminal legislation once again: a law may fail to base itself on a true apprehension of the social situation (the legislators exaggerate, perhaps, or underestimate the problem); or it may fail to gain effective control over the situation (by imposing inappropriate standards of proof, perhaps, or inadequate sanctions). Either way that law fails as judgment, and so is "unjust."

(4) The object of judgment is the *new public context,* and in this way judgment is distinct from all actions that have as their object a private or restricted good. This requires us to set certain uses of the word "judgment" on one side. To speak of simple intellectual acts as "judgments" — as in Kant's use of the term *Urteil* to refer to aesthetic comprehension — belongs, as Thomas and Grotius both insist, to a wider semantic field that has grown up around the core use of the term, which is political.[6] Yet when these are taken out of consideration, some further distinctions remain to be made. Judgment, even in its core political sense, is an analogical notion.

The private citizen, in the first place, may be responsible to the community simply in the way he or she pursues a private avocation; and in this minimal sense we may echo the psalmist who says that "the mouth of the righteous utters wisdom, and his tongue speaks judgment" (Ps. 37:30). An act with a private object cheerfully undertaken within the terms of the political order may be an act of judgment in a marginal sense: when in hiring a housekeeper I dutifully pay the National Insurance as I ought, I enact my judgment on the judgments that others have made, judging it right to conform to them. Less marginal is the use of the term in relation to the *public* engagements of a private citizen, who may take responsibility for the public order by joining in arguments, debates, or elections. This kind of activity has a directly public object, not a private one, having in view what is requisite for the good order of the community. We commonly call it "political," though the term "public" expresses its scope and rationale rather better, I think. The views that we express when we complain that the burden of National Insurance prevents full employment, are clearly intended to *contribute to* a judgment made on behalf of the public; yet they stop short of actually *effecting* such a judgment, in a third and stronger sense, in the way that an official person effects a judgment. A

6. Thomas Aquinas, *Summa Theologiae* II-2.60.1: *nomen iudicii amplitum est ad significandum rerum determinationem in quibuscumque rebus.* Grotius, *De imperio summarum potestatum circa sacra* 5.1: *Est enim iudicium a iudice; iudex autem ius dicens. Coepit deinde proferri ad definitionem qualemcumque etiam internam in omnibus quae contemplamur aut agimus.*

magistrate in court, for example, fining an offender for non-payment of National Insurance, gives a judgment that is something more than his own contribution to the debate. It is *ipso facto* an act of the community as a whole. Official judgment serves the public order in this much stronger sense of acting *on behalf of the public*. Because the magistrate acts representatively in this way, the act of judgment has an immediate effect, which private persons' judgments do not. Furthermore, it limits both the magistrate's freedom and ours: the view the law takes of non-payment may not correspond to his or her own view, yet it has to be upheld; and the upholding of it binds the rest of us to its terms. We are not free to take such a judgment or leave it, as we are with judgments expressed in a debate; we are not bound hypothetically, as with the judgment of a University examiner that is relevant only to certain limited projects and ambitions. It binds us, as the phrase goes, *semper et pro semper.* We are "subject" to it.

Of these points on the spectrum, it is the third that will provide the central and normative use of the term "judgment" in political discussion. That is because it provides us with the central use of the word "political," which is also capable of an analogical use. When an employer conscientiously pays the National Insurance contribution, or when a charitable organization mounts a campaign to relieve the victims of war, these acts, "private" and "public" respectively, may be thought of as "political" in a broad sense. Yet we have a range of actions that are primarily acts of judgment and have no meaning as anything else, and there is a restricted range of agents who may perform them, "political actors" in a narrower and more precise sense. To put our finger on this narrowly political role, we must single out its *representative* function: a political act with political authority occurs where not only the *interests* of the community are in play, but the *agency* of the community as well. To this latter point we shall return in the second part of this volume.

We should note a further point on the spectrum of analogy, the point occupied by the judgments of God. Here, too, responsibility for the community's good is determinative. The idea of divine judgment presupposes a context of covenant relations, in which "I shall be your God and you shall be my people" (Lev. 26:12; Jer. 7:23). YHWH's covenant with Israel constitutes the political relation in which he rules, and so judges; judgment is part of that covenant activity to which he has sovereignly bound himself. In other words, it is an aspect of *potentia ordinata,* not *potentia absoluta,* for God's absolute power can destroy but not judge. The story of the covenant with Noah illustrates the same point in terms of the whole human race: a God who will judge the human community, requiring "a reckoning for the life of a man," is one who has assumed responsibility for the good of the human community, and will not destroy it (Gen. 9:5, 9-17). Yet we do not conceive of God as undergoing the loss of personal freedom that characterizes the human official; nor is he a "representative" in the sense that his voice simply *is* the voice of the community. That is because God's freedom is not curtailed by his self-giving in covenant, but is wholly expressed there; and his agency *for* the community is *prior to* the community, not subject to it. In that sense it is sovereign, as no human political agency ever can be. In speaking of God's rule as the foundation of political authority, then, we speak of the point at which things separated and often in tension in our political experience find their true point of equilibrium. "All authority from God," the apostle said. And we know that that must be true, precisely because of the contradictions and tensions that arise when we are mandated to exercise authority over one another.

2

Imperfectibility

It is, perhaps, the most fundamental of all political questions whether and to what extent judgment is possible. How are we so to pronounce as to establish? How are we to make the truth appear effectively? Of God it is said that "He spoke and it was done." "God said, 'Let there be light,' and there was light." The word of God carries the power of God within itself; to echo the old phrase from sacramental theology, it effects what it signifies. But can the human word effect what it signifies? Are we given to renew the life of human communities by a word of truth, or is this an unattainable ideal, from which we have to fall back upon the "messiness" and "compromise" of politics?

This question, which divides the "idealist" from the "realist" strands of Western political thought, first became articulated in the Middle Ages in response to the Averroist separation of intellect and will. Marsilius of Padua, reflecting on a passage of Aristotle's *Politics* where the philosopher distinguished judges from soldiers on the basis that the judiciary was required against internal, the military against external foes, observed that this was neither the only nor the principal reason for the military class. Rather, that class existed so that "the sentences of the judges against injurious and rebellious men within the state [might] be executed with coercive force."[1] The distinction Marsilius perceives be-

---

1. *Defensor Pacis* 1.5.8 (commenting on Aristotle, *Politics* 1291a7ff.), trans. A. Gewirth. See Oliver O'Donovan and Joan Lockwood O'Donovan, eds., *From Irenaeus to Grotius* [hereafter *IG*] (Grand Rapids: Eerdmans, 1999), p. 428.

tween these two elements of political society, then, reflects that between rational and voluntative functions of the mind. The exercise of judgment requires the coincidence of discernment and coercion. The judge says "Guilty!" and the military leads the prisoner away. At the last judgment Christ will unite these two elements; but in the meantime human judgment is a composite act which depends on their fragile conjunction. They are not inseparable. Discernment may be exercised without coercion, which gives us, Marsilius thought, a secondary sense of the word "judgment," by which a priest may be called a judge: "a teacher of divine law" who "has no coercive power in this world to compel anyone to observe these commands."[2] In Marsilius's conception we may observe the first stirrings of that outlook which has come to be called "realism": the coercive act is a voiceless complement to an otherwise impotent word.

But it was possible to think of force in judgment quite differently. Later in the fourteenth century Oxford's John Wyclif proposed that it was the *non*-coercive declarations of the priest that comprised the essential reality of judgment. "A judge," he wrote, "is a contemplative ruler of the people operating solely with the moral authority of God's law." This office is distinguished from that of the king in terms of the contemplative and active lives: "a king is an active ruler of the people operating with human law." The judge as such uses no coercion: "It belongs to judges to direct the people solely by God's law, and to kings to use civil compulsion."[3] This "contemplative" government, which should be represented in Christendom, Wyclif believes, by the bishops, is a real alternative to coercive government, "nearer to the state of innocence," more apostolic, more like the heavenly state, and so "more perfect."[4] Only "accidentally" (i.e., "circumstantially") may the rule of kings be preferable in the face of extensive sin, though even so "human law and kingly office have no worth unless they are directed by the evangelical law." Here we encounter a form of the "idealist" tradition, derived from Plato's famous conception of the rule of philosophers in the *Republic,* where the whole action of government is contained in its expression of wisdom and rationality. Coercion is not essential to judg-

2. *Defensor Pacis* 2.8.5f.
3. *De civili dominio* 1.28.
4. *De civili dominio* 1.27. *IG,* p. 506.

ment; it is an ancillary for a less than ideal world, an accident that *be-falls* the act of judgment.

The question posed by this divergence of views has haunted political thought in the twentieth century. Is there in the nuclear core of human judgment a shortfall of reason, which generates an exertion of force to compensate for its lack? Or does reason reach all the way to express itself, where necessary, in forceful action? We found ourselves constantly reverting to such a question in our decade-long heart-searchings over the crisis between Iraq and the United Nations: was there a point at which the reasoned discourse of diplomacy simply "ran out"? The question may present itself in various guises: in terms of the practical fragility of human judgment, the insufficiency of propositions to pass over into action, the shame attached to force, the limitations on our perceptions of the truth, and our restricted capacity for constructive and forward-looking initiative. These different forms of the question are interrelated, constantly leading back to one another and to the theological root-question underlying them: can we imitate God's unity of thought and action so that the reasonableness of a judgment will be sufficient to give it effect?

It is not simply a question of whether we approve or disapprove of coercive force. The idealist tradition presents itself as the champion of reason; yet its upbeat account of the rationality of public action contains an *apologia* for force as a form in which political rationality may sometimes appear. So Eusebius of Caesarea, that arch-idealist, interprets Constantine's military victories as the conquest of the Logos, the final triumph of rationality.[5] The realist tradition, on the other hand, presents itself as the advocate of necessary force; yet its sombre account of human possibilities may sometimes contain a confession of shame in the face of necessity, a sense of tragedy about the cutting-short of reasonable interaction. So for Augustine the just man wages even just wars in tears.[6] The realist critique of idealism is that it fails to acknowledge the brutal rupture implied in the transition from speech to action. The idealist critique of realism is that it allows too little distinction between rational force and irrational violence.

5. *Speech for the Thirtieth Anniversary of Constantine's Accession* [= *Laus Constantini* 1-10]. *IG*, pp. 60-65.

6. *City of God* 19.7. *IG*, p. 149.

Let us pursue the question from each end in turn. What is implied, first, in speaking of the *truth* of a judgment? And what is implied, secondly, in speaking of judgment as an *effective action*?

*   *   *

The traditional definition of truth spoke of an "adequacy" of language to object, *adaequatio verbi et rei.* The sense in which language may be said to be "adequate" has, of course, given rise to much discussion. No notion of equivalence will fit the case, since language and its referent are things of a different kind, not to be commensurated. Yet language "refers." It is not condemned to be a new beginning, a venture into the world from outer space, like the Arminian conception of the act of will. Language enacts itself by referring to other performances; and the success with which it makes that reference is what we mean by its truth. But what does "success" mean? When language refers to an object, we do not think that it summons the object into existence, but that it corresponds with greater or lesser effect to the way things are with the object. Yet the way things are with the object is not given to us directly; objects are not known to us apart from our reference to them through language. The implication of this antinomy is that we conceive the object, as it is in itself before we refer to it, as the object of a *prior* reference that is somehow presupposed by our successful reference to it. Our reference appears to us as a kind of correspondence to the reference of God. Our judgment, therefore, can be said to judge truthfully when, within the limits of human understanding, we judge of a thing as God has judged of it.

A judgment on any act or situation proposes an account of it; yet it is not an open-ended account, but has a moment of closure, where innocence is separated from guilt. The moral *description* ends in a moment of *discrimination*. Description is complex and indeterminate, tracing and representing the dimensions and boundaries of the multiple relations which constitute and situate the object of judgment. But discrimination is simple and determinate: it draws a moral line through the situation, dividing its actors and their acts into two opposed moral categories. It is this simplifying moment that enables judgment to become action. Discrimination treats its object as an act, rather than an emerging sequence of happenings, by imposing closure on it: the conclusion is understood as the act's intention. At the same time it shapes itself as an act, emerging out of the observer's descriptive stance, where it simply stood by and looked on, into a practical posture of judgment.

Imagine with the aid of a hypothetical exercise how it would be if all our truth were purely descriptive, with no closure. Every transaction made in every shop is recorded on a central computer that identifies not only retailer, customer, and price, as with our present-day credit-card transactions, but also the precise description and quantity of the goods purchased. The computer then reviews each transaction, and if the price charged is above or below the average market value, it makes an adjustment in the form of a credit or debit on the retailer's and customer's accounts. Subsequently the computer tracks fluctuations in the market price of those goods, and makes ongoing retrospective adjustments as necessary. Such an arrangement, besides putting an end once and for all to the January sales, would ensure against unjust pricing — if that term could be thought to have a meaning anymore. But it would not be *judgment*, telling the truth about a human act. For the original transaction would never have been properly concluded. Sales subject to endless adjustments, like scientific theories open to infinite revisions, are not completed acts; and so they are not susceptible of attributions of guilt or innocence. It is characteristic, perhaps, of a totalitarian society that nothing is ever regarded as finished: everything is always open for higher review. Even the loser on the scaffold knows that with the next turn of events his memory will be rehabilitated. There can be no responsibility, no truth of human acts, because the point is never reached at which something has been definitely done. Judgment on a human action imports the moment of closure both in the performance of the act and in its description.

(i) How, in the first place, may our *descriptions* correspond to the judgments of God? It is not as though God has pronounced on each case already, so that all that is wanting is simple implementation or execution of what God has decided. When we judge, we venture our own pronouncement. But we do not have to do this in a vacuum, but in responsibility to the generic judgments of God known to us through divine law, natural and revealed, and through salvation history. God's judgments illumine the categorical structure of all events, and so teach us how to appraise particular events. The word of God illumines the works of the flesh and shows them up for what they are: fornication, impurity, licentiousness, idolatry, sorcery, enmity, and so on. That John Doe did or did not practice a sorcery on Tuesday last is not, however, illumined by the word of God, but is given in the first instance to us to decide.

Descriptive truth is a matter of appropriate predication. This act, this event: of what kind is it? Are we looking at an assault, or at an innocent accident? At a lie, or at the careful statement of a truth? To answer this question requires a kind of reasonableness that is neither deductive nor inductive. It is not inferential at all, but cognitive: it is the recognition of a *kind* in a *particular.* One must see past the bare particularity of the object (the *haeccitas,* in scholastic terminology) to its *quidditas:* it is not simply "this" or "that" but "a such and such." From the philosophical point of view, this is one of the most mysterious acts there is: it seems that it either happens or does not happen. I either recognize this slithery floppy object as a fish, or I do not; even if I can be taught to recognize a fish by looking for gills, scales, and fins, I either recognize this orifice as a gill, those membranes as scales, that limb as a fin, or I do not. But though recognition is unanalyzable, it is not haphazard. We prepare for it by acquiring competence with the relevant moral categories. To be sure of answering the question "Was that a lie?" we have to learn in general what *constitutes* lying. We learn to feel out the boundaries between categories, determining where one ends and another begins: "In those circumstances an evasion might have been innocently meant, but in these it could only be a lie." A particular act may plausibly belong to more than one category at once: there are fish, there are dogs, and there are dogfish; and so, we may say, there are idolatries, there are enmities, and there are idolatrous enmities — and more ambiguous combinations, too, such as maternal jealousy, protective lying, and so on. The first and most obvious categorical description of any human act may require a number of qualifying categories.

It is a sign of inadequate judgment to rest content with the superficial description, a hallmark of "summary" justice. This is why laws must be drafted with a certain complexity, so that courts may have sufficiently developed categories in which to form reflective judgments. It is a great weakness for a law to be under-specified. In ancient societies this complexity was sometimes achieved by the device, confusing to modern readers, of letting two apparently contradictory laws stand alongside one another in a law code. This device allowed judges to weigh up different possible interpretations of a given act. A society more used to discursive thought, however, rightly prefers to express the relation between the different provisions for different possibilities clearly, so that the determination of the judge is less likely to be arbitrary.

(ii) As well as appropriate predication, however, true description implies a reflexive contextualization. A further truth comes into the picture, which is the truth about the community that judges; and only by taking that truth into account can we attain a satisfactory discrimination of innocence and guilt. In the story of Jesus and the woman taken in adultery, which has shaped so much of Christian jurisprudence (John 8:3-11), Jesus does not challenge the generic categories in which the judges describe the act, nor does he challenge the application of those categories to the accused woman. But he demands that another dimension of description should be included: the ambiguous relation in which those who accuse others of adultery stand to the adulterers. And so he challenges the discrimination they have made. Were *that* community to carry out the death penalty on *that* woman, the line between innocence and guilt would have been drawn wrongly.

We may treat this story as a paradigm for the problem confronting all idealistic legislation. The trouble is not that law hopes to express some moral truth, for law must express moral truth if it is to command authority; the trouble is that it underestimates the complexity of the moral truth it must express. The truth of a law must also be a truth about the society in which the law will function. An over-demanding or over-restrictive law bears false witness to the totality, while intending to bear true witness to the part. Consider, for example, the legislative proposal that, irrespective of harm done, it should be criminal for parents to slap their children. The idealist character of this proposal is betrayed by its assumption that parents can always command forms of rational persuasion, and always have sufficient social support, to discharge their responsibility for their children's behavior without physical expression of their displeasure. Even were we satisfied that everything this proposal supposed about the moral character of parental slapping was true, we would still know that its view of the realities of parenthood was an idealized fiction.

Accommodation to human weakness, then, which the Greek Fathers called *oikonomia*, is not simply a matter of *how* a truthful judgment is implemented. It bears upon the truth of the judgment itself. So when

Jesus says, "Moses for the hardness of your hearts commanded you to give a writ of divorce," we should not take him to mean that the Mosaic law was, from a moral point of view, a second-best law. This regulative arrangement, rather, was the *right* way to condemn divorce, because it told the truth about the Israelites' hardness of heart.[7]

All this helps us to understand why laws differ from one society to another, and, indeed, ought to differ. A false inference is often drawn from the truth of social imperfectibility: that it implies a *uniform minimum* of law (or, in a more modest version, a uniform minimum of criminal law), which will safeguard the bare essentials while renouncing the attempt to maintain by legal means moral standards in excess of them. Without pursuing all the various objections to this inference, we may simply observe, as Aristotle did long ago, that sin is manifold.[8] The *universal* sinfulness of humankind is not a *uniform* sinfulness. Some societies tolerate a measure of violence, some tolerate offenses against property, some sexual offenses, and so on.[9] Societies differ in their besetting sins as well as in their distinguishing virtues. The uniform minimum law risks ending up with the worst of both worlds: it neither appeals to our sense of value to motivate us, nor provides us with protection at points where we feel we need it. It is idealistic in the vicious sense of the word, i.e., it supposes some other kind of society, with other problems and possibilities, than the one it actually has to serve.

Apart from differing moral possibilities within society, other changeable factors require variations in law. Local expectations differ from place

---

7. Mark 10:5. In *Resurrection and Moral Order* (Leicester: Apollos; Grand Rapids: Eerdmans, 1986), pp. 96-97, I observed that "the forging of compromises does have a legitimate place in Christian moral thought when it addresses . . . norms for the conduct of public life." I also noted, however, that "it would be better to find another term." I now prefer to speak of the "imperfectability" of human politics. This logic framed one of the most interesting and disturbing experiments in legislation of recent years, the law on euthanasia in the Netherlands.

8. The extensive discussion it received from Basil Mitchell a generation ago in *Law, Morality, and Religion in a Secular Society* (Oxford: Oxford University Press, 1967) is still well worth reading.

9. Thus the ironic bookseller whom George Borrow met at St. James of Compostella asked: "By the bye, I have heard that you English entertain the utmost abhorrence of murder. Do you in reality consider it a crime of very great magnitude? . . . The friars were of another way of thinking. . . . they always looked upon murder as a fiolera." *The Bible in Spain* (London: Dent, 1906), p. 249.

to place and need to be respected; local conditions for detection and execution have to be taken into account. The European Convention of Human Rights declares: "Everyone arrested or detained . . . shall be brought promptly before a judge . . . and shall be entitled to a trial within a reasonable time"[10] What is prompt? What is reasonable? It must depend in part on the distances to be covered and the topography, the means of communication, the local laws which govern evidence at a trial, the pressures on courts' schedules, and so on. The principle must be universally upheld, but cannot be uniformly implemented. Yet that does not mean that implementation may be indefinitely elastic; some intervals are not "prompt" or "reasonable" by any criterion.

Furthermore, law must change with historical circumstances. A generation ago, in common with many other Western countries, Britain decriminalized suicide and attempted suicide. The law continues to disapprove of suicide, for it remains a serious offense to counsel or assist one. But it was judged, surely correctly, that suicide was better dealt with by discouragement. We should not conclude that because we now judge it right to deal with it in this way, it was always a mistake to have had criminal legislation. That was for our grandparents, not ourselves, to judge, in the light of how they thought their contemporaries would react to the presence or absence of sanctions. To take a contrary example: in the seventeenth century it seemed evident to all the more civilized and reflective thinkers that war-crimes could not be prosecuted. Though many common acts of war ran counter to basic principles of lawful conduct, they had to be immune from prosecution, for if every war was followed by a systematic attempt on the victor's part to punish the crimes of the defeated party, not only would justice be intolerably one-sided but belligerent parties would be deterred from making peace. Today the trial of war-crimes is popular, and for good reasons. But it is not the case that either the seventeenth or the twenty-first century had to be wrong. The existence of international institutions makes some things practicable now that were impracticable before.[11]

10. §5.3. In *Basic Documents in International Law,* ed. Ian Brownlie, 5th ed. (Oxford: Oxford University Press, 2002), p. 246.

11. I have discussed this question further in *The Just War Revisited* (Cambridge: Cambridge University Press, 2003), pp. 109-23.

It is difficult to evaluate the judgments of a past historical period, because we are not "at home" in it to assess its possibilities realistically. But is it any easier to evaluate the judgments of our own? Is it given to us to know our own society more clearly than a past one? Our society is not an object set before us for scientific examination. It is a historical, shifting and changing context, constantly emerging out of a past society and constantly developing into a future one. It is of infinite complexity, and we who assess it are part of it, and assess it from a partial point of view. We may sometimes suspect that there is no more misleading view of a society than the one it takes of itself, a blend of hopeful and despairing self-images, sectional perceptions, and so on. Once grant the reflexive movement, in which the particular case is set within the context of the society, and the search for the truth looks like a voyage towards a landless horizon. Contextual truth, so important to assessing the case, is in principle unlimited.

But some limit must be set to the reflection that any case requires of us, and so human judgments settle for functional simplifications. While requiring some degree of complexity, the practice of judgment precludes an indefinite search for insight and understanding. Neither the court nor the legislative chamber is the place to explore some aspects of a situation that more extensive and humane reflection, not to mention divine insight, would uncover. They have to cut things short, and act. So when we describe what a court does in relation to the case before it, we say simply that it "declares the law"; it terminates the quest for truth within those categories of determination that human law has provided. Our judgment is never more truthful in its correspondence to God's judgment than when it acknowledges its own severely limited capacity for truth.

*   *   *

What makes a judgment an *effective action?* We have spoken of establishing "a new public context." That is to say, the shape of what any member of society may and may not do is determined by judgment *on behalf of* the community as a whole *for* the community as a whole. The verdict of a court on a crime is addressed not only to the offender and the victim's relatives, but to the whole of society, which is to conduct its affairs on terms that repudiate such crimes. So there is a directive function even in judgments that are primarily reactive. In other forms of judgment the directive function is primary, most notably in lawmaking. Responding to no particular events and formulated in wholly generic terms, legislation is still a reaction to wrong, for otherwise its restriction of our freedoms would be unwarranted, but to wrong as a tendency or threat, not as a concrete past event. Its primary role is to direct us to avoid the actualization of the wrong. With legislation there is in view the ideal horizon of a law needing no enforcement since its directions are simply observed. It is an ideal horizon only, since, were that to happen, the suspicion would arise that the law was unnecessary and exhortation would have sufficed; yet this horizon has important implications, for it underlines the necessary coherence between the directive content of law and the directive content of moral belief. The fashion for denying the connection of law and morality was based on a privatized conception of morality as comprising those directive judgments which each person makes for him or herself autonomously. But that concept of morality is untenable. While it is certainly the case that moral thought deliberates upon areas of individual conduct which the law cannot reach, moral deliberation is not and cannot be confined to the self-directing inner discourse of the agent. There is no area for which we legislate on which we do not also deliberate morally. It is well for the legislators if our conscientious moral deliberations approve, rather than disapprove, what they instruct us to do or not to do.

Political judgment prevents the fragmentation of the public space into myriad private spaces, each construed according to the differing perceptions and emotions of individual agents. This is necessary because the dissolution of the common world into mutual incomprehension is always possible. The alternative to public judgment is not *no* judgment, but *private* judgments, multitudinous and conflicting, frustrating each other and denying everyone the space of freedom. "There was no king in Israel; everyone did what was right in his own eyes" (Judg. 21:25). A private person acting only on his or her own behalf could not establish a new public context, and so could not perform an act of political judgment. The private act of vengeance, even if it is intended to serve the common good, is not done "on behalf of" the community. There was a popular story-line used by more than one author in the heyday of the detective story, which concerned a public-spirited individual resolved, in a spirit of disinterested justice, to settle society's unpaid debts by killing off its unpunished murderers. The pleasing paradox in the idea was that the objects of this disinterested justice inevitably became victims rather than executed criminals. Such informal dealings could never give society what it needs in response to crime, which is judgment.

I am inclined to believe that the moral rule prohibiting private vengeance is an example of that much-controverted category, the "exceptionless" moral rule. Apparent exceptions arise only because the concept of political authority is extended to other forms of social authority with limited rights of public vengeance: to the authorities of a school, for example, which have the right to expel students and censure staff, or to the management of a business which has the right to dismiss employees for misconduct. These exercise judgment within the sub-political institutions where they hold office. Theirs is not political judgment in the strict sense, but in serving a public institution it has a quasi-political character, as the law recognizes when it allows a court to intervene to uphold the principle of "natural justice." Other apparent exceptions arise from emergencies, in which provisional political authority may be assumed on a temporary basis. The citizen-groups in the Romanian revolution of 1990 who caught, interrogated, and executed members of the secret police may or may not have acted rightly, but they were certainly not acting privately. They claimed a provisional authority for a political action that the emergency required.

What, then, is private vengeance? It is something more than the merely malicious desire to inflict retaliatory injury. It is a desire for reckoning, a need to bring the private sense of injury into the public space for vindication. There is a *private* desire for *public* vengeance, which becomes a *private* desire for *private* vengeance only when the desire for public reckoning is frustrated, unsatisfied, or despaired of. So it belongs to the art of politics to persuade those who nurse grievances that judgment can provide the satisfaction they desire. Institutions of judgment are in principle at the service of the aggrieved, whose cause has an indefeasible claim upon the public interest. When a woman lies bleeding on the pavement, the contents of her handbag strewn across the road, the street is galvanized into action; she commands assistance, creating a community of action around herself. Victims have the authority of injured right to claim the interest of mankind and God. But they do not have the authority to enact judgment; that authority resides with those who respond to the claim by making their injury the object of public vengeance. So although private vengeance has to be condemned, the desire for vengeance must be allowed its proper point of entry into the public realm, where it both commands and legitimates political authority.

A decisive view on the relation of private vengeance to public judgment is given us in the ancient Jewish institution of the Cities of Refuge, described at several points in the biblical narrative of conquest.[12] It bears witness to a difficulty: how to overcome the strongly felt religious duty on the part of the next-of-kin of a slain person to kill the slayer. Normally such a sense of family obligation must have produced blood-feuds and inter-clan warfare. The institution aims to restrict this by providing a court that had, in effect, only one thing to decide: whether the violent death complained of was a true murder. The accused was protected within the bounds of the city until the decision had been made, and, if the verdict was favorable, thereafter. If there was true cause, the retaliatory slaying was allowed, and the demands of vengeance satisfied; yet this was no longer *private* vengeance, since the duty of the next-of-kin had been subjected to the terms of a public act of judgment.

In all texts the manslayer who may benefit from the court's protection is described in two Hebrew phrases: *bibli da'ath* and *lo shone lo mithmol*. The first, "without knowledge," means "accidentally," as the illustrations make clear. The court has to distinguish between intentional and unintentional killing. The second, "without previous evidence of hatred" (not "malice aforethought"), is a supplementary criterion, supporting the appearance of lack of intention. On the historical context of this institution only speculation is possible. It looks like an institution designed for a society with minimal juridical organization, and there is no narrative record of its functioning. It is therefore possible to suppose that it was very ancient, and died out with the growth of local courts of justice. But the emphasis laid on it in Deuteronomic writings invites an alternative suggestion. In Deuteronomy itself we encounter it twice; the first occasion, most unexpected, is as an appendix to the First Speech of Moses (4:41ff.), which suggests that the editors and promoters of the Deuteronomic code set some store by it. This code was claimed to originate from Beth-Peor, on the East Bank of the Jordan, and we notice that this text is only acquainted with Transjor-

---

12. Num. 35:6-28; Deut. 4:41-43; 19:1-10; Josh. 20:1-9.

danian Cities of Refuge. In the other texts the distribution still favors Transjordania, with three cities located there and only another three for the whole of the rest of Israel. Were these Cities, perhaps, an East-bank institution, the device of a frontier-territory with certain features in common with the Wild West of American imagination? When the Josianic Reformers found in Transjordania a law-text around which they could promulgate reforms in Judah (and, as they hoped, in the former Samaria), did they attempt to extend this institution to the West Bank? Perhaps they conceived it as a bridgehead for monarchical authority, a point of appeal against local jurisdiction. So far as we know, the project of West-bank Cities of Refuge was stillborn. But it was a sufficiently attractive idea to encourage the post-exilic Pentateuchal editors not only to preserve the record, but to attempt to integrate these cities with Levitical cities and the High Priesthood (Num. 35:6, 25).

There is, however, something in the private yearning for vengeance that political judgment can never satisfy. The inner logic of grievance is to demand a *cosmic* reckoning. Wrong, as Hegel described it, is "infinite," and demands infinite judgment.[13] The victim demands that the wrong should become the whole business of the universe. In confronting his adversary and striking him down he will command the world, which is reduced to that one event on which it appears to depend for its vindication. Like all sin, vengeance makes the world a small pseudo-infinite, a substitute for making contact with the true infinite. (This is the psychology explored so brilliantly in the book of Job in a portrait that is neither unsympathetic nor uncritical.) The pseudo-infinite can appear in history only as infinite bloodshed, the unending retaliation of the feud. It is a false god that the avenger has called to his aid, and the role of public judgment is to provide a place of provisional satisfaction, where we may open ourselves to the infinitely reconciling judgment of the true God. The victim is required to accept a moment of renunciation, even disappointment, in allowing the community to give finite and limited recognition to the wrong by enacting judgment on it. An age that champions victims' rights is familiar enough with the grieving spirit that clings defiantly to its wrongs, unsatisfied with public vindication and always in pursuit of the illusory hope of infinite reckoning.

13. *Philosophy of Right,* §102, trans. T. M. Knox (Oxford: Oxford University Press, 1952), p. 73.

In Scripture the issue is posed in the story of Cain and Abel, the first offender and the first victim. Cain, the murderer, is founder of the political and civilized arts; and so the myth conveys that the purpose of political life is to set a limit to the infinite reckonings of justice. The blood of Abel cries from the ground; but God, having heard the cry, protects Cain from it. The vengeance demanded by Abel's murder would put an early end to the human race. How could the universe concede to Abel's reproach, except by dying? The author of the Epistle to the Hebrews commented, "Abel, being dead, yet speaks" (Heb. 11:4): his cry for vengeance is never silenced, satisfaction never having been given, for only God's decisive judgment *against* the world could set that cry to rest. But God will not give him judgment. Or, as the Christian author adds, he *has* given it, though in a manner quite different from what was demanded: "the sprinkled blood of Jesus speaks more loudly than the blood of Abel" (Heb. 12:24). Infinite judgment has been given in infinite sacrifice, but with redemptive, not destructive purpose. Abel's cry for cosmic vengeance has been met, but not on its own terms.

Here, then, is the crucial point: there is a limit to the extent to which we are capable of accommodating a disclosure of right as the basis for our future public freedoms. The inner brooding of the victim may conceive of cosmic reckoning, but such a settlement cannot appear among us under the conditions of common social life. Public judgment is constrained by this limit, and in its struggle to wrest the initiative from private judgment, it loses the ground of its authority if it succumbs to immodest pretensions. It is not only that there is more truth to be known than it can know; there is also more judgment to be given than it can give. Its work lies on the surface of things, and only anticipates the deep judgment of God by not pretending to forestall it. To the extent that it exceeds its limits it loses credibility as a community undertaking, and appears in the world as a prophetic, didactic, or ideological force, armed with an authority springing from beyond community discourse.[14]

14. We may recall Hannah Arendt's memorable comments (*On Revolution* [Harmondsworth: Penguin, 1963], pp. 84, 87) on Herman Melville's *Billy Budd*, which she took to be a criticism of the "natural goodness" invoked in the French Revolution: "The absolute — and to Melville an absolute was incorporated in the Rights of Man — spells doom to everyone when it is introduced into the political realm. . . . Passion and compassion are not speechless, but their language consists in gestures . . . rather than in words. . . . Good-

What, then, are the limits of practicability that constrain a judgment performed in public on the community's behalf? They are three: (i) that not everything known can be publicly expressed or certified; (ii) that judgment has only certain modes of expression open to it; (iii) that it lacks final authority.

(i) God knows the thoughts of the heart, and will publish them. We, too, may know some thoughts, but they are inexpressible in the public sphere. Certainly, thoughts are the well from which we draw our public utterances and deeds; but the source remains hidden, and in drawing from it, we transform what we draw. Thoughts are not simply utterances that we have held back. To the extent that it is possible by introspection or with the aid of drugs to render a succession of thoughts verbally in speech or writing, it is incoherent. But that simply means that it does not have the coherence of *utterances;* to make sense of it one would have to have *thought* it. The famous observation of Elizabeth I, that she did not wish to make windows into men's souls, is simply a concession to the inevitable, for political surveillance cannot, as a matter of reality, make windows on souls. When governments have thought they could do so, they have caused untold misery, because what is actually done is to destroy spheres of community that are not "hidden," as thoughts are hidden, but are "private": family, friendship etc., spheres in which we justifiably expect freedom from political control. In catching us out in our careless utterances, political surveillance can only exaggerate their significance, since *careless* utterances are precisely not utterances vested with high political significance.

(ii) Divine judgment is "final" in that God alone has the power to cast the devil and his angels into the lake of fire. Human judgment has no such ultimate power at its disposal; it commands only the same resources for exertion as any other human action does, including wrongdoing itself. The Noachic *lex talionis,* "Whoever sheds the blood of man, by man shall his blood be shed," gives expression to an invariable limit on human judgment. How much more we should like to accomplish when confronted with a murder! Best of all would be to cause the murderer to step forward, confess himself, and repent; failing that, we

---

ness that is beyond virtue . . . is also incapable of learning the arts of persuading and arguing. . . . Innocence . . . cannot be proved but must be accepted on faith, whereby the trouble is that this faith cannot be supported by the given word."

would identify him and cause him to remove himself from the community in shame, without our having to raise a hand against him; and in either case we should like to demonstrate the wrong of murder so irrefutably as to deter all future murderers. We can do none of this. We can only watch the sin of Cain repeat itself, and only, as it were, repeat the murderer's crime back to him, responding to force with force. In doing so, of course, we give force a new rational and moral context, that of judgment, and so we transform it. But it is still force. Irrespective of whether the death penalty is in question, it is the murderer's mortality and vulnerability that expose him materially to the act of judgment, just as it was the victim's mortality and vulnerability that exposed him materially to the murderer's criminal intent. Judgment exerts contrary force for the simple reason that, materially, there is nothing else to exert. Spiritually, there is rationality and persuasion, and these are not empty of power; but by the time a case comes to judgment they have already failed once, and if they are to have a chance of success on the second attempt, a new situation must be created first.[15]

(iii) Lacking transcendent power of action, human judgment also lacks transcendent authority that can withstand contest. When a judgment fails to elicit acquiescence, the issue reorganizes itself as a quarrel between the judge and the contestants, in which the judge's independence is subverted, and the judge's authority with it. The arbiter ends up being party to a wrangle. The extensive machinery for police complaints and appeal courts indicates how the right to judge needs protection against the threat of attrition by challenge. Precisely because force cannot accomplish persuasion, and may even make persuasion more difficult, the very legitimacy of political organs can be worn away by protest.

Human action is always subject to limits that make it fall short of its intellectual conception, and the action of political authorities, despite the illusion of being able to transcend limits, is peculiarly subject to them. This is the source of that universal phenomenon of shame and embarrassment before political power, a phenomenon at least as

---

15. There could be no clearer illustration of this than the circumstances leading up to the Dayton Agreement of 1995, which ended the Bosnian civil war. Until serious external military force was thrown into the scales, every deal that was signed was broken before the ink was dry.

perennial and deeply rooted as shame before bodily sex, though these days much less well understood. The comparison between the two is illuminating, not least because the same philosophical temptations arise in both cases: to misinterpret the shame as guilt (the idealist temptation), and to face it down as a mere misunderstanding (the realist temptation). To appreciate sexual shame we must recognize the exposure and belittlement before God which human action encounters in its highest pretensions to transcendence. And in the political instance, too, the correct response to shame lies in the virtue of modesty.

3

Justice and Equality

Justice-as-right is a presupposition of justice-as-judgment. It corresponds to "general justice" as Plato and Aristotle conceived it, embracing all the various virtuous practices that might appear in a well-ordered person or society. Theologically conceived, it is the successful determination of our ways in the light of God's law. Justice-as-right envisages the possibility of injustice, as success envisages the possibility of failure; but that does not mean that it presupposes actual injustice. Justice is founded on the *posse peccare aut non peccare*, "the capacity either to sin or not," which is a moral feature of the original createdness of humankind. In discovering that we are determined by God's law, we discover that, in another sense, we are apart from it. We can determine ourselves as we are determined, or we can determine ourselves in defiance of our determination. We can be either just or unjust — not that these are equal alternatives in an ontological sense, since injustice is ultimately unreality; but they are alternatives practically, as deliberative possibilities. Justice-as-right is the correspondence of self-determination to the determination of God's law; it is obedience. For this reason Grotius, in the first of the three senses that he ascribed to the word "right," *ius*, propounded a *negative* formulation: *ius* means "what is just — 'just' being understood in a negative rather than a positive sense, to mean 'what is not unjust', and 'unjust', in turn, meaning what is inconsistent with the nature of a society of rational beings."[1] This definition points us behind

1. *De iure belli ac pacis* 1.1.3. *IG*, p. 797.

31

the concept of justice to the nature of rational society, which gives content to what we may do positively; and it conceives right simply as the negation of the negation of that prior order: "what is not unjust."

Judgment, on the other hand, presupposes actual injustice, for judgment (in its central political sense) is response to wrong. Of justice-as-judgment we cannot say what we can say about justice-as-right, that it is simply obedience to God's law. On the other hand we can say about justice-as-judgment what we cannot say about justice-as-right, that it is founded on principles of justice. By "principles of justice" is meant not simply the nature of rational society, but specific ways of acting in conformity with them. General justice knows no principles of justice other than God's law itself, the ways of life. But the ways of judgment are more specified than the ways of life, and the possibilities open to judgment are more limited than the possibilities of life. We are told "judge not, that you be not judged," but never "do not do right!" Judgment is a special activity that must be taken up and put down; there is a time for practicing it and a time for abstaining from it, like the other activities in the Preacher's list. As a special activity it is governed by special principles, the principles of "politics." This activity has its corresponding discipline and virtue, which we call political virtue. That is what should be meant by "special justice," or, as a common but unfortunate translation of Aristotle has usually put it, "particular justice."

But justice-as-judgment is the only special justice there is. There is no special virtue of justice that is *not* a virtue of judgment. There is no distinct mode of practice with distinct principles that are neither the law of the universe nor the political principles of rendering judgment. The special virtue of justice, which Aristotle thought to describe and which philosophers have never ceased to talk about, is an apparition that arises on the borderline of political and non-political existence. If we single out practices as "just" in this special sense — paying bills as soon as they are presented to us, and so on — and then attempt to describe a practice of justice made up of these, we are either failing to see how they are, in fact, virtues of a distinctively political kind, aspects of our role as fellow-citizens in an ordered state constructed by judgment, or we are failing to see how they are laws of universal neighborhood, no different from everything else that we owe one another as the children of God.

If we fail to pay a craftsman's bill, we may be failing to show him due regard as a child of God, in which case the injustice of our action in this case is not interestingly different from making him the victim of some other species of contempt. If, on the other hand, we propose to acknowledge his labor by offering to take his small daughter to play in the park on Saturday afternoons, we are failing to recognize the labor contract as a political form. Our failure is either a failure of neighborly charity or a failure of political obligation. When Proudhon, promising to prove that property is theft, declares, "Justice, nothing but justice, that is the sum of my argument. I leave to others the task of bringing the world to order," we can only fear that he is promising to dance, like an angel, on a point of infinitely small dimensions.[2] In looking for justice while ignoring government, do we not abolish human existence altogether along with poverty? On the one hand we exclude the general virtues of social existence that might make property seem intelligible; on the other hand we exclude the special virtues of political existence that might make property seem necessary. There is no principle of justice that is neither of these two things, not even the abstract principle that has most shaped the political conceptions of the modern world, *equality*.

It was Aristotle who imprinted upon the Western mind the idea that the essence of justice was equality. His great insight into equality, that it cannot be a univocal term with a quantitative application, has not restrained the later modern tradition from a kind of literalism in its understanding of it. When a univocal and quantitative notion of equality assumes a controlling role in the concept of justice, what is true about any case is subordinated to the bureaucratic or revolutionary concern for equalization, i.e., for making things equal rather than treating them equally. Either an undetermined object is equalized to the measure of a determinate one, which yields the conservative justice of bureaucratic precedent; or two determined objects are equalized in relation to each other, which yields the revolutionary justice of redistribution. In this way equality-arguments become the politicians' alchemy, producing the gold of judgment from the straw of noncommittal stances. They create the illusion of settling questions justly without needing to determine the truth of them. Should homosexuals be treated equally to heterosexuals in the matter of the age to consent

2. P.-J. Proudhon, *Qu' est-ce que la propriété?* (Paris: Lacroix, 1873), p. 15.

to sexual intercourse? Should the Palestinians have a state of their own, to make them equal to the Israelis? It depends on whether there actually *is* a natural class of sixteen-year old homosexuals different from a natural class of sixteen-year old heterosexuals, i.e., on whether that is a plausible description of human sexual development; it depends on whether the Palestinians *actually are* a political society like the Israelis, or whether they are merely scattered refugees.

Aristotle's *isotēs* is a relation not of two, but of four terms, a kind of proportion: the *treatment* meted out to *one* person must match the *treatment* meted out to *another*. But the type of proportion represented by *isotēs* depends on the kind of action that is to be done justly. Justice in distribution is marked by "geometric proportion," where the treatment differs in proportion to the difference of the two persons, while justice in rectification is marked by "arithmetic proportion," which strikes a mean between gain and loss so that neither party scores off the other.[3] In this attempt to divide the concept of equality into two streams, acts of "rectification" or "compensation" on the one hand and of "distribution" on the other, lie both the strength and the weakness of Aristotle's legacy to the theory of justice. Its strength lies in its recognition that different types of judgment employ different types of justice. Its weakness lies in its determination to maintain the notion of equality as the common point of reference.

The paradigm case for Aristotle's rectificatory or compensatory justice is that of just exchange. Exchange is not reducible to the simple notion of equalization, as Aristotle recognizes in refusing to accept that justice in punishment is no more than "return-suffering."[4] Exchange-justice is *equalization within difference*. Without the difference there can be no point in aiming at equalization. Both in nature and in art there are objects and experiences that so closely resemble one another we could have no practical interest in distinguishing them. We call them "identical," not meaning that they are one and the same thing, but that they are indefinitely replaceable by one another. Replace a screw with an identical screw, and things run as they did before; it makes no difference which of the two screws holds the machine together. Such replacements have no point; the only reason to replace one screw with another

3. *Ethica Nicomachea* 1132a1ff.
4. τὸ ἀντιπεπονθός, 1132b21.

is that one is broken and the other is not, one is the wrong size and the other the right size, one is made of a stronger material than the other, i.e., that there is some respect in which they are not identical. Replacements with no point pose no questions of justice. Issues of justice arise by virtue of the difference that makes the objects worth exchanging. Together with the difference there is a functional equivalence: each party to the exchange has to gain a proportionate satisfaction from it. We do not exchange a screw for a car, but may exchange a sports car for a sedan, since two people with different uses for their cars may reap equivalent benefits from the exchange. Matching equivalencies to differences is the work of cooperative practical insight, yielding the justice of reciprocity.[5] These comparabilities are represented in money-terms as equality of value. Aristotle's famous remark that coinage "measures everything" should not be misunderstood, credulously or incredulously, to suggest that money eliminates differences. On the contrary, the point of the observation is that difference is necessary in order to establish the appropriate comparability.[6]

It is possible to be too impressed by the purely formal possibilities of reciprocity, and to see in it the fundamental idea that lies behind all justice, not only in the "special" but in the "general" sense. So Wolfhart Pannenberg, seeking to identify natural-law principles that find expression in all societies, proposes as the chief example "reciprocity in giving and receiving."[7] On his account this embraces not only the *lex talionis* but also the Golden Rule and all the provisions of the Decalogue, on the basis that "community depends upon its members' mutual recognition of one another, both in themselves and in what they

5. When St. Paul, in promoting the cause of relief for the Jerusalem poor, urges upon the Corinthians the importance of ἰσότης, it is not material equality but the justice of reciprocity that forms the point of his argument: "I do not mean that others should be eased and you burdened; but as a matter of ἰσότης your abundance at the present time should supply their want, so that their abundance may supply your want, that there may be ἰσότης. As it is written, 'He who gathered much had nothing over, and he who gathered little had no lack'" (2 Cor. 8:13-15). The quotation from Exod. 16 enforces the point: when the Israelites gathered manna, those who were not very successful had the same amount in their bowls as those who were. The unequal material yield of each person's effort did not matter; what mattered was the equality of the effort in the common cause.

6. *Ethica Nicomachea* 1133a20.

7. *Grundlagen der Ethik* (Göttingen: Vandenhoeck and Ruprecht, 1996), pp. 58-61.

lawfully possess." In justifying the very wide scope he gives this principle Pannenberg argues correctly that the universality of a natural-law principle does not reside in its formulation, which may vary, but in the basic "anthropological" conditions for social existence that are expressed in it. Yet reciprocity is not an anthropological datum at all; it is a formal principle that brings together a number of anthropological data of quite different kinds: the practices of exchange, punishment, gift, etc. Personal recognition is different from giving and taking. The search for a fundamental idea of social ethics should lead us not to the idea of reciprocity, but to that of communication.

Treating reciprocity as the sole matrix of justice has its practical result in that totalizing of market-theory which was such a feature of late twentieth-century political and social thought. In order to find exchange equivalencies within complex political and social relations, we are sometimes forced to treat as loss what any sound philosophy regards as gain. Work, for example, a good gift of God and an expression of a person's intellectual and physical powers, is spoken of by the negative term "labor" in order to represent the relation of worker and employer as an exchange rather than a partnership. We are also forced to conceive of bizarre exchange-values. In the cost-benefit analysis beloved of planners, we are told, the economic viability of any project is assessed by a balance of gains and losses in which even the deaths of human beings are assigned a quantified value; and it is said that government has sometimes reclassified "economic" road-building schemes as "uneconomic" by the simple means of adjusting the token sum which represented the loss of a human life in a road accident! A sound theory of justice must recognize that some goods are not exchangeable, and that some transactions are not exchanges.

It was Aristotle's refusal to confine justice to reciprocity that gave his account such resonance, especially in a Christian culture formed by the parables of Jesus and Paul's doctrine of justification. But Aristotle proposed that *distribution* was the alternative model of justice, and this created serious difficulties. Distribution suggests that something hitherto held in common is assigned to private ownership; unowned goods are looking for owners. But if there are just and unjust answers to the question who should own the goods, it appears there must already be *putative* owners, and that the distributor's task is to determine the right person to own each portion of the common property. So distributive justice shadowed exchange-justice; it was founded on the notion of *suum cuique,* an existing property-in-right that gave ground for possession in act. But distributive justice was more conservative than exchange-justice, for where the latter equalized differences, distributive justice replicated and reinforced them. Distributive justice was an idea arising from that noteworthy feature of ancient Greek political experience, colonization, where societies with already formed hierarchies of honor were transplanted into new and empty lands. It answered the question of how a society's existing shape could be preserved in a materially new beginning.

The disruptive effects of the distributive idea in the context of a more continuous political experience is obvious. On the one hand, the hint of new beginning carries revolutionary potential. The idea of unowned resources waiting for distribution has served as a kind of "state of nature" lurking in the wings ready to challenge and unsettle any actual historical moment in a society's communication of wealth. On the other hand, the weight given to the existing balance of merit encourages the notional separation of a distributive "economic justice" from the variety of ways there are of spending public resources creatively (educating children, caring for the sick, fostering the arts, and so on). And that is true even, or particularly, when the balance of merit is interpreted in an egalitarian rather than an aristocratic fashion. In positing a scale on which every condition of welfare or deprival is commensurated, it has set us the task of bringing the well off and the badly off closer together, thus ignoring the incommensurable differences between ways of being well or badly off: being rich, being well educated, being able to appreciate beauty, being securely situated in a functioning community, having productive work to do, living with those one loves, adoring God, and so on. The imperatives of "distribution" (the conversion of public wealth into private) and of "redistribution" (the correction of disparity by transferring wealth from one private owner to another) become a serious rival to almost any genuinely *public* undertaking which seeks to disseminate worthwhile but incommensurable goods: education, job-creation, or whatever.

Let us take an example which appears at first glance to fit Aristotle's distributive paradigm rather well, the child-allowance in modern welfare states. Clearly, it is not a form of compensation, as though to make good the losses of child-rearing. Child-rearing is not a loss (though there are losses incurred in it), but a form of worthwhile human living. It is no part of the work of justice to equalize differences between parents and childless persons, nor any other differences arising from the pursuit of different forms of living. Is its point distributive, then? Does it place spare resources of the community at the disposal of those who have something worthwhile to do with them? No, for if that were the case, we would need to measure the worthwhileness of child-rearing against the worthwhileness of other projects laying claim to public money. The child-allowance would be determined in a proportionate relation, say, to Arts Council grants and money for hospitals, conceiving the whole distribution of public money as a competition of merit. The justice in setting the allowance at a certain level would depend on answering the question: who *deserves* the resources more? But this account would be as mistaken as the compensatory one. The point of a child-allowance is that the community should assist a crucial social function in which it has a strong interest. Its justice depends not on comparative judgments between the merits of child-rearing and other enterprises, but on judgments about the extent to which the parents' role needs assistance.

The best Christian revision of Aristotle's theory, that of Hugo Grotius, takes issue precisely with the place assigned by Aristotle to distribution. The real difference between the two kinds of justice, Grotius argues, is that the first has to do with reciprocity and the principle of *suum cuique*, while the second concerns "the prudent allocation of resources in *adding* to what individuals and collectives own."[8] That is to say, it emphasizes the prospective, forward-looking aspect of judgment. This, too, is justice — but not "strict" justice. Grotius re-names it "attributive justice," and proposes his revision in a simple formula: "To a faculty corresponds *expletive justice*, justice in the technical or strict sense of the term. . . . To a fitness corresponds *attributive justice*."[9] A "fitness" is a moral quality that is "less than perfect," i.e., which does not amount to a right in the strict and proper sense; while a "faculty" is a "right in the technical or strict sense," i.e., which would entitle one (in

---

8. *De iure belli ac pacis* prol. 10; *IG*, p. 793f. See further my essay, "The Justice of Assignment and Subjective Rights in Grotius," in Oliver O'Donovan and Joan Lockwood O'Donovan, *Bonds of Imperfection* (Grand Rapids: Eerdmans, 2004), pp. 167-203.

9. *De iure belli ac pacis* 1.1.8; *IG*, p. 798. The term "expletive" means "compensatory."

juristic parlance) to lay claim on something as "one's own." He invites us to consider, among other examples, an appointment to a post for which there is only one fully qualified candidate. One may make such an appointment justly or unjustly. Yet the qualified candidate has no greater right to that post, on the one hand, than he would have were he competing against a dozen fully qualified rivals, nor, on the other, is there any place for distribution. Distributing is not something one can do in abstraction. It is an operation performed in the course of doing something else, whether private (making a will) or public (funding education). These other acts provide the relevant criteria for the justice of the distribution, but they apply just as well when there is no distributing to be done. Justice does not always have to make comparisons between one person and another; it may simply be attending to what action will be fitting to the salient features of the situation. Through his concept of "fitness" Grotius effectively sets justice free from equality.

Grotius resists Aristotle's assignment of the different types of justice to different spheres of action: the one exercised in voluntary exchanges and punishments, the other in distributions of common goods. In almost any context, he believes, the two types of justice must be coordinated. In the justice of war, with which he is especially concerned, "mere expletive justice" is always a bad guide. Consideration of rights must be supplemented with consideration of prudence, the need of populations for peace and welfare. Yet expletive justice may not simply be overridden; it is not sufficient but it is necessary, and attributive justice is secondary to the satisfaction of its demands. Prudence which simply ignored the demands of exchange justice could not be attributive justice, for it could not be justice at all.

The key difference between the distributive and attributive ideas is brought out when Grotius remarks that attributive justice "depends on what is being done in each case and what the business in hand requires."[10] Aristotle thought that while people could disagree about what the criteria for distribution were, whether egalitarian or aristocratic, there was in principle one set of criteria that should be applied to all acts of distribution. Grotius thinks that the criteria must vary from one enterprise to the next. There is no one ground on which we should always prefer one person to another; the right ground at any

10. Prol. 10; *IG*, p. 793.

moment depends on what it is we prefer someone *for.* Attributive justice, then, comes in innumerable forms corresponding to the innumerable types of action we may prudently undertake. We could simply say that the attributively just judgment *gives appropriate expression to the moral situation by undertaking a new act.* It answers the circumstances by representing them in innovation.

*   *   *

If equality is not a "principle of justice," what is to be said about it? Two things: first, that the only equality that need or ought to interest us is the equality of each individual human being; second, that this is, and can only be, a theological assertion.

Duncan Forrester begins from the right place when he stipulates: "At the heart of the notion of equality lies the conviction that each person is of infinite, and hence equal, worth and should be treated as such," and he draws the right inference when he adds, "But it is difficult to see how this core affirmation can be justified without theological reference."[11] And then he continues in the right direction, adding irrefutably, "there is huge disagreement about how best this equality of worth may be translated into policy and practice." But at that point we look for the explanation of the disagreement, and it is not forthcoming. It should run as follows: the *relevant* sense of equality (i.e., the infinite worth of each person) is not *self-evidently* convertible into norms of social practice. Many conceivable, even attractive, policies of equalization (e.g., the leveling out of all University degree classes to a universal Upper Second) do nothing to respect the infinite worth of human beings, and may even disrespect it. But instead of providing us with this explanation, Forrester proceeds to cut the Gordian knot by asserting a universal presumption in favor of equalization, subject only to an argued rebuttal in certain cases: "Although some inequalities may be justifiable or even necessary, they still require explanations as deviations from the norm." But the knot is too tough for his sword, which bends at the last five words, "as deviations from the norm." Of course, all justified inequali-

---

11. *On Human Worth* (London: S.C.M. Press, 2001), pp. 30f. Justifiably, Forrester makes a great deal of the role the theological foundation played in the thought of R. H. Tawney.

ties are capable of explanation, but not as *deviations* (how could that be an explanation?) but as *differences* implied in the various forms of human flourishing and achievement. The general norm that we should treat all persons at all times according to their infinite and equal worth allows of no exceptions or deviations, no evasion of its universal force. As for the *specific* norms of equalization that give shape to the general requirement, Forrester has not told us how we may discern them. He lists some negative examples: "Equality as such is incompatible with racism, anti-Semitism, sexism, apartheid, and other systems that celebrate and enforce human inequality." But to this list he could equally well have added multiculturalism, the protection of threatened linguistic communities, the exercise of political power, the pursuit of excellence in education, and competition in sport, all of which "celebrate and enforce" inequalities of various kinds among human beings. What he has failed to provide is a criterion to identify where equal treatment is required of us, where respect for equal worth is really at stake.

Morally significant equality, as Aristotle knew, is a relation of relations. It supposes a description in which more than one person stands in a like relation to some other thing. And so the equality of all human beings cannot simply be posited, as in the notorious Rawlsian program which attempts to derive it from self-interest veiled in ignorance; it has to be grounded in a truth that is to be told about humankind's relations to that which is not humankind, and the only relation which answers the point is that in which each human being stands to the creator. The equality of human beings is an aspect of the doctrine of creation. It locates every human being equally to every other as one summoned out of nothing by the creator's will, one whose life is a contingent gift, created for fellowship with others and answerable to judgment. Only when social differences, which may be inoffensive or even constructive, tend to deny that created equality, do they expose themselves to such radical critiques as those which Christians have directed against slavery and, more recently, racism — to take two examples that commended themselves ecumenically to all Christian consciences.

Equality is something that is true about human beings. The language of "ideals" confuses the most important distinction between "equality," as the reality of the relation between any two humans created in the image of God, and "equal treatment," as the norm of behavior that gives some practical expression to this reality. It is a demand of *faith* that we should lay hold and act upon the truth of human equality; it is, in fact, an aspect of the belief that God created the human race, and without the one belief the other must be undermined. But it is a truth "beneath the surface" at the metaphysical level, a truth that has to be seen through to, past the differentiated and complexified structures of human society. Human society does not and cannot yield us a clear and unhindered view of our equality; to insist that it shall do so is to want to "live metaphysically," that is, to confuse the foundations with the superstructure of human existence, and the result of that is to annul the created forms in which the elaboration of human society is possible. The fate of all revolutionary equalization is to make human life unlivable.

Attributive justice elaborates differences. It strengthens relations of affinity and bonds of loyalty, it promotes talent and makes wise appointments to office, it gives opportunities to those who can use them. It represents the very opposite tendency to the demand for equal treatment, a demand that can only dissolve and degrade social structures, since differentiation is the law of every social organism. We depend on the justice of differentiation from the moment we take our first breath and are placed in the arms of our mother, rather than being handed to whoever may be next in the queue for a child. Nevertheless, the justice of elaborating differences can never be presumed on, and there are many kinds of difference which seem to promise enriched social possibilities, but are in fact simply unjust.

How, then, does our real equality shape our differentiated moral and social engagements? In the first place, it provides an interpretative key for the conduct of special relations, keeping them open to the recognition of the underlying inter-human realities. There is, as Kierkegaard understood, a close connection between equality and love. The reality of our human position before God sharply defines the character of love between human "neighbors," and distinguishes it from divine love for mankind on the one hand, and human love for God on the other.[12] The concept of equality shapes the love-of-neighbor "as yourself," and so gives form to the whole moral endeavor. If our elaboration

---

12. If we wish, we may name these *philadelphia, agape,* and *eros,* so bringing the point into connection with a famous debate; but we must understand that this is not a distinction made by the authors of the New Testament.

of differences is to serve the love of neighbor, it must allow scope for the recognition of equality *within* the difference. Person must remain distinct from role, and the distinction must be marked by recognized limits on the degree to which the differentiating role controls the person's conduct. When rulers, for example, are surrounded by ceremony or security that makes it impossible for them to conduct themselves with others as ordinary people, the role looks like becoming demonic. The reason we value the virtues of modesty and candor especially in those whose role separates them from others, is that it suggests that social difference and human equality are being successfully combined.

In the second place, positive acts of equal treatment may sometimes be required of us. The difficulty is to know when this is the case, and when, on the contrary, equal treatment would be anti-social and destructive. This question can be paraphrased by another: when is it right and proper to ensure that the underlying metaphysical condition of human equality should be brought to the surface, taken as the direct norm of human action? We may identify two moments at which substantive equal treatment is a decisive norm of attributive justice admitting no appeal. These moments are situated at key points of threat to human existence, where the only relevant fitness to be acknowledged is the minimal fitness for bare human existence itself. The equal treatment demanded at these points is to support the existence of one human being as we support that of another.

These two moments form an eschatological framework of equality, within the bounds of which social differentiations can safely be developed. In a school, for example, which is an institution constructed around the difference between teacher and learner, many inequalities of privilege necessarily arise. The teachers, not the students, have the last word on the syllabus, on homework requirements, and on discipline. And in support of the privileges essential to their role they may properly have others: a common room where they may work in quiet, removed from incessant student demands, a place to eat where they may learn to know and trust each other away from the distracting noise and crowd. It would destroy the institution to insist on immediate application of the principle of equal treatment, so that the Head Teacher and the youngest student had equal votes on everything. Differentiations are necessary in the education of the young. Yet if the Head Teacher and some students were involved in a road accident and admitted to intensive care at the local hospital, all thought of teachers' privilege would be forgotten. As so many human beings fighting for their lives, they would require strictly equal care.

The first threshold on which we are called on to give immediate practical effect to human equality, then, is the threshold of death, when the continuance of life itself is at stake. The ethics surrounding the struggle against death and the saving of life is always one of strict equality. Controversies about "quality of life" judgments in medicine illustrate our sense that at certain points qualitative discrimination becomes inadmissible. The claim of a patient with a poor prognosis upon our active assistance is no less than the claim of a patient with a good prognosis. In what sense do we use the term "equality" here? It is clearly not some kind of exchange equivalence. The value of a human life is equal, because equally infinite, not susceptible of any exchange value. One life is not worth one tenth as much as ten lives, and ten lives are not worth ten times as much as one life. The equality of human lives is simply the metaphysical datum of their unsubstitutability: each has a fitness for human existence that is unique and incommensurable. It is not the justice of exchange, but the justice of attribution that refuses to make differences in treating them.

Only in a serious social emergency, where further lives may be at risk from equal treatment (such as the *triage* situation on the battlefield, where life-saving resources fall far short of the demand) do we justify the selective prioritizing of one patient over another. The case for this is not generated by a differential value assigned to human lives; it is simply generated from a principle of efficiency that ought to govern an enterprise with over-stretched resources. The decision not to offer life-saving treatment to a patient who could benefit from it can be made only on a conjunction of two grounds: (a) that it would exclude other patients equally urgently in need; and (b) that it would be a more effective use of the resource to save another patient. The consideration that the single available ventilator is likely to accomplish less for a brain-damaged patient than for a non-brain-damaged one will justify the choice of the latter over the former. But this argument from efficiency does not constitute a general license to conserve scarce resources in all circumstances. *Possible* future patients are not *equally urgently* in need of the same resource. We cannot withhold a resource simply because we can imagine a possible future case where the resource would be more efficiently used. In the emergency of over-stretched life-saving resources we do not decide *whether* to save a human life, but only *which* human life to save when we cannot save them all. Outside the situation of emergency we expect hospitals to attend to critical patients in the order in which they arrive, and to provide each patient with whatever immediate care he or she can benefit from.

We are called on to give equal treatment to human beings, in the second place, when they lack essential resources to participate in social communications as such. Here we make contact with the long tradition of Christian concern for the poor. The term "poor" has been disconcertingly fluid in its application: understood by Chrysostom to mean someone who has to work for a living, today it is more likely to mean someone who does not have any work to make a living from. To the Franciscan friars it meant the lack of legal title and modest use of goods; to the early modern period it meant the lack of access to an education. The consistent element in poverty, however, is an insufficient command of material resources to take a part in the communications of society, so that one's social role is impeded or denied altogether.

It is necessary to insist that equality is the *appropriate* point of access for a discussion of poverty, which can otherwise either be sentimentalized or politicized. There is a moving sermon of Bossuet, *Sur l'Éminente Dignité des Pauvres dans l'Église,* in which the preacher argued that "In the kingdom of Jesus Christ, preeminence belongs to the poor, who are the firstborn of the church and its true children. . . . In the church the rich are allowed in only on condition that they serve the poor. . . . In the church of Jesus Christ the graces and blessings are meant for the poor, and the rich have no privilege save through the mediation of the poor."[13] It is impossible to impugn the good intentions of this, delivered to a well-heeled congregation in support of an orphanage; but it suggests no interest in overcoming the inequalities of poverty. The permanence of poverty, which in Jesus' saying "the poor you have always with you" is a somber acceptance of the reality of economic differentiation in a fallen world, has now become the proud boast of a class that is forever to enjoy pride of place. Bossuet is too good a theologian not to remember 2 Cor. 8:13 — but it has to be dragged in in defiance of his logic. In following this false trail Bossuet was immediately indebted to Vincent de Paul, but further back stand John Chrysostom and Ambrose. And have we not heard very similar things from

13. *Oeuvres de Bossuet,* vol. 12 (Versailles: Lebel, 1816), pp. 1-22.

Liberation Theology? Nor was Liberation Theology the first to discover in the class-solidarity of the poor a significant resource of power. Ambrose's strategy was overt: "If they complain that I shall ask for the support of the poor, I do not deny it. I actively seek their support. . . . The blind and the crippled, the powerless and the aged, are stronger than mighty warriors."[14]

By contrast we may consider the approach of Old Testament legislation to poverty, which is directed to preventing the poor from falling out of their ordinary social capacities through the economic floor. The Deuteronomic legislators, adapting a law-code of rural provenance to a nascent money-economy with an element of international finance about which they are frankly enthusiastic (15:6), protect against chronic indebtedness by confining interest-loans to dealings with foreign merchants while encouraging Israelites to borrow on pledge. (This extends to all Israelites the protection offered only to the poor in the Law of the Covenant, Exod. 23:25.) An innovatory septennial pledge-release (15:1-6) provides an elementary measure against bankruptcy, presented in the confidence that the increased prosperity created by a ready money-supply will reduce the level of defaulted debt and enable commercial lenders to absorb the loss (15:4). In addition to these general measures, the poor are further protected by a special casuistry. The weakest class of borrower is protected against the drying-up of credit in a remarkable provision (15:7-11) that confers, in effect, a right of access to short-term lending. Following the Law of the Covenant (Exod. 23:26f.), the Deuteronomists require the release of a garment given in pledge for a loan at sundown (24:10-13), thus restricting the very poor to very short-term liabilities. They retain specifically for dealings with the poor certain provisions of their source-text that probably originally applied universally: wages must be paid daily (24:14f.); a millstone may not be taken in pledge, because it is a means of livelihood, nor a cloak if the borrower is a widow (24:6, 17f.). Certain taboo-like provisions in the source-text concerning gleaning, reaping, and fruit-picking are interpreted as intended for the benefit of the "sojourner, fatherless and widow." These requirements are supported by arguments from the history of Israel in Egypt, which should create sympathy for the poor (24:18, 22), and that the poor man's cry is heard by YHWH (15:9; 24:15), who counts mercy to the poor as righteousness (24:13), and blesses the merciful (24:19).

The famous Levitical law of jubilee (25:8-55), while not primarily concerned with poverty but with establishing a leasehold structure for land-transfers so as to protect the continuity of family landholdings, has, nevertheless, three special provisions to assist the poor: The first requires a public maintenance allowance for the poor, and repeats the prohibition of lending to them on in-

14. *Sermon against Auxentius* (*Epistle* 75a), 33. See *IG*, p. 74.

terest (25:35f.). The second prohibits the enslavement of an impoverished Isra-elite (39-46), assigning him the status of a servant hired for a limited period. The third (47-55) provides a legal structure for the redemption of an Israelite debt-slave who has ended up in the possession of a foreigner not governed by the previous provision. These provisions have in common with the Deutero-nomic ones the aim of retaining the impoverished Israelite within the social world. He is given such status and protection as makes it possible for him to expect to return to his alienated property when the lease runs out at the year of jubilee. Clearly they are responding to disturbing social and economic develop-ments in which large numbers of Israelites are caught up helplessly. Yet they treat of our obligations to the "poor man" in the singular, an individual mem-ber of the community whose poverty is an accident that has befallen him and who is in need of assistance and restoration.

The critique of poverty (and of wealth with it) is not founded on a demand that *material resources* should be equally distributed. There is no moral significance in distributing goods equally as such. At gradua-tion ceremonies one may present every child with a Bible, or an eco-nomics textbook, just as one may present a political leaflet to every passerby in the street; but in the absence of anything sensible the recip-ients can do with their new possessions, this scrupulous impartiality will not amount to a serious act of justice. To ask about the justice of possessions is to ask about their human significance, i.e., how they em-power the possessor to act, how they work as a resource for the exercise of human freedom. And only in certain well-defined contexts can equal distribution confer something like an equal increment of freedom. The children at the mealtable may demand fair shares, but that is because they have roughly equal appetites; it would make no sense to insist on piling Granny's plate as high as that of the ravenous nine-year-old. For the most part, freedoms won from a given material resource will vary as widely as our different histories and projects vary. Equality of treat-ment never guarantees equality of outcome. "Outcome," indeed, is a chimerical notion. Economics can draw lines under its predictions only when it functions in an abstract mathematical mode. Reinsert the pre-dictions into history, and they are no more than trends. New commu-nications will always ensue to produce new inequalities.

Measures of equal distribution, then, can achieve only momentary states of equality, and are not a universal response to poverty. They may or may not be a sensible strategy for dealing with it in any given cir-

cumstance. Yet there is a categorical case for undertaking them on the
threshold where social participation itself is threatened or denied. Let
us imagine a society confronting a serious problem of refugees, who
have lost their homes and their possessions in a disaster or a war, and
are sitting in large numbers in camps. The first call they make, of
course, given the predictable threats from starvation and disease, will
be for a program of food, shelter, and medicine. That is their claim to
equal treatment on the threshold of death. But when that provision is
in place, something will have to be done about their resettlement and
the provision of basic equipment for them to earn a living. This, too, is
simply the claim of equal humanity for equal treatment. As we must respond to them on the threshold of death, so we must respond to them
on the threshold of social exclusion. Both responses are concerned
with a minimal provision equally necessary to all human beings. There
may then be very good reasons to do *more* than the minimum: to provide their children with educational opportunities, to assist them to
learn new skills that might avert future such disasters, and so on. But
these further measures will not apply universally to every person by virtue of his or her bare humanity; so the argument for them will be made
in terms of relative attributive claims, where one claim competes with
another. The criteria of human equality establish the minimum demand, the demand on the threshold, which takes priority over all other
possibilities of attributive justice.

This may perhaps be taken as a variant of equality of opportunity,
one close to what Amartya Sen has described as "basic capability." It interprets the claim of poverty in a way restricted in scope but demanding in terms of practical urgency. There are all kinds of opportunities
that history denies to most of us, and justice has no business trying to
universalize these, if only because we none of us have life enough to exploit them all. But the opportunity to live, and the opportunity to participate in a society, are metaphysically foundational; they correspond
to our universal created nature as human beings; they can seriously
and unqualifiedly be demanded from fellow human beings. On this account, as the example makes clear, "equality of opportunity" is not the
purely *spiritual* equality given in the metaphysical condition of free
agency, nor the merely *formal* one of having an equal chance of winning
or losing in the lottery of life — Tawney's "tadpole philosophy" — objections that may, perhaps, reasonably be made against some more expan-

sive accounts of it.[15] It is a definite social disposition of material resources, to achieve which we may have to take definite action. It is a
norm of general justice and therefore a proper goal of political judgment. To the objection that by focussing on elementary social enablement it does nothing to promote justice among the enabled, the answer is simply that not all justice can or should be thematized under
the head of *equality*. Much that we ought to do for people, we ought to
do for reasons of attributive justice: employ them to the level of their
abilities, reward them for their labor to the point that they can afford
appropriate housing, marry and have children, and so on. But these are
things we cannot do, and should not pretend to do, equally.

How elementary social enablement must be, will, of course, be determined by reference to social conditions. British farmers, who would
count as wealthy by African standards, were committing suicide in record numbers some years ago because they found nothing left for them
to do to stave off disaster. That suggests, at least, a measure of social
disenablement. Financial indicators alone cannot tell us whether people have the necessary minimum; only the human economic reality of
people finding, or being unable to find, the opportunity to work can
do so. Taken in these terms, however, the threshold must be understood as a *human* one, on which all human beings are equal. We cannot
move the threshold up and down on impulse, at one moment offering
the public some heady moral idealism by making large minimal demands on behalf of British farmers, and the next relieving their embarrassment by declaring how little it takes to support an African refugee!

For along with these two threshold-instances, at which human
equality directly shapes the requirements of attributive justice, we must
mention a third form of equal treatment that is immediately binding:
what is called, "equality before the law," and would be better called,
"equality before judgment." Our judgment, like God's, must be without *prosōpolēmpsia,* "respect for persons." This is partly a purely formal
condition of the act of judgment as such. We cannot judge unless we
can describe particulars as instances of a kind; and this requires them
to be ranged alongside one another as equal instances of the relevant
kind, to be treated in equal ways. To make a judgment "without prejudice" is to import no differentiation between one particular case and

15. See Forrester, *On Human Worth,* pp. 143-44.

the next which is not justified within the descriptive aspect of the judgment itself. For this reason it normally imposes only negative requirements, that we *refrain* from offering inducements to the judge, tampering with the evidence, according privileged status or information to one party, etc. Yet over and above its formal character this, too, implies a substantive acknowledgment of the metaphysical equality of human beings. The critique of slavery, for example, was concerned as much as anything with the absence of recognized legal and moral relations between two human beings who were in principle capable of cooperation and fellowship. All human beings, because they are endowed with language, are open to answer for their behavior and to question other people's. Courts may not deny standing to those who are capable of speaking for themselves. Practical reason equalizes those who dare to engage in it.

In all these three instances we are dealing with an equality of *individual persons*. It is those who have direct standing before God who can call in question the claims of complex social organisms. Classes, communities, and other collectives have no such standing. We should always exercise care in the face of statements of the form, "class x must be treated equally to class y." Some such statements may be robustly defensible — who, for example, would doubt the wisdom of equal power-sharing between Catholics and Protestants in Northern Ireland? — but they stand at the *conclusion* of a train of thought about the requirements of justice in the situation, and do not arise immediately from the moral principle of the equality of all human beings. So St. Paul judiciously framed his most famous statement of human equality as a negative proposition: "There is neither Jew nor Greek, slave nor free, male nor female" (Gal. 3:8). That is to say: there are certain decisive junctures at which it is irrelevant to which of these categories a person belongs. The generic claim that women should be treated equally to men may sometimes be intended simply as a shorthand for that negative proposition. But at other times it may be intended in a quite different sense: that the *class* of women should have equality of treatment to the *class* of men, a social-engineering proposition which could be valid only in certain special contexts and which would need to be argued contextually. Does anyone think that the right amount to spend on women's health-care is necessarily what is spent on men's health-care? Or that the right amount to spend on boys' education is precisely what is spent on girls' education? The right amount to spend on women's health-care and boys' education is what women's health and boys' education *require* — or as near to it as can be afforded. The drift from a claim about equality of persons to a claim about equality of classes produces some of the more laughable examples of political prudery current today, such as the expectation that women and men must be equally represented in every trade or profession regardless of natural preferences. What applies to women and men applies equally to races in multi-racial societies. The right number of black police in the force cannot be determined as an arithmetic equivalent to the number of white police, as though the whole of society were a bilateral contract between black and white populations; neither can it be determined as a proportional figure corresponding to the ratio of blacks to whites in the population. The right number is whatever it takes to provide understanding and sympathetic policing in black areas without serious loss to the policing of white areas, to assure a valuable experience and a useful contribution of black members at every level in the force, and to encourage well-equipped black candidates to think they can make a successful career in policing. In the present circumstances in Britain it is rather more, one may suspect, than strictly proportional number — and certainly more than we actually have!

4

Political Judgment

The most distinctive feature of political judgment is its universal and categorically binding character. We should distinguish this from the *free* self-binding which any individual agent may impose on him or herself in the pursuit of projects. "Absolute" freedom is the freedom to deliberate on our actions wholly in teleological, forward-looking terms. If I am invited to review a book, I may not have to ask myself any questions other than about the goods that may be achieved by doing it: "Will the book be instructive? Will it be entertaining? Will it assist my thought on an intriguing subject? Will it provide an opportunity to give instruction to the public?" These questions — about realizing aims, satisfying wants, and so on — have a teleological form. But that kind of freedom gets me no further than *beginning* something. As soon as I actually set my hand to the review, I cannot confine my considerations to forward-looking ones. I have assumed a responsibility: to do justice to the contents of the book whether they intrigue me or not, to complete what I have undertaken whether I am pleased by the task or not, and to do it thoroughly whether it can be done in the time anticipated or not.

The loss of freedom I have incurred in accepting responsibility is an aspect of freedom itself. The condition for realizing freedom is that I shall accept limitations on it. All that can be done in absolute freedom is to begin; finishing implies responsibility. Someone who is free only to begin is not free to act. So freedom itself implies the dialectical movement by which we limit it in order to realize it. This dialectic lies at the heart of all social roles, which are defined by other people's expectations of them. If I am not a reviewer but a reviews-editor, even my initial decision as to whether to commission or publish a review of a given book is not wholly forward-looking, because my role allows me no true beginnings. Expectations and entitlements are there before me: I must ask what is due to the author, what the journal is obliged to include, and so on. I am part, as we say, of an "institution." Any role in an institution is defined by its responsibilities, so that there is no moment at which one may simply please oneself. Those who occupy such roles are allowed a certain freedom of discretion, but not a freedom of choice. When they retire, they say, "Now I am free to do what I want!" though everything they have done in their institutional position has been an implication of their freedom. The self-binding of freedom is not confined to institutions, but institutions involve it in the highest degree. If self-binding is the price we pay for freedom to act, this enhanced self-binding is the price we pay for freedom to act in cooperative ways together with other people.

But the way in which political judgment binds our freedom is not like either of these examples. Political binding, too, operates with the dialectic that limits freedom to realize it. But with free engagements it is the logic of our own pursuit of our ends, whether individual or social, that restricts our freedom. Self-limitation is a means to self-realization. Political authority, on the other hand, realizes goods that never were the ends of our action, and political authority is not itself a means to realize anyone's end. It has been the hallmark of much political theory since the seventeenth century to conceal this difference, and to argue that political authority is precisely what we would devise, or perhaps even did devise, in the pursuit of the freedoms we desire. But the goods we value in political relations could not from any conceivable practical perspective have been desired, or the means to realize them calculated. Those whose freedom is limited by political judgment are not limited by the inherent logic of their own actions. There is no point of view from which the question, *shall* we have such a thing as political authority in order to achieve *these* goods? could be imagined as having been asked. Political freedoms and the practices of restraint in which they are embedded are simply *discovered within* our human experience of the world. This is the heart of what is said more simply by speaking of political authority as a work of "providence."

The judgments of political authority, then, have a radically *other-*

binding character; they bind those who have not bound themselves. They form a framework within which freedom, however exercised, is to function, and that framework is the same for any action of any agent. Although much of the time we are not aware of the constraints of the political order, that is because we have learned in general terms to exercise our freedom within its constraints, so that we never have to become aware of them. They shape what we are doing, even when we are not immediately confronting them. In that sense the dictates of political authority are "universal and universally applicable" *(semper et pro semper),* which is simply to say that they are categorical, not hypothetical. Political authority makes requirements to which we must all conform.

This conformity, looking at it from one side, we call "obedience," using the traditional term which stresses the particular self-denial that may be required of the political subject. But looking at it from the other side, we may call it "solidarity." For this conformity is a way of acting *together,* of *all* doing something or refraining from doing something. Within the corporate response, of course, there are special performances assigned to special roles. Only military personnel perform bombing raids; only tax collectors send out tax demands. But what they do, they do in a role that has meaning only within our collective solidarity. If their roles were not so constituted, their actions would have no political authority; they would merely be bizarre forms of crime, which is how libertarians are inclined to see them. This solidarity is something quite different from *community,* which is a sphere of free action, pure and simple.[1] More precisely, solidarity is a way of *suffering* together, rather than acting together, since the corporate character of what we do in response to legitimate authority consists essentially in allowing ourselves to be restricted in our own freedom of action by others' necessities. In community we may deny ourselves for the sake of achieving something together; in solidarity we deny ourselves for the sake of meeting a threat together.

---

1. Against Robert Spaemann, *Zur Kritik der politischen Utopie* (Stuttgart: Klett, 1977), p. 9, commenting on Aeschylus's *Eumenides:* "Was in diesem Zusammenhang interessiert, ist die formelle struktur des ethischen Handelns: erstens die Unmittelbarkeit einer Wertschätzung, die sich nicht durch Gründe vermittelt, zweitens eine ausschlaggebende Entscheidung durch die Vernunft, die die Impulse zum Schönen koordiniert und am Ziel des guten Lebens im ganzen kritisch mißt. Hier . . . wird der Ursprung der Polis, der griechischen Stadtstaates, dargestellt."

Yet political judgments, too, preserve freedom and do not merely limit it. How, then, do they function differently from the hypothetical limitations we impose upon ourselves? In the first place, they compel us to conceive of a sphere of freedom wider than any we might project from our private undertakings. We must conceive of a "public realm" (to use the phrase made popular by Hannah Arendt), which we do not devise but which exists antecedently to us.

In liberal and neo-liberal discussions it is usual to find the terms "private" and "political" (or sometimes "public" in the sense of "political") dividing the whole sphere of human social engagement between them. This expresses the thought that political structures are justified solely by private interests, and it results in the persistent late-modern dilemma of "hard" versus "soft" liberalism: either we accept a diffuse extension of political authority throughout public life (the "hard," totalitarian corruption), or we glorify private experiences, especially sensual or emotional experiences, as the good which social interaction serves (the "soft," individualist corruption). But the rationale of political structures is not to preserve private freedoms, though they will also be preserved, but to preserve public freedoms, i.e., the free communications that we undertake simply because we are, as human beings, helplessly social. Public freedoms are in an important sense the fulfillment of private freedoms, for the pursuit of private satisfaction can never satisfy our actual human aspirations. Yet they are not the *goals* of our private actions, but are over and above them, a framework that we discover rather than devise. These are the freedoms which political authority serves directly, binding our private freedoms in order to safeguard our public freedoms.

Terminology in this area is a jungle of incompatible conventions, and there is no hope of doing anything other than cut a path through it. (1) The adjective "political" is sometimes used with wider reference than the noun "politics." "Politics" has to do with government, but any kind of socially aware activity may be called "political," from writing poetry to organizing a drop-in shelter. (2) "Political" and "politics" are sometimes confined much more narrowly to those activities remotely concerned with elections and elected office, so that civil servants, judges, etc. are spoken of as "non-political." (3) The term "public" is used in a time-honored legal sense to mean government-promoted, and "private" to mean independent of government promotion. So a "private university" lacks government funding, and "public law" controls the activity of government departments. This terminology has influenced the social-theory distinction between "public associations" and "private associations." (4) Hannah Arendt influentially used the pair of terms "public" and "private" to denominate the difference between a widely conceived sphere of the common good, on the one hand, and a sphere of domesticity or consumption on the other. For the purposes of our present discussion, "politics" and "political" are used more narrowly than their widest current sense and more widely than their narrowest, to indicate those activities with a direct relation to government, but not only those with a direct relation to elected office. Our term "political," then, corresponds roughly to the lawyers' term "public," and our term "public" to the lawyers' "private." Our terms "public" and "political" divide between them the pursuit of the common good, which Arendt treated as a unified "public" sphere; and in this we follow a traditional line of disagreement between Christianity and classical antiquity. We use the term "private," on the other hand, more flexibly and favorably than Arendt, who was somewhat hypnotized by the household as the paradigm alternative to public engagement, characterizing it wholly negatively in terms of consumption.

The important point is more than terminological; it is conceptual. Activity impinging on society divides three ways, not two: "political," "public," and "private." Public activity and political activity are both concerned with the common good; but public activity pursues the common good directly, political activity defends it reflexively. Private activities engage the common good only indirectly; they serve a restricted sphere of communication, like a family or a corporation. The private finds its decisive focus in the familiar, those formal and informal spheres of emotional intimacy, family and friendship. Public activity, on the other hand, has the good of the community in view. But public activity is not restricted, and often better not restricted, to political means. We may organize relief of the destitute and homeless, which is a public activity, or we may campaign for government action to relieve the destitute and homeless, which is a political activity. It is fashionable to deny the possibility of distinguishing these two aspects of a charitable enterprise, and, indeed, they may often be difficult to separate sharply in practice. Yet there are certain purposes for which the distinction is important. Charity Commissioners administer a favored tax-status, i.e., a form of governmental patronage; it is important that such governmental patronage should not be used to subsidize one side against another in an open public debate on matters of general public concern. Those who accept government patronage for good purposes, then, must accept also the need not to use it to promote their own view of public affairs. So a condition of enjoying charitable tax-status is that engagement in political debate is strictly limited; one may advise the public that there are certain serious obstacles to humanitarian work, but one may not advise it to remove the obstacles by opposing, or supporting, a political party.

We should not suppose that the only reason for engaging in political rather than direct public action is to make our voluntary efforts more effective, or, indeed, to replace them with action by governments. There may be crises where the scale or political dimension means that nothing is effective without action from governments (one's mind goes to the militarized refugee-camps of eastern Zaire during the great Rwanda crisis, or to the escalating AIDS crisis in southern Africa). But for the most part, the most effective way to relieve the destitute is simply to relieve them, not to condemn them to the clumsy processes and eternal procrastinations of government. The value of invoking political authority is a political value: to recognize that this *promotion* of the common good by voluntary agents acting in public is also a *defense* of the common good for which the community as a whole must take responsibility. The reason for getting governments involved in such matters is that it is not right for them to be left out of them.

In the second place, political judgments do not limit freedom *in order to realize it*, but *in order to defend it*. Public freedom is not a project, like private action, that requires realizing; it is an ensemble which gives coherence to private undertakings. And so political authority has no special mandate to pursue a public goal, "the common good" conceived of as a giant millennium dome. Mankind in his and her native social existence, to the extent that that is not impeded and hindered by sin, serves the common good simply by being *societas humana*. Government's task is to respond to *threats* to the common good, repelling whatever obstructs our acting freely together.

Here, then, we can identify a distinctive way in which political judgment discriminates between right and wrong. All analogical forms of judgment make these discriminations in some way, whether intellectually or practically; but political judgment discriminates in order to *defend against the wrong*. In an intellectual discernment of justice-as-right, the wrong may be identified simply as what contradicts the right: in affirming that Caesar was consul for the first time in 59 BC we reject a potentially infinite number of suggestions that he was consul first in some other year — 58 BC, 60 BC, etc. The same goes for a private practical judgment: in deciding to invest £1000, we exclude an infinity of possible decisions to invest less or more. In each case the right is determined, the wrong left indeterminate. But in an act of political judgment it is the right that is indeterminate, the wrong determined. No judge can declare comprehensively what is right to do — for what is right to do lies in the sphere of freedom, and is the subject of an infinite number of decisions by an infinite number of people. What the judge can determine is the wrong done at a given point, and this focus on the determinate wrong is what gives the political judgment its distinctive condemnatory character. In political judgment wrong has epistemological priority over right — which is to say that there are no formal "principles" of justice before we render actual judgment on some concrete wrong, which, in its turn, is measured, not in relation to some prior principle of justice, but in relation to created order as such. The wrong is not a mere negative of some right, but *guilt and injury*. Guilt and injury, however, cannot be elucidated *a priori*, only condemned *a posteriori*. The determination of wrong, then, is constantly repeated in an ongoing practice of judgment, which elaborates general categories of guilt and injury out of concrete condemnations.

What is the difference between speaking of "wrong" and speaking of "harm"? Wrong denotes a moral relation, harm an objective detriment. One can do wrong without doing harm, and harm without doing wrong; but one cannot do intentional harm without doing wrong, nor can one do *effective* wrong without intending something harmful, even if one does not intend harm as such. For the purposes of defining political judgment, then, the two are interchangeable. To react to objective wrong is to react to harm. But in the context of liberal antipaternalism, a distinction is often introduced: harm is wrong done to others, not to oneself. The contention that only harm permits the intervention of authority amounts to the same as the contention that authority cannot intervene to prevent one wronging oneself. This contention is in turn predicated on a distinction between a purely "private morality," which concerns the way an individual governs his or her own life, and a "public morality," which concerns the way in which the individual impacts the lives of others. But this distinction cannot be substantial. Though harming oneself is something different from harming others aspectually, they overlap substantially. Classical ethics was never tired of pointing out that one who wrongs others wrongs himself, and the one who wrongs himself deprives others of a worthy fellow-citizen.

The paradigm cases which are meant to prove the possibility of doing wrong without doing harm make the point only by begging it, i.e., excluding *a priori* from the category of harm anything other than the direct assault on another person's autonomous self-disposal. The antipaternalist thesis is founded on the denial of such a thing as the common good. This can only be doctrinaire. Even if we resolve to allow all alcoholics and drug abusers to follow the logic of their self-destructive lifestyles to its doom without an attempt to rescue or rehabilitate, we shall have to find some way of speaking of the sheer damage done to society by the presence of its members lying about the streets in various stages of self-destruction. To refuse to call it "harm" looks like terminological willfulness. Society has a clear and obvious interest in people not conducting their lives in certain ways, even if there are no immediate victims of their doing so. It is partly to limit such wider damage that we think that simple *laissez-faire* is not a civilized option, though partly also out of charitable concern. The motivational distinction between what we do for another individual and what we do for society as a whole can never be made precise, since the altruistic motivation implies precisely a sense of identification of oneself with the interests of the other within a wider community of interest.

*   *   *

Political judgment, then, is a response to wrong as injury to the public good. We may call this "the reactive principle." The earliest Christian reflections on the origins of civil government, led by the Yahwist primeval history, located the origin of government *post lapsum,* a doctrine that prevailed throughout the patristic period. "In the beginning," Chrysostom declared, "there was only one kind of government, that of the man over the woman. But when our race had run adrift into every kind of disorder, [God] instituted other kinds, those of masters, rulers, etc." And Augustine: "the rational creature made in God's image was given dominion over irrational creatures, no more: not man over man, but man over beast."[2] An earlier generation of historians used to attribute the doctrine to Stoic sources, but these would have had little influence upon patristic thought, had they not chimed so well with Genesis 1–11, a constant source of images that contrasted the historical state of society with a state of innocence.[3] This line of reflection intersected with another, also primitive, which stressed the role of government as a mediation of divine wisdom. The meeting of these two thoughts generated an important tension in Western political thought. St. Thomas's departure from the *post lapsum* account under Aristotle's influence and his elaboration of an administrative view of government that might have served unfallen man, has been singled out as a dramatic departure. The fourteenth-century reaction to it, however, by Scotus on the one hand and Marsilius on the other, must equally be noticed.[4] The tension proved resolvable. By the sixteenth century an Augustinian such as Luther can find the germ of political life in Adam's naming of the animals in the garden, while his Thomist contemporary Vitoria can assign the origins of the city to Cain and Nimrod, and see its purpose as to ward off attack.[5] The two emphases converged upon a consensus, that while powers of association, organization, and management are among the creaturely possibilities of human existence, the crystallization of these into political functions of command and restraint presupposes a threat to social relations. *Politia* may represent the original social powers of humankind, and it may also represent the measures that divine providence devises to protect them.

The reactive principle is one and the same with the anti-totalitarian

2. Chrysostom, *Homily on 1 Corinthians* 34. Augustine, *City of God* 19.5; *IG,* p. 157.

3. The "coats of skins" (Gen. 3:21); the city of Cain with its arts and crafts (4:17ff.); the use of alcohol as a sedative (5:29; 9:20ff.); the confusion of tongues (11:6ff.).

4. John of Paris, in the first generation after Thomas's death, can be associated with him, as can Dante. But in the second generation political Aristotelianism took an Averroist turn, which recovered a distinction between the age of politics and the age of perfection — now conceived eschatologically rather than protologically.

5. *Commentary on Genesis,* WA 42.87 [= LW 1.115]; *De potestate civili* 4. Vitoria's polemic concern is directed primarily against the idea that political society is conventional. That is the real issue in the sixteenth century, one which cut across the Augustinian-Thomist divide.

principle that has been so important for Western politics in the past century: not everything we do is to be determined by political judgment; not everything is to be either forbidden or commanded. This is in strong opposition to the conception, which the Renaissance recovered from Aristotle, of government as an architectonic practice: "Someone who sings a given part in a consort may sing very well, but is only a singer; only the conductor of the whole consort who commands all the parts at once is the master of music. Someone who carves the columns and raises a wall of a building is a mason; only the one who conceives the whole building and has all the proportions in his head is the architect."[6] If we think of the art of government in this way, political authority becomes totalitarian in principle; that is to say, it is the agency that constructs a social whole out of diverse individual strands. How vicious it is in practice will depend on how abstract the concept of the social whole turns out to be. But it is implied in the conception that *some* abstract social design must be imposed if harmony is to emerge from the variety. The reactive principle, by contrast, supposes that harmony is not a design conceived in a ruler's head, but a nexus of social communications that exist and flourish antecedently.

The reactive principle is not, however, to be confused with the libertarian insistence on "minimal government." Even if government is limited to defense against injurious wrong, we are not bound to a narrow or restricted concept of what injurious wrongs may require defense against them. If we confine our idea of wrong to crime or tort, of course, we shall end up with a very shrunken role for political authority, or else lose patience with the reactive principle altogether. But wrong includes failures of wisdom, and the exercise of political judgment overlaps significantly with the exercise of prudence. We may exercise prudence in ways that do not imply judgments on wrong, where the only question is how to act in the most beneficial way, e.g., in making the most profitable investments; such exercises of prudence are not

6. Fénélon, *Les Aventures de Télémaque* 17, *Oeuvres* II, ed. J. Le Brun (Paris: Gallimard, 1997), p. 294: "Celui qui dans un concert ne chante que certaines choses, quoiqu'il les chante parfaitement, n'est qu'un chanteur. Celui qui conduit tout le concert, et qui en règle à la fois toutes les parties, est le seul maître de musique. Tout de même celui qui taille les colonnes, ou qui élève un côté d'un batiment, n'est qu'un maçon. Mais celui qui a pensé tout l'édifice, et qui en a toutes les proportions dans sa tête, est le seul architecte."

political judgments. But prudence is also involved in avoiding harms, and the failure to avoid avoidable harms may constitute wrong. When wrong is done by private neglect or ignorance, it is a properly political judgment to impose the prudential provisions that the primary agents ought to have imposed on themselves. It is a properly political judgment, furthermore, to *anticipate* harm from private neglect or ignorance, and not to wait for it to happen. We may speak intelligibly of a prospective judgment, at once *reactive* to wrong and *proactive* to avert the threat of harm.

Suppose, for example, that the question arises in a developing country of founding a national university. As the debate unfolds, it becomes apparent that the chief interest-groups are opposed to it. The existing foreign-educated elite does not want its privileges diluted by more ready sources of expertise; primary producers are threatened by the prospect of a skilled economic sector; organs of cultural tradition fear cosmopolitan deracination; and these all come together in agreement that a university is something the country does not need. Yet that opposition could be profoundly unwise, for if higher education is available to citizens only in foreign languages and alien settings, both cultural and political integrity could be at risk. Here, then, there could be a *wrong.* We may call it a wrong "to future generations," but that means simply that the wrong has no *determinate* victims, though still doing harm to many people in the long term. It is not a crime or a tort; it is not the product of malice or ill-will, but merely of restricted sympathies; it is a wrong simply by being a failure of attributive justice.

Wrong, and nothing else, is the necessary condition, but also the sufficient condition, for governmental intervention. The attempt to define certain spheres of social life as in principle beyond the reach of such intervention is a mistake. This attempt began with the claims of the Christian church leadership to have a parallel and alternative authority to that of secular rulers: "two there are, august Emperor, by which this world is ruled, the consecrated authority of priests and the royal power."[7] The Reformers, with the exception of Calvin, swept such claims to independent church authority aside: for Anglicans the monarch had "the chief government of all estates of this realm, whether they be ecclesiastical or civil," and for Grotius the term "wrong" in

---

7. Gelasius I, *Letter to Emperor Anastasius.* In *IG*, p. 179.

Romans 13:4 must include wrong done in religion.[8] The exemption of religion from the competence of rulers implied an alternative authority competent to rule in this sphere, usually the papacy. The confusion which followed in the modern period, with neither the secular nor the spiritual power generally recognized as having authority to govern the church, is evident from the ideological chaos of modern secularism, which imposes on government a distance from religion that is anything but benign. Yet in the modern period we have encountered an efflorescence of similar claims to exempt status, on behalf of the family, of educational institutions, and even, in the higher flights of neoliberal fervor, the economy.

Education was historically an area in which government began to intervene by way of prospective judgments quite early, with Byzantine emperors extending their concern for the training of state officials to the general enlightenment of society, a trend taken up in the West both by a regulatory regime and through royal foundations and endowments. But in recent generations the most expansive development of prospective judgment has been in economic affairs. The complexities of this development are too great to explore here, and we shall have to be content with a single observation of principle. The intervention of government to control the economy may be justified, like every other activity of government, only as a measure to remedy or avert wrong. But as such it *can* be justified, and this is sufficient in principle to justify many of the extensive economic undertakings of modern governments.

Western doctrine on this point is at a peculiar juncture. At the level of popular expectation "managing the economy" still looks like the single most important function of government. Urged on by the media, politicians continue imprudently to parade taxation plans before electorates to the exclusion of almost everything else. Yet the newly dominant orthodoxy teaches that the "free-market system" brooks no intervention, and we have seen strategic renunciations of domestic economic control by governments, combined with hot pursuit of market-liberalization at the international level. The new orthodoxy has, however, itself fallen into disrepute, especially as it affects interna-

---

8. Article 37 (1571); Grotius, *De imperio summarum potestatum circa sacra* I.2: *Dicitur a Paulo apostolo 'Dei' esse ministra, vindex ad iram ei qui malum fecerit. 'Mali' autem nomine comprehenditur etiam omne id quod circa sacra committitur.*

tional markets. The metamorphosis of that angel of light, G.A.T.T., into the Satan of the World Trade Organization is one of the more notable transvaluations of our age.

Conceptually, the problem lies with the reification of "the economy." The habitual use of the definite article with that noun is revealing, suggesting a kind of *corpus mysticum*, over which the same battles have to be fought as were fought over that other *corpus mysticum*, the church. Does civil government exercise control of this sanctuary, or must it bow down and worship? The socialist identification of society and state encouraged the idea that total state-management of the economy was necessary to human self-direction. In response there arose a kind of anti-socialism: the economy was a spontaneous wellspring of human vitality to be protected by religious reverence from the impious tamperings of government. The two perspectives agreed in conceiving the economy as a *pleroma*, a complete embodiment of human endeavor and energy.

What is needed now is a demystification. The economy is no *pleroma;* it is simply the way in which our various endeavors and engagements appear when observed at a certain cross-section, the point at which transactions occur in markets. The meaning of these transactions is not to be found in the market through which they pass, but in the forms of life that generate them. These are very various: education, worship, cultivation of crops, transport, child-rearing, etc. None of them is like any other, and though all of them may generate transactions, the extent to which they appear in the market, and so can be observed there, is very varied, too. A snapshot of the market is a snapshot of life, but one taken from an unnatural angle. The attempt to regulate all that appears in the market would not only be an attempt to control all life, but an attempt to control it through its most incidental feature — like directing a herd of buffalo by pulling their tails. Yet this does not mean that markets are a nullity which can be allowed to regulate themselves with the same confidence that we trust well-kept books to balance themselves. Exchange is a distinct kind of human undertaking, and, because it involves the comparing of unlike with unlike, it is full of opportunities for wrong, whether deliberate (as with false weights or counterfeit money) or unwitting (as when a market falls under the control of a few dominant interests). It is to restrain these wrongs that governments intervene into the mechanisms of economic transactions.

The almost insoluble problem of international markets provides the clearest illustration of how a reactive response to wrong requires selective control of economic processes. Markets do not regulate themselves. They *adjust* themselves, but like the brutish and short-sighted Leviathans they are, they trample people beneath their feet while they do so. It is not believable that government disinvolvement and absence of control could ever foster economic justice. Nature, as every groundsman knows, abhors a level playing-field. For just and ordered exchanges to take place, there must be means to safeguard them. So any program with the single aim of liberalizing trade, however beneficial it may be in its early stages in removing unnecessary tariffs, is doomed at some point to fall into the service of uncontrolled private interests. And in the absence of international regulatory institutions which command general confidence, the only way to tackle the injustice of international trade, as with all international injustices, is piecemeal and *post eventum*, by a kind of "just war" that includes the possibility of defensive tariffs or restrictions.

Economic wrongs may be of many kinds, but they converge on the lack of reasonable resources to work, understanding "work" in the broadest way, not narrowly as paid employment. The responsibility for confronting economic wrong belongs to those who have the responsibility for confronting wrong of other kinds, that is to say, governments. What measures they need to discharge this responsibility may vary from time to time. They may need their own currencies if alternatives are unreliable, but they may judge their people better served by sharing a currency with others. They may need arm's-length mechanisms to regulate money-supply, or in other circumstances may need direct control. Policies on such matters resist universalization, and derive such validity as they have from immediate practical circumstances. But the principle is clear, that whatever measures are necessary to remedy wrongs as they arise are the responsibilities of governments. And no government can afford to ignore the perpetual inventiveness of wrong.

All this by way of elaboration of the reactive principle. That principle must be construed broadly, but is not vacuous. There may be wrongs to be righted when no group in particular is to blame and no group in particular is victimized; yet the idea of defending the common good cannot underwrite *any* project of community self-expansion. We can understand, whether we approve or not, why the government of Quebec has consistently attempted to privilege the use of the French language in public places. We would not understand if the government of Ontario were to privilege the use of English in the same way. Where there is no threat, there is no reason for government action. Not everything that ought to be done by someone ought to be done by governments. The doctrine that a government ought to have a policy for absolutely everything is one of the aspects of totalitarianism.

Although minimal government is not the right conclusion to draw from the reactive principle, then, it is not wrong to insist on an *economy* of government. Economy requires that authority may be exerted only where there is *prima facie* threat to the common good. Every abridgment of freedom must be justified by a proportionate danger to freedom. Over-deployment of political judgment frustrates the achievement of its goal. Throughout the Hebrew Scriptures we find an acknowledgment that the purpose of civil institutions is not only to administer true judgment, but to limit it. In Genesis 4, by skillful deployment of his mythological sources, the narrator interprets the protective "mark of Cain" as the city which Cain founded: civic existence defends the murderer against the cry of the blood of Abel, and is a bulwark against an outraged natural justice that cannot tolerate the continuance of murderous humanity upon the earth. Again, the narrative of the punishment of the tribe of Benjamin (Judges 20-21) comes to a climax in the realization that the very existence of the twelve-tribe nation is imperiled by the judgment that it must impose upon its smallest tribe. Judgment has to be restrained in the interest of human welfare; and God's judgment, too, is restricted this way, as Noah learned from the bow in the sky (Gen. 9:12-17). Civil government must operate on the principle expressed by T. S. Eliot, that "human kind cannot bear very much reality."[9] Societies that approximate to the totalitarian ideal that everything not forbidden is commanded, suppress the public realm by quelling the free initiative of society's members.

---

9. *Murder in the Cathedral*, in *Collected Poems and Plays* (London: Faber, 1969), p. 271.

5

Freedom and Its Loss

To speak of the "defense" of the common good is to envisage a threat, and that threat is the loss of public communications, the disappearance or erosion of those patterns of holding things in common, which constitute the point of our individual lives. This brings us to a crucial point in any description of society, the point at which we have to speak of how society consistently fails. For in describing human sociality we are on the same ground as in describing any other aspect of the image of God in humankind: a description is possible only from the viewpoint of loss. As scattered stones on an archaeological site allow the skilled eye to reconstruct the city that was built there, so the fallen shards of social existence allow us to understand the sociality that human beings were made for. There is no other route to that understanding than one which lies through the disappointments of unsociability. From an objective point of view unsociability can be described as a loss of *order,* from a subjective point of view as a loss of *freedom.*

"Freedom" is a term with a range of meanings. First and most formally, it is simply *the power to act,* that ownership of one's behavior which distinguishes the intelligent agent from creatures of instinct. Stripped bare of all social context, this is a power of individual human nature, which may usually simply be assumed. The *assertion* of freedom in this form always belongs with some kind of individualism. Here is the freedom-as-defiance of the existentialist, and of the teenager who refuses to get out of bed in the morning. But freedom so conceived is abstract and unproductive. To give the term a moral significance, we must understand it in terms of the orientation of the individual to social communications.

And so there arises a second and more substantial sense of freedom: *the realization of individual powers within social forms.* This is the sense in which we can say that the objective correlate of freedom is authority.[1] Authority (in the broadest sense, not political authority alone) attaches to those structures of communication in which we engage in order to realize freedom. And this is the sense in which freedom may be lost. Loss of freedom does not mean that the social orientation of human beings can be utterly thwarted. But we can be deprived of the structures of communication within which we have learned to act, and so we can find ourselves hurled into a vacuum in which we do not know how to realize ourselves effectively. "What I have built I am breaking down, and what I have planted I am plucking up," said YHWH to Baruch. "And do you seek great things for yourself? Seek them not!" (Jer. 45:4-5). In such a circumstance one is free to go where one will, but one has lost the forms that made it worthwhile to go anywhere. They have to be painfully reinvented, step by step, out of the bare struggle for survival. But what we can say of the individual in these circumstances, we can say equally of the society. It is not free unless it can sustain the forms that make for its members' freedom.

Freedom is a term used almost exclusively to focus attention on the possibilities of its loss. In English we have no corresponding negative term in regular use — to talk of "slavery" in this context has a quaintly old-fashioned exuberance — yet when we speak of freedom it is almost invariably to warn against, or object to, that negative possibility for which we have no regular term. Freedom is the looking-glass in which we search our features anxiously for signs of "unfreedom." But the collapse of any vital condition can occur in a multitude of ways, so what appear to be straightforward descriptions of freedom turn out to be hugely various political ideals, some of them in tension with others. Freedom can be said to be the absence of legal restrictions or the security of lawful government; it can be said to be the independence of a people owing nothing to any other, or participation in an

---

1. Cf. *Resurrection and Moral Order* (Leicester: Apollos; Grand Rapids: Eerdmans, 1986), p. 122.

international network of commitments and communications; it can be revolutionary innovation or the cherished tradition; it can be a participatory republican constitution, or a monarchy in touch with the soil and language of the people; it can be the liberty to argue and disagree in public, or it can be the private security of home and property, all depending on where we see the threat arising. That is why it is no easy thing to construct a positive program around the idea of freedom. Politicians who praise freedom too profusely in flourishing circumstances are viewed with understandable suspicion. Yet when some concrete threat appears, whatever it may be, "freedom" is the first word on all our lips.

If freedom is the self-realization of the individual within social forms, the twin guiding lights of sociality and individuality mark the runway along which any discussion of freedom must get airborne, whether its flight path then turns in a socialist direction towards securing individual freedom by way of social structures, or in a liberal direction towards securing social freedom by way of individual liberties. A people that boasts of having freed itself from foreign domination or tyranny, whose citizens all live in misery or frustration, has achieved no freedom worth the name. There is, of course, no condition of society so terrible but that somebody somewhere does well out of it; but a society's freedom is not proved by the success of a few buccaneers, but supposes that the majority of members have some openings into social forms in which they realize themselves to some degree. "Freedom" speaks of a certain conformability of society to individuals and of individuals to society. It is a measure of fit between the communications which the individual hopes for and those which the society sustains. As such, it is a matter of more or less. Even in the most oppressive circumstances it is not wholly absent. Those who have survived under totalitarian regimes have learned, and taught us, that the all-important thing is simply to persist in exercising freedom in whatever fragmentary ways remain open, sustaining communications to the fullest extent that they may be sustained. Yet this insight is compatible with reflection on "lost" freedoms, the forms of communications that should be available and are not.

Communications are sustained by tradition, and tradition is a continuity of practices, learned, repeated, and developed. In specialist communities these practices revolve around skills and around the knowledge that supports skills. But what kind of practice forms the tradition of a whole society, the matrix within which many specialist communities cohere within a given place? Supremely, the practice of recounting. History sustains the identity of societies, not only the history of the distant past, but that of the immediate past, too. The news bulletin contributes to our sense of political identity as decisively as the history of the last war. The subject of histories are places. But because places are materially different from one another, so are their histories; and because histories are different, so are the societies which recount them. The indexical difference between one society and another is the difference of the places they inhabit; but this results in a material difference, too, in the content and character of their traditions.

Freedom, then, has to do with a society's particular historical way of existing. Societies cannot be free if they cannot sustain their historical identities. They are not, as a distinguished tradition supposed, unchanging or immortal.[2] Not unchanging, because the continual process of communication transforms them by the accumulation of new experience and the operation of forgetfulness, so that over time the continuity of their identity become unclear. The sense in which the society of Great Britain today is continuous with the early medieval societies that first constituted it — Romano-British, Anglo-Saxon, Pictish, Gaelic, Norman, etc. — is highly debatable, even given the comparative stability of political institutions on that island. Societies, unlike individuals, do not have *absolute* identities; they are only more or less the same with themselves. But like individuals, when subjected to sufficient pressure they die.

That a society should be free is not merely a matter of its being situated in its place, but of having a tradition of communications shaped by the place, handed on from generation to generation. What it means for the Greeks to be free is that there is a place, Greece, where they may live together and share a society; and that the traditions native to the place, its language, intellectual discourse, geographical experience, and

---

2. See the anonymous *Vindiciae, contra tyrannos* (1570): "If it be objected that kings were enthroned and received their authority from the people who lived five hundred years ago and not by those now living, I answer that the commonwealth never dies. . . . And further, as we have at this day the same Rhine, Seine, and Tiber as was a thousand years ago, in like manner also is there the same people of Germany, France, and Rome (excepting those transferred to colonies in the meantime)." *IG*, p. 719.

the cultural practices formed by it, may be sustained unimpeded and be mediated by each generation of Greeks to the next with the enrichment of their own experience and achievement. To "be" Greek supposes that one has been educated among Greeks since one's youth, though not necessarily that one was born in Greece or had Greek parents. A national identity can, to a limited extent, be exported and sustained even away from the place that gave rise to it (though not indefinitely, and not without continuing interaction with the home society). It can also be disrupted and broken, not only by calamities but by new experiences, traumatic or otherwise, which put in doubt the significance of previous generations' experience. Revolutions in knowledge or technology have the power to disrupt cultural communications and destroy political identities.

Social identity, then, is an important contributing element in the freedom of an individual. There can be no "freedom" in having many spheres to participate in, unless one can rationally conceive of a whole that connected those spheres together. From the communications of youth, in the first place, which confer certain powers and evoke certain efforts, and, later, through the communications in which we are given to act in this or that way, making decisions which form a path across the terrain of society's traditions, we each become who we are. For Greeks to be free implies not merely that they can live in Greece and communicate with other people there; but that they can receive from previous generations of Greeks accumulated stores of experience and practice related to the place, and can contribute constructively to their transmission to younger Greeks. In realizing personal freedom we come to understand that the material content of our own communications was all provided through the communications of others; and as we discover the extent of what we have received, we recognize the significance of our social identity. Even the rebel depends upon his society to react against. When the conditions for social identity collapse, it is felt as personal injury by every member, and the resulting loss of a sense of personal significance may often be expressed in outbreaks of wild and irrational violence.

However, there is more to personal freedom than simple participation in a tradition. The individual is called by God to his or her own vocation. When William Temple, at an early stage in his career, declared that he was "not first myself and then an Englishman. . . . I am, so to speak, 'the Englishman' expressed and interpreted in a particular way," he spoke preposterously. There is a loss of both Christian and liberal perspective in the conclusion: "Consequently to England I owe all that I value and every ounce of my energy. I shall find the fulfillment of my own will precisely in the service of the country to which I belong, and I can find it nowhere else."[3] It is an imprisoned self-knowledge that cannot distinguish one's calling from one's social identity. There can be no freedom in a social identity unless it is a context to discover what one is *personally*. Roger Scruton understood the matter better when he wrote about his early "glimpses of England": "At the time they were like revelations; in a certain measure they told me who I was, and why; and their very fragmentariness inspired me to complete the picture — to complete it not in the ruined world around me, but in myself."[4] There is an eloquent difference between the term "identity," used both of societies and of individuals viewed objectively as members of societies, and the term "vocation," used only of ourselves as subjects. Two interlocking histories, the history of the society and the history constituted by the vocation of the individual, are complementary to one another, but are not fused. Neither of them is susceptible to straightforward observation and description, but each has to be sought and made the goal of reflective moral commitment. "Vocation" takes us beyond identity, to a fulfillment in service that is extended to us personally by God. And this provides us with a third sense of the term "freedom," as *the individual's discovery and pursuit of his or her vocation from God*. It is to this that Christians have pointed when they have spoken of "evangelical liberty," the liberty of baptism.

*   *   *

The success of a society lies in enabling its members to imagine their own fulfillment within the context of the whole, and where this imagination fails, so does freedom. When I sense a contradiction between the law of my being and the law of my society, I feel trapped. Such a sensation is not at all uncommon in the small change of life. It may be a perennial accompaniment to other, more pleasant experiences of sociality.

3. *Mens Creatrix* (London: Macmillan, 1916), p. 210.
4. *England* (London: Chatto and Windus, 2000), p. 42.

But when it is widespread and unrelieved, it produces acute symptoms of social collapse: conflict, suspicion, and violence.

At the root of these is a failure in the communication of wisdom. "Keep listening, but do not comprehend," the prophet was to tell his people, "keep looking, but do not understand." The prophet was enjoined to "make the mind of this people dull" (Isa. 6:9, 10). The gross and uncomprehending mind, the eyes no longer capable of observation, are a feature of every profound social malfunction. Wisdom is our appropriation of the good afforded to humankind, inexhaustible, limitlessly open to participation, defining the relations of the other goods that we encounter and the communities that they sustain. Society fails in wisdom above all when it fails to comprehend its own communicated goods in relation to the supreme good — God himself, and also the Word and Wisdom of God which gives form to the universe of beings. Its structure of shared meanings becomes falsified, and it comes to be held together by a distorted idea of itself. This may take form as an overt ideology of the traditional kind, a legitimating theory based on claims for some class, race, or civilizational form. Or it may take form as the pretended refusal of an ideology — "pretended," because communities have to have some understanding of themselves: the understanding that there is no need for an understanding is the falsest of understandings, since it refuses to admit the very question that should never be refused, the question of how true it is.

We sometimes speak of the need for a social "vision" which can make sense of personal identity within the social ensemble. This language will serve us well enough as long as we remember that not any vision will do, only a true vision. There are visions that offer reconciliation, making mighty promises of individual fulfillment within the social whole, only to shepherd us into some project of domination or some struggle for a material Utopia. We are right to distrust a certain kind of social visionary. False visions have a certain measure of success in attuning identities, since their falsity preys upon, and so incorporates, a measure of truth; yet their loss of touch with reality causes them to fail in the end. So Augustine understood the success of the Roman empire to be the fruit of "good traditions" *(boni mores)* which yet fell short of real virtue because they were founded on imperialistic delusion.

Yet human societies are not infinitely capable of wisdom, and all societies fall short of truth in some measure. How, then, can there be any degree of success, even relative success, in sustaining freedom? We find answers to this question offered from two sides.

One answer, with an emphasis that may fairly be called "communitarian" but might also be called "conservative," stresses the strongly formative role of a society in shaping its members' self-understandings. It is through the enfolding perspectives of a society's tradition that our attention is first drawn to ourselves, and our self-awareness must accommodate itself to reality as our society conceives it. Even a limited social truth may offer some scope to the individual to discover a role. Personal self-projection has to be rescued from the indulgence of pure fantasy and fitted into the constraints of reality by disciplines of observation and critical intelligence. It is the task, perhaps the principal task, of education, necessarily a conservative and directive undertaking, to equip us with the skills to distinguish fantasy from objective truth. Even art — or should we not say, especially art? — depends on and perfects such disciplines, for its whole power of expression turns on the capacity to render the artistic vision within the canons of public communication.

In forcing us to come to terms with reality, society eases us into social roles that are actually available, tasks that can actually be performed. Its first duty is to prevent us from becoming crackpots; and so it warns us to let go of certain unrealizable notions: not to try to manufacture gold by alchemy, not to try to bring peace to the world by conquest, etc. But then, we object, it used once to warn us not to think we could fly through the air like birds. Does that not discredit all society's views on what is and is not possible? Not at all. It was no credit to the Tailor of Ulm that he thought men could fly, since he failed to imagine the modalities of flying correctly. The people of Ulm were right: the tailor was a crackpot, and met the end of all crackpots. But what of the Wright brothers, who succeeded where the Tailor of Ulm failed? They succeeded because they took society's warnings seriously; only by taking the measure of what experience has shown to be impossible can anyone discover the narrow crack in the rock that leads to the hidden chamber of new possibility. Society does not have to know everything; it is enough if it knows what its members need to know in order to lead effective lives. Attunement of identities can take place in the half-light of a *sufficient* wisdom.

So much for the conservative point, and all strength to it. Yet when everything has been said along these lines, there is a further point to attend to, which may equally fairly be called "liberal." The social mediation of reality has to act as midwife to a personal vocation that is not simply a social role. Out of the communicative process there must come a moment at which the individual stands apart and looks upon the social system as it were from outside — the famous "view from nowhere." From this moment there arises the uniquely historical character of human communication, as each comes to hold as "mine" what began as "ours," and then gives it back to the community as "ours" again. For a moment society must withdraw, like John the Baptist, and point its disciple beyond itself, to the place where this reflective stance is accessible. "Blessed is the *man*": that is how the moral catechesis of ancient Israel begins, focussing our attention on ourselves as individuals. "Blessed is the man who does not stand in the counsel of the ungodly, walk in the way of sinners, or sit in the seat of the scornful" (Ps. 1:1).[5] The "counsel of the ungodly," or the "company of evil-doers" (Ps. 22:16; 26:5), is the first object against which society arms the individual, warning him that it is moral weakness to be too gregarious, too wholly responsive to social pressure. And the society which so arms the individual admits that it is itself a "company of evil-doers," that it is arming him against itself. The moral horizon which Kierkegaard called "becoming an individual," anti-social though it may seem, is in fact the horizon to which a society must direct its members if it is to fulfil itself as a society.

It is all the more important to appreciate the liberal insight at this juncture of our civilization, when appreciation is inevitably mingled with a sense of loss. A de-natured late-liberalism, shaping itself ideologically even to the point of religious persecution, indistinguishable in some ways from the Marxism it once combatted, parts company with classical liberalism precisely at this point. The liberal tradition used to defer to a point of transcendence in the individual, something which social identity could not account for, something which gave the individual an independent point of view upon society. This was not a point

---

5. This is not by any means the only occasion on which the recourse of recent English translators to the plural to avoid the word "man" has made nonsense of a text that depends on the singular noun.

of view "from nowhere"; it was a point of view from "the conscience."
By instructing the individual that conscience had precedence over every social demand, the liberal tradition did not throw him back upon
the chances of an untutored imagination. It presumed that conscience
had a source beyond both society and individual, that it was more than
an echo of social claims, more than a projection of individual dreams.
It presumed this because of the monotheistic faith that lay at the heart
of its logic. Until the early years of the twentieth century Augustine's
now controversial thesis, that there can be no "right" in a society that
does not acknowledge the right of God, appeared to be the incontrovertible bedrock of a liberal society.[6] A polytheistic society negotiates
multiple claims with no cohesion but what it can impose on them, so
that, in effect, it enforces its own sovereignty. Late-liberalism, one may
say, in taking up the banner of "pluralism," has made itself self-
consciously polytheistic.

If modern (i.e., early and mid-modern) liberal societies were successful to any degree in securing their members' cooperation and participation — and it is hard to deny them that — it was due to the moment
of self-abdication instilled by their monotheistic faith. Through that
religious moment they directed their members to become critical
moral intelligences, and taught them to see themselves as answerable
directly to God. So they envisaged themselves as open to authoritative
criticism and correction, and this lay at the heart of the reconciliation
they effected between individual and social identities. In the face of
conflicting expectations and hopes, a liberal society could make itself
answerable to pleas before the throne of God's justice. This opened up
a variety of self-understandings for the dissenter, who could assume
the role of critic, prophet, even martyr — all categories that could be socially learned and socially acknowledged. Society could even move a
dissenting member to sense its moral need, and so to respond to it not
merely with revolt but with compassion.[7]

In abandoning their deference to the transcendent, late-liberal societies followed a perilous course. Losing the conciliatory strength of religious humility, they have gambled on securing majority support for a

---

6. *City of God* 19.21. In *IG*, p. 161.

7. See the moving words of Simone Weil on "compassion for our country," in *The Need for Roots* (New York: Harper, 1971), p. 170.

narrowly materialist and sensual sphere of public communications, inculcating by every means at their disposal the purely material expectations that would conform to them.[8] This strategy of moral undereducation presumes as impoverished a view of human nature as classic liberalism presumed an exalted one. In the long term it can only have the effect of creating alienation among the spiritually more alert, those to whom a society ought to be able to look for its renewal. And it must finally run aground on the fact that the sensual majority to which it appeals is no more than an abstraction. The discontent that any human being, gifted or ungifted, educated or uneducated, feels at being underestimated can, and surely must, erode the majority, generating high waves of inarticulate dissatisfaction. The warning is commonly enough heard that if liberalism does not look out for its own foundations, it may "provoke a reaction"; and such a warning is solemn enough, given what the loss of liberal traditions would mean. But the warning that needs hearing is more solemn still: by proceeding along its present lines, liberal society may *deserve* a reaction, because it is incapable of taking the spiritual capacities of its members seriously.

The loss of wisdom that we have to fear, as the prophets have always said, is idolatry, the refusal to acknowledge God as the sovereign authority of any human society. Under the shadow of this refusal, all kinds of penultimate acknowledgments may arise. "I do not want you to be communicating with demons," St. Paul warns (1 Cor. 10:20). Does he imply by this decisively realist phrase, that "food sacrificed to idols is anything, or that an idol is something?" Apparently not. The demon may be a rebel spirit distinct from the community itself, or it may merely be a projection of the community's own spiritual powers; but in either case it is a rebel spirit. It is enough that "what pagans sacrifice, they sacrifice *to* demons, and not to God." The demon is the content of the community's self-understanding. It hardly matters in what sense this object "exists," because the community's self-understanding in its rite is so radically *false,* and yet at the same time so palpably *effective* in setting terms for common existence that exclude obedience to the source of all goods.

---

8. On the curious intensification of communications in late liberalism I have commented in *Common Objects of Love* (Grand Rapids: Eerdmans, 2002).

*　　*　　*

We have taken the loss of freedom back to a failure of wisdom. But Augustine is famous for the privileged place he assigns to *pride* as the first cause of sin, an account remembered especially for the deep influence it had upon Milton's portrayal of Satan.[9] He is also famous for his application of this idea to the history of Roman civilization, and especially to the growth of empire: "the swelling pride of an ambitious mind claims for itself, and loves to hear quoted in its praise, the verse, 'to spare the lowly and strike down the proud.'"[10] His account of sin as pride, then, has two poles: a protological pole, which finds the source of all sin, down to the meanest motive of the meanest individual, in an original act of pride, and a historical pole, which finds pride embodied paradigmatically in the ambitions of political empire. This proved attractive to the realist school of political thinkers in the mid-twentieth century. Reinhold Niebuhr found Augustine's bipolar analysis of sin an ideal model for focussing on the totalitarian developments of that period. "The religious dimension of sin is man's rebellion against God, his effort to usurp the place of God. The moral and social dimension of sin is injustice. The ego which falsely makes itself the center of existence in its pride and will-to-power inevitably subordinates other life to its will and thus does injustice to other life."[11] This suggested a democratic strategy of checks and balances to control the will to power in any one group. It was a congenial theme to a democratic tradition rooted in the seventeenth-century problematic of controlling tyrannical tendencies in absolute monarchs, and inclined (until better instructed by more penetrating analyses) to see the problem of totalitarianism as a replication of the old question of absolute rule.

But there are difficulties in harnessing Augustine's interpretation to this democratic program, and they arise at both poles of his theory. When we explore the protological pole more fully, pride is seen to be a

---

9. *City of God* 12.6, depending in part on a mistake in the Latin translation of Sir. 10:13(15), though other biblical foundations were plentiful, notably the anonymous prophetic invective against Babylon, preserved at Isa. 14:12f., which represents it as a fallen angel, "Daystar, son of the Morning."

10. *City of God* 1, pref., quoting Vergil, *Aeneid* 6.853.

11. *The Nature and Destiny of Man*, vol. 1, *Human Nature* (New York: Scribner, 1964), p. 179. I owe the quotation to Gene H. Outka.

thread within a complex weave. Satan's pride, as Augustine understood it, was not directed downward against subordinates, but upward against God. It was more envious than tyrannous. A synonym frequently deployed is "complacency," or "self-love — *to the extent of* contempt of God," suggesting that the core of this primal sin is composed of narcissism.[12] A further complexity arises when Augustine turns to describe the sin of our first parents. Here the model of open-eyed defiance will not fit. Only an angel could sin in naked pride, because only an angel could stand before the presence of God. Eve was deceived.[13] Human offense is veiled in epistemological ambiguity. Beneath the ambiguity it was a true echo of the angelic sin of rebellion; yet it was a human mediation, different from the angelic sin. Social rather than solitary, human sin was evoked by false communications that concealed the rebellious character of the will. And yet a third stage in Augustine's account is reached with the sin of Adam and Eve's descendents, different once again in that the "wound" of human nature is always presupposed as a constraining necessity, manifest in the passionate resistance of carnal instinct to the control of human reason.

Already, then, at its protological pole, the concept of sin as pride is not a monothematic one, but opens out into a psychological spectrum where deception and shortsightedness play a part as well as impotence and envy. One might sum up the difference between Augustine and Niebuhr by pointing out the role of the "will" in Niebuhr's analysis, contrasting it with Augustine's dominant motivational category, which is "love." Talk of "will" focuses upon a point of sheer choice, and brings everything to the issue of who conquers whom. Talk of "love" opens up the motivational structure to perception and misperception.

When we turn to the historical pole, the complexity is still in evidence. Rome's imperial self-aggrandizement is the result of an illusion. Polytheism, a deception practiced on Rome by demons and willingly acquiesced in, is the natural accompaniment of empire, and enslavement to the sensual is its natural corollary. So the paradigm of social sin that Rome presents is not narrowed down to the question of unbridled power. "Will-to-power" fails to capture the kind of ascendancy which Augustine conceived Rome as thirsting for. He borrowed from

12. *City of God* 14.28.
13. *City of God* 14.11.

Sallust's invective not only the phrase *libido dominandi,* but also *cupido gloriae.* The lust that consumed Rome had everything to do with the way it would be seen by others. It was not merely a matter of imposing will, but of eliciting admiration. There were brutish and oppressive moments in Rome's conquest of the world; but the ambition which drove Rome to its high achievements was the glory of "sparing the lowly," being the benefactor of humble dependents, bestowing communications, law and peace, being the focus of the world's appreciation. Its pride was the pride of a civilization, rather than the pride of an oppressor. From this we see how Augustine can also offer other unitary accounts: "It can sensibly be said that all sin is falsehood."[14]

Within the New Testament, too, we find protological accounts of sin which focus the paradoxical essence in a single word, e.g., "sin is lawlessness" (1 John 3:4). More characteristic, however, are those descriptions which unfold the various manifestations of sin in a broad phenomenological sweep, often in an eschatological framework. "In the last days distressing times will come. For people will be lovers of themselves, lovers of money, boasters, arrogant, abusive, disobedient to their parents, ungrateful, unholy, inhuman, implacable, slanderers, profligates, brutes, haters of good, treacherous, reckless, swollen with conceit, lovers of pleasure rather than lovers of God, holding to the outward form of godliness but denying its power" (2 Tim. 3:1ff.) The obviously rhetorical formation of such a passage should not lead us to overlook its detailed phenomenological interest: here is an account of evil as the collapse of sociality, society being presumed throughout as the organism on which these disturbances take hold. Individualism is conceived as a *post*-social development, a withdrawal from communications, beginning with preoccupation with the accumulation of material goods, and proceeding to aggressive competitiveness, the collapse of relations of responsibility and trust, personal degradation, and godlessness.[15]

A single protological concept such as "pride" cannot do service as a complete phenomenology of sin, which will always be diversified. As Aristotle observed, sin is multiple. The function of a protology is to *locate* sin in relation to the freedom of human agents vis-à-vis God,

---

14. *City of God* 14.4.

15. To this type of account, despite its protological appearance, belongs the observation of 1 Tim. 6:10 that the love of money is the root of all other evils.

rather than to *describe* it.[16] There is scope, certainly, for seeing the pride of the primal sin worked out in the will-to-power; but an exclusive focus on power will restrict our observations too narrowly. Lord Acton's over-quoted dictum that "all power tends to corrupt, and absolute power tends to corrupt absolutely" deserves the modest credit of noting one among many psychological phenomena that can produce the loss of freedom. Individual power-holders may indeed be corrupted by power; but they may be corrupted by weakness, too, and by indolence, compassion, or stupidity, by not having to take responsibility and by being protected from it by others. And when corruption does associate with power, who is to say which is the active element in the mix? Is it not as true to say that "the office displays the man"? The blame for a society's corruptions cannot be laid uncomplicatedly on power, since the exercise of power is always determined by the possibilities which the society itself affords. In a social description of sin we are taken beyond the idea of a particular agent's distorted acts to the distorted relations which constrain the possibilities of acting. Here Niebuhr's stress on the *collective* seat of the will-to-power is a helpful warning against liberal simple-mindedness. Are Israeli *governments* alone responsible for a decade of disastrous and oppressive policies towards the Palestinians, or must not Israeli *voters,* not least those in the weakest groupings, take their share of the blame?

There is scope, too, then, for seeing the rebelliousness of the primal sin worked out in anarchy and loss of social disciplines. But neither can this be passed off as a complete phenomenology of social failure. A popular version of this thesis points to the narcissism implicit in the primal sin and exploits its implications with the aid of developmental psychology: sin is self-absorption, *Ichverfangenheit*.[17] Each individual is held to progress from childish solipsism to adult sociality, and individ-

16. The distinction is well made by Eberhard Jüngel, *Justification: The Heart of the Christian Faith,* trans. Jeffrey F. Cayzer (Edinburgh: T&T Clark, 2001), pp. 93-95: "Sin has its real place in the relationship to God. But sin tries to make even this place unrecognizable. . . . For that very reason we must *locate* sin, we must give it its true place. . . . Sin dissimulates. . . . And that is precisely why we must not only locate, but also *identify* sin and evil. . . . It loves anonymity, even pseudonymity."

17. Thus Wolfhart Pannenberg, *Grundlagen der Ethik* (Göttingen: Vandenhoeck and Ruprecht, 1996), p. 120. A fuller anthropological account is given by Robert Spaemann, *Glück und Wohlwollen* (Stuttgart: Klett-Cotta, 1989).

ual sin is an under-developed capacity for social recognition. We have not broken out of our self-referring egg into the world of relations in which we confront the other as a subject like the self. So social sin is simply *under*-socialization. This forms the obverse of the Niebuhrian picture: not "moral man and immoral society" but "immoral man and moral society." We may concede a considerable measure of truth to the psychological observation underlying this; yet in locating the essence of wrong in heightened self-consciousness, and the overcoming of wrong in a heightened consciousness of other people, we would fail to notice ways in which heightened self-consciousness can be virtuous, over-awareness of others vicious. Kierkegaard, as though to parody this theory, reverses it: it is *becoming an individual,* he tells us, not becoming socialized, that is the test of spiritual maturity.

There is scope, finally, for the insight of Liberation Theology that the envy of the primal sin may be worked out in *excluding structures.* Social failure may consist not only in under-socializing, but in wrong socializing. Patterns of community may be erratically or irresponsibly formed, to exclude participants who ought to be included. Vigorous communications are unhapppily compatible with narrow circles that leave large numbers out. Of the three over-simplifications we have considered, this is certainly the least misleading. Failure to communicate is a failure in the functioning of society itself. Yet though failing communications may often take the form of structural exclusion, this account, too, fails to provide a general phenomenology of social wrong. For exclusion is the means by which communications are structured and specialized, and so is necessary to the very development of communication; there could be no practice of medicine or law, for example, unless insufficiently skilled persons could be excluded from offering these arts in public. Correspondingly, there are forms of inclusion that simply subvert community: we may reflect on what "inclusiveness" means when the criteria for welfare-provision or tax-breaks to help the needy are too loosely drawn.

So it is that we are sometimes required *not* to communicate — the lesson that Ezra taught to post-exilic Judah, little to our modern taste.[18] This focuses a painful paradox about exclusion: it can be *both*

---

18. As illustrated throughout the books of Ezra and Nehemiah. From the New Testament, cf. 2 John 11, 1 Tim. 5:22.

necessary *and* potentially destructive of community. We have not learned the lesson of Jesus' dealings with the Samaritans unless we have learned that barriers need to be overcome. The openness of God's communication creates a presumption in favor of more inclusive rather than less inclusive communications. Yet this presumption cannot simply be wielded as a weapon against all defined boundaries. There is a way of demonizing "structures" which is naïve and unhelpful. A measure of definition is necessary to all spheres of communication if they are to be aggregated in a society. Excluding barriers create inclusive communities; inclusions result in barriers that exclude others. To take one fundamental example: a sphere of privacy is among the social possibilities created by orderly exclusion, and without it we could not experience the intimate inclusiveness of a family. Totally inclusive communication belongs alone to the communication of the kingdom of God, which God holds in reserve, while human communications, called to "partake of the divine nature," must first "flee from the corruption that is in the world through lust" (2 Pet. 1:4).

We cannot arm ourselves with a single explanatory principle of evil and hope it will yield us a complete phenomenology of evil communications. Descriptions of social evil must be prepared to range in an exploratory fashion, and will always have a provisional and prospective quality. Nevertheless a well-focussed protology equips us with certain perennial points of reference. Here we have identified two complementary ones: in any society there will be a question both of *what* is communicated, and of *how*. In relation to these two interlocking questions we can see failure as a failure of truth, and as a failure to admit participation. Our experience of freedom's loss arises at the point where falsehood converges with envy.

6

Mercy

It was a celebrated thesis of the Reformation that the political judgments we enact are *Mosaic* and not *evangelical*. The Christian legal tradition from Gratian to Grotius, blending Roman-law jurisprudence
and scholastic theology, had thought that *lex divina* was available to
knowledge from a variety of sources, natural and revealed, but that the
capstone was *lex evangelica*, the "Gospel law," which both extended and
interpreted what we knew of God's judgments from the other sources.[1]
In challenging this the Protestant thesis agreed that God's will was revealed as divine law, but it denied that this divine law included the decisive judgment of God on which our hope for the future hangs, the Paschal judgment rendered in the death and resurrection of Christ. The
term *lex evangelica* appeared a hopeless paradox, for Gospel was not prescription but promise. Faced with that ultimate disclosure of judgment in condemnation and forgiveness we could only tremble, and believe in our hearts. The judgments that we fashioned in the public
realm, on the other hand, were founded upon natural reason, Old Testament law, or some combination of the two. This meant that they
were un-evangelical. Which was not the same as saying that they were
harsh or inflexible, for neither natural reason nor the Old Testament
are dumb about the patience and forbearance of God. But it did mean
that they stood on the near side of the great Law-Gospel divide between terror and freedom. We are conscious, on this view, of a certain

1. See Jean Porter, *Natural and Divine Law* (Grand Rapids: Eerdmans, 1999).

alienation in performing them, for they are cut off from our hope, and can tell us nothing of God's final word of grace in Christ. "Execution is the life of the Law; but then, it is the death of the Man."[2] "Do you want to know what your duty is as a prince or a judge or a lord or a lady, with people under you? You do not have to ask Christ about your duty." With this answer of Luther much of the Protestant tradition rested, treating of ethics and politics alike under the heading of "the uses of the law."[3]

We should note initially that such a formulation may have disturbing implications for the moral life as such. For if the Paschal judgment is not prescription, we cannot obey it. Ethics, too, not politics alone, must become un-evangelical. But this, we may think, is to conceive the Paschal judgment in too exclusively an apophatic fashion. The act of divine discrimination that took place there is left with no dimensions; God's acceptance and rejection is narrowed to a mathematical point without length, breadth, or height. He has accepted a faith "apart from works" in a sense so silent as to works that no distinction remains between one work and another.[4] Where, then, do we find faith "working through love"? Where, if works demonstrate a continuing relevance of law, are the "works of faith," those by which faith appears and is attested?

This apophatic approach corresponds to a characteristically Western concentration on the cross at the expense of the resurrection. For while the cross discriminates between God's righteous servant and the world that rejects him, and brings every question down to the point of which side we stand on, it is the resurrection that vindicates the pattern of humanity that Christ lived for us and commanded us to follow.

2. *The Sermons of John Donne*, ed. George R. Potter and Evelyn M. Simpson, vol. 1 (Berkeley: University of California Press, 1953), p. 173.

3. Luther, *The Sermon on the Mount*, WA 32.390 [= LW 21.110]. See *IG*, p. 599. The Law is supremely the condemning force of divine judgment — to the extent that the *Formula of Concord* §5 can even find the Law in the "preaching of the passion and death of Christ" — but into this category of condemnation every *prescription* is swept up, so that the two notions of condemnation and prescription are combined in a single compound definition: "The law is properly speaking the revealed teaching of God which instructs us what is right and pleasing to God and which also condemns whatever is sin and opposes God's will." *Legem esse proprie doctrinam divinitus revelatam, quae doceat, quid iustum Deoque gratum sit; quae etiam, quicquid peccatum est, et voluntati divinae adversatur, redarguat.*

4. Cf. Luther's paradoxical thesis, "In this faith all works become equal, and one work is like the other" (*Treatise on Good Works*, WA 6.206 [= LW 44.26]).

The resurrection does not leave God's judgment as a mathematical point without dimensions, but unfolds it and expounds it in the life of the Second Adam.[5] That life, though not wholly disclosed, is not undisclosed either: "Thy judgments have been revealed" (Rev. 15:4). Here there is a prescription we may embrace as a promise, a prescription that wholly presupposes that God has given us back our human powers of active life renewed. In the Apocalypse (Rev. 20:12) the dead are judged not out of one, but out of two books, one a multi-volume library that contains a history of all that has been done in the world, the other a single volume with a catalogue of names, a way of saying that the final judgment, too, involves both complex description and simple decision.

Yet all this does not settle the matter with respect to the judgments that we ourselves pass. Before we attempt to follow God's evangelical judgments with our own, we encounter a warning: "Judge not!" (Matt. 7:1). As we take the responsibility of judging upon ourselves, we set ourselves at a distance from the evangelical disposition of obedience and acceptance. The faithful *shall* sit on thrones and judge the tribes of Israel with God's own judgment, we are told; but that transparent identification with God is not theirs to command as yet. Not everything about God's kingdom has been disclosed, but only the path of evangelical faith and obedience. To step across into the role of judge is to leave the position of evangelical strength and to enter the sphere of human weakness and political shame. If there is service to be rendered there, we may enter that sphere without ourselves ceasing from faith and obedience or leaving behind us the strength of God; yet that sphere is paradoxically related to the sphere of faith. Its way of confronting sin is not the evangelical way of patient suffering. Its way of hearing God's judg-

5. It is in this sense Clement of Alexandria speaks of Christ as "lawgiver": "The true lawgiver not only promises what is good and fine, but knows it. His is the law that can be a 'saving prescription'; or, better, the law is 'the prescription of knowledge', for 'the word of God is power and wisdom'. He, then, is the exponent of laws through whom 'the law was given'; he is the first exponent of divine prescriptions who expounds 'the bosom of the Father', the only-begotten Son" (*Stromateis* 1.26; *IG*, p. 35). And Karl Barth, in his famous programmatic essay, "Gospel and Law" (*God, Grace, and Gospel* [Edinburgh: Oliver & Boyd, 1959]), defines Law simply as "the manifest will of God." In this sense we may understand sympathetically his thesis that the law is "the form" of the Gospel, though not without hesitation at the implications of the definite article. On this see my *Resurrection and Moral Order* (Leicester: Apollos; Grand Rapids: Eerdmans, 1986), pp. 11-27.

ment is not the evangelical way of humble and trusting obedience. God's redeeming judgment pours out the promised Holy Spirit upon all who believe and obey; human judgments convey no such power. The human judge may know the Holy Spirit's help in judging, but cannot shed the Holy Spirit abroad on those who are judged. Human judgment cannot assure mankind regeneration and new life.

A temptation has to be confronted here, the temptation to overlook the distance of human judgment from divine, to pretend to achieve politically what God has achieved in the Paschal judgment We cannot condemn and redeem at once. Idealist political orders have become tyrannous by ignoring this limitation, and pretending to redeem when in fact they are doing no more than condemning. The practice of punishment has never been in more danger of becoming cruel than when it is most confidently believed to regenerate the offender and renew society. Political order has never been more penetratingly oppressive than when it was framed with the pretension of bringing about a transformation of the world. There is in God's life-giving judgment something that our own judgments cannot, and must not try, to imitate. "In one respect man will never in all eternity come to resemble God, namely, in forgiving sins."[6]

We see, then, in what sense our political judgments are "Mosaic." The undisclosed aspect of the new creation means that our judgments cannot achieve a completely self-contextualizing truth. Our judgments form a kind of reverse image of God's judgment in Christ. Where he expounded the discrimination between sin and righteousness concretely in the risen life of the man he accepted, we expound our discriminations concretely only by describing the offenses we reject. We cannot give concrete and effective approval, as we can give concrete and effective condemnation. This is most evident, of course, in the criminal court, where acquittal is simply a failure to convict, a relatively indeterminate conclusion. It is less obvious in the civil courts, which reflect the balance of condemnation and vindication more evenly, finding against one party and for the other; and in other forms of political judgment we may point to the conditions of renewed life even less indirectly, as in a peace-treaty. Yet even in so positive an example our deter-

---

6. Søren Kierkegaard, *The Sickness unto Death* 2.2.2, trans. W. Lowrie (Princeton: Princeton University Press, 1941), p. 253.

minations remain negative. We are limited to specifying the conditions for cessation of hostilities, prohibiting acts on either side that would be to the detriment of the other. The treaty cannot prescribe the process of cooperation itself, because it cannot describe the many ways in which that has yet to be developed. It can only clear a space for peace, not create it.

But this negative word is not the last word. The wisest of those who have thought about what might be implied in an evangelical politics have looked first to the social life of the church. There we may expect to see the Paschal victory take effect in judgments that immediately serve the creation of mutual love and the forgiveness of enemies. The church is not yet manifest as the self-standing political society it is destined to be, acting together with the free obedience of all mankind in the worship of God. Its political character is worked out through engagement with the secular political societies among whom it lives, witnessing to the risen Christ and claiming their judgments in obedience to him. Political judgments belong to these political societies; and if they belong to members of the church, it is because they, too, are members of these societies. They can be evangelical to the extent that they respond to the witness of the church's evangelical social life. They are shaped by the presence of a society in which redemption is taking effect and assuming a social form; so they witness to the Paschal judgment, but indirectly. They are not part of the immediate witness to resurrection life; they are a witness to the witness. Even politics is not driven back to a point from which the triumph of Christ is invisible; it is merely situated at a distance from it. The ministry of condemnation is a reverse image of the Paschal judgment, but as such it attests it. It cannot preach the Gospel like an apostle, but it can carry out its work of condemnation in the conscious awareness that the Gospel is being preached. It can point indirectly to the living hope of which it cannot speak directly.

*   *   *

The indirect but real relation of human judgment to divine mercy has exercised us a great deal in recent years in the question of how revolutions are to cope with the legacy of the past. Can an act of judgment incorporate *forgiveness*?

Since patristic times the theological tradition of political thought has consistently wished to answer this question positively. In A.D. 414 Augustine responded, politely but firmly, to a frontal attack by a provincial governor who strongly disapproved of what had become a traditional practice of bishops, intercession for condemned prisoners. He argued that this practice did not imply condoning offenses, but was motivated solely by love of the offender. "It is easy and simple to hate evil men because they are evil, uncommon and dutiful to love them because they are men; thus in one and the same person you disapprove the guilt and approve the nature."[7] By interceding the bishops act out of religion towards God, who is infinitely patient to us in this life, punishing only a very few offenses as exemplary warnings and saving up the majority of punishments for the last judgment. The implication, Augustine concludes, is that in human courts there must be different roles: as there is both prosecutor and defense counsel, so there may be both judge and intercessor. All these "quail before the divine judgment, recalling that they have need of God's mercy for their own sins, and they do not think they do an injury to their office if they show mercy to those over whom they have the lawful power of life and death."[8] They have different functions, and justice, such as may be done on earth, is the result of the dynamic interplay of these different functions. There is good in severity, and there is good in intercession that restrains severity. In this groundbreaking text Augustine opens up the question more than he resolves it. In sharp contrast to some later Augustinians, such as Luther, Augustine sees no other context for exploring this than the church's mission of reconciliation and redemption. The secular magistrate is simply caught up into that project, and his wholesome severity, when exercised, is a service to it. Does this tend to subvert the function of secular authority? May the wholesome dialectic of terror and mercy collapse altogether if pastoral authorities are too insistent and magistrates too obliging?

Forgiveness may appear to be a project of more or less antinomian sympathies. If an act of charity is, as John Milbank puts it, "unprecedented," it must be in conflict with a law operating by conformity to precedent. Milbank's own program for a radical Christian ethic, advo-

---

7. *Ep.* 153.3, trans. W. Parsons. See *IG,* p. 120.
8. *Ep.* 153.8; *IG,* p. 122.

cated under the description of "poetics," is consistently opposed to measuring the deeds of the present by the deeds of the past. It is founded on a fundamental opposition between "the right" and "the good," the one based on a notion of absolute limit, the other based on analogy, the one associated with repetitious Aristotelian "praxis," the other with innovative Platonic "poiesis." The poetic ethic, conceived by analogy with the creative imagination of an artist, has no element of repetition, so that grace is incompatible with "reaction," and charity "breaks through existing representations of what is our duty." It explores in an analogical and metaphorical way the possibilities of goodness opened up through the concrete universal, the "figure" of the mediator or of God himself. And so it is forgiving towards the past. Evil is "not rightly 'to be known' but rather, in this aspect, to be 'forgotten about.'"[9]

Yet such a conception of the moral life can hardly be *social.* Recollection and response, it would seem, are essential to society, which requires relational continuity and recognition. In society we are not "unprecedented" to one another, but already known; were there no recognition, there could be no encounter. Our engagements are constituted by the histories we bring to them; if those histories contain evildoing, our encounters must recognize that evildoing. Whatever "loving the sinner and hating the sin" may entail, it cannot be forgetting. In a social context forgetting would be indistinguishable from admitting evildoing as the basis for further engagements. The sacrifice required by forgiveness would seem to be the sacrifice of justice itself.

The usual conclusion, then, is to reject the possibility of forgiveness within the context of judgment. Insofar as forgiveness waives the demands of justice, justice is compromised by forgiveness. This may be illustrated from the practice of executive pardon. In pardoning some, the executive discriminates against others. That was oppressively clear in the use of pardon for the death penalty, so that in sophisticated jurisdictions executive pardon became, in effect, merely an instance of final review, applying public and objective criteria of desert and so mak-

---

9. John Milbank, "A Critique of the Theology of Right," *The Word Made Strange* (Oxford: Blackwell, 1997), p. 23. Cf. in the same volume "A Christological Poetics," pp. 132-34; "Can Morality Be Christian?" pp. 219ff. We may compare Hannah Arendt's observation that we must "of necessity forgive."

ing the term "pardon" a misnomer. The objection concludes that pardon has no point of access into the administration of justice. To the extent that political life is not governed by justice, it is compromised by expediency, and although we may acknowledge the necessity of acts of political expediency, we may not recommend them. We may admit that we sometimes "have" to forgive, but can never admit that we ought to do so.[10]

This objection is jealous of the *retrospectivity of justice,* as a response to a wrong that has been done, and it arises from an anti-consequentialist posture of more or less Kantian inspiration. We may be inclined to lump it in with the "new retributivism" which has arisen as a reaction against utilitarianism in recent legal philosophy; and this is not entirely mistaken, since the retributive theory of punishment has everything to do with the retrospectivity of justice.[11] But the class of retrospective actions contains more than acts of justice, including such acts as "recognition" and "answering"; and the class of acts of justice contains more than retribution, including such acts as just payment, just performance of citizen duties, just award of prizes in a competition. So the claim that justice is essentially retrospective is actually much wider than the claim that justice is essentially retributive, and more defensible. The objection to forgiveness can be made on behalf of other kinds of justice than that of punishment. It can be made against the writing off of bad debts, as we saw in debates about the millennial proposals for international debt-cancellation. The objection to public forgiveness conceives justice simply as the discharge of some existing liability or obligation. And, of course, justice does have to do with liabilities and obligations, for judgment cannot be a forward-looking act, like "initiating," "enabling," and "pursuing." It is by definition responsive.

If one objection defends the retrospectivity of justice against the compromising prospectivity of forgiveness, there is another, a kind of mirror-image to it, which defends the *retrospectivity of forgiveness* against

---

10. David A. Crocker, "Retribution and Reconciliation," *Philosophy and Public Policy* 20, no. 1 (2000): 1-6. "Powerful practical reasons may explain the decision to spare oppressors from trial and criminal sanctions. But . . . no *moral* argument . . . justifies rejection of the Nuremberg paradigm" (p. 1).

11. For example: Michael S. Moore, *Placing Blame: A Theory of Criminal Law* (Oxford: Oxford University Press, 1997). See my review article, "Payback: Thinking about Retribution," *Books & Culture* (July-August 2000), pp. 16-21.

the compromising prospectivity of public justice, reversing the assumptions about what is forward- and what is backward-looking. Forgiveness is not true forgiveness, it argues, when subject to forward-looking ends such as reconciliation or reform. "Pardon is not responsible — must *never* be responsible — to a therapy of reconciliation."[12] But no justice that takes form as public order can be detached from such ends, since it accommodates pure desert to the conditions of practicality. Forgiveness, therefore, cannot take public form; it can arise only as a private or inter-personal reality, an inner attitude with no political expression. If forgiveness assumed the form of public order, it would not be unconditional, and so would not be true forgiveness.

Yet this convergence upon the separation of forgiveness as a private matter from justice as a public matter has a disconcerting implication: forgiveness is excluded from human relations altogether. For the proposal that forgiveness can flourish as a private response to personal wrongs suffers from a fatal incoherence: "wrongs" cannot be purely personal. "Wrong" is distinguished from "harm" by the fact that it implies a breach of moral relations, which makes it liable for punishment. A forgiveness which functioned solely on the personal level could not have regard to the wrong *as* wrong, but only as personal injury; and it could not lead to the remission of punishment, but only to the renunciation of private resentment. Such "forgiveness" could even insist on punishment, though without personal rancor — an intolerably paradoxical conclusion. The notion that any *moral* transaction could proceed in absolute privacy is an illusion. Forgiveness will always have a measure of public reference, and the only question is how formal and institutionalized that is. The first martyr prayed, "Lord, lay not this sin to their charge!"

The fact that it is possible to invert the roles and either defend retrospective justice against forgiveness or retrospective forgiveness against judgment, should warn us that there is a misapprehension at the bottom of the discussion. Simple retrospectivity cannot be the whole story either about justice or about forgiveness. Both are forms of recollection, defined by their purely retrospective objects, but both need the authorization of forward-looking purposes. Though they are defined by their object and subject to criteria of truthfulness about it, they cannot, any more than any other act can, be undertaken intelligi-

---

12. Jacques Derrida, "Le siècle et le pardon," *Le Monde des Debats* 9 (Dec. 1999), p. 7.

bly without a purpose or goal. To forgive, or to punish, is to address the past; but it is to address the past with some definite aspiration for the future. Retrospective acts, too, have their teleology. To recount a history, for example, involves concentrating attention on the logic of past events — and we all know what corruptions can ensue if the historian's attention is distracted by the agenda of his own time. But historians are not averse to explaining, in their prefaces, the goals they have had in view: to correct misunderstandings; to rouse interest in forgotten personalities and events; to help readers understand their own times better, and so on. Historiography would not be undertaken without such objectives. Neither is judgment undertaken without the goal of establishing, or maintaining, a just social order.

By insisting on a purely retrospective criterion for punishment or forgiveness, the two objections both deny something that Christians have found themselves compelled to assert: divine "justification." God's decisive act of justice was a *constitutive* act, just by virtue of the justice it brought about, not solely by its response to obligation, and it took form as an act of forgiveness. "Making just" is equally alien to the thought of a purely retrospective justice and to the thought of a purely retrospective forgiveness; and this discloses the deist character of these objections, in which divine judgment is conceivable only mechanically as a perfectly reactive response, divine forgiveness only as indifference. Neither way can it inaugurate the kingdom of heaven. If we question the assumption that created the dilemma, we may reconsider the question presented by John Milbank: how there may be a point of purchase for forgiveness within the logic of justice. Can we think of forgiveness in the same terms as judgment, i.e., as an act of recollection rather than an act of forgetfulness? May we entertain the thought that what is "unprecedented" in forgiveness is simply *what* we remember and *how* we remember it?

The point of purchase becomes clear when we recall that judgment is a social practice with its own context and conditions. The possibility of mercy arises when judgment reflects upon the conditions of its own performance. In judging we can take cognizance not only of what was done and who did it, but of ourselves who now recognize it, and of the means by which it has come to our recognition. The act of public recognition itself is publicly recognized. Forgiveness corrects the established pattern of justice as the pattern of justice corrects itself by attending to itself and passing judgment on itself. Apart from such a context of public self-reappraisal, forgiveness must appear monstrously arbitrary, as we see from certain notorious uses of the power of executive pardon. We are accustomed to take such moments of self-transcendence for granted; but they represent an important achievement in the understanding of justice, not easily accomplished. Ancient societies, as is well known, believed in the eternity of law: in early law codes it is common to find contradictory provisions side by side, since there was no way to conceive the act of repealing law. The book of Esther splits its sides laughing over the comic postures in which this doctrine landed the autocrats of the Medo-Persian empire. Only with the conception of "natural law," the critical and transcendent law above law, could legislators self-consciously abolish the laws their predecessors had made.

The paradigm case of self-transcendence in Western legal thought is the ending of war. Immunity has been seen as the sole condition upon which each can be assured of the other's good faith in making peace; for without it the settlement would not be full and final, and the war could at any time break out afresh in the pursuit of unfinished business.[13] For the classic just-war theorists, the implication of all this was clear: crimes committed *in bello*, however grave, were not justiciable; crimes committed *ad bellum* might possibly be punished, but only very selectively and against responsible leaders. No belligerent party would be willing to come to terms if by doing so it opened the floodgates to indefinite juridical recriminations.[14] The ending of war was an imperative that required judicial business to be set aside. Nuremberg broke with this long tradition by making crimes *in bello* liable to inquisition and punishment, and for very necessary reasons. But it has raised in the sharpest way the question of those traditional immunities from prosecution which used to surround every treaty of peace.

Immunities have also played a vital part in the resolution of other forms of conflict. Amnesties mark the division between the politico-

13. It was an alarming aspect of the human-rights-driven campaign for compensation for former British prisoners of war in Japan that it ignored the obvious dangers of trying to unpick a full and final treaty of peace between warring parties. If that peace treaty were opened to re-negotiation forty years on, what issues might not surface? How, for instance, could the nuclear bombings of Hiroshima and Nagasaki not become a matter of active recrimination between Japan and the former allies?

14. Cf. Oliver O'Donovan, "Can War-Crimes Trials Be Morally Satisfying?" in *The Just War Revisited* (Cambridge: Cambridge University Press, 2003), pp. 109-23.

judicial orders of the past and of the present, and signal the non-pursuit of claims outstanding from the previous order. In the republican revolution of Florence in 1494 Savonarola famously insisted upon amnesty, *la pace universale*, for supporters of the ousted Medici. Under circumstances of revolution, he insisted, no attempt to do "justice" could be anything more than "vendetta." "What others have done is what anyone could turn out to have done, if the record were examined," he urged. "So don't ask for justice, since equal justice for all means that not many escape punishment." "A special time demands a special mercy."[15] In recent years there have been many contexts in which this proposal has been repeated. The Federal Republic of Germany, in putting former East German border-guards on trial, rejected it. In South Africa, on the other hand, it was taken with great seriousness: the Truth and Reconciliation Commission arose from a common recognition among South Africans that their society had undergone not merely a change of government but a change of moral perspective, which made the penalizing of past attitudes irrelevant to the task of overcoming them and replacing them. Northern Ireland provides a less comforting illustration. The Good Friday Agreement of 1998, which established the fragile power-sharing Executive, included prisoner-releases from both communities of those convicted of terrorist crimes. But these were widely objected to within the majority community, precisely because of the unwelcome implication that there had been a breach of regime.

The practice of amnesty in public life, then, arises from a discontinuity in the judicial regime, a reflective self-transcendence evoked by the recognition that judgment is imperfect. The crises of revolution and war evoke such moments of transcendence acutely; but this recognition is a constant possibility, and there is place, also, for an ordinary recognition of limit and an ordinary practice of mercy. It must tell the truth not only about the cases that come before it for judgment, but *about itself.* Because the truth of judgment includes a *reflective* truth about its own practice of judgment, it can take a variable view of a given case.

Where do we find such a moment of self-transcendence in the ordinary administration of justice? We may consider first a half-way case, that of legislation. Legislation is the product of critical reflection upon

15. *Prediche sopra Aggeo*, a cura di L. Firpo (Rome: Edizione Nationale, 1965) 13, p. 227; 14, p. 247; 16, p. 273: "Uno speziale tempo vuole una speziale misericordia."

the law as it currently exists; yet it is normalized in the political life of a community as a continuous task. The making of a new law creates inequities of treatment between those judged under it and those judged before its introduction. In any change there will be privileges for some which are denied to others, with no difference between them except the time at which their cases happened to arise. The most striking example of this was afforded by legislation to abolish the death penalty, which created the sharpest problems of inequity between the last generation of convicted persons to be executed and their successors. Yet we rarely pause to worry whether the practice of legislation is, as such, unjust. We accept that amendment of law is a process that must be built into the ordinary life of a community.

To amend the law is not the same as claiming that the law was *wrong,* as concerns its judgment on the object. This would result in the over-moralization of every change in the legal regime, so that, for example, the state's erstwhile attempts to regulate sexual conduct, abandoned for very practical reasons, would be written retrospectively into a popular history of persecution, while the death-penalty, once abolished, became part of popular history's record of torture. There may indeed be occasions when a society must accuse itself collectively of some crime; but such self-accusations are by their nature exceptional. The reflection that we are concerned with here is different: it is the simple recognition, which may arise at any time, that it has not been possible to achieve by the existing law everything which it was hoped to achieve, that legal provisions have fallen short of their aims. This is not a matter for guilt, though it is, perhaps, a matter for "shame." This recognition belongs together with a *practical* commitment to provide the effective judgment that a political society needs. There may be justified anxiety that a society may so lose confidence in its judicial practice that it drifts into less and less decisive responses to crime, a climate, as the Italians have called it, of *perdonismo.* If to understand all is to forgive all, how are we to think of criminals other than as victims of our misunderstanding?[16] And what can this mean for the reform of law other

---

16. The common phrase is anyway a misquotation. What Mme. de Stael wrote was more intelligible: "tout comprendre rend très indulgent" (*Oxford Dictionary of Quotations,* 3rd ed. [New York: Oxford University Press, 1979], 517:15). The absolutized version has meaning only as a projection about the relation of justice and forgiveness in God.

than the minimizing of criminal penalties, not as a concrete exercise of mercy but simply out of a helpless sense of guilt? The bulwark against this logic is the practical judicial responsibility of government, which must, if it is to exist at all, maintain effective judgment. Changes in law, then, are properly governed by an ordering of practical priorities in the pursuit of judgment, neither abstractly moral nor abstractly amoral, but mediating the demands of social morality as effectively as possible within a range of possibilities that are not infinite and are constantly shifting. In any change to the law some moral beliefs, hitherto definitive, become less central to public order, others, hitherto marginal, become more central. The role of our various moral beliefs in shaping public order is changed, without our beliefs themselves, or their public relevance, being impugned or denied.

But there is, Christians have believed, a more extensive ordinary application of the principle than legislation. The moment of self-criticism must be present even in routine administration of justice. The dialectic between satisfying the requirements of justice and rising above the existing order of justice takes form as a constant duty to temper justice with mercy, which yields a practice characterized by "moderation." "Moderation" is the normal translation of the Greek noun *epieikeia,* which appears in the Epistles of the New Testament as a virtue of reasonableness, mercy, and low affect. The term disappears from subsequent Christian thought, to make a sudden reappearance in Western thought of the thirteenth century with the Latin translation of Aristotle's *Nicomachean Ethics,* which contains a discussion of how *epieikeia* relates to justice. The two, Aristotle says, are distinct, but not heterogeneous. *Epieikeia* is just, but not strictly according to law; it corrects legal justice, and so is superior to it. Law is limited to prescriptions suited to the generality of cases, and can therefore fail to encompass a special case adequately. *Epieikeia* provides the correction that the lawgiver would have made if he could have been present. The individual who displays *epieikeia* as a virtue is self-effacing, not pressing legal claims to the limit but accepting reasonable accommodation.[17] This Aristotelian passage made a deep impression upon medieval thinkers. *Epikeia* (the Latinized form) was "half way between natural and legal justice," and was shown in a judge's reluctance to punish infringements of law that did not offend natural jus-

---

17. *Ethica Nicomachea* 1137a3-1138a2.

tice, as when legal but unreasonable exactions were resisted.[18] The reference to natural justice shows how Christian *epikeia* had gained a new context in medieval legal conceptions; Thomas Aquinas identified it with legal equity *(aequitas)*, and argued that it belonged to the virtue of justice rather than to temperance.[19]

With the Renaissance and Reformation, there was a shift in emphasis in the interpretation of *epikeia* from reasonableness to mercy. Seneca's *De clementia*, popular in the period, had described clemency as an "inclination of the mind to mildness," characteristic of judges who were not enslaved to statute but had the freedom to "create" the most just resolution by their decisions, supremely the Roman emperor.[20] So described, clemency was readily seen as a necessary modulation of Christian justice.[21] Yet the ground for the judge's freedom was transformed under the influence of the Gospels, especially the story of the woman taken in adultery and the parable of the unforgiving servant, to make judicial moderation a display not of sovereignty but of humility. *Epikeia*-equity-clemency was a humble modesty in passing judgment, such as befits those who know their own sinfulness. So William Perkins, basing his discussion on the text, "Let your moderation be known to all men. The Lord is at hand" (Phil. 4:5), takes the latter half of the text as a clue to the whole. The nearness of divine judgment demands humility in judging, showing mercy as we hope to receive it. We are "flesh and blood and full of infirmities," and society cannot endure if we judge with the rigor that an angel might use. But that is not a reason to abandon justice, for justice must shake hands with mercy (cf. Ps. 85:10, understood as a prophecy of the cross in exegetical tradition). The prince's laws cannot be "perfect and absolute" as God's laws are;

---

18. Thus Robert Grosseteste of Lincoln, pioneer of Aristotle translation, in the course of a dramatic denunciation of the papal curia delivered before Innocent IV at Lyons in 1250. See S. Gieben, "Robert Grosseteste at the Papal Curia: Edition of the Documents," *Collectanea Franciscana*, vol. 41 (1971), p. 386.

19. *Summa Theologiae* II-2.120.1

20. Seneca, *De clementia* 1.5, 2.4-7.

21. J.-B. Bossuet, "Sermon sur la justice," *Oeuvres de Bossuet*, vol. 13 (Versailles: Lebel, 1816), p. 396: "Il n'y a rien de plus juste que cette loi de l'Apôtre, 'Supportez-vous mutuellement en charité, et portez le fardeau les uns des autres,' et cette charité et facilité, qui s'appelle condescendance dans les particuliers, c'est ce qui s'appelle clémence dans les grands et dans les princes."

but the prince may practice a merciful judgment, witnessing to the divine work of reconciliation.[22]

In conclusion, within the New Testament the sphere of public judgment constitutes a carefully circumscribed and specially privileged exception to a general prohibition of judgment. "You have no defense, then, whoever you may be, when you sit in judgment — for in judging others you condemn yourself" (Rom. 2:1). To judge, Paul argues, is to set oneself above one's fellow; it is to claim an innocence which one cannot claim, and so to ignore the truth of the universal judgment of God. Yet renouncing our own judgment is simply the respect we owe to God's. The word of Jesus, "Do not judge, and you will not be judged," the advice to reach a settlement with our opponent while we are still on the way to court, the prayer to be forgiven "as we have forgiven those who have wronged us," the command, "Love your enemies and pray for your persecutors": all these reinforce the inference that we are not to be the subjects, but the objects of judgment.[23] We shall appear before the throne of God as offenders in need of mercy; and justice itself, as in the parable of the unforgiving servant, requires that those who ask for mercy shall show it.[24]

How are the two spheres, of judging and not judging, related to each other? Are they simply opposed, representing in antithetical and irreconcilable ways different facets of the being and acts of God, who alone can judge in forgiving and forgive in judging? Or do they approach each other, and so bear witness in fragmentary ways to the unity of judgment and forgiveness in God? There are good reasons for giving the former of these two answers. It is necessary to exercise reserve in speaking of the representation of God in human institutions; human judgment does not have the Holy Spirit at its disposal to renew the moral consciences of offenders; it cannot raise their victims from the dead, nor restore moral relations to what they were before they were violated. There is much to caution us against conceding to human authority any pretension to redeem. Guided by such warnings Christians have rejected a conflation of roles that ought to be distinct: of priesthood with royal authority, and of church discipline with secular courts of judgment.

---

22. William Perkins, *A Treatise of Christian Equitie*. See *IG,* pp. 772-77.
23. Matt. 7:1; Luke 12:58; Matt. 6:12; Matt. 5:44.
24. Matt. 18:23-35.

Nevertheless, we cannot treat the sphere of human judgment as though it lay outside the reach of redemption, walled off from the grace of God. Even judgment is exposed to the effects of the church's mission, the word of the Gospel, and the transforming work of the Holy Spirit. We may and should look for a reflection of redemption in the work of civil justice, too, as the ordinary practices of public judgment are themselves affected by the demand for renunciation. They, too, must resign their judgment to God's in accepting the limitations that their accomplishments betray; but as they do so, they are permitted to mirror the unity of truth and grace which we discern in God's deed of justification. The reflection, to be sure, is not luminous. It is liable to prompt the complaint that true forgiveness is something more profound than the occasional amnesty and immunity, which is the best that public justice can arrange. Yet we should not be deterred by this, for in this respect public forgiveness is on no different footing from private forgiveness. It is true that the generosity of God's redeeming act is far removed from the tortuous negotiations that lead a warring community to make peace; but it is equally remote from the anguished inner wrestling by which we force ourselves to put away persistent private resentments. Christians, at any rate, believe that none of us forgive, even on our deathbeds, without the prior knowledge that we have been forgiven. The act of private forgiveness, too, is not generated from nothing, and to this extent we may agree that public forgiveness is prior.[25] But whether privately or publicly, to forgive as we have been forgiven will always be a matter of limping painfully after. The original act of generosity is God's alone, beyond replication; yet that should not make us despise the partial and conditioned reflections that we may from time to time be given to display.

25. Cf. Bernd Wannenwetsch, *Political Worship: Ethics for Christian Citizens*, trans. M. Kohl (Oxford: Oxford University Press, 2004), p. 310: "The political character of forgiveness is at the root of all individual forgiving acts."

7

Punishment

The account of justice-as-judgment which we have developed up to this point must now be put to a test: whether it can shed light upon the question of punishment, about which a vigorous, if rather too self-contained philosophical debate has been sustained for the past two centuries. This requires, initially, some introductory observations on the proper scope and task of a theory of punishment as such.

"Punishment" refers to a practice found in many forms — slapping, depriving of pleasures or satisfactions, physical beatings, pecuniary confiscations, imprisonment, maiming, killing — and in many contexts (families, schools, businesses, and armies, as well as political societies) in every major type of human community, extant or historical, primitive or developed. The name "punishment" means "requital" or "return," deriving from an Indo-European root meaning "exchange," and is therefore not very remote semantically from the term "retribution," which means "giving back." The practice consists in responding to a wrong which somebody has done by inflicting an evil upon the wrongdoer. It is described formally by Hugo Grotius as "suffering harm for having done harm."[1] These words name the practice, they do not theorize about it. The task of a theory of punishment is to make this practice of requiting and returning intelligible.

---

1. *De iure belli ac pacis* 2.20.1; *IG*, p. 801: *Malum passionis quod infligitur ob malum actionis.* Grotius qualifies this definition as *generali significatu:* it is the *common reference* of the term *poena*, i.e., the initial datum about which he will later propound a theory. It is not itself a theory.

It is common to refer to a "retributive theory of punishment," a paradoxically redundant expression that would seem to mean a "penal theory of penalty." The sense that may be given to this will emerge as we proceed. But together with the expression there has often been heard a claim that the number of possible theories of punishment are three: those which find its purpose in retribution, those which find its purpose in reform, and those which find it in the protection it affords society. This "three-theory theory" was until recently learned as a text-book axiom by every undergraduate — and, indeed, could be learned in no other way, since no rational argument for it was to be found. The three-fold division of the alternatives is either *a priori* or *a posteriori:* either it exhausts all logical possibilities, or it is an induction from a comprehensive survey of all actual theories. Since almost everyone who advances the three-theory theory offers to "overcome" it by presenting a fourth theory that combines the advantages of them all, the ground for advancing it can hardly be *a posteriori*. On the other hand, the appearance of exhausting the possibilities is swiftly dispelled. We can make a division of *those affected* by punishment along these lines: victim, offender, and the rest of society. But this does not license the conclusion that there are three kinds of theory, one for each category of those affected. On the contrary, it would seem to be a condition for the success of any theory that it should take account of all three categories of those affected. A theory that set out to notice only one of them would be a worthless theory. The three-theory theory encourages a style of argument like a race of hobbled horses. None of the beasts are capable of finishing the course, so the victory goes to the jockey who knocks his rivals over.[2]

---

2. We illustrate this all-too-common way of pleading from an otherwise sober discussion by Wolfgang Huber (*Gerechtigkeit und Recht* [Gütersloh: Kaiser, 1996], pp. 337-41). Having sketched the three theories and shown the weaknesses in each of them, Huber promises, predictably, "a coherent conception" that will accommodate elements of all three. What then follows is an unvarnished social-utilitarian theory in the Benthamite tradition. How did that come about? By a decision that it was not, after all, *punishment* that his theory would explain, but *law*. We may, of course, be sympathetic to the idea that the criminal law must be justified in terms of the function of law, not in terms of the idea of punishment — *if*, that is, we are first clear about what the idea of punishment is, and what it would be like to justify the criminal law in terms of it. But we were offered an account of "disagreements about the meaning of punishment" ("der umstrittene

Better reasons, it would seem, can be produced for a "two-theory theory." More recent debates sometimes divide possible accounts into "utilitarian" and "retributivist" types.[3] This distinction corresponds to two elementary ways in which action as such can be envisaged, as "forward-looking" and "backward-looking." Action may be seen as setting off in a direction, "pursuing some good" in Aristotle's famous phrase; or it may be seen as closing a circle, setting some prior matter to rest. Complex action-types often presuppose one or the other of these two ways of constructing action: "founding" an institution and "broaching" a question are necessarily projective, while "enlarging" an endowment and "answering" a question are necessarily reactive. Punishing and requiting belong to the latter group of action-types. The reason for this, of course, is not simply definitional or philological, but has to do with the nature of the practice of punishment and its conditions of rationality. To explain why you punish you refer to something that has gone before. Either you punish someone *for* something, or you do not punish at all. A theory of punishment has to shed light on a practice constituted by its backward-looking system of justifications. Theories of punishment cannot therefore be divided into those which see it as backward-looking and those which see it as forward-looking. The latter category would not be theories *of punishment* at all.

Does this mean that all theories of punishment must simply accept retribution as an idea, without being able to criticize or repudiate it? No, it means simply that they must accept the reality of retribution as an established practice and offer such wider accounts of it as they can devise. There is no point in discussing punishment as though it were an optional extra, something which human societies may choose to do or not to do — in general terms, that is, for they are always in a position either to punish or not to punish in a particular case. All theories must accept that human communities do punish and always have punished, for that is what they are required to explain. This challenge is not met sufficiently if one "begins with some existing, historically contingent practice," e.g., "criminal punishment as practiced in contemporary

---

Sinn der Strafe"). All we get is a proposal to talk about something else *instead of* the meaning of punishment.

3. Michael Moore, *Placing Blame: A Theory of Criminal Law* (Oxford: Oxford University Press, 1997), pp. 91f.

Western societies, such as Britain and the United States."[4] The inherent logic of this very specialized form of contemporary Western practice cannot be understood aside from the wider cultural practices out of which it has developed, and from the wider anthropological regularities of which it is a part.

Yet a theory of punishment may criticize the practice of retribution. Four different levels of critique suggest themselves at first glance:

First, one may object to *the practice of punishment in its entirety* — in effect, conceiving punishment as a manifestation of original sin. It is possible to think that, while communities do punish and always have punished, it was always a fault to have done so. This is, to be sure, a headily idealist way of dismissing a practice so deeply rooted in human society, but its daring would not be unprecedented, in the theological tradition at least. Jesus considered even such a universal practice as hating enemies sinful; or, to take a less happy example, Augustine thought of spontaneous sexual excitement as a trace of original sin in our bodily constitutions. Such a critique will inevitably have a whiggish flavor, hoping to defeat what is to all appearances an anthropological datum, i.e., to conquer nature by civilization. The condition it will have to meet is to show what societies would be better advised to do about offenses *instead of* punishing them. It will have to venture on a description of a new non-retributive practice. Of what kind might that be? Radical deterrence, perhaps, such as Jeremy Bentham sometimes advocated? Or a reformative practice, fostering behavior-change in offenders and potential offenders? Such hypothetical proposals are to be distinguished from the theoretically more modest suggestion that punishment *in the normal sense* should serve goals of deterrence and reform. These proposals would be for practices to replace punishment in the normal sense, and so, while limited by respect for human dignity — not even to reform an offender's behavior-pattern should you keep him in a drugged stupor indefinitely — they would not be limited by any notion of retributive justice. We would never ask how prolonged, or how severe a behavior-modification was *merited* by a given offense; we would never ask whether someone *deserved* to be made a deterrent example of.

And here we must mention a third possible alternative practice:

4. R. A. Duff, *Punishment, Communication, and Community* (Oxford: Oxford University Press, 2001), p. xvi.

"Love your enemies and forgive those who persecute you" (Luke 6:27). If this is the practice to be commended, then radical reform takes an ecclesiological turn, and looks to a community in which radical forgiveness is possible. It will then be confronted with a well-known line of questioning about the relation of church and society: can society *become* the church, or can the church only coexist *with* society? At one end of the scale we find the view that in human affairs no meeting is possible: as the proper business of the preaching of the church is the Gospel of forgiveness, so the proper business of the state is the terror of punishment. "If anyone attempted to rule the world by the gospel and to abolish all temporal law and sword . . . pray tell me, friend, what would he be doing? He would be loosing the ropes and chains of the savage wild beasts and letting them bite and mangle everyone."[5] At the other end of the scale we may think of human punishment as simply redemptive and regenerative, as God's is.

The failure to develop a convincing alternative is the chief weakness of Timothy Gorringe's *God's Just Vengeance,* a recent essay, as I read it, in the genre of radical critique.[6] When the author finally, and briefly, addresses what he sees as hopeful developments, they consist of constructive ways of handling *punishment* (largely in the prevailing contemporary mode of imprisonment), and constructive ways of situating it within wider social practices. These are welcome indeed, but fall short of what the critique appeared to promise. The cause lies in the usual confusion of retribution as a practice with retributivism as a theory. A rebuttal of the theory is taken to have effected a replacement of the practice. In Gorringe's view, the theory is nourished by satisfaction-theories of the Atonement: he sets out to illustrate a correlation between phases in medieval and early modern penal practice and phases of the satisfaction theory, as well as between the exemplarist theory of the Atonement and the "new sensibility" (i.e., dismay at the cruelty of early-modern practice and an interest in the reformation of offenders) which began to emerge in the Enlightenment period. Gorringe's purpose is less to illumine our dilemmas about punishing than to warn us off the notion of Atonement as satisfaction. But this supposes that he has stable ground beneath his feet in the matter of penology, that the difference between good and bad penal practice is too well known to need discussing. The deliberative question —

---

5. Luther, *Temporal Authority* (WA 11.251), trans. J. J. Schindel and W. I. Brandt (*Luther's Works,* vol. 45). *IG,* p. 587.

6. *God's Just Vengeance* (Cambridge: Cambridge University Press, 1996).

how *are* we, after all, to respond to crime? — is taken as having been answered, as it were, on the page before the book began.

Here a contrast with Foucault is instructive, whose melodramatic exploitation of history Gorringe imitates, and with whose modernity-criticism he occasionally appears to compete, offering an alternative, more whiggish narrative. Precisely because Foucault *is* a modernity-critic, he can put us on our guard against our culture's current truisms about punishment, and show us how the ideals we take for granted were spun out of practices we would rather forget. Gorringe, confining himself to the correlation of historical practice with historical thought, avoids confronting modern penal practice directly, together with the dilemmas it faces.

Secondly, one may offer a *conceptual* critique of the way in which the practice is designated as "punishment," "retribution," or "suffering harm for having done harm." We may argue that the same practice could be described more adequately without resort to the old Indo-European root meaning a "return." This line of criticism is one I shall pursue in the following discussion: the term "judgment," in my view, affords a clearer and more intelligible idea of what is being done. There is a place for the thought of "return," but it must be located within the context of judgment. But the condition for proposing a new description is that it must fit broadly the same phenomena. This critique cannot support revision in the practice, only in the way we think and talk about it.

Thirdly, we may criticize *theories* of punishment, including those which misunderstand the role of the idea of retribution, whether to promote it or to oppose it. And, fourthly, we may criticize specific *forms* of retributive practice. These last two types of critique are common coin in discussions of punishment, and there are examples of them both in what follows.

This list is probably not exhaustive, but it will serve to give an impression of the critical scope still available to theories that proceed as they ought, by trying to *understand* the practice we call "punishment." Even the first and most radical of these will need to understand the practice if it is to show how it is mistaken; that is to say, it will need to know what the mistake is *about*, just as an account of our duty to love our enemies has to understand what an enemy is and why we naturally hate one. Any other forms of theoretical criticism that there may be will have to proceed in the same way. Thought can only be corrected by clarification; we cannot shovel ideas out of the way like a bulldozer, but must get to the bottom of them. What is it to get to the bottom of punishment? It is to relate it to the way we understand other aspects of human social existence, to "locate" it on the map of our social experience where it belongs, to explore its connection with the goods of social experience, with justice, love, worship, and loyalty, etc., and with the transcendent goods in which these are rooted.

* * *

We propose as our thesis, then, that punishment is best understood as *a judgment enacted on the person, property, or liberty of the condemned party.* The following comments help to explain this:

(a) Punishment is *judgment,* in saying which we presuppose all that has been said about judgment up to this point: it is an act of moral discrimination, that pronounces upon a preceding act or existing state of affairs to establish a new public context. A rational act of condemnation, it is neither irrational, like impulsive revenge, nor inactive, like reflective disapproval, but an "expressive act" or "communication."[7] It is not a private act, but an authorized act undertaken in the defense of the order of society, an act of social definition. When we speak of God's own "punishing," we are speaking of his judgment within the quasi-political context of his covenant-faithfulness. Divine punishment is executed, as in Jeremiah's prayer, $b^e mishpat$ "with judgment" (Jer. 10:24), and so is contrasted with God's absolute wrath, which will "bring me to nothing." It is God's disclosure of himself as our good, revealing the truth of our wrong. For this reason Christians have always found it necessary to speak of divine punishment in connection with the Atonement, for the Atonement is the supreme demonstration of God's covenant-faithfulness.

(b) Punishment is *judgment enacted,* not an additional act subsequent to judgment. The misconception of punishment as an "extra," a level of retaliation that goes beyond the enactment of justice, is encapsulated in the negative sense of the adjectives "punitive" and "vindic-

7. The one phrase is from Joel Feinberg, *Doing and Deserving* (Princeton: Princeton University Press, 1970), p. 95; the other from J. R. Lucas, *Responsibility* (Oxford: Oxford University Press, 1993), p. 95.

tive." It may possibly derive from the medieval theory of penitential satisfaction, which distinguished between satisfaction for *reatus* and satisfaction for *culpa* as two successive levels of punishment; or it may merely be a recurrence of the same intellectual mistake, which is to treat aspects of an action as though they were incremental: as though the unlawfulness of the offense and the lawlessness of the offender were two different things that had to be set right in two successive ways. The judge punishes when he sentences or awards damages. The punishment is not something *else* that must be done as a supplement to the judgment; what follows the giving of sentence is merely the carrying out of sentence.[8]

(c) Punishment is judgment enacted *against the person, property, or liberty of the condemned party*. On this three comments are in place:

(i) The distinction between "person" and "liberty" is unlikely to raise many doubts, though traditionally a judgment against liberty was understood necessarily to imply a judgment against the person. Concerns about physical abuse have given rise to the proper intuition that a decision to deprive someone of liberty does not authorize the use of force against the person beyond what is necessary to enforce the judgment against the person's liberty.

(ii) There is no fundamental distinction between what is done in criminal courts and what is done in civil courts and elsewhere. The "condemned party" is the party the judgment finds against. Civil courts, too, assign innocence and guilt in a conflict between two parties; they vindicate one and condemn the other; and in some branches of law, e.g., tort, they even enact their judgment on the property of the condemned party by requiring compensation. It is philosophically correct, if legally incorrect, to say that they "punish." It is true that judgment for tort is also enacted on the property of the successful plaintiff who is awarded the damages, and that this introduces a distinctive limit into judgments for tort which is not present in criminal judgments: the defendant, however great his guilt, may not be punished beyond what is required to compensate the plaintiff for his loss. Yet the

8. Cf. John of Salisbury, *Policraticus* 4.2: "For although it may be seen that the prince has his own public executioners, we ought to think of him as the sole or primary executioner to whom it is permitted to allow a substitute hand." Trans. C. Nederman (Cambridge: Cambridge University Press, 1990). See *IG*, p. 284.

opposite also holds true: the plaintiff, however great his loss, may not be compensated beyond the defendant's liability. In this way the criteria for just retribution also operate as a determining constraint in judgments on tort.

There is judgment outside the courts, too: some of this, but not all, may imply punishment. The legislative branch of government cannot punish, since it cannot enact its condemnations on the person, property, or liberty of particular parties; it condemns only generically, i.e., classes of offenders. The provisionary branch of government, on the other hand, may condemn particular offenders when it intercepts them by arrest or act of war, and in some circumstances these condemnations may be punishments. In a law-state arrest is always a provisional procedure, to facilitate the action of a court; but in a police-state, where arrest is not routinely followed by court proceedings, arrest would of itself constitute punishment. (Even in a law-state a sentence of imprisonment is counted from the moment of first detention.)

(iii) The enactment of a judgment may lie in a bare pronouncement, and when this is the case the enactment is not a punishment. A legislator gives effect to judgments simply by passing them in due form and promulgating them. Courts sometimes give effect to judgments by issuing an injunction. Even a more concrete enactment may not be a punishment. A court may enact its judgment on the property or liberty of the *vindicated* party, as when a successful writ of *habeas corpus* results in his release from restraint, or when compensation for criminal injury is awarded from the public purse. (As for the *person* of the vindicated party, we may remember Socrates' proposal that the court should order him to receive a public banquet!) Or a court may enact a judgment by causing certain performances to cease, as in an interesting case from Brazil, where the judgment that a rancher failed to fulfil his obligations to squatters resulted in the withdrawal of police protection from his ranch.

In many cases, however, enactment on the person, property, or liberty of the condemned party is the only effective action open, and this is especially true of the judgments on crime and tort typically given by criminal and civil courts. Punishment is thus justified in general because the person, property, or liberty of the condemned party is the only possible, or the most apt, *locus* for the enactment of a judgment. Punishment singles the offender out for especially disfavorable treatment, and is thus coercive in a way that other forms of judgment are not. Punishment excludes the offender from some elementary form of respect for person, property, and liberty that citizens customarily accord to one another.[9]

With these preliminaries in place, we may reflect further on the idea of "retribution," or "giving back." The justice that we look for in punishment is the justice of an act of judgment, i.e., its truth and effectiveness. Since an act of judgment is true by correspondence to the act on which it reflects, punishment is an "expressive" act, telling the truth about an offense. Yet the truth told is ontologically distinct from the reality told of. The relation between them cannot be an exchange, which only occurs between commensurables. If I stand in front of a house and utter the statement "This is a house," my statement corresponds to the thing I see; yet the statement is in no sense *exchanged* for the house, since it is an entity of a different order. It *represents* it. In the same way the expressive act which fines or imprisons or even executes a convicted offender corresponds as a statement corresponds; it is of a different order from the act of robbery, kidnapping, or murder that was committed. Materially, there is a reciprocation of coercion to coercion; morally, the two acts are quite different. Wrong, as Hegel correctly saw, is infinite. It cannot be repaid, but only represented.

The core of the retributive idea is the thought that in punishment something which the offender has put forth comes back. This thought is true, as far as it goes. But it comes back *as a representation.* Judgment brings an old act back by a new act, an act that corresponds to the old and so expresses it truthfully. What the offender gets back in being punished is different from what was put forth, not an echo but an answer. More precisely, it is a "judgment." This explains both why the idea of retribution is persistent, and why it is so open to misunderstanding and abuse.

One way of conceiving retribution as exchange is to suppose that the return of the offense to the offender must involve an experience *materially* the same as that inflicted on the victim. The burglar deserves

---

9. I am not attracted, therefore, by R. A. Duff's proposal to distinguish unjustifiable from justifiable punishments on the basis that the former are "exclusionary," the latter "inclusionary" (*Punishment, Communication, and Community,* pp. 77-79).

to be burgled, the rapist to be raped, the torturer to be tortured; and all actual punishment of these crimes is a kind of commutation, for decency's sake, of these ideal demands.[10] This proposition, which for convenience we label "retaliationist," misses the essential difference between punishment and crime, which is that punishment pronounces judgment. If you take what the thief stole and return it to its rightful owner, that is not punishment, merely restitution; if you take the life of the murderer who took your brother's life, that is not punishment, but vengeance. In punishment the only experience that is necessarily in common between victim and offender is that of suffering. They are, in turn, the object of another's unwelcome practical attention. There is no further specification possible. A crime may be performed by depriving someone of money, and a punishment may be performed this way, too; a crime may be performed by depriving someone of liberty or life, and so may a punishment. But the idea of punishment does not imply a correlation between the kind of suffering that befell the victim and the kind inflicted on the offender.

A more sophisticated exchange-view, emancipating itself from the thought of material retaliation, hopes to identify some moral or spiritual *value* that could be the object of the exchange. John Finnis, in an article which proved of great influence in the growth of the "new retributivism," argued that a criminal seizes an "unfair advantage," an "excessive freedom in choosing . . . something that his fellow-citizens have denied themselves."[11] This advantage can be annulled only by subjecting the offender's will to the representative will of the society. Punishment effects a return of the extra value of the unfettered will-act, leaving everyone in the same relative position that they were in before. Finnis's will-act theory suggests a disturbingly autarchic conception of social benefit, and appears to make frustrated criminals of us all. But even if we locate the extra value somewhere else, there is a deeper problem in the exchange-concept itself. The sense of a restored "equality" is so remote from our normal conceptions of equality as to be merely mystifying. There is no "equality" between how things were before the

---

10. This view is represented by both the rival protagonists in *The Death Penalty: For and Against*, by Louis J. Pohman and Jeffrey Reiman (Lanham, MD, and Oxford: Rowman & Littlefield, 1998).

11. "The Restoration of Retribution," *Analysis* 32 (1971-72): 131-35.

offense and how they are after the punishment. Redemption itself does not carry us back to the state of innocence before the first sin. Whatever we mean by "giving back" the offense in the punishment, it is not that we pay it off and leave the account clean. Hegel's proposition, "Coercion is annulled by coercion," with its suggestion of a *status quo ante,* set the imagination of the nineteenth century off on a false trail.[12]

And with this perception we ought to make our minds up once and for all to have done with the metaphor of "debt" and "payment." In the first place, there is something that distinguishes a punishment from the price paid for a commodity: the purchase of a commodity is an honorable undertaking, which confers a right to the commodity, but the performance of a crime is not an honorable undertaking, and we never gain a right to it, not even when the penalty is fully "paid." This distinction is not accounted for by Aristotle's observation that the payment in the one case is "voluntary," in the other case "involuntary." I may be forced involuntarily to pay for some commodity I had hoped to get free; but when I have paid for it, however unwillingly, it is a purchase, which confers on me the right to enjoy the commodity. But in no sense is crime a right that can be purchased by punishment. There may be industrial firms that routinely pollute air and water on the calculation that they get a good bargain even if prosecuted. But that does not mean they have a right to pollute. The second difficulty is that no punishment, however fitting, can restore the world to an equivalent condition to that obtaining before the crime. There are crimes, including some crimes of pollution perhaps, which may be set right if the cleanup is sufficiently stringent. But most crimes do irreparable harm, especially those which cause great human grief or loss of life.[13]

---

12. *Philosophy of Right,* trans. T. M. Knox (Oxford: Oxford University Press, 1952), §93, p. 67. In the context of Hegel's philosophy of history this suggestion was well constrained: ultimately there could be no return, and annulment is something more like "reaffirmation," a negation of the negation, in which neither the original negation expressed in the crime nor its subsequent negation expressed in punishment ever *amounts to nothing.* Yet the mathematical abstraction effected by Hegel's logic was a temptation.

13. Christian thinkers have wrestled uncomfortably with the implications of Aristotle's classification of punishment as a case of involuntary rectification-justice. Thomas classifies it as *iustitia commutativa,* but also argues, not wholly consistently, that God can practice only distributive justice (*Summa Theologiae* II-2.80.1, I.21.1). The paradigm case of

The justice manifest in punishment is not exchange-justice, but is correctly understood as attributive. Grotius's reason for rejecting this conclusion, towards which he pointed, takes us to the heart of the logic of punishment. Attributive justice, he argues, involves the conferral of something new, whether benefit or burden, something not already in principle included in the reckoning of "to each his own"; but punishment is a return of what has already been put forth. To which we may reply that a return may be a new act, an answer rather than an echo, and that something new is conferred upon the offender, something not generated by the disorder of the offense. Society accords him notice. He is given a standing within a truthful judgment that founds a social order, the standing of "offender." (One of the problems of crime and punishment within a fragmented society is that there are those who find this notice the only social dignity they ever acquire, and become addicted to it.) The punishment of an offender requires the community to devise a truthful response to the offense, which is a purposive action, not a blind consequence or an instinctive reaction. The concept of punishment as an automatic and impersonal return of evil to the doer is a seductive but dangerous one. Seductive, because it offers to relieve us (and God) of the responsibility for fashioning hostile judgments, so permitting us (and God) to be wholly friendly towards offenders while the just deserts of crime are worked out behind our backs with the rational impersonality of a law of nature. Dangerous, because it carries the high price-tag of a despairing fatalism about evil. There will be no forgiveness or escape in a world where cosmic justice operates apart from anyone's intention; we will quickly be given over to the implacable Furies. The best theological tradition asserts God's responsibility even for what look like chance occurrences of justice. When the Psalmist observed that the "nations have sunk in the pit that they made, in the net that they hid has their own foot been caught," he con-

---

exchange-justice for Thomas is not punishment, but restitution (II-2.62). Grotius, who successfully banished the notion of debt-payment from atonement theory, establishing the notion of penal atonement as an alternative to it, is well aware of the difficulty with Aristotle's classification: "they consider this a business transaction, as though something were paid to the wrongdoer in accordance with the usage of contracts. They are deceived by current idioms of speech whereby we say that punishment is 'owing' to him who sins" (*De satisfactione Christi* 2.8-11, *De iure belli ac pacis* 2.20.2; *IG*, pp. 818f., 802f.). But Grotius himself is unable to make a convincing break with the tradition.

cluded that "the Lord has made himself known, he has executed judgment" (Ps. 9:15f.).

*   *   *

When God himself punishes, argued Hugo Grotius, he exercises his right of supreme dominion. But only divine punishment can be self-justifying in this way; human judgment "is never inflicted for harm's sake."[14] At this point we can measure the distance between Grotius and the utilitarians of the eighteenth and nineteenth centuries, whom he is sometimes said to have anticipated. They held that punishment was justified *solely* by its good results, for in itself, as Bentham said, "all punishment is mischief."[15] Grotius thought that retribution was a good in itself, justified on its own terms; but when practiced by humans it needed to be justified *both* on its own terms *and* in terms of consequent goods. Ontologically native to God, punishment takes some excusing in terms of extrinsic goods, when practiced among consanguineous humankind.

We can reformulate Grotius's distinction in terms of judgment, protecting its distance from utilitarianism but shedding its hint of retributivism. A judgment, as we have said, by pronouncing on the past, establishes a new public context. The "goods" of punishment are simply aspects of the new public context. In divine retribution, we may say, the new context is sufficiently apparent in itself. In disclosing the truth of human offense, God discloses himself as our preserver, the ground of our future right. But only divine judgment can be self-verifying. Human punishment needs to prove its relation to the preservation of the world. The benefits that flow from retribution are extrinsic only to the bare act of retribution, not extrinsic to its character as judgment. As judgment, punishment is integrated into a web of social and political practices that serve social and political goods. Herein lies

---

14. *De iure belli ac pacis* 2.20.4. *Celebre est Platonis dictum, οὐ γὰρ ἐπὶ κακῷ δίκη γίνεται οὐδεμία. Sed haec in hominibus punientibus vera sunt; nam homo ita homini alteri ipsa consanguinitate allilgatur, ut nocere ei non debeat nisi boni alicuius consequendi causa. In Deo alia res est, ad quem Plato dictas sententias male extendit. Dei enim actiones niti possunt ipso summi dominii iure, praesertim ubi meritum hominis speciale accedit, etiamsi finem nullum sibi proponant extra ipsas.* For translation, see *IG,* p. 804.

15. Jeremy Bentham, *Introduction to the Principles of Morals and Legislation* 13.2.

the methodological weakness, as I would see it, in the proposal to justify retribution on the basis of a foundational moral intuition.[16] Intu-
itions are not dismissible, but neither are they self-sufficient; they are
open to correlation with each other and with other elements of moral
experience. The retributive intuition must be socially situated if we are
to claim for it the dignity of an intuition of justice.

The character of divine punishment, it might seem, could be side-
lined as a purely theological question, leaving practical measures of human punishment unaffected. But in reality what is at stake in this
question is the relation of retributive practice to the goods it secures. In
utilitarian theory punishment is conceived entirely instrumentally, as a
means to produce goods that have nothing to do with it. It is introduced, at arm's length as it were, into the offender's calculations as a
"motive."[17] This is a deterrent "annexed," as Bentham put it, by a legislator to a law. The good end is simply the "general prevention" of crime
"at as cheap a rate as possible."[18] Indeed, Bentham dared to say that the
exercise of punishment was necessary "only for the sake of producing
the appearance of it."[19] The whole theory was premised upon the
unintelligibility, even the undesirability, of retributive practice as such,
and may be viewed, in effect, as proposing an alternative practice that
saves some of the appearances of punishment, that of deterrence. (But
there were appearances that deterrence could not save; utilitarian accounts, therefore, have often assumed a reformist cast, revising the
practice to suit the theory.) The Grotian theory of the goods of punishment, on the other hand, had in view a succession of goods that naturally followed from the good of retribution in itself.

What are these goods? A tradition with classical roots identified
three possible beneficiaries of punishment: the victim, the offender,
and society at large. In Christian thought, however, the victim's benefit
was removed from consideration. The importance of this move can
hardly be over-emphasized. The satisfaction proper to the victim,
Christians thought, was simply that his or her grievance was God's
concern, a matter of public judgment. Over and above that, any satis-

---

16. As exemplified by Michael Moore, *Placing Blame,* pp. 83-188. See my review, "Payback: Thinking about Retribution," *Books & Culture* (July-August 2000): 16-21.

17. Cesare di Beccaria, *Dei delitti e delle pene* 1.

18. Bentham, *Introduction to the Principles of Morals and Legislation* 14.6.

19. Bentham, *Rationale of Punishment* 1.5.

faction the victim might take in the punishment of the offender could be no more than personal vengeance. Even those theories generally called retributive, such as that of Kant, have emphasized not the victim's interest, but that of society.[20] It is a measure of the deep de-Christianization of our times that it is once again possible to speak in public of the victim's interest in punishment — to the point of providing victims' relatives with the opportunity to watch the execution of a murderer on closed-circuit television — an interest which those who followed Jesus' teaching thought could be no true interest at all.

Abandoning the first supposed beneficiary of punishment, then, Christian thinkers refashioned the doctrine of the three goods into a new shape: there was a *primary* good, the good of punishment itself, the active pronouncement of the truth; and there were two *secondary* goods, the good done to the offender and the good done to society. Sometimes this was expressed in terms which made God the primary beneficiary. So Benjamin Whichcote wrote in the mid-seventeenth century: "The end of punishment, with respect to God, is the vindication of his uprightness and righteousness; with respect to the sinner, it is the reformation and amendment of his life; with respect to the innocent, it is warning to fear and do not such sin."[21]

The benefit of punishment to the offender is a doctrine owing a great deal to Plato, who taught that just punishment purged the soul from evil, which greatly attracted Christians in the patristic period.[22] Augustine spoke of a "benign harshness" taking thought for the conversion of the offender, which stamps the Christian ruler's actions with paternal affection.[23] It is a conception with its own dangers. We could express these by saying that paternal and political authority are not the same in human society, though we believe that they are one and the

20. Immanuel Kant, *The Metaphysic of Morals,* §49E, trans. M. Gregor (Cambridge: Cambridge University Press, 1991), pp. 140-45.

21. *Aphorisms* 309. For a recent statement of the doctrine, see *Catechism of the Catholic Church,* §2266: "The primary effect of punishment is to redress the disorder caused by the offence. When his punishment is voluntarily accepted by the offender, it takes on the value of expiation. Moreover, punishment has the effect of preserving public order and the safety of persons. Finally punishment has a medicinal value; as far as possible it should contribute to the correction of the offender."

22. *Gorgias* 476a-478e.

23. *Ep.* 138.14.

same within the authority of God. Parental chastisement, intended for moral improvement, is necessarily different from civil punishment. The family as a social structure has as its goal the communication of tradition, not the enactment of judgment. Precisely because a family may suspend judgment before the destructive energies of an incorrigible member, it can reconcile the offender more effectively than a civil society can ever do.

Attempts to replicate within political society the reconciling potential of the family often end up by being ideologically deceptive. Augustine's doctrine of paternal affection was put to disturbing use in justifying the persecution of heretics. More recently, the penitentiaries conceived at the end of the eighteenth century by evangelical philanthropists as an alternative to capital punishment are generally frowned upon as a paradigm of paternalist oppression. Believing that the world could be made better, but not believing sufficiently in miracles to know that penal techniques were insufficient to that end, they made a use of unrelieved solitary confinement and enforced silence that were sometimes enough to make prisoners mad, but were not enough to make them good. Nineteenth-century prison reform was an uneasy coalition of utilitarian ambitions for deterrent efficiency and Enlightenment-Christian aspirations for techniques of redemption. The idea that punishment benefits the punished should lead us back to the redeeming work of God, and so on to the last things. The point at which judgment and redemption meet lies hidden in the counsel of God and can only be pointed to.[24] Christian thinkers of the patristic era displayed a wise insight in applying the idea primarily to the sufferings of the wicked after death, so giving an initial impulse to the medieval doctrine of Purgatory.[25] The element of truth in that doctrine lies in its conception that divine judgment is at once both condemnation and mercy; so that we may say paradoxically, *bonum damnatis sic damnari,* "such a damnation is good for the damned."[26]

Within the relations of civil society we have to acknowledge that there are things we may hope for the offender which we cannot achieve,

---

24. Even Plato (in the *Phaedo*) was driven to the myth of reincarnation to give his theory of punishment a satisfactory development.

25. Origen, *De principiis* 2.10.5; Gregory of Nyssa, *Oratio catechetica* 8.

26. John Wyclif, *De civili dominio* 3.24.227c.

and so we must be content with the one good always owed to the offender in punishment: the truth about his offense. That is something to which the offender is entitled whether or not it benefits him, for it affords the occasion to acknowledge the social conditions of his own existence. Hegel spoke of punishment as the satisfaction of the offender's "explicit will" (though the language of "will," as often in Hegel, is misleading, for it is, in effect, the moral *rationality* of the offender which the punishment addresses), expressing the law of his existence as a rational — and we may add, social — agent.[27] From one angle, then, the good of punishment for the offender is simply and solely the good of judgment; yet it is not trivial to recognize that judgment is good for the offender, and it may make a difference to the kinds of punishment we allow ourselves to administer. If punishment addresses the offender with a truth to be grasped, we will wish to shape our punishments, as far as possible, to facilitate, or at least not to obstruct, the grasping of it.

Something similar must be said about the good of society. This is not some *further* good, such as the security of a crime-free society; it is simply the good of judgment itself, the basic condition of a common life, which points to God's work in upholding society. Punishment is good for society because it is through judgment that "the good live more peaceably in the midst of the evil."[28] If we speak of a "deterrent" good of punishment, we are not to understand it as introducing any further terror than that which is already presented by the truth that constitutes society. The terror is not "annexed" to crime as an afterthought; it belongs essentially to the act of condemnation, by which society declares the moral terms of its existence. Judgment offers society the truth about itself, just as it offers the offender the truth about himself. Each needs to grasp its own truth in order to flourish in relation to the other. We may note the moral-educative turn given to this good in the quotation from Whichcote: "warning to fear and do not such sin." A contentless "security" will not suffice for society's good.

In the normal exercise of judgment within civil society we have no need to ask whether any given act of punishment will serve the social good or not; it serves it by being a just and consistent application of a practice on which society depends. In relation to any new experiment

27. *Philosophy of Right,* §97-100.
28. Augustine, *De natura boni* 37; *Ep.* 153.16; *IG,* p. 125.

in justice, however, whether the introduction of a new law or the prosecution of judgment in an extraordinary form such as war, the question of whether it will serve the just order of society as a whole is a pressing and important one. For example, the introduction of international war-crimes tribunals, admirably intended to bring a range of the gravest crimes against international law within the scope of judicial enquiry and punishment, has had to prove itself against a series of skeptical questions: will they make peace-settlements more difficult to implement? can they proceed equitably? can they establish sufficient levels of proof to secure public confidence in their judgments? and so on. These questions are relevant precisely to the *justice* of the tribunals. It is not that punishing war-criminals is certainly just but only doubtfully prudent, but, rather, that if these questions cannot be answered satisfactorily, the tribunals will be a parody of justice.

The two goods of punishment, then, the good of the offender and the good of society, are not the basis of distinct or competing "forward-looking" theories of punishment, but belong together within a unified account of punishment as a form of judgment. This relation of the ideas is at its clearest in Hegel's masterly discussion, which, for all its ambiguities, describes a convergence of the interests of offender and society upon the common need for a vindication of infringed right that will effectively express the moral and social "nullity" of the crime. In many ways Hegel's account of punishment brings to theoretical completion the scattered insights of patristic Christianity. What it lacks, however, is a way of relating penal practice to the wider range of practices that constitute political and social life. It remains abstractly suspended in the psychological context that is the matrix of so much of his thought, and so appears to be merely ingenious. That is why a satisfactory penal theory must be couched within a theory of judgment.[29]

29. The lateness of this theoretical achievement may be due to the dual institutional development of parallel courts — ecclesiastical and civil — that came in the later Middle Ages to be thought responsible for pursuing the different goods of punishment. Ecclesiastical jurisdiction, founded on penitential practice, was taken to provide a punishment directed to the offender's welfare. So Nicholas of Kues saw it as a mark of "ecclesiastical coercion" that it was undertaken (a) with consent, and (b) for the salvation of the punished (*Concordantia* 2.261, trans. Paul E. Sigmund [Cambridge: Cambridge University Press, 1991]). With the responsibility for the two goods thus distributed, there was no need to insist upon the conception of punishment underlying both.

*   *   *

Judgment enacted on the condemned party displays justice if it discriminates correctly between innocence and guilt; but also, as we have said, it must observe descriptive truthfulness. In punishing we pronounce on a range of different offenses. How may we pronounce articulately, marking the differences between one kind of offense and another? What scale of proportioned actions may we deploy?

The scale which relates punishments to offenses is inevitably a conventional one. There is no absolute tariff. Many penal systems in the course of history could claim to satisfy the formal demand that punishment should respond proportionately to different kinds of offense. Differing languages of punishment have expressed differential judgments comprehensibly to the societies that gave rise to them. Some have been more severe, some milder; but they have not tended to severity or mildness arbitrarily, but in relation to the capacities of the society to feel. Montesquieu observed famously: "Experience shows that in countries remarkable for the lenity of their laws the spirit of the inhabitants is as much affected by slight penalties as in other countries by severer punishments."[30]

The notion of an absolute tariff is a chimera that has proved irresistibly tempting to thinkers about penal measures. The principle called *lex talionis* by the Romans, and most famously expressed in the phrase from Pentateuchal law, "an eye for an eye, a tooth for a tooth" — the idea, that is, that punishment should consist in the infliction of an equal and opposite harm — has seemed to promise an objective rule for the correspondence of punishment to crime.[31] Even so subtle a thinker as Kant was persuaded that this was the logical implication of the practice of retribution, and that the death penalty was universally required by it. In fact, the only practical application of the *lex talionis* ever advocated is the death penalty for murder. To apply it to other kinds of

30. *L'Esprit des lois* 6.12, trans. Thomas Nugent (New York: Hafner; London: Collier Macmillan, 1949).

31. In Pentateuchal law it is not deployed as a general principle for determining punishments, but is invoked only in a limited number of contexts: for careless injury to a pregnant woman, for inflicting lasting disfigurement (Exod. 21:23ff.; Lev. 24:20); and, in an instance of especial interest, in the law of false witness, to punish malicious intent even though it was never carried through (Deut. 19:21).

crime would be impractical fantasy.[32] The correspondence of punishment to crime must be a symbolic construct of some kind; once we grasp this point, we can see the necessity of different societies having different "languages" of punishment that correspond to their different sensibilities about the meaning of different coercive acts.

But we should not confine the significance of Montesquieu's observation to a simple scale of mildness and severity. Societies feel differently about different things. Some are more sensitive to the infliction of physical injury or death, others to social humiliation. These differing sensibilities are themselves not arbitrary, but are shaped by the practical resources available for punishment and by the expectations of life formed from daily experience. It has meant a great deal for Western society that it has been wealthy enough, peopled enough, and has enjoyed sufficiently effective communications, to organize and maintain a humane system of long-term imprisonment. Western sensibilities about the death penalty changed as doing without the death penalty became a practical proposition. Similarly, sensibilities about corporal punishment changed as medical advances spared us the daily sight of people in pain and spared us also the moral task of bearing pain with fortitude. Effective and technologically sophisticated policing facilitated more relaxed parole and probation. All these features of the Western penal system are dependent upon social conditions that have not always existed, and which do not exist everywhere today. They are also dependent upon certain moral dispositions that favor them. A society inclined to immoderate anger and revenge will be driven to harsher forms of punishment. Mild practices of punishment are not an irreversible achievement; nor does Montesquieu's observation mean that society can be made more sensitive by making its laws milder, like economists who try to control public expectations from the supply-side. It simply inverts a remark that goes back to Gregory the Great: God visits unruly societies with harsh governments.

The relativity of penal languages should alert us to the danger of over-hasty disapproval of penal practices other than our own, whether historical or contemporary. In evaluating the practice of another soci-

32. This generalization embraces even such practices as the Shari'ah requirement of the amputation of a hand for theft. This is not an application of *lex talionis*, which would require amputation for amputation and theft for theft. The appeal of the Shari'ah rule is purely symbolic, lying in the perceived fitness of inflicting punishment upon the bodily member used for the deed.

ety we must see it as a whole; it is not enough to feel a *frisson* at some feature which we find barbarous. But can we, then, disapprove of anything at all universally? May it not be that even torture is accommodated within the symbolism of some penal languages? And if we define torture purely anatomically, as performing certain painful acts upon the human body, perhaps it may be so; and perhaps it may be lack of imagination that makes it seem incompatible with respect for human dignity — we need only think of the measures used by admirers of the Japanese samurai culture to commit suicide! As things stand, however, the practices we condemn as torture are clearly not viewed in that light by the societies which practice them. They are performed in secret, without due process, without legal specifications as to duration or intensity; and they in no way seek to tell the truth about the crimes they punish. These features identify such practices as subversive of the norms by which those societies formally operate. Understood in this sense, as the infliction of "cruel and unusual" suffering outside prevailing norms, torture may be regarded as universally prohibited.

So the scope for relativity is not infinite. Our metaphor of penal "languages" should, perhaps, speak of penal "dialects," made up of the same linguistic elements with differently nuanced uses. A kiss is a sign of love, though in some cultures a polite greeting, in others an intense endearment. A blow in the face is an insult, in some places a mortal offense, in others merely vulgar loutishness. There are basic conditions for any penal system, and they can be derived from the words of Genesis 9:6, promulgating the Noachic covenant: "Whoever sheds the blood of man, by man shall his blood be shed." This is not a formulation of the *lex talionis* as a determination of penalty; it is, rather, an expression of the basis of retributive practice itself. We are all mortal, and our life has a limited expectancy. That fact gives all crime and all punishment its meaning. Two years in prison are "two good years of my life"; if we were immortal, they would count for nothing. A heavy fine is a drain on resources needed for food, clothing, and shelter. Corporal punishment weakens the bodily constitution. Every serious injury is an assault, directly or indirectly, on the victim's life; so every punishment, too, is an assault on the offender's life.

What we look for in a system of punishment is a flexible range of intermediate measures that hedge that infringement on life around with alternatives, so that we are not driven too quickly back upon the ultimate resort of taking life directly. The art of penal development is the multiplication of a carefully differentiated range of intermediate assaults. Yet its horizon is the ultimate possibility of death itself. Even if a society formally removes the death penalty from its criminal sanctions, it does not abolish death as its ultimate recourse, for when crime becomes uncontrollable by normal means, society resorts to making war upon it. The armed patrol takes the place of the hangman.

The saying, "Whoever sheds the blood of man, by man shall his blood be shed," speaks not only of judicial retribution but of private vengeance, too. If the manslayer's blood is not held forfeit by the first, it will be held forfeit by the second. It is the task of all government to bring grievance out of the sphere of private action into the field of public judgment; and if its judicial and penal arrangements fail to do that, informal vendettas will take their place. This is not to say that government has to satisfy every last victim of crime. The decisive test is not the residual existence of a grievance, but its capacity to arouse general sympathy. Many a smitten Abel has gone on crying from the ground after his Cain has been sealed with the mark of limited judgment and marched off to prison. The question is whether Abel's protestations can subvert the solidarity of society, shaking its confidence in judgment. Sympathy is a great fomenter of discord, and that is what must be avoided at all costs. It can happen when penalties are generally felt to be too low, too unpredictable, too insecure; and it can happen also when they are generally felt to be too high, too implacable, too pitiless, so that Cain himself becomes an Abel crying for justice.

Here, then, is a positive condition that a system of punishment must always meet. Can we describe any comparably universal negative conditions? In the first place we should always criticize a system that fails to differentiate between discernible levels of guilt, between the guilt of one acting under necessity, for instance, and one committing the same crime wantonly. We should always criticize a system that fails to minimize within reason the incidental sufferings of the innocent, those of the family and dependents of the condemned, for example. And we should always criticize a penalty that fosters attitudes of contempt towards the condemned. The Deuteronomic code limits the number of stripes to be administered in a flogging to forty, "lest your brother should be degraded in your sight" (Deut. 25:1-3). There is, to be sure, a difference between this "degradation" and shame: shame is inseparable from punishment, and, within bounds, is a healthy by-product of it, showing that the condemned person is not insensible to social influences and tending to reinforce the general will to obey the law. Degradation is a function not of the sensitivity of the condemned person, but of the insensitivity of everyone else. When the suffering of punishment becomes an object of vulgar curiosity and fascination, even experiment, the condemned person ceases to count among us as a human being deserving of neighbor-love, and ordinary human respect seems to vanish. A penalty that has such an effect on the community fails to achieve the public moral self-definition that judgment aims at; in fact, it demoralizes the community. In this connection we should criticize every attempt to devise a penalty more grave than death. The attempt to enhance the deterrent effect of the death penalty by torture betokens a cruel mind, rebelling against the constraints of mortality that define the practice of retribution. And besides these failings, subject to criticism in any possible penal system, we should be ready to criticize any specific untruths that a given system may embody: one that treats offenses against property as equivalent to offenses against life, or offenses against government as equivalent to religious blasphemy, or offenses against women as of less account than offenses against men, and so on.

These general constraints apply to any system of punishment. In the history of Christian thought they have been articulated, sometimes more clearly and sometimes less, as part of that clarifying task that has been understood as the explication of natural law. They are necessary if punishment is to fulfil its function in society as judgment. Though their application may be relative to social conditions — what counts as degrading punishment may vary from the Deuteronomic forty strokes — they represent the formal limits that define proportion in punishment. We must distinguish their logic from that of the Christian prejudice in favor of mildness, of which we wrote in the last chapter. This does not propose *limits* on what may count as just punishment, but introduces *substantial considerations* into our assessment of what is proportionate, presupposing a certain evangelical self-consciousness. This evangelical logic, not the formal natural-law logic, is what has guided Christian reflection upon the death penalty.[33]

---

33. On which see my discussion, "Todesstrafe," in *Theologische Realenzyklopädie* 23, hsgb. Gerhard Müller (Berlin: Walter de Gruyter, 2002): 639-46.

PART II

Political Institutions: Representation

8

Political Authority

"Be subject to the governing authorities" (Rom. 13:1). An apologist for St. Paul may wish to cushion the impact of the verb by pointing out that what it demands in the first instance is simply a developed political consciousness. Paul's outline of political responsibility, though schematic and limited by the possibilities of the early Roman empire, may be filled with appropriate content as we learn to operate intelligently within any political structure whatever. "Subjection" *(hupotassesthai)* corresponds philologically to God's "arrangement" *(tetagmenai)* of authority, words formed from the root meaning "order." This line of defense is neither inappropriate nor unfruitful; yet, when everything possible has been said along these lines, "be subject" is hardly the favored language of republican citizens who see themselves as participating in the reciprocal relations of self-government. Between St. Paul's model of political structure and the dominant model of our era there is a decisive difference, which turns upon the non-reciprocal relation of subjects to rulers.

Non-reciprocality is the stumblingblock from which the dominant problematics of modern politics have arisen: on the one side authority, on the other side obligation. The history of the emergence of political from pre-political concepts, the slow evolution from clan to state, indicates how the experience of being commanded and responding required a lengthy and difficult clarification before civilized man could speak clearly of what it was that imposed the obligation. And clarity is not guaranteed even to civilized man. When civilization thinks of political authority as one of its own artifacts, it conceives it in terms of institutions rather than events, and then, equally naturally, begins to resent being asked to defer to institutions of its own making. That is why "authority" has little place in late-modernity; yet late-modernity continues to encounter it and respond to it, even if it does not know how to explain itself as it does so.

The contract myth of Bodin and Hobbes was an attempt to justify the non-reciprocal relation by deriving it from reciprocality. The attempt ended with Rousseau's republican reaffirmation of reciprocality. Political subjection was owed not to the rulers themselves but to the collective whole; consequently, everybody owed precisely the same to everybody else. This turning of the contract through three hundred and sixty degrees derived from a failed attempt to resolve the paradox of political subjection. Political subjection is not servitude; the political subject is freer *as* a subject. Political authority may abridge freedom in certain of its exercises; but it does so only to ensure it and secure it. That paradox refuses to be resolved into a *stratagem* of freedom; it can be grasped only at its center, the experience of being subject to a governing authority.

This experience is generated by a *political moment* of non-reciprocality that accompanies the performance of the *political act*, the act of judgment. Initially we recognize authority simply as an occurrence: it appears to us in the acts of a given agent, and summons us to defend the common good. Presupposing no institutions, political authority arises as judgment is done. In Scripture we find it said that God "raises up" those through whom he exercises judgment. The clearest example of this truth is in revolution. By definition an extra-constitutional act, it must also, by definition, have authority, for otherwise it is not a revolution but merely a seizure of power. But what kind of authority does a revolution command? To say it is authorized by the will of the people is like saying that fire is started by combustion. The will of the people is precisely what needs explanation. Why did *this* person's speeches spur the people to act as one? All we can say is, God raised him up.

There can be no sensible deliberation as to whether we shall or shall not have such a thing as political authority. It is something we simply stumble upon. Yet we may devise institutions to channel it, and these may be more or less successful. A train of constitutional thought running from Ockham to Suárez conceived the matter this way: to design political forms and to prefer persons to occupy positions within them is a human undertaking; it nonetheless presupposes the providential gift of authority. That the ruler we elect and the forms we devise should be able to assert and retain authority, *that* is something we cannot undertake. We can only entrust them and ourselves to God's providential authorization.[1]

So it is that theologians have asserted at one and the same time that a ruler was the people's representative and the "minister of God" (Rom. 13:4). This latter phrase does not remove political authority from the sphere of the human; it does not imply a *special* intervention of the divine to appoint a particular ruler, but a *general* provision of non-reciprocal relations under which we may flourish. That which God has arranged is, in another New Testament phrase, a "human institution" (1 Pet. 2:13), i.e., a relation among human beings for the benefit of human affairs.[2]

Our situation in the face of political authority, far from being out of the ordinary like an encounter with an angel or a divine revelation, is simply a special case of a situation deeply woven into our experience as human agents: finding ourselves under obligation to do something. Being obliged is different from being compelled, for it is only in a minimal sense that one "does" what one is compelled to do. The prisoner walks into the cell on his own two legs because the prospect of being manhandled is too painful, but his choice in the matter is limited to the means; for all the real difference he can make, he might as well be trussed up and carried in. To do something one is obliged to, on the

---

1. An older tradition learned from the Litany of the *Book of Common Prayer* to pray for "the Lords of the Council and all the Nobility . . . grace, wisdom and understanding," and for the Magistrates "grace to execute justice" — "grace" here being meant precisely in the sense of divine authorization. Our recent liturgists, unable to share the perilous sense of contingency in government, have thought it enough to ask that politicians should be clever people: "Endue the high court of Parliament and all the ministers of the crown with wisdom and understanding" (*Common Worship*, p. 285).

2. We may well share Wolfgang Schrage's discomfort with this traditional translation while not feeling that he has shown us how to improve on it (*The Ethics of the New Testament*, trans. D. E. Green [Edinburgh: T & T Clark, 1988], pp. 277-78). His proposal, "every human creature," ignores the theme of social structures that controls the context. But whatever we take the precise sense of κτίσις to be, the key to the sense of what follows is ἀνθρωπίνη: whatever it may be by which the polity and the household are governed, it is *common among humankind*. The word has a consistently leveling tone; it conceives the "human" as the *ordinary usage* of human beings, sometimes in contrast to the greater scope of divine and angelic powers, and sometimes suggests the need for indulgence.

other hand, is to do it freely, not under compulsion. But it is also different from acting *spontaneously;* the spontaneous act is entirely our own, an act which nobody has laid upon us. In being obliged by an authority we have an action laid upon us, even though it is still free action. A large number of human actions are "laid upon us" in this sense, for there is a multitude of non-political authorities, constituted by the ordinary relations of society, which direct us to perform certain actions: doctors, teachers, parents, employers, all whom the catechism called our "pastors and masters." In these relations, where two parties are not equally capable of envisaging the goods of action, one is dependent upon the direction of the other.

If we overlook the role of authority in these non-political relations we can never understand their effect on us. We are used to hearing them characterized, inaccurately, in terms of "power." In the eighteenth century Joseph Butler could claim the distinction between power and authority as one that "every body is acquainted with," a claim that could hardly be made today.[3] In its widest sense "power" is simply the capacity to accomplish something, by whatever means, and in this innocuous sense authority is a species of power. But in a narrower use, "power" is the power *to compel,* which is not what authority is, though political authority does depend on power as a precondition. The confusion of these senses gives the word "power" its fashionably sinister sound, as, for example, in the alarms promoted by Foucault about the power of the medical profession. Actually, physicians exercise power over patients only when the latter are unconscious or exceptionally weak, and there are strong professional constraints upon how they use their power in those circumstances. What a physician does exercise is a great deal of authority: the patient will submit without protest to physical examinations, medical treatments, surgical operations, and so on, perfectly freely, but at no other instance than the physician's prescription. This authority may be, and sometimes is, wrongly coveted or wrongly used; but its abuse is not the same thing either as the abuse of power, nor the same thing as the abuse of political authority.

To oblige us freely to do something, authority must present us with a reason for doing it. Action is free only as it is intelligible — intelligible,

---

3. *Sermon* 2.19, in *The Works of Joseph Butler,* ed. W. E. Gladstone, vol. 2 (Oxford: Clarendon Press, 1896), p. 63. Butler's "mere power" is, I take it, the power to compel.

that is to say, to the one who acts. A free action must seem, in some sense, "a good thing to do." Some actions occur to us effortlessly: a beautiful sound invites us to stop and listen; a truth dawning on our intelligence inspires us to apply our minds. We have reasons for doing such things, but do not usually stop to ask what they are, since reason and response flow delightfully together into an unruffled stream of experience and action. But other goods of action are intruded into the stream by the intervention of another agent, and these require an effort in response. We perceive them as obligations laid upon us by authority. We attend to sounds that do not appear beautiful, or struggle with thoughts that do not appear significant, because the teacher who trains our ear or mind instructs us to do so. Authority is not, as has been said, "a reason for acting in the absence of reasons," for the goods of action are reasons in either case, whether effortlessly present or painfully mediated. Yet reasons are "absent" to the extent that they are not conspicuous. An authority is someone I depend upon to show me the reasons for acting. The authority of the expert, the person with a special knowledge, teaches me what I cannot work out for myself, e.g., how to operate a computer. Even if I hope to learn enough to be independent of my teacher one day, I still need help for the time being. Less obviously, but no less cogently, the same principle applies to relations grounded in emotion. When the poet writes of "that not impossible shee, that shall command my heart and mee," he points to the meaning of erotic love as a form of dependence on authority.[4]

At this point the exposition of authority I gave in *Resurrection and Moral Order* is in need of improvement.[5] Tempted by the project of compiling a list of basic goods of action (such as is pursued in the Reformed thinker Herman Dooyeweerd and the Catholic thinkers Germain Grisez and John Finnis, not to mention ancient models in the Old Academy and the Stoics),[6] I identified four "immediate natural" authorities of beauty, age, community, and strength; one "reflexive" natural authority, that of truth; and one "supernatural authority," the

4. Richard Crashaw, "Wishes. To his (supposed) Mistresse." The poet desires that a "divine Idaea" (punning the word "idea" with the title of the goddess Cybele, associated with Mount Ida, who overmasters her devotees with ecstatic rites) will "take a shrine of chrystall flesh" in his mistress, who is to direct all his practical engagements.

5. *Resurrection and Moral Order,* pp. 124-27.

6. Cf. Cicero *de fin.* 2.11.33f., 4.7.16f.

divine. Clearly, my list did not account for actions arising out of the instinct for self-preservation, nor, perhaps for the good of play, or *mimesis*. I was able, however, to exploit the provisionality of my undertaking in invoking a compound authority, "tradition," which combined the authority of age and community, and by allowing "strength" to diversify into every kind of *aretê*, or virtue, from might to wisdom. I do not feel a need to modify my insistence that authority is intimately connected with the basic goods of action, and is therefore not a reason for acting in the absence of reasons. An end of action must be intelligible, not only from the actor's point of view but from the observer's point of view. Reasons for acting are not mere "goals" which we set ourselves, they are also "grounds" which integrate our action into the intelligible structure of events. But I was injudicious in using the term "authorities" more or less interchangeably with "goods" in the objective sense, i.e., "grounds of action." This usage failed to identify the key difference about authority, which is that the ground of action is not immediate, but mediated through another agent.

Where authority is, freedom is; and where authority is lost, freedom is lost. This holds good for all kinds of authority. Without adults who demand mature behavior, the child is not free to grow up; without teachers to set standards of excellence, the scholar is not free to excel; without prophets to uphold ideals of virtue, society is not free to realize its common good. To be under authority is to be freer than to be independent. The centurion of Capernaum addressed Jesus with the memorable words, "I, too, am a man under authority. I say to this man 'Go' and he goes, and to another 'Come' and he comes" (Matt. 8:9). He exercises authority because he is under authority. Authority communicates itself through him, liberating his capacity for effective action and command. We catch the idea in our expression, "to be authorized to do something," a condition in which one is at the same time dependent upon authority and freed by that authority to act. When a group of followers identify themselves with a leader, they experience their leader's command as freeing them. That is true of any social movement: a political party, a school of intellectual criticism, an artistic fashion, or a gang of thugs — Augustine famously understood that certain social principles apply equally to kingdoms and to robber bands!

Together with freedom there is awe, a wonder that is both delight and terror. Freedom begins in delighted astonishment: at the beauty of the object which the artist will paint, at the complexity of the thought which the philosopher will tease out, at the God who reveals himself in the burning bush. This is a normal element in the genesis of any worthwhile project: a rational action which looks from one point of view like the pursuit of a good may from another point of view look more like being stopped in one's tracks. The parable of the pearl of great price is a parable about how any great thing comes to be done. Wonder contains dread as well as delight, and it is this that is especially prominent in response to authority. Those who present us with something we must do impose responsibility on us as well as freedom, and they become the immediate object of our fear of responsibility. The police officer waving down the car, the teacher setting the exercise, the physician recommending the operation, are all in varied ways our judges, should our response prove inadequate or unseemly. Only desire can make this dread tolerable, only love can make it welcome.

Confronted with political authority in particular, we respond with the same combination of freedom and awe: "fear to whom fear is due, honor to whom honor is due" (Rom. 13:7). Yet in the political case there is an all-important difference: political authority is non-transparent. It does not wait upon a mature perception of its rightness, and an understanding of its ways is granted only as we obey. There is a spontaneity in the mixture of delight and dread with which we bow to our teacher's wisdom or our mistress's beauty; our responses will need discipline if they are to come to anything, yet the discipline is supported by an intuitive appreciation. With political authority the disciplines must support themselves, for there is no intuitive perspicuity to call upon. Faced by some government official who behaves discourteously and issues foolish instructions, only a reflective belief engendered by civic virtue will instruct us to see his office as a service of the common good. Undisciplined responses oscillate between two poles: ogling fascination with political leadership on the one hand, angry resentment on the other — fetishism without fear, fear without admiration.

Rousseau was only the most celebrated of many who have concluded that political authority is peculiarly artificial, a "subjection" of nature to device.[7] But it was not *devised*, this invasive obligation that in-

---

7. *Discourse on Inequality*, trans. Maurice Cranston (Harmondsworth: Penguin Books, 1984), p. 77: "What exactly is the object of this discourse? To pinpoint the moment in the

terrupts spontaneous pursuit of social goods. It is, of course, possible to devise invasive strategies, which is why the ancient comparison of the statesman with the surgeon has always had an appeal; a surgical operation attacks the pathos of illness with the pathos of surgery. But political authority is more disturbing than that. It is not a device, of which we might say, "How clever!" nor a strategy, to which we might be a consenting party. It resembles our confrontation with the divine. Like God himself, political authority is peremptory.

The demands of political authority take us beyond our natural social responses and instincts, and direct us towards an aspect of our human destiny. They are, to be sure, an invariable accompaniment to social life, for the only examples of de-politicized societies we know are also de-socialized societies, i.e., societies in collapse. Yet we can distinguish society quite clearly from the authority that accompanies it. Authority is an *epiphenomenon*, not a *phenomenon* of society. To use Aristotle's famous expression, it concerns the step beyond "living" to "living well."[8] The good that it serves is the perfection of our social selves. From its defense of the common good it wins something new for society, a common history, a self-conscious tradition of purposes and goals, achievements and disappointments, which connects one political undertaking to the next.

History is connected with the difficult category of "progress," an idea from which it is impossible for political reflection to be disengaged. Progress cannot be perspicuous, like nature; it cannot be observed as a system. To conceive of it, we must think in terms of hidden purposes transcending brute fact, which is to say that we must think of divine providence. Theologians, in pointing to providence as the source of political authority, understood it as a service of human progress, securing the social world in the face of disintegration and preparing it for its goal in redemption. When every allowance has been made for the lines of connection between political authority and natural social authorities such as parents and teachers, it is the summons to the perfection of the kingdom of God that makes the crucial difference. In the

---

progress of things when, with right succeeding violence, nature was subjected to the law; to explain by what sequence of prodigious events the strong could resolve to serve the weak, and the people to purchase imaginary repose at the price of real happiness."

8. *Politics* 1252b29f.: γινομένη μὲν τὸ ζῆν ἕνεκεν, οὖσα δὲ τὸ εὖ ζῆν.

light of that summons the ruler can appear "like the angel of God to discern good and evil" (2 Sam. 14:17), the herald of the hidden future to which God summons human society.

* * *

To recognize political authority is, in the first place, to recognize a *particular bearer* of authority. We hear the summons to defend the common good mediated through this or that political actor. This does not imply that we approve of the way that bearer acquired authority, nor that we judge the bearer better suited to the responsibility than alternative candidates. It simply means that this and not some other power is, for us at this moment, "the government" — the one that "actually is"[9] — and may be expected to make dispositions for the defense of the common good which require our obedience.

We are obliged to sustain that bearer in place, to achieve continuity of regime. Complex constitutional arrangements, of course, make continuity of regime compatible with change of administration, and in democratic constitutions there is due provision for a "loyal opposition." But interruption of authority is an evil to be avoided. If we find ourselves in a state of sub-political social chaos where no bearer of political authority is to be found, our obligation is to facilitate the emergence of one. Here arises the famous moment of political "foundation" on which constitutional and contractarian thought became exclusively focussed. But this moment arises only in the pathological, not in the normal case, and even when it does arise it is not so much a "foundation" as a kind of midwifery, attending on events as providence directs them. In either case, normal or pathological, the goal which we are obliged to promote is political *institution* — that is, a series of common practices in which the exercise of political authority has a regular position. Institutionalized authority does not supplant the "moment" of authority; it provides the framework within which such moments may easily occur and easily be recognized.

"For this reason," as St. Paul says, "you pay taxes" (Rom. 13:6), which is the fundamental way that we facilitate political institutions. The duty to pay taxes is unconditional in the sense that the citizen-taxpayer does

9. Rom. 13:1: αἱ δὲ οὖσαι. . . .

not acquire a right to make terms. Taxation is for the support of government. It is not for specific policy aims of government at any given time, to be withheld if one disapproves of them, which would make taxation a kind of standing plebiscite on policy, a way of directing the state's counsels. Such direction can be given only by a critical political discourse, and the duty of sustaining such a discourse cannot be discharged by paying or withholding taxes. If a government pursues an unpopular war, those who disapprove are bound to propose articulate and reasoned objections, which they may do precisely because it is their government supported by their taxes. If they merely withhold the proportion of taxes supposedly designated for the war, the government could be content to buy their silence and pursue its policy as an optional extra which supportive citizens would buy into. But that would be a collusion to undermine political authority. A voluntary subscription can support a voluntary enterprise, but not a policy of government.

The second form the obligation takes is to discern the demands of authority as they are made from moment to moment. This is distinct from the first form. From the fact that I acknowledge some Caesar as the bearer of authority it by no means follows that I see myself as presently confronted with a binding demand to act in a certain way. Even if Caesar has this moment made a demand, there may be no obligation. For Caesar may make demands that do not pretend to political authority: he may urge us, for example, to buy something from him like a government-bond or a state-owned railway, or he may press upon us the need to vote for his party in elections. Our usual discretion as purchasers or voters is not diminished by the fact that the vendor or canvasser is Caesar. Alternatively, Caesar may lay claim to an authority that he does not have. The competence of any political authority is limited both by the rightful competence of other political authorities and by the proper immunity of social bonds to unwarranted political interference. Conscientious subjects will understand the formal limits of political authority no less clearly than they understand the moral weight of its substantive demands.

There is an element of discretion that can never be removed from the obedient subject: it is always the subject's business to be clear in his or her own mind that this or that command actually *requires* obedience. The duty of obedience carries with it the right and duty to decide what constitutes obedience at any given point. The subject's discretion has sometimes been misrepresented by the suggestion that political commands present us with an alternative in which we are free to make a choice: either obey or be punished, whichever we prefer.[10] But this is sheer confusion, for if Caesar has the right to punish he has the right to be obeyed; and if we have the right not to obey, we have the right not to be punished for not obeying. Obedient decision is not a choice between alternatives, it is an aspect of recognition. Responsibility for ascertaining that the demand is duly authorized belongs inalienably to those who must obey it. One cannot be obedient without making sure that it is the right demand one is obeying. "That thou mayest rightly obey power, her bounds know."[11] Agents of government will, of course, have their own views on where the limits of their competence lie; but agents of government are not infallible, whether in politics or in any other sphere, and they cannot relieve the subject of the burden of intelligent obedience. This was the principle upheld so starkly in the Nuremberg war-crimes trials.

Prior to these two forms of political obligation the subject has a more basic obligation — not, as such, the obligation *of a subject* specifically, but the obligation of a *member of society,* something owed to the neighbor before anything is owed to the ruler. This is the duty to preserve the public truth of social engagements by exercising candor in the public realm, a candor which necessarily includes appraisal of the conduct of political authority. Freedom of speech strengthens the public social bonds and prevents their being swallowed up by political demands. If there is one special virtue in constitutional arrangements that incorporate formal opposition into the regime, it is to encourage freedom of speech. Yet free speech can only be encouraged, not conferred, for free speech is participation in the word of God, not a privilege which one form of constitution may confer, another refuse. Nor is it a "right" that one citizen may claim, another forgo. That would imply that only the private citizen who exercised it had an interest in it, whereas candor is of the greatest importance for the public realm itself.[12] Candor is a

10. The sixteenth-century theory of the "purely penal law" interpreted certain inconvenient measures of taxation as not binding in conscience, since government purposes seemed to be served equally well by collecting taxes or by collecting fines.

11. John Donne, "Satyre" 3.100.

12. The Universal Declaration of Human Rights (19) declares "the right to freedom of opinion and expression," and the European Convention for the Protection of Human Rights (10) "the right to freedom of expression." We may be grateful for the insistence

simple public duty, often unperformed, or performed badly, out of simple reluctance to take responsibility for the truth on which the community depends. Behind many a story of tyranny lies collusion between oppressor and oppressed, a community that prefers to accept a shrunken public realm rather than pay the price of discerning and articulating complex truths in public.

The duty of public candor is not a duty of public office alone. Subjects who hold no office may discharge it by the way they tackle their business in the public realm, look to safeguard the common good in their commercial engagements, articulate and discuss the common good with those they deal with, not isolating themselves by technical narrowness or professional mystique, but advocating, justifying, listening to others' advocacy and justification, seeking a common understanding and approach to common tasks, avoiding the sins of rhetorical exaggeration and administrative impatience. Citizens who are comparatively "unpolitical," in the sense of having little to say about the conduct of government, may influence their community effectively by exercising the pre-political social virtue on which any good political community is founded. Living in a society that deliberates about its common good, they may contribute vigorously to its deliberation. And if their political role is no more than that of "recognizing" political authority without playing any active part in the machinery that sustains it, we can at least be sure that they will do that much with discernment and freedom. A society is free vis-à-vis its government when it is free vis-à-vis itself.

*   *   *

But *what* do we recognize, when we recognize that political authority has arisen? What does the bearer of authority bear?

The common good which government defends includes, in the first place, *right*. This is not self-evident, because it is possible to construe

---

that freedom of speech is a presupposition of political organization, not conferred by it. Yet the rights-orientation conceals the truth that the Declaration of the International Labor Organisation (1, annexed to the Constitution), from its more socialist perspective, observed quite clearly: that "freedom of expression" was "essential to sustained progress," i.e., of the workers' movement in particular, but also of the public realm as a whole. For all these documents, see Ian Brownlie, ed., *Basic Documents in International Law*, 5th ed. (Oxford: Oxford University Press, 2002).

the common good too narrowly as something short of right, a prosperity like material wealth or peace without justice. It is also possible to construe "right" too narrowly as something less than the *common* good, restricting it to private goods and immunities, as is constantly done in late-modern talk about "rights." But understanding common good and right as the good and the right *of a community,* that is, the sphere of social communications in which each member communicates within the whole, we must say that for political authority to defend the common good, it must command the authority of right. "Right" is at one and the same time the right of the community to its participants and the right of the participants to their community. Here, we may say, is the only fundamental and inalienable human right that can be thought of, at once subjective and objective: the right of society as such, the right of each member of society to be social.

In a famous passage[13] Hugo Grotius defines *ius* "right" in three ways: (a) It means *"what is just —* 'just' being understood in a negative rather than a positive sense, to mean 'what is not unjust', and 'unjust', in turn, meaning what is inconsistent with the nature of a society of rational beings." (b) A secondary and derivative sense is "attributed to a subject," a "subjective right" in our modern sense: "a right is a moral quality attaching to a subject enabling the subject to have something or do something justly." (c) The third sense "means the same as 'law', understood in a broad sense as a rule of action obliging us to do what is correct." This lapidary terminological summary has an acknowledged place in histories of the early-modern development of subjective right; but we will appreciate it better if we observe how Grotius conceives subjective right as a subject's participation in a prior and objective social right.[14] And we

13. *De iure belli ac pacis* 1.1.3-9; *IG,* pp. 797f. On the sources and interpretation of this passage, see "The Justice of Assignment and Subjective Rights in Grotius," in Oliver O'Donovan and Joan Lockwood O'Donovan, *Bonds of Imperfection* (Grand Rapids: Eerdmans, 2004), pp. 167-203.

14. Contrast Grotius's formulation here with that of Jean Gerson (*De potestate ecclesiastica* 13; *IG,* p. 528), propounded two centuries earlier but infinitely more "modern" in its leaning to rights-positivism: right is defined as "a proximate faculty or power which belongs to some subject as prescribed by primary justice." "Primary justice," we are told, is the disposition of God, so that the right-bearer derives his power directly from God's disposition through God's law, with no *social* right to mediate between God and the subject.

need add only one comment in order to make it serviceable also as a *material* summary: law is just one form of *political enactment,* i.e., the act of upholding or defending right in senses (a) and (b). "Judgment" is the broader term that encompasses any act of right-giving.

In the second place, the common good implies the flourishing of a particular society with a particular identity. An abstract defense of right which destroyed one society and founded a different one would not be an exercise of political authority, since one could not identify *whose* common good was served. (That is the force of the story of the Deluge in Genesis.) The idea of an identity introduces the idea of a community's "tradition." Tradition is "what is established"; and "what is established" is not the past, but the present as determined by the past. The authority of tradition resides in the way the community functions now to sustain its identity. But a community's identity depends on its historical provenance, so the authority of tradition is that of its *continuity with immediate history.* In Heidegger's terms, "tradition" is "historicality."[15] It is constituted by actual and diachronically communicated memories, relations and practices that determine the community as this community rather than some other. If these are corrupted or destroyed, the community is corrupted or destroyed. If innovations fail to connect with them, it is not *this* community that innovates, but some new community that has sprung into existence as a predator upon it.

These two aspects of the common good, "right" and "tradition," represent the essential ground of political authority. Authority belongs to those who, embodying the identity of the community, enact right on its behalf. With these two components, the idea of political authority is given. Yet for the idea to become actual a third component must be present, power. Power adds nothing to the idea as such. This is important to be clear about, since the thought that coercive power is the *essential* determinant of political authority, though periodically discredited, periodically returns. "The modern state can only be defined sociologically in terms of a specific means, which is peculiar to the state . . . namely physical violence," wrote Max Weber in 1920. It is, of course, true, and not only of the "modern" state, that "a state . . . lays claim to the monopoly of legitimate physical violence within a certain

---

15. *Being and Time,* trans. John Macquarrie and Edward Robinson (Oxford: Blackwell, 1962), pp. 19f. "Historicality" translates "Geschichtlichkeit."

territory."[16] Any apparently legitimate use of private violence (e.g., in private self-defense) is lawful only as the state has authorized it, not on the basis of some pre-political individual right. But it is not true that violence (or, better, "force") is the *foundation* of the state. The state's claim to monopolize legitimate force is secondary; it derives from the harnessing of power to the service of right and tradition. "Legitimate force" is power deployed in the service of right within a given community. The definition of the state, its founding rationale, is not the monopoly of violence but the monopoly of the community's right, its claim to be the last instance in a society's defense against wrong.[17]

What we should rather say, then, is that power is a prerequisite for the *realization* of the idea of the state. That is why we cannot recognize an agency that has no power as having political authority, though it may have moral authority. Political authority enacts judgment, and action expends power. If a representative agency has no power to act decisively, it cannot command the authority to require action of us. No political authority is possessed by a "government in exile," since a government that does not govern is nothing. Ousted regimes may at best have the status of a worthy opposition, which does not entitle them to command disobedience to government since it is the duty of subjects to ensure that they are actually governed, wherever their sympathies may lie.[18] In the moment of conflict, of course, when posses-

---

16. *Political Writings,* ed. and trans. Peter Lassman and Ronald Speirs (Cambridge: Cambridge University Press, 1994), p. 310. The term *Gewaltsamkeit,* "violence," is ill chosen, however, and too broad. A private entrepreneur may deploy a stick of dynamite to clear a building site; it is *force against persons* that the state monopolizes. "Violence" and "legitimate force" are exclusive alternatives.

17. And for that reason Weber's hypothetical formulation, "If there existed only social formations in which violence was unknown as a means, *then* the conception of the 'state' would have disappeared," is not true either. We can conceive in thought the idea of a state maintaining its political authority without calling on force against the person — confining itself to resort against goods, liberty, and social participation. The conditions for such a state would be an utterly pacific society, where offenders complied unresistingly with orders of house-arrest or expropriation. But however implausible in themselves, such conditions would not destroy the form of the state, which would continue to rest upon its monopoly of community right and of such power as was necessary to exercise it.

18. In the seventeenth and eighteenth centuries monarchical governments uncertain of their tenure attempted to evade the moral logic of this principle by exacting

sion is contested, the matter may be different: a revolution acquires power as it acts, recruiting the power it needs as we respond to its summons. But in this case, too, authority lays its obligation on us by what it can effectively achieve for justice. If it can achieve nothing, it lays no obligation on us, and therefore is not an authority.

We sum this argument up in a theorem we have broached before: *Political authority arises where power, the execution of right, and the perpetuation of tradition are assured together in one coordinated agency.* Neither power, nor right nor tradition alone, nor any two of them without the third, can constitute political authority. It cannot arise except where one and the same agency can dispose of all three.

In *Resurrection and Moral Order* I propounded this theorem tentatively in the form that political authority was a compound of *might, injured right, and tradition*. In *Desire of the Nations* I reached the present formulation (p. 46), and interpreted it in terms of the kingship of YHWH as salvation, judgment, and possession, seeing this reflected in Jesus' works of power, announcement of judgment, and interpretation of the law. The source of this triad, as I now realize, was Paul Ramsey's analysis of authority as *lex, iustitia*, and *ordo*. By *ordo* Ramsey meant "order" in the late-modern sense, i.e., control of the situation, something more like power than I would understand by the term.[19] In *Desire of the Nations* I added a fourth strand to the analysis of YHWH's kingship, *worship*, to which the equivalent in the Gospel account of Jesus' ministry proved to be *faith*. In the present discussion this fourth strand is represented by the term "recognition." The fourth strand is not a constitutive element of political authority alongside the other three. For it is not recognition, or consent, that *constitutes* political authority; yet the presence of political authority is *demonstrated* in recognition. "In acknowledging political authority, society proves its political identity" (cf. *DN,* p. 47). The orchestra does not make someone its conductor by playing in time to his beat; but by playing in time to his beat they recognize him as their conductor.

---

oaths to the person of the monarch whatever should become of him. So the nobility of Ireland, bound by oath to James II, was creamed off into unnecessary exile with the fallen monarch after the Treaty of Limerick in 1691, to the incalculable loss of the country. But an oath to a monarch is an oath to the monarch *as* monarch. It can do no more than render explicit what is implied in the subject-monarch relation.

19. "The Uses of Power," in *The Just War* (New York: Scribner's, 1968), pp. 3-18. I have discussed this important essay at length in "Karl Barth and Ramsey's 'Uses of Power,'" in *Bonds of Imperfection*, pp. 246-75.

My earlier discussion in *Resurrection and Moral Order* required correction in four respects. (a) "Might" is the capacity to deploy force, which is an element in political power, since a society without the resources to mount a determined defense against an assault on its order can only act tentatively at best. St. Paul says that the ruler "does not bear the sword in vain," i.e., that the symbolic sword which is the mark of his office is not an empty symbol, but points to the fulcrum of political authority in the capacity for coercion. But "power" is a wider notion than "might." It implies wealth, a good deal of it these days, to support and train government officers, to house the administration, to equip it for its routine work, and, of supreme importance, to enable efficient communication among its officers. And so Paul continues, "For this reason you pay taxes" (Rom. 13:6). (b) The epithet in "injured right" is misleading. The sense of "right" in question is the *enactment* of right, and authority is commanded by all active resistance to wrong. (c) For reasons explained above, it was a mistake to describe the authority of tradition as the authority of "age." (d) In *Resurrection and Moral Order* I assumed it as typical of all political authority that the authorities of might and tradition were "put at the disposal of" the authority of injured right (p. 128). By the time I wrote *Desire of the Nations* I had reached the conclusion that this subordination of two to the third is "not imposed by the nature of political authority as such" but "by the limits conceded to secular authority by Christ's kingdom" (p. 233). This significant change of mind was not acknowledged in *Desire of the Nations,* and, indeed, it went unnoticed by the author until his attention was drawn to it by Jonathan Chaplin.[20]

Every conflict over political authority is played out before two horizons of de-politicization, on which political authority simply disappears. One of these lies where the claim of injured right is systematically ignored by those holding power, the other where those holding power have no right of tradition. On the first horizon we locate those powers that are not political authorities because, while they maintain traditions, they ignore the tasks of right.

The cultural imperative of tradition can assume far too great an urgency. The book of Deuteronomy, while calling upon tradition to maintain Israel's identity, and making much of educational transmission in the home (6:20-25), yet insists that this domestic tradition needs always

---

20. "Oliver O'Donovan's 'Christian Liberalism': Political Eschatology and Responsible Government," in C. Bartholomew, ed., *A Royal Priesthood* (Carlisle: Paternoster, 2003), pp. 265-308.

to be normed by law. Tradition is corruptible. In Israel's case the authentic national tradition was in danger of being overwhelmed by local traditions which had lost their connection with the original memory of Exodus, Horeb, and conquest. Law is the only safe form of cultural memory, Deuteronomy thinks, the only way in which crucial patterns of tradition can resist assimilation to rival patterns (6:1-19). Tradition needs to be a tradition *of* right, which is upheld as such. The prophets express even more reserve about tradition. Jeremiah looks for a form of communication in which the urgency of the task of tradition is relaxed, since all participants will enjoy equal and direct possession of God's law (Jer. 31:34). Diachronic communication is characterized by dependence: of receiver upon giver, pupil upon teacher, later generations upon earlier. How is this dependence to be overcome, since no communication can be imagined that is not in time? Only by fashioning the tradition around practices of judgment that are answerable to the law of God.

But practices of judgment are not perfectible. It is in a *tradition* of judgment, not in absolute justice itself, that political authority resides. Doubtless, if we were to know the full tally of false convictions in our courts, not to mention false acquittals, failures to prosecute for lack of evidence, evidence unheard, mistaken decisions in civil causes, honest witnesses put to shame under hostile cross-examination and rogues creating a fine impression, justice denied or delayed for budgetary reasons, we would find it all very depressing — and that within the sphere of justice where the reaching of precise decisions has been made a fine art! What if we were to think of contracts badly awarded, appointments badly made, inquiries badly conducted, and so on? Yet to explain them we do not need to suppose one moment of malice or neglect on the part of any office-holder. Non-culpable ignorance, misunderstanding, excessive pressure of work, and perhaps the very procedures meant to ensure adequate consideration — committees, reports, inquiries, etc. — all conspire to choke the administration of justice. The greatest reason for injustice is simply human limitation. The element of failure is insurmountable, and sensitive people who have to make decisions affecting others know how doubts and uncertainties can persist forever after.

But then we must add that sometimes there *is* malice or neglect among office-holders. Do these invalidate the claim of government to political authority? Not if they are acknowledged as the defects they really are — an acknowledgment sometimes made, paradoxically, in the form of a cover-up! To this, again, we must add unjust laws, mentioning among many possible examples one of the most widespread: those that permit unborn children to be unreasonably killed by their mothers with the assistance of gynecologists. Does the existence of such laws in Western states, as protesters have claimed, invalidate those states' claims to obedience? Not at all. As one swallow does not make a summer, so one bad law — even a handful — do not make a refusal of right. But consider the hardest case of all: when a section of society marked by some arbitrary characteristic is systematically exploited, not only as it happens to fall into one or another category, as "unborn child," "tenant," "day laborer," or whatever, but perennially and on all fronts, chased by the law from pillar to post, so that wherever it turns it finds itself forbidden to exercise ordinary freedoms, prevented from ordinary social participation, hemmed into a fixed place to fulfil a fixed role. Can the slave-state or the apartheid-state command real political authority? Not, to be sure, over the group it persecutes. Allowing them no right, it can lay on them no obligations. Those whom it treats as citizens by enacting justice for them, however, may owe it the ordinary duties of citizens, though they do not owe it cooperation in its policy of planned injustice.

Short of the horizon, then, lie powers which *are* political authorities because they take up the tasks of justice, but which are guilty of such grave faults in their performance that we are bound to ask ourselves whether something better may be put in their place. What is required in this case is an act of political reform. "Justified revolution," around which most discussion of the latter case has been organized, is, when properly conceived, an exercise of political authority governed by constitutional law. There are circumstances (the classic scenario of the "class war," for instance) in which the cause of the oppressed, reinforced with public identification, generates the appearance of informal authority in the name of which defiance may be hurled at official authorities. But that is a perilous appearance. The fact of a wrong needing to be righted will always provoke some kind of common action, which will in turn command a certain moral authority. Injury unavenged attracts protest; it wins the support of morally responsive people not immediately affected. Yet its authority, based on the claim of right, does not amount by itself to political authority. Lacking the authority of tradition, it can neither demand obedience nor refuse it. Defiance uttered in its name can only weaken government, and tend to make its already disappointing services even more disappointing. Classical political theology spoke of a duty of "non-resistance," which, properly understood, was simply the duty to preserve the tradition of relations between ruler and ruled. Reform itself is a way in which this duty is honored. If it is to be of service to the political community, it must be constitutionally carried through.[21]

So much for what lies *this side* of the horizon, still within the parameters of a political authority that enacts justice somehow or other. On the horizon itself, however, there is simply a political vacuum, and any action taken there is an act of punishing criminality. This was treated schematically by medieval thinkers under the heading of "tyrannicide." The tyrant controlled the polity not for the common good but for his own private good; which is to say, the public sphere of action and interaction was effectively shut down, and government was abandoned in the pursuit of private interest. Alongside this paradigm, we may put a rather different one, which we may call "tribalism": here there is indeed a public order, but it is wholly a phenomenon of communal solidarity, not of enacted judgment. Both cases are ideal types. The thinkers who discussed tyrannicide in the fourteenth century, doubting whether the pure tyrant ever existed, spoke more qualifiedly about the problem of "tyrannical rule," i.e., a political regime which *tends towards* the horizon of tyranny. In the same way we may doubt whether a purely amoral solidarity can exist for any sustained period of time. But ideal types may usefully display tendencies that emerge at critical moments when political order begins to disintegrate. The horizon is remote, but not unreachable. As the recent histories of Rwanda, Somalia, and Bosnia have demonstrated, from time to time it draws frighteningly close.[22]

---

21. The Reformed theologians of the sixteenth century and after disagreed on whether only some historically particular constitutional arrangements provided for the possibility of removing a supreme magistrate (thus Calvin and Grotius) or whether such a structure was implicitly present in all states (Beza and Althusius). But all agreed that the structure of any state was governed by natural and divine law, which provided a necessary and universal limitation ("constitutional," as we would call it) on the power of magistrates to command obedience.

22. And, to go further back in recent history, Uganda, where the murder of Archbishop Janani Luwum on February 17, 1977 (an event commemorated in the Church of England as a martyrdom), focussed the question of tyrannicide in its simplest form. There is no reason to doubt that the Archbishop was complicit in a failed attempt to de-

On the opposite horizon we may locate the situation where a breach of tradition causes political authority to disappear irrespective of success in enacting right. Here medieval thinkers spoke of the *usurper*, who seized power in defiance of existing constitutional law and custom. Usurping regimes they thought void of authority, but added one significant qualification: if in its day-to-day dealings the community tacitly accepts the usurper's rule, it confers by tacit consent the legitimacy that he lacks by law. It does not matter that the community did not want him; it is enough that it came to terms with him, wove the intrusive thread into the fabric of its tradition. By this means medieval thinkers avoided the nightmarish conclusion that no regime has more legitimacy than lay in its original entitlement – a conclusion that would perpetually set loose past wrongs to destroy present right.

In this they understood correctly that tradition is a function of what the community as a whole is doing. Tradition inherited passes without pause into tradition developed; continuity, like a stream, flows down the most convenient bed. There is no core of tradition which in every case *must* be carried on; in a crisis a community will preserve *what* it can, *how* it can. Recognizing the right of tradition, therefore, is an amoral business, depending on *post hoc* judgments about how things have actually gone. This truth returns to haunt every attempt to regulate the process of political constitution by law. Even in untroubled times what constitutes the authorizing tradition is open to gradual renegotiation; at a moment of breach the negotiation intensifies and widens its scope.

This observation sheds light upon another case familiar from recent history, that of the regime deserted by its tradition overnight, deprived of its authority by a massive and sudden relocation of the community's identity. The Soviet government was no usurper in 1991 when it was brushed aside by its constituent republics, and until very shortly before it had not even been weak. Neither was the Yugoslav government

---

pose the arbitrary and bloodthirsty leader who had demolished the rule of law in his country. Yet his death was a murder, not an execution, since the power that ordered it had lost the last shred of political authority and the intentions of the Archbishop must have been to stop the war of one against all by the only means available. If in doing this he maintained a profession of belief in Idi Amin's legitimacy, he was doing no more than was suggested in John of Salisbury's coolly ironic statement, "Him whom it is permitted to flatter, it is permitted to slay" (*Policraticus* 3.15, trans. Cary J. Nederman; *IG*, p. 281).

an imposition when Slovenians and Croatians suddenly ceased to think of it as their own government. These renegotiations were carried on apart from, and in disregard of, the existing political structures, which suffered fatal damage from them. In such a situation it is tempting to see the right of tradition as lying with the discarded regimes. Yet we will understand the phenomenon better if we see that the right of tradition itself was what lay in dispute. The tradition of a community is not a homogeneous whole but the confluence of a multitude of streams, and when streams submerged since 1918 burst to the surface, they washed away the more formal but weaker representations of identity, which the regimes — successfully, according to their lights — had upheld.

9

Representation

When we recognize a political authority summoning us to act together in defense of the common good, we recognize ourselves. We conceive ourselves as a "people," a community constituted by participation in the common good. On the relation between the "people" and the authority that summons it, hangs the delicate question of political representation.

The term "people," echoing the classical Latin *populus*, the Greek *laos* and the Hebrew *'am*, is unavoidable, despite the irrelevant associations of its corresponding adjective, "popular."[1] Attempts to find alternative expressions for this moral society constantly lead astray. On the ambiguities of the term "nation" we shall have more to say; it is tied to the historical phenomenon of the "nation-state" of early-modern times, being unsuitable for use either of the ancient *polis* or of an ancient empire, and it is hardly appropriate either to culturally heterogeneous peoples formed by immigration, e.g., the U.S.A. and Canada, or to peoples formed of parts of larger quasi-national groups, e.g., Austria and Bangladesh. To invoke the term "state" plunges us prematurely into the political organization that serves the moral society; but the moral society has to be conceived in its own right first. "Political society," preferred by Maritain, also sounds too structural a note, and is cut

---

1. In this terminological preference I coincide with John Rawls, *The Law of Peoples* (Cambridge, MA: Harvard University Press, 1999), pp. 23-30, though differences in our conceptions emerge below.

off by self-conscious voluntarism from natural affinities. The term "perfect society," favored by the Aristotelian scholastics, is founded on the idea of material self-sufficiency; and though a measure of self-sufficiency may be supposed in a "people," there is no such thing as total self-sufficiency; moreover, a people is defined by its external relations to other peoples, not only by its internal relations to itself.

To see ourselves as a people is to grasp imaginatively a common good that unifies our overlapping and interlocking practical communications, and so to see ourselves as a single agency, the largest collective agency that we can practically conceive. A people is a complex of social constituents: of local societies, determined by the common inhabitation of a place; of institutions, such as universities, banks, and industries; of communities of specialist function, such as laborers, artists, teachers, financiers; of families; and of communities of enthusiasm such as sports clubs and musical organizations. To have identity as a people is to be able to conceive the whole that embraces these various constituents *practically*, as a coordinated agency. When it is no longer possible to discern the constituent elements within the whole, each with its stock of tradition, its reserve of memory, and its communal habits of practice, then the whole dissolves before our eyes. It also dissolves when it is no longer possible to think of these elements as acting, in some sense, together and for one another.

What is it that gives unity to these various focal points of social tradition? They are likely to have certain things in common: the use of a language, the observance of a religion, beliefs that are accepted as premises for discussion among strangers, a mythology, a literature, spheres of administration, law, and economic interaction. All peoples have some such cultural features that unify them internally, though there are great differences in what carries most weight: sometimes it is a common language, sometimes a religious tradition, sometimes a trading pattern. Yet a people is more than an ensemble of its cultural features. These are simply the precondition, the channels worn by habits of communication that have brought the people to birth. To be a people is to put these culturally unifying features to the service of collaborative action, and that is what makes the difference between a group of homogeneous tribes and a viable political entity.

In framing the possibilities of common action, one feature has come to assume a special significance: a defined territory. The more complex the content of the tradition, the more varied culturally and racially it has grown, the more depends on this formal mode of demarcation. There was a "king of the French" before France had defined borders; but today we depend on the borders to know who the French are. Territory gives objective form to the infinitely varied cultural elements that comprise the people's communications. This point is illustrated by the conquest-traditions of Israel. It was not through the promised land that Israel became a people; it was a people already, by descent from the patriarchs, by the common experience of Egyptian bondage and miraculous delivery, by the shared nomadic existence in the desert, and supremely by the law. Territorial existence was an enhancement of Israel's identity, one which the prophets never forgot could be reversed if it were abused. It offered opportunities for growth and maturity, for establishing a civilization with internal disciplines of cultural transmission and ordered relations to surrounding peoples. Territorial boundaries mark the division between the domestic and the foreign. But the effect of the division is not merely to set a limit. It is to form a horizon which will stimulate neighborly relations between the people and other peoples. It defines a "You" in relation to which the people acts as a corporate "I."

To see ourselves as a people is a work of moral imagination. Not arbitrary imagination: it is an insight into reality, the reality of what we are given to be and do together. Nor does it imply "creativity" — the less the better, one might say! When those who wanted to unify the kingdoms of Kent, Wessex, Mercia, and Northumbria into one kingdom urged their claims and fought their battles, it showed creativity of a kind, since the English people was not yet a reality; yet these were merely ambitious warlords, and we need not credit them with any special moral insight. Only when former Mercians, Wessexmen, and, later, Normans called themselves English without thinking, could such a thing as the English people be spoken of untendentiously. Moral imagination has no business with the unheard-of or the merely possible; its concern is with the familiar and the actual, and its task is to comprehend a multitude of familiar communications in relation to each other, as an identity.

"Identity" refers to a sphere of common action open to us. The people is the largest corporate agent capable of evoking consistent and all-inclusive cooperative action. Treaties provide for areas of cooperation between peoples, but outside the scope of the treaty each people acts and answers for itself. The European states have expanded the scope of their cooperative endeavors far beyond the range of occasional treaty-based collaboration; yet when a disease strikes the cattle, each state acts by itself and for itself. By contrast the community of action achieved by a single people may be described as "universal," meaning that it embraces every area of the common life within its scope. Yet it does not comprise the real universe, but only a provisional one. There is a wider horizon, "universal" in a fuller sense. Human fellowship reaches more widely than even the largest corporate agent. The common action of a people is set against the background of other human communities with whom common existence, though not common action, is possible. Peace has a broader scope than coordinated activity; it involves respect and letting-be. If the people is the largest common "I," the agent to which we commit our energies for cooperative action on a global scale, there is always a "You" for this "I" to confront, and a goal of peaceful fellowship to be sought, the horizon of a "We." So the people's common good of practical cooperation is directed outward towards a truly universal common good of reciprocal acting and being acted upon. Those who plan to overcome our international quarrels by devising a form of world-government fail to understand the distinction between the people as acting subject and the world of reciprocating others. A world-government would have to be predicated on a world-people, but a world-people could come into existence only, one might say, when the Martians arrived — a "You" for a world-people to be an "I" to. With no Martians there can be no external communications, no foreign relations; and without these the moral imagination will not furnish it with identity as a people. If a world-people has no identity, a world-government is an idle imagination, a surplus entity.

In saying that the people is the *largest* communal agency conceivable, we show why it cannot be included in a list of typical social organizations, as "federal" theories often suggest. One may reach cities by federating households, provinces by federating cities, nations by federating provinces; but the *people* does not have a place on this scale between a smaller and a larger unit. It is the "universal association," as Althusius called it, the last point on any possible list. So a people may be any size of social unit, provided that no larger unit is practical. How large is largest changes with historical and circumstantial possibilities. The city, the nation, and the continental bloc may each, as circumstances dictate, encompass a people, as each becomes the largest practical unit of agency. Kent, Wessex, Mercia, and Northumbria could each constitute a people for a while; but when operations on the English scale had become natural to their citizens, England was the people they constituted, and then, when communications with Wales and Scotland became so necessary and natural that they could not be excluded from any thought of corporate agency, there was Great Britain. And Europe may possibly follow, but only when European citizens naturally construe their relations with each other in that way. When the Italian who moves in next door is not a foreigner, but merely from out of town; when it requires no comment or explanation that the chief of police for Northern Ireland is hired from Denmark, or a Spaniard heads an elementary school for the children of Prague, and everyone automatically speaks English, then a European people is at hand. Of course, only misplaced moralism makes such a development out as somehow virtuous — as though it were more charitable to travel further! — and only ill-informed dogmatism supposes that history always underwrites the development of larger units. The tide did, indeed, flow that way for the greater part of the second millennium A.D. as a result of improved communications; but in the last century it turned, and the general trend for the past hundred years has been towards separation, not unification. Italy and Germany were the late flowers of early-modern agglomeration; nationalism since then has scattered the map with new and smaller peoples like Slovakia and Macedonia.

We pause over the limits implied by the word "practical." There may be tempting designs of the political imagination which fail to envisage daily communications practically. We are free to think of an independent Scotland, a United States of Europe, or a passport to Pimlico. But to think our existing patterns of communications into the shape of such a thing is quite another matter. The inhabitants of the ancient Greek city-states, with the example of a vast empire before their eyes, could easily imagine themselves its subjects. But they could not conceive practically how the communications to which they were accustomed, and which they thought fitting, could ever be accommodated in such an agglomerate. They could not imagine *its* undertakings and *their* undertakings woven into a single fabric of common responsibility.

Such an empire seemed to them merely imposed. Its inhabitants, as they saw it, were not "free." The danger of dreaming up abstract schemes of political union on paper — a danger never far from the European Union — is that they do not accord with the way the member-peoples actually conceive their practical engagements.

What is practical about a people is its defense of the communications that make it up. The largest practical unit within which communications can be sustained is the one that can gather the appropriate resources for defending them. Political thinkers influenced by Aristotle liked to refer to the "perfect society," conceiving this as a society independent of its neighbors. Although in a literal sense no such society could exist, since mutual dependence is as much the rule for political entities as for individuals, the term can be understood sympathetically to mean a society capable of its own defense. But as the common good is many-faceted, so is its defense. A large military empire may be capable of defending its borders but incapable of defending anything else; the diversity of its elements may make it unable to sustain the mutual sympathy and interest essential to more subtle forms of defense, such as good lawmaking. A society is "perfect" when it is not too small to rally against a threat, not too diverse to be interested in doing so.

The people is imaginatively envisaged when and as its common good is in need of defense. The idea of the people and the idea of the authority that summons it to defend its common good arise together. The summons evokes the idea that the ensemble of communications is in fact a people. Yet here it is easy to leap too far too fast. The idea of the people is not the same as that of a juridical or law-based entity with a political order. Political authority does not "make" a people; it "finds" it. The governing state-structure serves the defense of something other than itself. The point of the state is not to defend the state but the people. The people, the subject of the common good, must be imagined apart from its political and juridical arrangements if either people or state is to be imagined properly at all. Otherwise the juridical unity of the state is simply imposition, not protection.

Here we touch upon the chief point at issue in the theories of constitution that occupied the minds of sixteenth- and seventeenth-century thinkers, culminating in the absolutist conclusion of Hobbes: "it is the unity of the representer, not the unity of the represented, that maketh the person one. . . . And unity cannot otherwise be conceived in multitude."[2] Without a full-blown government, that is, the people is precisely nothing. There is no community prior to the uniting of many under one sovereign, no social order to mediate between the unity imposed by government and the fragmented disorder of a multiplicity of wills. This gave a radical turn to opinions already entertained by such a respectable constitutionalist as Suárez: "Unity arises in large measure . . . from subjection to a single rule"; and "if there were not a government, this body could not be directed to one end and to the common good."[3] Suárez, of course, would not have wished to contradict the more traditional view, expressed by the anonymous Huguenot "Stephanus Junius Brutus," that "the people may subsist of themselves and are prior to the king."[4] Yet the people's subsistence, Suárez thought, was already implicitly political, "as by a special act of will or agreement it comes together to form a single political community, bound by a single tie of association for mutual assistance in the pursuit of one political end."[5] Hobbes understandably saw nothing to recommend this hypothesis of a political order prior to political order, and so went all the way to state-totalitarianism.

If state-totalitarianism prioritizes government over society, the constitutionalist postulate of a political order prior to political order yields the "nation-state," an idea perfectly expressed by its hyphen: first we have the "nation," a self-evident political totality, and then the "state," which is the nation in its organized form. Our political obligation then consists in attaching the second to the first.[6] Given the nation, we must fashion a state to its dimensions and demands. Any political failure is traceable to a failure of constitution. Where the contractarian approach failed to grasp the fact of popular unity prior

2. *Leviathan* 1.16.13. Later in the seventeenth century a similar thesis is maintained by Bossuet, *Politics Drawn from Holy Scripture*, 1.3.3, trans. P. Riley (Cambridge: Cambridge University Press, 1990), p. 15: "It is by the sole authority of government that union is established among men. . . . Otherwise there is no union; the people become wanderers, like a flock dispersed."

3. *De Lege et Deo Legislatore* 3.2; *IG*, p. 732.

4. *Vindiciae, contra Tyrannos* 82; *IG*, p. 719.

5. *Vindiciae, contra Tyrannos* 82; *IG*, p. 719.

6. For a fuller exposition of this problem see Joan Lockwood O'Donovan, "Nation, State, and Civil Society," in Oliver O'Donovan and Joan Lockwood O'Donovan, *Bonds of Imperfection* (Grand Rapids: Eerdmans, 2004), pp. 276-95.

to political constitution, the constitutionalist approach failed to see that this popular unity was a moral unity, comprised by a common good rather than by a political structure.

Misconceived in this way, society is impregnated with an ideological self-consciousness from the beginning. In a contemporary form this is done when we think of society as a network of quasi-legal rights. When John Rawls, for example, distinguishes "liberal peoples" (fully democratic) from "decent peoples," the qualification "decent" is not meant in a moral sense — decent *to each other* — but denotes an elementary political structure: "whose basic institutions meet certain specified conditions of political right."[7] Instead of imagining our membership of one another in terms of what we communicate in — our neighborhoods, our businesses, our wisdom, our songs, and stories, we are taught to think of ourselves as united wholly by a political vocation, which, precisely because it is not rooted in ordinary life, requires constant reinforcement by indoctrination. This overwhelms the simple and honest work of government, that of judging between a man and his neighbor, with a constant need to see the political vocation realized; political functions bear too heavy a burden of identity-conferral.

But mankind is communal by virtue of God's creation, not by political invention. Political order discovers and defends the social order; it does not construct it. At the heart of the false turn of the early-modern period away from pre-political society there lie two mistakes, one methodological, the other moral. Methodologically it was wrong to depend upon the narrative myth of constitution to perform the task of political analysis. Rightly judging that pre-political society could have no self-standing existence in the world, outside the Garden of Eden at least, they wrote it out of their "history" of the foundation of states, forgetting that that was not history that they were concerned with, but political analysis, and that pre-political society was indispensable for focussing the political, even if it never occurred. The moral mistake was a false suspicion of the ordinary, a doubt of human nature as known in the simple communication of food, wisdom, and affection. It could not

---

7. *The Law of Peoples*, pp. 3f. "People" so clearly implies for Rawls this apparatus of political order, that he judges the term unusable without it; collectives lacking even this elementary constitutional "decency" must be referred to by another noun, as "outlaw states" or "burdened societies."

see that a common good could be composed of such humble engagements, and thought the only worthwhile mode of human cooperation lay in jurisdiction. It failed to hear the word of Jesus, "Judge not!"

* * *

In awakening our sense of ourselves as a people, political authority simultaneously awakens us to itself. We become aware of an authority that commands us, not abstractly but in a concrete form, as "our" government. Political awareness always has this double object, people and government, two corresponding subjects that cannot be collapsed into one. Politics arises only in the vis-à-vis of government to people and people to government. But they are not equal and opposite subjects: a government exists to preserve and secure its people, not vice versa, and the condition for its doing so is that it is "ours," i.e., that it "represents" the people. Through its agency the people assumes a concrete judicial form. The representative bears the people's image, makes the people visible and tangible, to itself and to others. Yet the representative does not bring the people into existence, but simply makes it appear.

The notion of representation in the Western political tradition is grounded on the relation of redeemed humanity to Christ, the representative of all humanity in his death and glorification. "One has died for all, therefore all have died."[8] "In Christ" the world is judged, "in Christ" redeemed; that much-discussed prepositional phrase sums up the belief in moral identity. But the identity of mankind with Christ is not merely posited as a unique, cosmic event. It is described by two Christological titles, which related him to the social and political structures of Israel: he was priest, and he was king, both of them representative roles. The priest stood before the altar of YHWH bearing the names of the tribes of Israel on his shoulders, and by his acts of confession, prayer, and sacrifice involved the whole nation in the identity conferred on it by God. The king marched at the head of Israel's armies, and upheld Israel's identity in its struggles with neighbors and enemies; furthermore, he embodied and safeguarded Israel's identity by the careful study of Israel's laws, a matter of some importance to the Deuteronomic reform-

---

8. 2 Cor. 5:14. Cf. also St. Paul's extended comparisons of Christ and Adam at 1 Cor. 15:22 and Rom. 5:12-19.

ers.[9] These models, constantly discussed in the Reformation period, are potently influential on the early-modern sources of our conception of political representation. In one direction they were deployed as paradigms for political constitution in general; in another, they were regarded as irreplaceably fulfilled in the person of Christ and unavailable for direct imitation or replication. By this dialectic of affirmation and negation an analogical structure of representation was conceived: the representative solidarity of a people in its ruler reflects, while it cannot eclipse, the universal solidarity of mankind in its head.

King and priest both represented Israel; but neither of them was appointed *by* Israel or was answerable *to* Israel. They were chosen from Israel, and given to Israel to represent them, it was said, by God.[10] To Thomas Hobbes we owe the decisive assertion that political representation does not subordinate the representative to the people's will. The relation of owning and serving which binds political society to its government is different from that in which a delegated agent represents a principal. Hobbes used the word "personation" for this special form of representation underlying political authority. The weakness of monarchism in his day, Hobbes thought, was that it failed to understand that the "sovereign" was in fact "the sovereign representative," and so allowed the idea of representation to be appropriated exclusively by Parliament.[11] The representative acts for the people, and in his action the people acts, which "is more than consent or concord; it is a real unity of them all, in one and the same person." Despite this major borrowing from the theopolitical tradition, Hobbes insists on the popular will, rather than the appointment of God, as the original source of representative authority. The multitude, in a famous passage, "confer all their power and strength upon one man . . . that may reduce all their wills . . . into one will . . . which is as much as to say, to bear their person; and every one to own, and acknowledge himself to be author of whatsoever he that so beareth their person shall act."[12] So the high

---

9. See, e.g., Deut. 17:18f.

10. A point made explicitly about the high priest by the author to the Hebrews (5:1-4). Forms of *acclamation* were, of course, in use with respect to the king — a point out of which Huguenot and other constitutionalist thinkers of the sixteenth century squeezed the maximum possible yield.

11. *Leviathan* 19.

12. *Leviathan* 17.13.

claims for the binding force of political obligation are taken back to "every subject": "Every subject is author of the actions of his sovereign."[13] Yet since the popular will was an ideal will, not bound to any particular act of choice in history but always presupposed and irrevocably given in the existing fact of the political community, Hobbes could return a distant echo to the theological conviction that representation was given de facto. This distinction of ideal and actual will, perpetuated by Rousseau, was fatefully abandoned by Locke. The false turn lies in the thought that representation is founded in the *will*. It is founded in the *imagination*. That the representative may act for us, and we in him, it is necessary that we see ourselves in him. Representation is a case of symbolization; the representative "stands for" our consciousness of our common association.

Political representation is a special case of a wider phenomenon. Many kinds of practical cooperation which have no political authority depend on the emergence of a representative to provide them with what we imprecisely describe as "leadership." Representatives afford us a sense of ourselves in action, an "identity" that is not the whole of what we know about ourselves, but locates certain specific endeavors as part of a larger corporate undertaking. Every activity generates its representatives, who are authorized to speak and act for everyone else. Identifying ourselves through our representatives, we construct a picture of the world in which our collective endeavors are significant. Community yearns to make its mark upon the world. The picture may be true or false, realistic or delusory; it may disclose real occasions of cooperation with our neighbor, or it may hide them behind an illusion of practical involvement. The successful and the prominent will always gather a following of hangers-on, who need the sense of being part of something to which in fact they cannot contribute. "Therefore the people turn to them, and find no fault in them" (Ps. 73:10). Film-stars, pop-stars, and, more recently, football heroes function as surrogate representatives for the masses of our identity-starved public realm. True or false, the picture we construct is important to us; and when it is challenged, we respond with defensive pugnacity. There is no reason for surprise that the ecstasies of a crowd of sporting fans are so often violent. The self-esteem of any social body has a demon inhabiting it,

13. *Leviathan* 18.5.

which may always break out when there are no structures of responsibility to restrain it.

Popular identity, however, serves also as a structure of responsibility. It directs the energies of solidarity to serve the constructive political tasks of judgment, and in so doing subjects them to constant testing against reality. Yet it may itself become the problem rather than the solution. The demon is never fiercer than when it inhabits the largest practicable agency of common action. The romantic primitivism of the national idea can breed a popular identity obsessed with the vision of itself as an ideal and incapable of interesting itself in the complex communications which actually comprise the social content of its experience. The terrible fate to which nationalism condemned many communities was to be ruled by visionary-terrorists, the violence to which they were addicted reflecting the breach that had opened up between the ideal people of their imaginations and the reality.[14]

The representative commands the authority of the community's "tradition" — not, as we have said, the authority of its *past* but the authority of its *present*, the continuity of the acting community with its own history. To command the authority of tradition is to be the link between what the community has come to be and what it is to undertake, the cord which attaches new actions to existing identity. The question, Who bears the authority of tradition? is equivalent to the question, Who represents the community? There can be no political authority without an effective claim to the authority of tradition, because there can be no political authority which does not represent a given community in its actions. An unrepresentative power might do all kinds of good, but it would do it from the outside; it would not be good done *by* that community.

To illustrate this we may point to the long and still ongoing struggle to establish a "power-sharing government" (so-called) in the province of

14. Seán South, a young IRA terrorist killed in a cross-border escapade in January 1957, was remembered for the telling phrase with which he would dismiss the claims of the Irish government: "Ní ionnann Éire dúinn" — "We have a different Ireland!" Mainchín Seoighe, *Maraíodh Seán Sabhat Aréir* (Baile Átha Cliath: Sáirséal agus Dill, 1964), p. 10, in a commemorative poem by Críostóir Ó Floinn. Another insight into the mind of the romantic terrorist is given in the author's observation (p. 122) that the dead influenced him more than the living: "Ba mhó a d'oigbrigh na mairbh ar Sheán ná na beo."

Northern Ireland, an arrangement which, if "tradition" were no more than what was done in the past, would have to be judged very untraditional. What politicians from Britain, Ireland, and Northern Ireland have labored for so patiently and courageously is a *more representative* government. But a more representative government is a government that will be more *effectively tradition-bearing*. That is to say, both the constituent communities in that society must be able to see themselves and their histories reflected in it; it will be capable of carrying into a common enactment of right the parallel and antithetical historical identities in which each community has been formed. Only by achieving this extraordinarily delicate balance could a government in Northern Ireland have political authority over its people — a warning against every attempt to resolve the problems of that province by imposing a "program" of liberal rights conceived and developed in some other corner of the world as a patent medicine suitable for curing all maladies.

We speak of this "seeing" of ourselves in the representative as "recognition." To "recognize" something is not simply to know it, but to know it in relation to oneself. We may recognize an element of past experience, like a place we have been before; or we may recognize a vocation for the future, as when one recognizes a duty or a life-partner. The second kind of recognition is involved in political authority: through this particular actor we recognize ourselves as summoned to a collective action. It is an affective as well as a cognitive movement. Political recognition is like the recognition we accord to a face or form, the recognition of *Gestalt*, grasped at once in a moment of acknowledgment and welcome. Underlying many ancient political conceptions, there is a visual aesthetic. The language of light, radiance, and display permeates classical political symbolism, in notions such as "splendor," "magnificence," "glory." These elicit something akin to erotic fascination. Eros is that form of love which responds to visual beauty; through it we respond to the sight of ourselves reflected in another, the familiar within the strange. Ancient societies reckoned, one might say, to fall in love with their ruler's image. The thought that the king marries his kingdom is found in folk narrative of every provenance, and is taken up in the eschatological visions of the Apocalypse. In Scripture the story of David and Abigail (1 Sam. 25:2-42) is a paradigm case. Abigail, the beautiful wife of the quarrelsome and violent landowner Nabal, the "fool" who is incapable of recognizing or supporting the political authority of David as the Lord's anointed, propitiates David's anger with her husband and teaches him the restraint that is necessary for a true king. In marrying her after her husband's death, David marries his own kingly vocation to rule Judah mercifully; and she marries her own political destiny, which is the sovereignty of the Davidides.[15]

The coronation of a monarch used to be such a moment of recognition. In modern democracies the general election, not so overtly ceremonious but every bit as instinctual, takes its place, sealing the bond of identification between people and rulers. These two forms of ceremonial recognition differ in one important respect: where the coronation of a monarch suppressed all sign of political rivalry to present a tableau of unanimity, the election actively exploits the affective power of contest and victory, like those primitive kingships attested in myth in which the throne was won by slaying the incumbent in single combat. The "election behavior" of politicians, party organizations, media, and ordinary voters is an important trace of this deeper political imagination buried beneath formal theories of popular sovereignty. The overflowing of collective feeling in hyperbolic rhetoric, the drowning-out of measured reflection, the ritual enactment of conflict between unreal enemies, the crude attempt of contenders to make symbolic contact with powerful sectors of society, all serve to affirm a common political identity binding the people to its government. The reflective critic naturally feels disturbed by it, as one might feel disturbed by being forced to take part in a tribal war dance. The wise, however, will not mouth the time-worn objections to "the low level of debate." An election is not the time for debate; if debate has not taken place already, it never will. Debates are about issues, elections about people. Which is not to say that serious decisions cannot be taken in elections, or that electorates are incapable of deciding rationally — those gloomy and anxious doubts which continue to surface in our higher democratic cultures — but simply that these decisions, however serious and rational they may be, still require the orgiastic ceremonial of a formal investiture. The media must strike up their drumbeat, the politicians must dance their steps, and we must all let out the whoops and cries that the occasion demands of us.

---

15. A grimmer aspect to the erotic character of political bonding is given in the Succession Narrative, where Absalom's beauty is the basis on which he can alienate political authority from his father David (1 Sam. 14:25; 15:6).

The affective dimension is entirely absent from official theories of representation in the modern West. The understanding of ceremonial recognition was lost to Western political philosophy at the point where God was lost to it; for it is essentially an acknowledgment of providence. The representative is recognized because he is there; God "raises up" leaders of the peoples. That God does so with patient regularity is no reason to suppress our wonder at it, let alone imagine that we ourselves arranged for it to happen. The first sign that this was being forgotten occurred, paradoxically, in a development which seemed to take it seriously, the early seventeenth-century reworking of the older theory of the divine right of kings. This sought to restrict providence to underwriting the legal claims of a given dynasty. Instead of the mysterious political *happening* which attests God's action in the world, it argued for a simple right of possession, inherited and bequeathable, the irrevocable gift of a providence which had made its dispositions and had nothing further to say.[16] This theory was at once a reaction to, and a cause of reaction in, the momentous train of thought which has come to be called "contractarianism." This, too, dispensed with the moment of recognition, conceiving the representative relation as achieved by a once-for-all act of the human will. The point was to establish lawful and binding authority for all existing political orders, deriving them from a supposed contractual agreement in the past, just as the divine-right theory, of which it was a mirror-image, sought to derive them from a past act of God. Once conceived as a purely contractual status, representation lost touch with the moment of collective self-discovery, in which the sociality of the people, reflected in the person of its representative, dawns on its recognition. In its place was a legal form.

---

16. Thus "indefeasible hereditary right," as maintained in England by Jacobites after 1688. But an alternative version of divine-right doctrine was held by Whigs and Hanoverian Tories, much more in tune with a doctrine of providence. See J. C. D. Clark, *English Society 1660-1832* (Cambridge: Cambridge University Press, 2000), pp. 105-23.

IO

Legitimacy

G od raises up those who will bear authority. The mysterious alchemy of the affections elicits recognition, a people sees itself in
the face of an individual thrown forward for the occasion, and representation occurs. When the representative enacts judgment, God's gift
of political authority is bestowed upon the people. But what when
that representative status is contested? Must human judgment not resolve how political authority shall be constituted in that case? And if
so, to what canons of justice may it be answerable? With questions of
this kind thinkers of the early-modern period brought *constitution* to
the fore of political philosophy, a fateful development that has influenced us deeply ever since. For those of us who fall under that influence, it is important to recall that there are other more pressing questions of political right. The more dominant the constitutional
question, the more abstract the political discussion, and the further
removed from reality. "A Constitution can be built," scoffed Carlyle,
"Constitutions enough *à la Sieyès:* but the frightful difficulty is, that
of getting men to come and live in them!"[1] In normal circumstances
we do not often have to found new regimes; and on the rare occasions
that we do, the situation is one of such disorder that we have little
practical scope for our discretion. Yet the question has its own theoretical weight: how are the responsibilities of government to be attrib-

---

1. Thomas Carlyle, *The French Revolution* 6.1 (London: Dent [Everyman's Library],
1906), vol. 1, p. 173.

uted justly? In this and the two succeeding chapters we shall consider three types of answer.

This is not the same question as the classical question about the best form of regime, in which theologians have generally displayed comparatively little interest. That was never seriously raised in Christian thought before the Aristotelian revival of the thirteenth century, and when at that point it began to be discussed, commonly in expositions of Aristotle's *Politics* 3.8, it was characteristically answered evasively: the best regime was a *mixed* regime.[2] But since the question meant, "Where should the sovereign power be vested, in a single figure, in an elite, or in the mass of the population?" this was actually no answer at all. It merely conveyed that a developed political society should have certain features: an identifiable head of government to ensure coherence; a functional governing class that could ensute communication, and adequate organs for popular consultation to ensure sufficient representative legitimacy. But since any constitution could with good will be developed to satisfy those demands, what made a good regime was not, in the end, its form of representation at all, but the exercise of political virtues by government and governed, allowing it to develop into a humane ensemble of relations.

The first of the three answers is given with the concept of "legitimacy." Legitimacy is the subjection of representation to law. Not only the conduct of government but its constitution, too, is to be lawgoverned. Legitimate rulers are not merely representative rulers; they meet *legal* conditions for their representative status; they have an entitlement to exercise political authority. Here we confront at once the disturbing abstractness of the idea of constitution: how can we be sure that any legal conditions for representative status will coincide with the reality on the ground? Representation is something that happens, a relation that arises between community and representative. If it fails, no legal entitlement will produce it. Entitlements were never proof against deep-rooted alienation of society from government. Constitutional law is neither natural nor divine law, but merely customary hu-

2. See, e.g., Thomas Aquinas, *Summa Theologiae* II-1.105.1. For a selection of texts commenting on *Politica* 1279b16-19, together with useful commentary, see *Cambridge Translations of Medieval Philosophical Texts*, vol. 2: *Ethics and Political Philosophy*, ed. A. S. McGrade, J. Kilcullen, and M. Kempshall (Cambridge: Cambridge University Press, 2000).

man law. The legal right it confers can do no more than reinforce relations that are sound and defensible in substance. This point was recognized early in Christian political history in a striking case from medieval history. As chancellor of the passive West Frankish King Childeric, Pepin, father of Charlemagne, was authorized by Pope Zacharias in AD 751 to supplant the monarch, with the argument that "it was better for the man who had power to be called king."[3] Royal dignity, that is, must be associated with practical responsibilities, and whoever had those responsibilities should have the dignity — a striking repudiation in principle of what today is called "constitutional," but might more properly be called "ceremonial" monarchy.

For this reason, to ensure the conjunction of title and substantial representation, there emerged from among the variety of legitimating titles that early-modern theorists acknowledged — inheritance, sale, dowry, conquest, etc. — one entitlement that came to be regarded as uniquely authoritative, because it seemed to promise political substance as well as legal form. Rulers are legitimated on the basis of *popular election*. Narrowly understood, the word "democracy" refers to this electoral concept of legitimacy.

We must comment first of all on the dramatic transvaluation of terms that is implied in the use of the word, "democracy." In the classical doctrine of the types of regime, it referred to something quite unlike our modern democracy: the immediate government of the *polis* by an assembly of the *dêmos*, that is to say, by the laboring and trading citizen-classes that lacked accumulated wealth. The anxieties surrounding this form of government concerned its liability to develop a malfunction ("ochlocracy") where the initiative fell into the hands of "the crowd." The crowd is a collapse of internal political relations. In the well-ordered polity everyone who participates enters the consultative process with a perspective won from the course of life he or she leads, bringing sufferings, skills, projects, and experiences to bear on common questions. In every debate there are privileged perspectives: the butcher, the baker, the candlestick-maker look out among themselves for the stock-grazing, agricultural, and petrochemical interests of society. But mix them all up in a crowd with students, teachers, trad-

---

3. Quoted from Brian Tierney, ed., *The Crisis of Church and State 1050-1300* (Toronto: University of Toronto Press, 1988), p. 20.

ers, business managers, and a shrewd politician or two to get them chanting a slogan, and the whole is much less than the sum of its parts. Aggregated in a mass, their separate contributions lose their distinctive basis in experience, and are reduced to a fraction of a decibel. The power of the crowd is the power of none. The price paid for strengthening its voice is for everyone to lose his own. "Demagoguery" was the name given to the reductive technique of political management that appealed to the crowd rather than the people, suppressing the relational structures that made for common practical reasonableness.

The verdict of antique and early modern thought on this technique was unambiguous. Savanorola urged that it should be viewed as tyranny to ring the tocsin in Florence, so causing the citizens to rush pell-mell into the city square where decisions could be thrust upon them by the cleverest operator. Curiously, it was the French Revolution, the scene of the most savage instances of destructive crowd-politics, that prompted a measure of reevaluation. This displayed Christian roots and post-Christian suppositions. It was not a Condorcet or a Proudhon that persuaded Europe of the nineteenth century that the French Revolution was, despite everything, a step forward in civilization. It was a handful of conservative Protestants, appealing to the legacy of Pentecostal aspiration, a prophetic view of history as the disclosure of divine purpose, and a romantic admiration for passionate feeling. In the fury of the masses it seemed possible to find an ecstatic freedom that answered Christian hopes for the goal of history. "Philosophy, too," as Kant had said, "may have its chiliastic expectations."[4] In calling its electoral legitimation "democratic," late-modern politics reawakened to chiliastic longings. We do not understand the democratism of our own time unless we appreciate its ambivalent attitude to the crowd: hoping to exploit its aggregative power in legitimating a regime, it is at one moment on its guard against its anarchic possibilities, and at the next moment toys with them.

Yet modern democratism is not confined to an electoral device for legitimating government. When we discuss democracy today, we have in mind a conjunction of two elements. One is the electoral device for

---

4. "Idea for a Universal History with a Cosmopolitan Purpose," in Kant, *Political Writings,* ed. H. Reiss, trans. H. B. Nisbet (Cambridge: Cambridge University Press, 1970), p. 50.

legitimation; the other is a substantive account of what good government requires. This account has a number of elements, all to do with
responsiveness to the real and felt needs of society: an elected Parliament as a formal court of pleas; local representative organs with local
autonomy; the admission of candid and open speech on all matters relating to the common good; the obligation of government to natural
and divine law; the recognition of basic individual rights at law as a
limiting constraint upon inequalities of social order; the independence
of courts from executive interference; due forms of consultation and
deliberation in preparing legislation and due process for promulgating
it, and so on. It is a defensible use of terms, which I shall follow, to call
this ideal of government "liberal," and so to use the phrase "liberal democracy" for the conjunction of liberal virtues in government and electoral forms of legitimation. For the purpose of this discussion, which
is specifically to explore its concept of legitimacy, I shall not treat here
a third strand in the late-modern idea of democracy, that of non-
hierarchical social organization, from which has sprung the recent de-
based fashion of counting the capitalist market-system as a founding
element of democracy.

One could almost say that there is only one political question worth
asking about liberal democracy: how firmly are the two elements, political freedom and electoral legitimation, bound together? Is their conjunction a matter of necessity? Or is it merely the product of a peculiar
socio-ecological niche, perhaps too fragile or too specialized to trans-
plant?

It is a matter of historical record that liberal virtues in government
were admired and cultivated long before the idea of democratic legitimation was at all widely countenanced. The common view of those
who admired and advocated these virtues was "that democracy or popular government is usually the worst."[5] The liberal ideal was the distil-
lation of the high period of political theology, the twelfth to seventeenth centuries, which reflected on an eclectic mix of Old Testament
and Hellenistic teachings about rulers' virtues that had grown up during the first millennium. Charlemagne was familiar with a prototype of

---

5. This is the title of chapter 6 of Richard Baxter's *The Holy Commonwealth* (1646).
The significance of the context of this writing in the English Civil War should not be
missed, nor the fact that Baxter was a prominent supporter of the Parliament.

the ideal. Fénélon urged a developed form of it upon the heir to an absolute monarchy. These virtues were sometimes referred to as "political rule," a term derived from Aristotle's list of six forms of regime.[6] More normally they were commended simply as "just rule," that department of the virtue of justice which had to do with the ruler's tasks.

History, then, does not allow the strong thesis that democracy is a *necessary* condition for the cultivation of the liberal virtues. Neither does it allow the equally strong thesis that it is a *sufficient* condition. This is ruled out by the illiberal behavior of many democracies. An argument for the conjunction of the two elements must adopt an indirect and partly historical strategy: they have proved congenial in practice, and aspects of the one are seen to reinforce the other. Either the liberal virtues favor the development of democracy, or democracy favors the practice of the liberal virtues, or both. Such an argument will have a partly narrative character. And given the hold that democratic institutions have on late-modern civilization, the narrative will have a progressive shape. But this raises the question that confronts every such narrative claim: is progress just a happy chance of history, arising from the capacity to learn from experience with a net balance of retentiveness over forgetfulness, or does it reflect an unfolding historical teleology, a revelation of the human destiny that has its own irreversible momentum?

The earliest, and surely the greatest, theological narrative of modern Western democracy made the latter assertion unashamedly. It was that of Girolamo Savonarola, who, claiming direct prophetic inspiration to discern God's purpose in the invasion of Italy by Charles VIII of France in 1494, announced that there was to be a root and branch reformation of the church as it entered the fifth of the seven eras foretold in the Apocalypse, which the city of Florence was to lead. Since church and civil society were coextensive, a reformation of the church implied the renovation of civil society, in which the common good rather than private interest would become the dominant motivation of every member. This in turn demanded a form of government that secured the liberty and cooperative endeavor of all citizens; and only a "civil" or "political" government — a republic in which all the citizens held the supreme

---

6. See, e.g., from the fifteenth century, John Fortescue, *On the Nature of the Law of Nature* 1.16, reproduced in *IG*, p. 533.

magistracy together as a General Council — could meet that criterion. As a Dominican, Savonarola had formally to admit the Aristotelian doctrine, taught in the pseudo-Thomistic *De regimine principum,* that monarchy was the best of all political forms. But this doctrine was, he thought, irrelevant — irrelevant to Florence, in the first place, because of its peculiar endowment of genius and temperament, and irrelevant to the new age of which Florence was the prototype, since new times required new forms. Any form of government would be irrelevant that did not express and embody the city's vocation as a reformed church, where every citizen and every rank of society was to participate directly in the worship of the angelic hierarchies. So the form of government was wholly dictated by the ecclesiological moment: "Christ will found his church better than he has founded it hitherto!"[7]

The thought that is likely to cause us most difficulty here, that a new dispensational era was beginning with the dawn of the sixteenth century, was so far from troubling to some of Savonarola's Protestant admirers that it could seem quite simply self-evident. Protestants from Hergot to Hegel made free use of this constellation of ideas. The philosophy of history was an irresistibly prophetic enterprise, a point brought out by the "postmillennial" eschatologies popular in progressive America in the nineteenth century. By the mid-twentieth century such prophetic narratives had fallen out of favor. In the heyday of Popperian suspicion it seemed that the greatest danger to the "open society" was the theological readiness to write the history of the future in advance. In recent decades, however, teleological narratives of the progress and achievement of democracy have reappeared in a secularized form, a development illustrated by the title of Francis Fukuyama's book, *The End of History and the Last Man.*[8] This change of intellectual fashion has coincided with a more strident ideological tone on the part of the democratic West.[9]

7. *Prediche sopra Aggeo,* especially nos. 13-15, 21; *Trattato circa il Regimento e Governo della Città di Firenze* 1, a cura di L. Firpo (Rome: Belardetti, 1965); *Compendio di Rivelazioni,* a cura di A. Crucitti (Rome: Belardetti, 1974).

8. London: Hamish Hamilton, 1992.

9. This was not prompted solely by the collapse of communism in Eastern Europe. A heightening of the pitch of democratic claims, fuelled by the need to invest the nuclear confrontation with a suitably apocalyptic justification, was already in evidence in the 1980s. On this see my remarks in *Peace and Certainty* (Oxford: Oxford University Press; Grand Rapids: Eerdmans, 1989).

Twentieth-century apologies for democracy offer a range of narrative possibilities, from the most metaphysically adventurous to the most metaphysically reserved. As a simple exercise in representative typology, we may consider three examples, at decreasing levels of moral pitch and predictive confidence. They are illustrations only, representing a variety of possibilities depending, for instance, on which of the liberal virtues are most emphasized — equality, freedom, accountability of government, etc., etc.

(a) At the highest pitch a narrative of democracy may aim to demonstrate irreversible ideological progress. Liberal virtues and democratic practices are simply the earlier and later stages in the forward march of a single idea: democracy is latent in liberal ideals, liberal ideals are explicated in democracy. This type of narrative is attractive to a progressivist theology looking to find the history of redemption expressed within the history of civilization. The writings of Jacques Maritain in and after the Second World War offer an example: democracy is "a temporal manifestation of the inspiration of the Gospel," in its progressive realization of "truths of evangelical origin" about the dignity of the human person.[10] In their religious form these narratives emphasize evangelical freedom.[11] Non-religious versions turn on the leading *motif* of individual rights. The early-modern rights to life, liberty, and property pointed the way forward to a right to participate in political power; property-right was the bridgehead through which democratic representation was established.[12]

One difficulty of this approach is to match the high moral pretensions of this narrative with the prosaic realities of electoral democracy as we know it. It seems to aim at nothing less than moral regeneration, and this is something altogether grander than the humdrum practice of voting in elections. There is something slightly ridiculous about talk of the dignity of human personality which comes to rest in a slip of paper where we set a cross against the name of someone we do not know! The

10. *Christianity and Democracy* (London: Bles, 1945), pp. 25, 30.

11. Cf. John Howard Yoder, *For the Nations* (Grand Rapids: Eerdmans, 1997), p. 32: "As the early Christians met for worship, all of them were free to take the floor.... From this original Christian vision have come the stronger strands of what we call 'democracy.'"

12. Cf. Fukuyama, *End of History*, p. 43: "The right to participate in political power can be thought of as yet another liberal right — indeed the most important one — and it is for this reason that liberalism has been closely associated with democracy."

argument would seem to require at the very least that each individual should make his or her judgments on substantive issues heard in the deliberative councils that shape public policy. And so this type of narrative is liable to conclude with the admission that real democracy has yet to be achieved. "The tragedy of the modern democracies is that they have not yet succeeded in realizing democracy."[13] But that is to overshoot the mark. What was wanted was a demonstration of the aptness of the arrangements for legitimating government that *do* exist, not a plea for arrangements that never have existed and perhaps never could.

There are other objections to the approach, more political in character. Its notions both of representation and of the scope of government are open to suspicion. Representative government is seen as a means by which each individual's power of action is granted a universal scope. Every individual was implicitly a sovereign ruler, waiting only for a representative mechanism to exercise powers of rule that belonged originally to the human personality as such. In summoning the representative to rule, then, nothing is added that the pre-political, ungoverned community had not in principle envisaged on its own account. The ruler is a delegated agent to administer the inalienable powers of others. This shrunken notion of representation greatly inflates the scope of governmental powers. For nothing can be excluded from the scope of government action that could be included in the scope of human action. Government is not assigned the special task of defending against wrong. The drift of such a narrative, as of all narratives that derive political goals directly from private or public goals, is totalitarian.[14]

(b) A second type of narrative attempts to demonstrate a less decisive form of progress, not ideological but institutional. The democratic

13. Maritain, *Christianity and Democracy,* p. 17.

14. With Rousseau the contractarian tradition takes a new turn, in which the multitude never alienates its sovereignty; actual rulers are only officials, appointed by the sovereign people. This removes the need for a concept of representation of the many by the one; but representation as such remains central to the contractarian theory of political authority. The sovereign, i.e., "the state, the nation," is a "legal person," an "artificial and collective body." Each member of the community understands its will to be his own will, his will to live under the protection of an ordered community. He commits himself to the principle that whoever refuses to obey the general will shall be "forced to be free" (*The Social Contract* 2.4, 1.6, 7, trans. M. Cranston [Harmondsworth: Penguin, 1968], pp. 74, 61, 64).

form has evolved in order to embody the liberal ideal of good government; but in embodying it, it also secures it and makes it easier of realization. Within this category arise a plethora of "restraint and accountability" arguments for democracy, which find in popular election the best guarantee — not strong prediction, but reasonable expectation — that government will continue along the broadly liberal lines we have hitherto valued. Reinhold Niebuhr's famous apophthegm that "man's capacity for justice makes democracy possible; man's capacity for injustice makes democracy necessary" can be taken as typical.[15] Democratic forms entrench and secure a general relation of rulers to people which is characterized by justice.

But what *is* the just relation of rulers to people that such a device secures? It can only be that envisaged by the contractarian myth, which sees political authority as derived from a founding act of popular will. Otherwise we would not look to *democracy* to achieve justice, but to intra-governmental "checks and balances." The power of an electorate to dismiss and choose its rulers can only be a guarantee of good government, if good government is understood as that which rulers exercise under the authority of the popular will. But this is to force too restricted an interpretation on the liberal ideal. To be sure, there are features in the liberal ideal that may encourage this interpretation: that government should consult, for example, and respond to complaints. But there is a great deal besides, much of which is not at all easy to ensure by popular election: the responsibility of governments to obey law, both their own and God's; the responsibility to temper justice with mercy; the responsibility to protect individuals and minorities against majority dominance. To accommodate these broader liberal concerns, some contractarian theorists drew a sharp line between the actual and the ideal popular will; but precisely this distinction makes popular election less attractive, since it is *actual* popular will, with all its injustices, that finds expression through election.

The claims made for democracy by this second narrative, then, are metaphysically more modest, but still very uncompromising. The claim that electoral democracy is the key to just government has the disconcerting flavor of social engineering that characterizes every attempt to ensure morality by managing systems. That certain constitutional ar-

---

15. *The Children of Light and the Children of Darkness* (London: Nisbet, 1945), p. vi.

rangements may tend to encourage the development of certain virtues we may easily believe. That there is one constitutional arrangement that will tend to encourage more virtues than any others we may believe with some effort. But that this arrangement consistently and predictably ensures the virtues of justice in whatever government, is a very large claim indeed to swallow, and democratic electorates, habitually on guard against their governments, show little sign of swallowing it.

However that may be, and with whatever modesty or lack of it, these two narratives of democracy have held sway within Western civilization, except where Marxism prevailed, until the late twentieth century, and the evolution of democratic forms was understood as a kind of moral progress. They have provided grounds for the Western democratic powers to commend democracy as the answer to every question, and generally to disapprove of non-democratic regimes. In the late- and post-Marxist period, however, liberal democracy has begun to fall under new suspicion in its traditional heartlands — one symptom of that flurry of intellectual restlessness and suspicion variously called "post-liberal," "postmodern," or "modernity-critical." Late-liberal suspicion of large totalitarian narratives has turned back on itself, to question the potentially totalitarian claim of democracy, too. One object of suspicion is the extension of the democratic apologetic to include a central role for market-economics. Another is the expansionist demand to impose democratic forms on all political societies. War, famine, bad communication, and under-education can all undermine democracy, and these are common enough conditions. Do not the shirt-tails of historical master-narrative hang out in the assumption that these can somehow be managed out of existence? Finally, there are doubts about the idea of legitimacy itself and its claim to maintain substantive justice. Do democratic governments win their legitimacy only at the cost of deferring or evading the most unpopular tasks of justice, not least those presented by the environmental crisis?

(c) A third type of narrative has seemed to be required, more modest still, the outline of which has begun to appear. Renouncing the claim of democracy to foster liberal government directly, we find its value solely in the good order it brings to the representational forms themselves. Rather than *underpinning* justice, democracy is a *task of* justice on the narrow front of political representation. By providing a just settlement to thorny conflicts of representation, democracy adds a further layer to liberal government. To take an illustration from the idyllic past: suppose that for generations the Duke's eldest son has sat for the county in Parliament, and everyone has been happy; the Duke has maintained his family's position, the county has enjoyed noble patronage. But now the tradition is challenged, feelings are running high, and the outside world, with no first-hand knowledge of the Duke and his ways, has to decide whether this relation is oppressive or constructive. So let the Duke's son stand at the hustings, it says; then, if the county wants him, it can have him. Election serves as a court of final instance, a point of constitutional anchorage. While it does nothing to ensure the just conduct of elected power-holders, it ensures at least the justice of their means of acquiring power, and that is not nothing. On this basis, it would seem, we are free to promote democracy where it has not hitherto prevailed, or, where it has prevailed to a degree, to "remedy the democratic deficit."

But this brings us back to the doubts we raised at the beginning. Democratic forms regulate representation, but cannot produce it. Behind the legalities of the electoral mechanism there must be the social event of representation, the cohering of a more complex network of relations — institutions, sectors, traditions, and loyalties — to forge an identification between a people and its government. Election can only be the lynchpin holding the wheel of tradition in place. So we must ask not only about the procedural justice of regulative electoral rules, but about their attributive justice — whether they express the identity and concerns of the people and their enduring loyalties; whether, in other words, they successfully *represent*.[16] Representative relations have to work at the level of the imagination. Do electoral mechanisms assist them, or may they even impede them?

A characteristically unpopular and yet universally necessary institution of electoral democracy is the political party. Democratic suffrage has given birth to this typically "aristocratic" formation, the function of which is precisely to counterbalance the expression of the popular will by creating strong political élites.[17] They are supposed to assist rep-

16. This distinction is sometimes made by contrasting the adjectives "representative" and "representational."

17. The struggle over the necessity of parties was decisive for the failure of Savonarola's democracy. See G. C. Garfagnini, ed., *Savonarola e la Politica* (Firenze: Sismel, 1997).

resentation by functioning as a permeable membrane through which the alarms and concerns that might rend the body politic are assimilated into the system of government and made susceptible to judgment. Parties are organs of representation in their own right, even apart from elections; they facilitate consultation between government and people. Their control of elections, sometimes brutal, sometimes delicate and unobtrusive, is an indication that the electoral form on its own cannot be relied upon to deliver representation, but can only be serviceable when put at the disposal of substantially representative institutions. Yet substantial representation is not guaranteed by the parties either. It is achieved only as the real issues that trouble society come to government notice through effective structures of consultation. Of parties, as of other institutions, we can ask how effective they are at representing, how successfully they express the concerns and loyalties of the people at large. The membrane can become sclerotic. Like other aristocracies, parties may lose their representative status, and become absorbed with the narrow concerns of the élites themselves.

When a government that is "democratic" by every constitutional canon ceases, by dereliction of duty, to be recognized by its people, or when a people undergoes a revolutionary change of sentiment that sets it at odds with its government, there is a crisis of representation. We were told that when Mr. Henry Kissinger was detailed by the U.S. cabinet in 1974 to persuade President Nixon to resign, he urged upon him the problem of "legitimacy," by which he certainly did not mean to cast doubt on the President's *electoral* legitimation, but on his ability, in his disgrace, to prevent his representative status from evaporating. A different case, and in some ways more fascinating, is that of the regime that has yet to achieve representative status. The European Union has difficulty in winning popular recognition for its infant institutions; they are too remote both geographically and in terms of population-numbers; the task of representing so many peoples is too diverse; the tradition of common cooperation is too recent and lacking in history, to secure any measure of imaginative identification; so the citizens of its member-states do not think of its actions as their own actions. To this problem of "disconnection," as they call it, European leaders propose an answer: to "remedy the democratic deficit." "More" democracy (measured out by the 15cm medicine-spoon!) will solve the problem of insufficient representation. And that while citizens of member-states stay at home in their hundreds of millions every time a European election is held!

Electoral forms cannot remedy a deficit of substantial representation, but they can repress and erode traditional representative relations. To return to our illustration, suppose that the Duke's son braves opposition at the polls and is handsomely elected. Has everything in the county returned to the *status quo*? Far from it. The whole balance of relations between the Duke and the county has changed, for now his son serves as the electors' current choice, not the ducal family's traditional service to its community. The regulation of the old informal pattern has left it eviscerated. This illustration from the idyllic past carries a warning for the less idyllic present: the policy of building up direct elections for European institutions runs the risk of sapping authority from national governments while *still* failing to invest European institutions with sufficient authority to replace them, so creating a dangerous vacuum of political authority. The greatest strength of the European Community in its early phases was to confer a dignity on its member-states, especially the smaller ones that could cut a figure in the world for the first time, and so strengthen responsible authority within them. The wise founders of European statesmanship began by building onto strong existing buildings; their foolish successors think they can scavenge stones from them to throw up weaker ones.

At a politically less weighty level we may consider the perennial desire to improve democracy by refining electoral processes. The enterprise of what is called "proportional" representation has this to be said for it: it recognizes the problem that electoral forms as such may fail to secure representation. But it underestimates the problem in hoping to solve it formalistically by fine-tuning the voting-system to get a precise proportional match of votes cast for parties and the assignment of parliamentary seats. As though our liberties depended on having *parties* adequately represented! To get the right number of Liberal Democrats in the House of Commons is an idle pastime, but to get the right number of British Asians is a most important matter, and no amount of finessing the electoral rules will help us achieve it. All formal electoral rules have the potential to betray our trust. One-man-one-vote produced minority exclusion in the old Northern Ireland, while proportionalism in Israel has constantly given bellicose minorities the power to frustrate the popular will for peace. "So pregnant with weight," as de Tocqueville exclaimed, "are hollow forms!"[18]

Electoral forms, then, not only fail to guarantee a just, or liberal, government; they are no guarantee of material representation either. The defense of Western democracy must, it seems, be even more modest than the most modest defense current among apologists. Perhaps it may take some form such as this: Modes of representation cannot be chosen in a vacuum; they are dependent upon the conditions of society and on the forms of spontaneous representation that arise unbidden. In a society that has lost most of its traditional representative forms to the unstable and shifting relations built on individualism and technology, but which can count on economic wealth, good communications, and general literacy, there is no serious alternative to the ballot box. Attempts to revive lost forms of loyalty are liable to be *Ersatz* and morally hollow; we had better secure ourselves against the temptations they present by setting a high procedural threshold for movements of spontaneous popular identity, and this electoral democracy provides. The case for democracy is that it is specifically appropriate to Western society at this juncture. It is a moment in the Western tradition; it has its own ecological *niche*. This allows us no universal claims of the "best regime" kind, nor does it permit the imperialist view that the history of democracy is the history of progress. Yet within its own terms it allows us to be positive about democracy's strengths. The best regime is precisely that regime that plays to the virtues and skills of those who are governed by it; and this one serves us well in demanding and developing certain virtues of bureaucratic and public discourse that the Western tradition has instilled. It is our tradition; we are bred in it; we can, if we are sensible about it, make it work.

We should, however, be suspicious of demands for continual improvements to our democratic credentials, multiplying occasions of electoral legitimation and sweeping away whatever vestiges of informal representation may still operate. A defense of democracy should be

18. *The Ancien Régime* 2.3, trans. J. Bonner (London: Dent, 1988), p. 41. For good measure, let us recall a witticism that circulated in Britain during December 2000. Why, it was asked, did a famously liberal newspaper time its latest campaign against the British monarchy to coincide with a U.S. Presidential election? Answer: a palace mole. At what point, then, should we expect it to begin its next campaign for proportional representation? Answer: to coincide with the Israeli general election.

content to persuade those who live in the West that they are *sufficiently* well represented to allow them to attend to the substantial tasks of just government. One of the most important of those substantial tasks is consultation. Much advocacy of democracy confuses two quite different things: electing governments and consulting about policy. Election is an aggregative exercise, roping different points of view together to form a majority. Consultation is a discriminative exercise, which entails weighing up different points of view. For representative action to have moral depth, the representative needs a comprehensive sense of what the people at its best, i.e., at its most reflective and considerate, is concerned about.[19] The "on behalf of" and "in the name of," which are proper to representation, must not displace the "with" and the "for." The representative does and says on the people's behalf what it cannot do and say by itself; yet what the representative does and says must be recognizable as what the community does and says. The people must be able to acknowledge as their own the common good that their representatives summon them to defend.

As the electoral system expands, organs of consultation ossify and fall away. The more the political classes are set to the task of fighting elections, the less they will be free to attend to what they hear. The roar of the heavy machinery of legitimation drowns out the very possibility of listening to voices that reason, plead, celebrate, or lament in public. The price of legitimist purity is a high one, paid in practical and moral impotence. Some democracies resemble nothing so much as the giant panda, needing to eat so constantly that there is no distinction between recruiting energy and expending it. So the state becomes cut off from the realm of public communications, and, by ignoring it, denies its own proper responsibility to it. "Democracy" can be alleged as a justification of this divorce, consciously wrapping all consultation up into a single movement of popular legitimation. Common deliberation on the common good is banished from the political realm, and replaced with rules-of-procedure. It was the sight of this bleak nemesis that led that great Christian advocate of democracy, John Paul II, to

---

19. The question of whether electronic communications assist democracy turns, in the end, upon whether they help the politicians reflect discriminatingly on what is said to them, or merely encourage them to count the messages they receive on one side or the other like votes. For further reflections upon this question, see Gordon Graham, *The Internet: A Philosophical Enquiry* (London: Routledge, 1999), pp. 62-83.

conclude: "A democracy without values easily turns into an open or thinly-disguised totalitarianism."[20]

*   *   *

As we have noted, democracy has generated its own critical reaction in late-modernity. But there has been a longer tradition of critique, which, though with a low theoretical profile, has exercised a significant operative role in European practice. This critique is directed against the part assigned to procedural rules in the democratic concept of legitimacy. The insistence on democratic legitimation, it argues, depends on abstract or purely formal relations, at odds with the rooted contextuality of substantial political relations. "Recognition," with its complex balance of the cognitive and affective, is essential to true representation; by narrowing the relation down to the fine point of election to office, we screen out those very moral sympathies that cement the bond between a people and its government. But these are an aspect of the people's identity with itself.

The substantial proposal to which this critique leads is this: representation is not a *preliminary* to government, but the *substance* of government. Securing the relation between government and people is the aim of all political activity. As a response to the democratic emphasis on formal representation this is a bold move: not to reduce the stress on representation, but to totalize it, expanding representation to include all political relations, formal and informal. The formulation of Rousseau's famous question, "How can it be made legitimate?," in which government is assumed as a fact and its relation to the people treated as the *next* problem, is declared to be perverse.[21] It can arise only from a pathological perspective, as, for instance, when a tradition has been disrupted by revolution or usurpation.

To this bold move the name most commonly given is "conservatism." The term "conservative," of course, has other uses, one of which is to be the name of a virtue, another to be the name of a vice. The virtue is a sensibility for traditional practice in practical decision-making, the vice a reluctance to question it. They are neither of them political

---

20. *Centesimus Annus* 46.
21. *The Social Contract* 1.1, trans. M. Cranston, p. 49.

principles, but simply *ways of holding* principles, political or otherwise. As a political principle, on the other hand, "conservatism" means making the continuity of tradition foundational to the political task. The identity of a people becomes the ultimate justification for the political structures that express it. As a contemporary advocate puts it, "One belongs to a continuing and pre-existing social order, and . . . this fact is all-important in determining what one ought to do." The "will to live which constitutes conservatism" is a matter of the "intricate entanglement of individual and society"; the vitality of the one and the vitality of the other reinforce each other, and of this the state is the expression and not the means. It is itself an "end," as social life is an end. Self-identity is one and the same with allegiance.[22]

But to what do we owe this allegiance? Not to the universal society of the kingdom of God, of which conservative theory disdains all knowledge — but to one particular society among others. Conservatism characteristically repudiates universals. Its strongest point in criticism of Western liberalism is precisely that, without a true kingdom of heaven, the pretended universals are suppositious and abstract.[23] The justification for any society's structures is simply what they are, not that they share something with other societies, nor that they approximate to any kind of ideal.

There is another "intricate entanglement" to consider besides that of individual and society, which is that of social and political institutions. As the individual finds him- or herself in existing institutions and practices, the state comes to birth. The unity of state and civil society is organic; from which it follows that there are no limits on the interpenetration of government and society. The term "state," indeed, comes in conservative theory to sum up precisely that interpenetra-

---

22. Roger Scruton, *The Meaning of Conservatism* (London: Macmillan, 1980), pp. 21, 38. This book was remarkable for its thorough conservative critique of that economic neo-liberalism which was at that very moment coming to power in Britain under the label "conservative."

23. This renunciation of universal perspectives was famously articulated by Michael Oakeshott's contention that politics was susceptible only of practical rationality, not of deep theory. Those who have advanced the claims of a conservative "doctrine" are content to view that doctrine as something of a second-order construct; the conservative theorist, in Scruton's memorable analogy (p. 195), "resembles the functionalist anthropologist."

tion: it is government institutions conceived as an expression of social identity. "Wherever states exist or have existed, their sphere of operations has embraced the whole life and aspiration of a nation with all its material and moral purposes," wrote F. J. Stahl in 1858.[24] "Military might and rank, public welfare, public education, public honors, the moral structure of the family, the education of the next generation in morality and learning: among civilized peoples all these have lain permanently within the sphere of the state."

But in what, we ask, does the *justice* of such a state consist? Here we may usefully refer back to Hegel, the inspiration of most subsequent conservative theory, and to his modification of Montesquieu's famous triad of "powers" of government. The legislature enunciates the justice of the state in universal (i.e., generic) laws; the executive acts to subsume particular decisions under the laws; but the judiciary is replaced in Hegel's scheme by the monarch (constitutional, not absolute), who embodies the personality of the state. The executive holds the whip-hand, generating the substance of the state's activities; neither monarch nor legislature needs any measure of independence from it.[25] Its obligation to act justly derives from the principle that all decisions must be subsumed under universal laws. But as the earliest and best critic of Kant, Hegel knows that law cannot embody right merely by being universalized, but needs a determinate social content.[26] Where is this to come from, if not from the practical activities of the executive? So we run into a disquieting circularity: justice in executive decisions consists in conformity to law, but justice in law consists in accommodation to the exigencies of executive decisions.

Our disquiet is increased by Hegel's observations on how the executive is to be prevented from abusing its position to serve bourgeois class-interests: it is restrained by "the sovereign working on the middle class at the top, and corporation-rights working on it at the bot-

24. *Der christliche Staat* (Berlin: Oehmigke, 1858), p. 3.

25. *Philosophy of Right*, trans. T. M. Knox (Oxford: Oxford University Press, 1952), §301, pp. 195-97. Hegel argues that if the aim of government were simply to get the best laws in the most efficient way, there would be nothing to prevent the executive from assuming the legislators' work, for by virtue of its own activity it acquires most of the necessary knowledge. The distinct importance of Parliament is to ensure the consent of the various classes of society; like the monarch, it exists to legitimate.

26. *Philosophy of Right* §135, pp. 89-90.

tom."[27] That is to say: government has to satisfy the demand for a coherent and unified state-policy and the various claims made by associations of common interest among the trading and manufacturing
classes. In determining the practical decisions of the state, the executive is informed by contact with these special interest groups, each
representing an abstract right of property. But justice so conceived is
no more than "adjustment," the negotiation of competing property-
claims in a moderate compromise. Here we see the point of Hegel's
remark that legislative business is comprised under the two heads of
provision for well-being and the exaction of services, i.e., benefits and
taxation. We need not elaborate on the difficulties which this creates
for claims that are not economic interests: the right to life of unborn
and handicapped children, for example, the right of threatened linguistic or cultural heritages, or the protection of environmental values against industrial development.

In conservatism we encounter the most self-aware and supple of the
modern doctrinal options, the only option of purely modern provenance, indeed, and wholly imbued with modern skepticism. It is tell-
ingly critical of the ideological rigidities of liberalism, yet offers the
strongest imaginable defense of liberal democracy. Its Protean capacity
for mutation allows it constant revivals of influence, most recently under the guise of "communitarianism." Though the lyre it plays is a
state-of-the art electronic instrument, its appeal rests on its ability to
sound in an antique mode. Founding itself on a certain self-
complacency as the generating principle of society, it gives a modern
look to the antique centrality of honor. Representation must take different forms, for there are different honors to be prized, different social
selves to be the object of self-satisfaction. What gives them their common cause is simply the need to disabuse themselves of liberal dogma
with its de-traditionalizing bent.

But here we must glance sideways at another manifestation of
"identity-politics," nationalism. Nationalism is a posture of demand or
recrimination: demand for a political order based on national identity,
or recrimination for threats made against an existing one. Its mood is
very different from conservatism, the revolutionary or protectionist
note sounding discordantly against the harmonious conservative reso-

---

27. *Philosophy of Right* §297, p. 193.

nance with tradition. And to single out national identity as a uniquely important cause repudiates the conservative faith that the *totality* of existing practices creates national identity. Yet for all these differences there is a deep affinity between nationalism and conservatism, which should not be missed. Both adhere to the vision of the state as expression. Conservatism is necessarily nationalist in a weak sense, in that it regards all social institutions as contributing to an organic whole which finds expression in the state. The strong nationalist is, one could say, a conservative who has lost his faith, for whom the sense of identity is no longer given immediately and on the surface of things, but must be recovered from the depths in which it has been buried. So nationalism stands to conservatism as a warning of dissolution, a constant reminder that a political vessel launched on the calm waters of self-satisfaction may founder in the neurotic waves of insecurity.

For Christian believers conservatism brings to light in the clearest possible way the problematic character of all political representation: in the representative the self becomes its own end. The peril of representation is idolatry, the projection of the collective self and the exaltation of man's honor over God's. When the identity of a society is held to be sufficient justification in itself for all the abridgments of social freedom that government requires, it has become an idol. In the political self-consciousness of Israel there was a polemic against national representation in the insistence that YHWH alone could represent his people. This conflict echoes through subsequent confrontations of kings and prophets. Even that most royalist of prophets, Isaiah of Jerusalem, argues the same point relentlessly: if the identity of Judah is to be protected by YHWH, it must be stripped of all its self-complacency. YHWH will "shave with a razor," as the prophet's violent metaphor puts it, "the head, the pubic hair, and the beard, too" (Isa. 7:20).

To ask about the justice with which any particular representative arrangement comes to obtain, is to ask about a *universal* justice. But that is to ask about the kingdom of God, and about the obedience to his rule on the part of a multitude of peoples and tribes and nations, not by one tribe on its own. To each particular identity, then, is put the question: how can the defense of *this* common good, focussed around *this* common identity at *this* time and in *this* way, be brought to serve *that* common good which belongs to the all-embracing identity, individual and collective, of God's kingdom? That question conservatism refuses to answer. But the liberal proceduralist answer, given in terms of electoral legitimacy, was too weak — a deist answer to a Christian question. It did justice neither to the particular nor to the universal: the abstract voluntarism of its idea of representative choice failed to acknowledge the binding force of historical and local particularities, while the abstract legalism of its idea of justice failed to recognize the kingdom of God in the Incarnation. God's kingdom is not first of all universal law, but universal representation: the disclosure of godhead and manhood at the river Jordan, which affords a universal identity in baptism. The representation decisive for God's kingdom is not that of any single nation by its ruler, but the representation of all mankind by the man anointed with the Holy Spirit. Savonarola was right to think that it was the social self-realization of the *church* that put the question of political constitution at the top of the agenda.

II

The Powers of Government

The doctrine of the "three powers" of government — legislative, executive, and judiciary — reached its decisive modern expression at the turn of the eighteenth century, when it was advanced in two quite distinct forms, one of which was to be decisive for the parliamentary democracies of Europe, the other for the presidential democracy of the United States. Each was more radical than the other in different respects. Montesquieu's familiar three-leaved shamrock pattern demanded a concrete "separation" (though this was not his term), each of the three powers being entrusted to different hands. In this way he went as far as any political theorist had dared to go in challenging the principle that government must be unitary.[1] Locke's earlier version, while not insisting on more separation than was implied in a popular legislature, took a more radical turn in assigning the legislative power a definite priority, so placing the executive and judicial powers in an ancillary role, as a kind of civil service mediating law to society.[2]

The modern forms of this doctrine can be traced back to a remarkably forward-looking fourteenth-century text, the First Discourse of Marsilius of Padua's *Defensor Pacis*. Marsilius recognized two classes of

1. *L'Ésprit des lois*, 11.6, trans. Thomas Nugent (New York: Hafner; London: Collier Macmillan, 1949).

2. *Two Treatises of Government* 2.13.151. The monarch was responsible for the two secondary functions of government; where, moreover, "the *Executive* is vested in a single Person, who has also a share in the Legislative; there that single Person in a very tolerable sense may also be called *Supream*."

magistrate, the judicial and the military, and derived the authority of these from a primitive authority possessed by the people as a whole, which he called "legislator," a title hitherto applied mainly to the jurists who codified and systematized Roman law. This was a classicizing innovation in more than one respect, recalling on the one hand the legitimating theory of the Roman empire, by which senate and people were said to confer powers upon the Caesar, and on the other hand invoking the memory of the founding *nomothetai* of the Greek city-state, such as Solon at Athens or Lycurgus at Sparta. Legislation, for Marsilius, was the constitutive act which founded the political society; correspondingly, the founding of a state was the paradigm act of lawmaking.[3]

Yet the crucial feature of this doctrine was not its classicism. Classical polities justified themselves by a narrative of origin, which could be appealed to only from within the particular polity itself. When the Roman-law account of the emperor's authority was generalized, its character changed; it became part of a natural-law theory to account for each and every polity. Neither was the crucial feature the striking anticipation of modern theories of popular sovereignty, for the popular act merely served Marsilius as a base line from which the natural-law account of government could advance; it was a theoretical foundation, but left no trace of popular powers behind it. The crucial feature was its differentiation of political powers. The founding entitlement has been cashed in for a principle of internal form. The state, it was proposed, would be founded well if its functions were appropriately organized and distributed, which means: differentiated.

Nevertheless, the classicizing features in Marsilius's doctrine were fateful in their influence on early-modern theorists, and especially the preeminent role assigned to the act of legislation. At an earlier moment of discovery in the thirteenth century, prompted by new adventures in civil law, theologians began to pay attention to the fact that government was not only subject to law but responsible for making it. That

---

3. An influential ancient source was Aristotle's rather confusing division of the political art according to types of prudence (*Ethica Nicomachea* 1141b23-33), on which Grotius (*De iure belli ac pacis* 1.3.6) built his classicizing account of "the moral competence to govern a state" as personal rule over universals ("legislative"), over public particulars ("political"), and over private particulars with public aspects ("judicial"). In this form, however, the doctrine never envisaged either a ranking or a separation of the powers, the distinction among which was purely aspectual.

emphasis can be seen at its most persuasive in St. Thomas's great treatise on law in the *Summa Theologiae*.[4] The structure of social order required, Thomas believed, not merely the application of divine law,
whether natural or revealed, but a *lex humana*, a "positive law" that determined matters otherwise left unresolved. The *ius ponendi leges*, the
"right of making law," was the mark of the sovereign prince. Yet the authority of human lawmaking still reposed on divine law. The positive
aspect of human lawmaking was thus controlled by a negative proposition, that legislation defying natural or revealed law is *ultra vires*, with
no standing as law at all. In repeating, gingerly enough, the Hellenistic
commonplace that the ruler was *empsuchos nomos*, the "living law,"
Christian use interpreted it with the assertion that in making law the
ruler was always under the law, charged, like anyone else, with keeping
it. The act of constituting law was a response to the law of God, which
determines the possibilities for human society.[5]

But now the drama of creating a sphere of lawfulness became the
principle on which political authority was to be understood. Early-
modern constitutional theory fulfilled the aspirations of ancient democracy only indirectly and, as it were, by accident; for its professed
purpose was not the rule of the people but the rule of law. Political society was lived rationality, and lawmaking was the source and spring of
it. As God, the supreme judge, was known to be "angry every day," i.e.,
to hold daily assizes (Ps. 7:11), so now the legislature neither slumbers
nor sleeps. An incessant stream of lawmaking is the proof of political
viability in the modern state.

The fact that the idea of differentiated powers came to the fore in a
populist context at the peak of the Enlightenment is responsible, perhaps, for its neglect by theologians concerned with politics.[6] Yet it of-

---

4. *Summa Theologiae* II-1.95.6.

5. Still, for Savonarola at the end of the fifteenth century the Grand Council of Florence is illuminated by God with all the right laws, "illuminati poi da Dio di tutte le
buone leggi" (*Trattato sul Governo della Città di Firenze* 3.2). A vigorous reassertion of the
extra vires proposition has recently been made by John Paul II: "Laws which authorize
and promote abortion and euthanasia . . . are completely lacking in authentic juridical
validity" (*Evangelium Vitae* 72).

6. Among the many surprises of John XXIII's *Pacem in Terris* (1963) was the endorsement of this doctrine in the name of "natural law": "We consider that it is in keeping
with the innate demands of human nature that the State should take a form which em-

fers an important corrective to an account of constitution which depends wholly on legitimate entitlement, helpfully directing our attention to the functional realities of how judgment is practiced, and so shifting the burden of proof away from appeals to legitimating events to the success with which justice is in fact done. And so it leaves the last word in legitimation to divine providence: if we have a functioning government, God has provided for our needs! The challenge in reappropriating the doctrine is to disentangle it from its modern preoccupation with legislation, and to situate it within the logic of political authority as judgment. In making the legislative moment foundational, the modern tradition made a serious mistake about law. It supposed that law and legislation, *nomos* and *nomothesia,* were one and the same thing, and that without the framework of founding legislation there could be no society of law. The Christian assertion, on the contrary, was that no human existence was ever prior to law. "Civil laws may be silent among arms," says Grotius, "but not those other laws, which are perpetually in force and are appropriate for every season."[7]

Law is the presupposition of every political act of judgment, because it is a presuppposition of every human act that is conscious of itself. It is the reality that determines how we conduct ourselves, the original bridge between the "is" and the "ought," the order within the world that is given to us. We find the law already there in place, we discern it, and we comprehend it. "The heavens declare the glory of God. . . . the law of the Lord is perfect, reviving the soul" (Ps. 19:1, 7). Law determines our ways without intermediary, because it is the order that determines whatever happens under the sun. It gives life to the soul because without it there would *be* no soul, and no energy. The energy and purpose of the law is not our *subjective* energy and purpose reflected onto brute

---

bodies the threefold division of powers corresponding to the three principal functions of public authority" (68). Further surprises were in store from the magisterium on the same theme: In *Centesimus Annus* (1991) 44, John Paul II reported that this doctrine had been propounded in Leo XIII's *Rerum Novarum* (1891), adding that "at the time . . . [it] represented a novelty in Church teaching." It takes determination to detect this sense in Leo's words, which ran: "Some there must be who dedicate themselves to the work of the commonwealth, who make the laws, who administer justice, whose advice and authority govern the nation in times of peace, and defend it in war. Such men clearly occupy the foremost place in the State . . ." (28).

7. *De iure belli ac pacis,* prol. 26; *IG,* p. 797.

facts that we must plot our path around. Law is not a brute fact to plot our path around; on the contrary, it is only under law and through law that we have a path to plot in the first place. Law is the all-comprising order to which we belong, and within which the idea of a path to plot makes sense. Law tells us "what we are made for," what it is that we seek. We never "discover" it, but "recall" it, for we have already known it for as long as we have ever known that there is anything to know.

Law may be encountered immanently in the world, without any conception of a God who created the world and its law. But once there supervenes the conception of law as an artifact and a gift of the commanding will, there arises a further thought: that law is something that we, too, may give to one another. Behind any act of human law-giving, there is always the prior reality of law already given. Only of God in his *potentia absoluta* may we say that law is absolute gift. Of ourselves we may say only that we make law out of law; we work on what we are already in possession of. And so it is that human law-giving is never simply an act of will, but an act of judgment, downstream from the source of law. It is an act that must discern: discern, on the one hand, the social context into which the law is to be given again, and discern, on the other, the form of the original divine command that must now be reiterated, given once again as human law.

That is why in the simplest model of government as judgment the monarch is a judge who sits in court. Ancient Israel knew, however, that the task of judgment required the monarch not only to sit in court but also to found courts. Three separate Pentateuchal narratives, each with a slightly differing emphasis, explore the logic of this move in relation to Moses. In Exodus 18, the first of these narratives in order of appearance, Jethro persuades Moses of the simple fact that the business pressing on any court is far too great for one judge to deal with. A unified system of justice requires a tiered system of courts, in which the ruler hears a case only as the last resort. In the second narrative (Numbers 11) it is recognized that the community possesses a variety of local, family, and tribal loyalties, which need to be harnessed to the task of judgment, since without their cooperation the ruler cannot achieve his purpose. The third narrative, which conflates elements of these two, stands in a programmatic place at the opening of that programmatic book, Deuteronomy, and employs the concept of law to combine the monarchical emphasis of the one with the tribal emphasis of the other.

The various courts, based on various social identities, are held together by the authority of one law, authenticated by the monarch.

Looked at from one angle this development anticipates the separation of the monarch from the judiciary, for as a court of last resort the monarch never acts personally, lest he should squander his last throw. From another angle, however, and more importantly, it defines a power of government beside the power of the courts, which is still, nevertheless, a power of judgment. To provide a court in which a judge sits is no less judgment than to sit in court oneself. The founding of a judiciary is a judicial act, giving judgment in favor of the oppressed — not one particular oppressed person in this case, but the oppressed as a class; yet not a universal class, for no ruler undertakes to remedy the wrongs of all oppressed people everywhere in every age, but a concrete historical class, the oppressed of *this* kingdom at *this* juncture of history. And what is true of the foundation of courts applies equally to their maintenance. The monarch's duty to keep courts open, to let "judgment flow like a torrent and vindication like a river in flood," as Amos picturesquely put it (5:24), is not something other than the exercise of political judgment. What is spoken of in early modern theory, then, as "the separation of executive and judiciary" is really a dialectical distinction of two institutional powers *within the one general function of judgment,* the first power to create and maintain courts, the second power to hear cases and give judgments on them.

The differentiation of roles is dialectical and complementary. Any given instance of wrong may be examined in more than one perspective, more broadly or more narrowly. Faced with a social crisis over drug abuse, for example, we must attend practically to the pressing problem of protecting our young people against the influence of drug dealers; but we must also attend to charges of drug dealing brought against *this* person at *this* time and place with impartial minds. We cannot attend to the second, more restricted matter if we are preoccupied by the first. If we ask, "What sort of a message will it send to drug dealers everywhere if this person is acquitted?" we will not be impartial. *Both* forms of practical attention are acts of judgment; *both* belong to a definite time and place and situation; but the second form is deliberately limited in scope, in order to protect against committing injustice on the narrow front while aiming at justice on the broad front. The public interest in justice requires its pursuit from both aspects, each on its own proper terms. The *sub judice* rule is a device for ensuring that the two powers function in a properly dialectical relation to each other, the first power not intervening in court cases and the second power not making judgments of general policy.[8]

Yet the policy which is the business of the first power is still a policy for *judgment*. We depend on rulers' keeping an eye on the running of the courts, just as we depend on their keeping their hands off particular cases. If courts prove incapable of dealing with a certain type of case, either they or the law they administer must be reformed. In the Republic of Ireland and in Northern Ireland at the height of the terrorist threat, jury courts were replaced by "special courts" to try terrorist offenses. This lamentable development was an appropriate response to the circumstances, and not merely for reasons of security, but precisely to ensure the probity of judgment. The first power of government must ensure that the second power functions well: reasonable expedition of legal process, reasonable restraint of legal fees, reasonable rules of procedure over such matters as the admissibility of evidence, the use of juries, and so on, all these are the proper concerns of the first power, ensuring that justice, not arbitrary whim, prevails in social relations. One way in which the first power discharges this responsibility is to give the courts law.

Courts are not, of course, wholly dependent on another power of government for their law. They have the law of God, natural and revealed, and they have the customary law of society. They also have a tradition of interpreting both of these which they themselves have developed by their decisions. The most general word for "law" in Hebrew, *tôrah*, means simply "decision." It referred to the "ruling" that a priest would give when consulted (Exod. 18:16, 20; Deut. 17:11). In the same way we say that the judge "declares the law" in relation to a case; which means that he announces a decision.[9] But since judgment is not a series of separate and discrete decisions but an institution, the law of each case is discerned in relation to the law of preceding cases. No act

8. Cf. Hugo Grotius, *De imperio circa sacra* 5: *Hinc fit ut iudicium ad actiones alienas tendens sit aut directivum . . . aut imperativum. Imperativum iudicium distinxit Aristoteles in* νομοθετικὸν καὶ δικαστικόν, *quorum illud esse ait* περὶ τῶν καθόλου, *hoc vero τῶν* ἀφωρισμένων καὶ κατὰ μέρος.

9. Cf. Thomas Aquinas, *Summa Theologiae* II-2.67.1: *sententia iudicis est quasi quaedam particularis lex in aliquo particulari facto.*

of judgment can simply invent law *de novo,* since that would defeat one of the canons of judgment, which is proportion. A law of precedent derived from many cases stands over and behind each new decision and is appealed to in support of it. Such a law requires no distinct legislator or statute. Divine law, natural or revealed, and mediated through traditions of right innate in the society, is sufficient to allow courts to develop law by way of their own judgments.

But when the authority of courts is undermined because their laws or operative principles are repugnant to the community's conscience, or because their orders are impossible to implement, the responsibility for correcting their law lies with the first power of government. All legal tradition may need correction from time to time. The obligation of the courts to maintain self-consistency makes them reluctant to innovate, but innovation may be necessary. That may be for either of two reasons: legal tradition may have deviated from natural right; or it may be ill adapted to the practical possibilities within society. These two grounds of law reform are easily confused. They are in principle different, moving in opposite directions: one brings law closer to the moral norm, the other removes it further from it. There are idealistic reforms that attempt to correct our unchecked vices; there are compromise reforms that make some kind of settlement with them. Either kind of reform may be necessary at one or another juncture, since acts of judgment must be at once truthful and effective. Every change in the law aims to squeeze out, as it were, the maximum yield of public truthfulness available within the practical constraints of the times. Sometimes it does it by attempting more, sometimes by attempting less.

But a further dialectical distinction arises between the power to reform law and other acts of political judgment. Legislation is *generic,* which is what distinguishes it from acts which concern bare particulars. When the first power of government is exercised in appointing a chief justice or supplying a sum of money for new courts, it decides only who is to be the Lord Chief Justice *next,* or where the money is to come from *now.* When a law is passed, on the other hand, it decides what is *always* to be done in such cases as the law specifies. Imagine two supposed miscarriages of justice, both uncorrected by the courts themselves, which provoke public anxiety. In one case there is public doubt about the evidence for identification on which a conviction was secured. In the other case there is dismay that evidence important to the defense was ruled inadmissible. Both are assumed to be miscarriages, but for different reasons. The first related to a particular, *"This* is the man who was observed at the scene of the crime"; the second related to a generic principle, *"This kind* of evidence is not admissible in defense." The two miscarriages must be addressed quite differently. In the one case the Home Secretary will review the case, and if it seems warranted, instruct the Court of Appeal to look at it again. In the second case the Lord Chancellor prepares new legislation to amend the law of evidence. These two different kinds of corrective action require different measures of public support. If the Home Secretary refers a case back, or simply issues a pardon, not much is needed by way of public consent. We understand that the minister must have these powers, and we require only that he use them reasonably. It is not possible to settle the validity of a conviction by public consensus. Nor does it matter to the public all that much in the long run if the minister actually reaches the wrong answer, provided that he is seen to reach it reasonably, conscientiously, and without prejudice. In the second case, though, where legislation is in question, it is a very different matter. Innumerable future cases yet undreamed of will be affected.

In order that no deep cleavage be allowed to develop between the general sense of what is right and what the law demands, something more is required in legislation than bare acquiescence in the authority of government: there must be a positive assent to the principles on which reform is proposed. Proposals for legislation need examination, not only to explore unforeseen implications but to test them against the attitudes and convictions of those who will be governed by them. Thus arises the English constitutional doctrine, maintained by Locke despite his advocacy of "separation," that the legislature in a government is *the monarch in parliament.* That is to say: not some other agent than the monarch, but the monarch in a certain relation to the people, engaged in a process of consultation. But what is the status of parliament as the monarch's consultation-partner? In England parliament began life as a "court of common pleas," a means by which the governed spoke to government about their frustrations, an organic line of communication between the two which served to legitimate government as pursuit of the common good. The extension of its role to a deliberative forum, first for the authorizing of taxation and then for the formation of legislation, recognized the need for politic government that would listen to the *vox populi,* respecting its deeply held convictions and taking the measure of its anxieties. The function of a parliament is not to *be* the government, but to speak for the people *to* the government, while acknowledging the government's right and duty to legislate.

We think of legislation as a third power of government, because it needs to be exercised in a distinctive way, in consultation with a representative parliament of the people. But since government, too, has representative status, it will also tend to bind this other representative into the closest possible collaboration with it. There thus develops a characteristic tension of loyalties within parliament itself: is it people, or is it government? Max Weber, who greatly admired the British parliamentary system, perceived clearly how the collaboration of parliament and government contributed to the strength of government, contrasting this with the "negative politics" of the German Reichstag in Bismark's constitution, which could only criticize and obstruct, never share responsibility.[10] What Weber failed to see was that this collaboration could cause the original vis-à-vis between the two representative bodies to collapse. In conforming itself to the needs of government, parliament could lose its representative independence, and its party bureaucracy could come to collaborate with government bureaucracy in irresponsible policy-formation. The risk had been appreciated by Montesquieu, who saw that a certain dialogue must accompany the formation of law if legislation was not simply to be another case of executive action, losing its distinctive lawmaking character.[11] But Montesquieu mislocated the dialogue we need, which is not a dialogue between departments of government, but a dialogue between government and people. By converting parliament into "the legislature," and so into government, he, too, lost the vital sense of the dialogue between governed and government as the heart of the legislative process.[12]

10. "Parliament and Government in Germany Under a New Political Order," in *Political Writings,* ed. and trans. Peter Lassman and Ronald Speirs (Cambridge: Cambridge University Press, 1994), pp. 165-96.

11. *L'Esprit des lois* 11.6: "When the legislative and executive powers are united in the same person, or in the same body of magistrates, there can be no liberty; because apprehensions may arise, lest the same monarch or senate should enact tyrannical laws, to execute them in a tyrannical manner."

12. Cf. Søren Kierkegaard's hostile commentary in *A Literary Review* (1846) on liberal plans to introduce constitutional restraints on the Danish crown: "The coiled springs of

This, I believe, lies at the heart of the malfunction which was perceived to have affected the British constitution in the course of the twentieth century. Those critics who were devoted to seventeenth-century analyses of twentieth-century problems identified the difficulty simply in terms of the excessive power of the (executive) government; but this analysis was one-sided, since the situation arose precisely from the sheer success of parliament in taming the willfulness of government and taking over some of its significant powers. The problem was an implosion of government and parliament upon each other, creating an unhealthy mutual dependence. Parliament (effectively one chamber) commanded ministerial appointments, so making ministers depend on parliament for their office. Ministers, for their part, commanded parliamentary agreement for legislative proposals with the threat of dissolution. The sense of dialogue was lost. Each side had too much power over the other, too little authority on its own ground. The stranglehold of the party system, effectively controlling the terms of political debate, was the worst symptom of this stasis. The price paid for co-opting parliament into government was loss of belief in the capacity of "politicians" — the term is an expressive one, bundling ministers and popular representatives together into a single professional class[13] — to respond to what actually moves the people. "Politicians" argue energetically about "the issues"; but what the issues are, they have settled among themselves, without consulting us.

If the first result of the legislative positivism of modern constitutional thought was the loss of consultative dialogue that ought to accompany the government's interventions into the making of law, the second and more recent result has been a radical assertion of the inde-

---

life relationships, which exist only by virtue of the qualitatively distinguishing passion, lose their resilience; the qualitative expression of the distance between those who differ from each other is no longer the law for a relation in inwardness to each other. . . . Inwardness is lacking, and the relationship to that extent doesn't exist, or it is a supine cohesion. . . . This is not the burgher who with cheerful loyalty pays homage to his king, and now is embittered by his tyranny; far from it, being a burgher becomes something else, it means being a *third party*. The burgher does not relate himself in the relationship, he is a spectator working out this problem: the relationship between a king and his subject. . . . But finally it will all end with the whole age becoming a committee."

13. Roger Scruton, *The Meaning of Conservatism* (Basingstoke: Macmillan, 1984), p. 18: "A professional class . . . that pursues power not for its own sake but as the by-product of professional advancement."

pendence of the courts over against laws once made. The widespread turn to the courts for relief expresses a frustration with parliamentary legislatures that claim to be a sovereign government while failing to be an effective court of common pleas. It was born of reaction against the modern notion of positively legislated rationality, a desire for that right which is prior to, and independent of, the "unequal constitutions of men." It thus responds to a religious, and historically to a Judaeo-Christian impulse. In the post-war documents which express late-modern faith in human rights, the use of quasi-religious concepts, though cloudy, is decisive, as in the U.N. Declaration, which speaks of the "recognition of the inherent dignity and of the equal and inalienable rights of all members of the human family." That the problem of autonomous courts should have come to the fore in this period, and in the nations most involved in those documents, attests the twentieth-century search to recover a pre-political moral ground of law.

The constitutional struggles of our age, however, attest that we have not in fact succeeded in breaking with the early-modern concept of positively legislated government. Neither we nor our courts have proved capable of acknowledging the claim of natural right without erecting a counter-legislature, an equal and opposite imitation, and so precipitating a crisis over the location of the ultimate responsibility for government. The would-be solution, like the problem, has arisen within the dialectic created by the separation of government from judgment. While government pursues policies of prudence only contingently related to justice, courts pursue justice with no relation to political prudence. Such prudence and such justice are purely formal and of little use. Legal positivism, which lies at the root of both, can only pit arbitrariness against arbitrariness, the ruthless on the one hand against the impractical on the other.

There is nothing wrong with the idea that law is made by courts. Courts must declare the principles on which they have decided cases, and those principles become a law to subsequent courts. The question is, how the law-giving of courts is to be integrated with the wider tasks of judgment for which courts do not take responsibility. There might be worse things, it is true, than dictatorship by courts; yet such dictatorship would not be good government, and for three reasons: (a) Good forensic practice requires concentration on the particular case, but good lawmaking requires attention to general policy (the *sub judice* principle).

(b) Good forensic practice requires insulation from pressures of public concern, but good law requires exposure through consultation to public concern (the principle of politic government). (c) Good forensic practice requires a conservative approach to legal tradition; but good law-making needs a critical distance on it (the natural-law principle). The root of the contemporary problem of autonomous courts lies in the faulty early-modern articulation, which, lacking a sense of the judicial character of *all* the powers of government, allowed the separation of powers to create competing jurisdictions. This is a situation which political authority cannot endure. The variety of functions within a complex government allows for an extensive diffusion of decision, but it rests on the hypothesis of a *summa potestas,* a unitary source to which in the last analysis the resolution of conflicts must return.

This was the rationale for the decision of the British Government to incorporate the European Convention of Human Rights within Scottish and English law. It was hoped both to overcome the existing liability to conflict and to protect the legislative supremacy of the Queen in Parliament. It allowed the Convention to be interpreted *as* British law by British courts, and British law to be interpreted within the interpretative context provided by the Convention, so presenting the Strasbourg court with interpretative decisions reached under British law by British courts. While stopping short of according Strasbourg's rulings *ipso facto* force in British law, it required British courts to consider those rulings, so admitting a serious contribution to the interpretation of British law from outside Great Britain. But it also deprived the Strasbourg court of its monopoly of interpretation, and so hoped to modify the interpretation of the Convention in the light of British legal realities.

One could say that this measure attempted to do *institutionally* what still remains to be done *conceptually,* which is to reintegrate the falsely dichotomized conceptions of statute law and human rights, the one enjoying a positive immunity from moral criteria, the other enjoying a natural-law supremacy over positive law. On the one hand, the truth of the natural-law principle, that for law to be valid it must be morally tolerable, must apply across the *whole range* of legislative endeavor, not merely to those cases in which individuals have claims to make against governments. On the other hand, the truth of the principle behind positive law must also be maintained: the rights of individuals cannot be respected simply by letting them cut across legal traditions, invading them, as it were, by sudden irruptions of court judgment at unpredictable moments; rights must be an essential aspect of the spirit of a well-tempered law, a "right" in the singular, which government takes responsibility for sustaining and correcting.

Whether the measure will succeed or fail will depend on whether the judiciary understands what is required of it, which is to apply statute law intelligently in the light of a body of general principles of natural justice, and so to make good moral and social sense of legislation that may sometimes have been incoherently or inconsiderately compiled. In handling law we cannot require that the courts be slavish; there can be no prejudice in favor of "strict construction." What is required of courts is simply a due acknowledgment of the authority of government to provide law, and a commitment to giving it the best interpretation of which it is susceptible, according to the most consistent interpretative principles (which are not necessarily the most literal) that can be developed. If the British courts do that, all will be well. But if, seduced by the remarkable success of Canadian courts in subverting the rule of law, or bewitched into thinking of "rights" as a whole new legal continent waiting to be discovered or — worse — invented, they imagine that they have been charged with leading a revolution (and some jurists have not hesitated to speak of themselves in those terms), we shall be subject to tyranny. For revolutionary courts are the most tyrannous of instruments, lacking both the wide-ranging prudence of government to innovate well and the judicial integrity of courts to observe precedent well.

But we must recall the root of the problem, which was a reaction to the idolatrously inflated conception of legislative power. The aggrandizement of positive legislation resulted in a cheapening of it and in a general contempt for legislative process: too much law made too fast and too carelessly. Law, as Montesquieu feared, had turned into a form of executive action, as parties competed at elections with rival legislative programs that they promised to ram through within one parliamentary term. In this ethos the shifting of real responsibility to the courts by no means occurred without the collusion of politicians. It enabled them to sustain a flurry of lawmaking without being ultimately answerable for the consequences. The *reductio ad absurdum* was reached when it came to be thought that the passage of legislation was merely provisional, and a new law not authoritative until challenged and upheld right through the court system. This signaled the spiritual demise of modern democracy itself, the great claim of which was to provide an answer to the question: how may a multitude of human beings live as a political society in obedience to law?

*   *   *

There having sprung two branches from the trunk of government, the judiciary to attend to particular cases, the legislature to engage in consultation over lawmaking, what becomes of the trunk itself? Does it disappear into its branches, like a shrub, or does it continue like the leading-shoot of a tree, to form a central stem around which the branches group themselves? In an attempt to describe the functions of the first power of government, two complementary paths lie before us to seduce us into error.

One is to suppose that once the second and third powers have come into being, the first is ordinarily subservient to them. Every initiative can be taken by one or the other of the two derived powers, and the ordinary exercise of the first power is merely "executive," giving effect to acts which the legislature and the judiciary have undertaken. So Locke conceived it, and his view was perpetuated in the Hegelian tradition of discussing "the bureaucracy" as a distinct branch of government — an idea that ought to cause alarm as soon as one conceives it. The bureaucracy cannot be a branch of government as the legislature and the judiciary are, for they are distinguished by their specific tasks of judgment, whereas bureaucracy has no task of judgment of its own. Bureaucracy is not so much a noun as an adverb: it describes the *way in which* every power of government is given effect and carries through its judgments in the modern state.

The other tempting path is to suppose that the first power of government, as the founding power, is required for *extraordinary* events, when for some reason the authority of legislature and courts is suspended. The operations of the first power are thereby associated with liminal moments in the life of the state with which the legal and judicial structure fails to cope. This is to conceive the first power as "sovereign," the *summa potestas* functioning as a last instance when the task of founding the legislature and judiciary has to be undertaken over again. "The sovereign makes decisions in an emergency," declared Carl Schmitt.[14] With an understanding of sovereignty related so decisively to the irruptive and uncontrolled — that is to say, especially with war —

---

14. "Souverän ist der über den Ausnahmezustand entscheidet," quoted in P. Manent, *City of Man* (Princeton: Princeton University Press, 1998), p. 173.

it is hardly surprising that the first power should come to seem ominous, and the claims of its sovereignty sinister. The mistake of limiting the first power to the case of last instance is simply a variant of the first mistake, supposing that the ordinary conduct of government requires only the powers of the legislature and the courts.

But there is an *ordinary* power of judgment that is distinct from the powers of the legislature and the judiciary. It is the power of *prospective judgment*, the proper criterion of which is attributive justice. We call its judgments "policies," and for that reason it could be described as the "political" power, though to avoid ambiguity we will do better to coin a term of art, and refer to the "provisionary" power. Its judgments arise at the interface between ordered society and disordered events, where initiatives require a high degree of discretion.

Every attempt to fetter that discretion to a merely executive service of the other two powers is, in effect, an attempt to bind future events — a procedure that infallibly leads to the ruin of political constitutions, since the future refuses to be bound. If every unforeseen initiative had to be accompanied by new legislation to permit it, action would be intolerably clumsy and the properly prolonged consultative procedures for legislation would be degraded. Most written constitutions include a provision for a formal declaration of emergency, an admission, perhaps grudging, that not all events can be provided for or foreseen, and that circumstances arise where improvisation is essential. Yet the emergency is only the limiting case of what is *always* true about new events. No new events, however reminiscent of old, present themselves spontaneously before courts and legislatures in obedient subjection to their authority; the unjudged has to be *brought to* judgment. To understand the logic of the provisionary function of government, then, we must begin from the ordinary, not from the extraordinary. And this may help us see how even its authority in emergency is not *wholly* extraordinary, but consists of an extension of ordinary functions in unusual circumstances. *The function of the provisionary power of government is to judge conditions as they arise, and provide for the further judgment of any occurrence that requires it,* so that courts and legislature may be presented with their proper business in an orderly fashion. This ordinary power, it should be noticed, is still precisely what the first power always was, namely, the power to initiate judgment and to provide for its continuance.

(a) The task of *preparing legislation* illustrates the function of the first power clearly. A legislature cannot make laws haphazardly, but must be presented with proposals that, taken together, form a "policy," i.e., a coherent approach to the emerging problems of the society. Formulating coherent policies is an ordinary task of the provisionary power, a necessary prerequisite for the work of a legislature.

But since the work of a legislature is frustrated if there are no material resources and personnel to give its law effect, the provisionary power must also direct budgets and appointments, so providing for the bureaucratic implementation of law. These provisions are not legislative acts, since they are not generic but once-off and unrepeatable. They are, indeed, not acts of judgment at all in themselves, but only as linked to policies that discern and respond to the threat of wrong in new events. But because resources in government are tied to acts of judgment, the provisionary power must have control over resources to enable acts of judgment.

But if resources are tied to policies, policies are tied to resources; and that means that policies are never separate and distinct from one another. All the policies which a government devises to meet all the contingencies that threaten society converge upon one budget and one determinate supply of qualified appointees. The responsibility of the first power is not merely to formulate policies, but to order them, converting them into a single coherent "government policy" for any one moment in history. This "policy of policies" is not a philosophy, or a comprehensive idea, like "modernization" or "consumer choice," which is destined to shape all the subordinate policies into a common mold. That is the route of ideology become stupid, made so, one can only think, by the dominance of electoral communication over political thinking. A policy is an *agenda,* which ranks policies according to their urgency and logical interconnections. This ongoing ordering of policies is the act of judgment that founds and supports all other acts of judgment in the state, the ordinary act of the first, the provisionary power of government.

As such, policy, too, needs consultation and consent. Not only at the stage of legislation itself, but at the stage of political judgment that precedes it, the consultative process that will secure the loyalty and obedience of those subject to these judgments is all-important. It was in recognition of this that modern democracy developed its characteristic institution of the *bicameral parliament.* Parliament stands at the point where government interacts with public consent to policy- and lawmaking; but this consent has two aspects, as *deliberation* and as *acceptance*. Deliberation concentrates on the proposal as such, the details and implications of its demands and restrictions; acceptance depends far more on the policy context in which the legislative initiative is proposed. The role of the "lower" chamber in a bicameral system is to effect acceptance. For in a constitution where the lower chamber of parliament acts, in effect, as an electoral college to appoint and dismiss the government, there is no room for open reflection on legislative proposals; the task of negotiating support for government policy is all-consuming, and determines the shape of debates and procedures (e.g., the division of members into "government" and "opposition"). The role of an "upper" chamber is to allow scope for full deliberation. The upper chamber has less power than the lower chamber, but more freedom. It is not in any way less important, even though its view can never be final, since the last word lies with the chamber that has the responsibility for keeping a government in office.

To observe the necessity for a second chamber, we need only reflect on the technical aspects of such policy areas as education or health care. If government is to make attributive judgments on the provision of services, it is exposed to the hazards of deciding specialized questions. And if it is to command the respect of the communities of professional practice who actually engage in education or health care, and of the public which is not without ideas about them, it must not only be well advised, but it must be seen to be open to a variety of views from within the specialist community, not falling captive to an official "ministry line" or held hostage by assertive pressure groups. (The unhappy failure of the British government to listen to the right advice when confronted with the new variant Creutzfeldt-Jakob disease is a cautionary fable with many applications.) The essential function of the second chamber is to ground the *public* side of that exposure to representative experience. How a credible upper chamber can be constituted is a question that has currently proved quite insoluble to the much-celebrated constitutional acumen of the British people, which once imposed constitutions upon half the nations of the world. I need only make one very obvious point — obvious, but alas unheeded: the more closely the upper chamber resembles the lower in the mode of its constitution and the manner of its debates, the less it is worth having. The upper chamber has a *different* task, and must be shaped to perform the task it is given.

(b) The function of the provisionary power is also illustrated by the task of *preparing cases for the courts*. It is not an accident that we use the term "police," philologically connected with "policy," for the agency that detects and prosecutes crime in the modern state. This reflects correctly the nature of police authority as an aspect of the first power of government.

When a stroller through the woods discovers a child's dead body bearing marks of violent treatment, help is sought not from judges or legislators, but from the arm of government that can initiate inquiries, make arrests, and present charges. The ordinary operations of the provisionary power react to *events,* and the police is the primary agency that reacts to events that ought to end up before the courts. The operation of the courts is the goal of police activity, not the starting-point. All that the police do, of course, is subject to law, but that is true of all the powers of government. Being subject to law is not the same as being subject to courts or legislatures. Indeed, the police possess a certain independent discretion about which laws they will give priority to enforcing, so that it may even be said that they act, as part of the first power, to reform the operation of law in minor ways that are not sufficiently weighty to justify legislative attention. Not every local lawmaking body that has passed elaborate regulations to control the traffic flow, has had the satisfaction of seeing those laws enforced!

We may identify two moments that illustrate the ordinary independence of the police:

(i) In a developed society the police is responsible for bringing cases to *prosecution*. There are, of course, various intermediary offices which may act as a channel between the police and the courts: the Director of Public Prosecutions in England and Wales, "investigating magistrates" in many other jurisdictions. But the logic of the process is clear: the courts cannot themselves bring the complaints that they will judge. Either these must be brought privately, or they must be brought by a public authority with a role independent of the courts, one that operates within the sphere of the first power of government. It is not essential to a political society that there should be any public authority to bring complaints. In the simplest judicial systems prosecution is left to plaintiffs. Yet there are powerful reasons why, especially though not exclusively within Christendom, the responsibility for prosecution has generally passed to government. These reasons emerge clearly from this radically Augustinian statement of Luther about vengeance: "The true meaning of Christ's words . . . 'Resist not evil' . . . is that a Christian should be so disposed that he will suffer every evil and injustice, not avenge himself, nor bring suit in court, and in nothing make use of secular power and law for himself. For others, however, he may and should seek vengeance, justice, protection and help, and do what he can towards this. Likewise the governing authority should, either of itself or through the instigation of others, help and protect him without complaint, application, or instigation on his part."[15] In drawing a clear line of separation between public judgment and private vengeance, Christians have wished to relieve the injured party of responsibility for complaint. Prosecuting a complaint has been seen as a matter of "caring for one another," rather than defending one's own right.

With the concept of public prosecution goes the distinction of crime from tort. There has been something of a fashion in libertarian circles of deprecating the extensive criminal law that has grown up in developed societies, and to urge a return to dependence on civil suits; but it is hard to think of this as other than deeply reactionary. It is necessary that authority should prosecute the more serious offenses. Although there are a few trifling crimes and some very serious torts, the general scope of criminal law is more weighty: battery is a crime, libel a tort. Crimes, furthermore, will include wrongs of which it is unreasonable to expect the victim to supply a proof, as well as those offenses committed indiscriminately against chance members of the public, as opposed to those arising from previous engagements of the victim with the offender, like breach of contract. Finally, criminal law is needed to deal with the class of offenses in which the victimization is indeterminate or diffuse, such as environmental pollution.

English legal authorities distinguish crime from tort not only by their different modes of prosecution, but by their victims, "the public" rather than "the plaintiff," and by their sanctions, "punishment" and "damages."[16] But the latter points are not fundamental; the decisive point where crime and tort part company is the first. Every wrong victimizes both its particular victims and the public.[17] And a tort is as

---

15. *Temporal Authority* (WA 11.259); *IG*, p. 590.

much a wrong as a crime; when the civil courts award damages for tort, they avenge wrong just as the criminal courts do.[18] Correspondingly, we ought to say that the civil courts "punish" when they award damages — though this is a philosophical point, not an objection to a convenient distinction in legal terminology. I have not found in Halsbury a definition of punishment that avoids the circularity of saying that punishing is what criminal courts do.[19]

Behind the distinction of punishment and damages there may lie the relics of the medieval penitential distinction of *culpa* and *reatus,* which did much to make punishment unintelligible by promoting the idea of "absolute" guilt apart from the relation between offender and victim. Thus punishment could seem to deal with absolute guilt, while damages provide restitution for the victim. But we should rather say, following the argument of Chapter 7 above, that any judgment against wrong is, as such and already, judgment in favor of the victim.

(ii) From the responsibility to bring cases to prosecution there derives the responsibility for detection and arrest. A system of public prosecution can, and in early modern Europe did, make do with surprisingly vestigial official resources for detection and arrest, relying heavily on the legal obligation of the public to report crime and the difficulty of concealment in a closely knit society. The modern police force, child of the early nineteenth century, came into existence not, as the utilitarian Sir Robert Peel claimed, "to prevent crime," but to bring more efficiency to the detection and arrest of its perpetrators. Deterrence, though a welcome side effect, could hardly justify its extensively intrusive activities.

The use of force in making an arrest illustrates the measure of discretion that is always associated with exercise of the first power. It is commonly, and correctly, said that the use of force in arrest must be subject

16. Earl of Halsbury, *Halsbury's Laws of England,* 4th ed., ed. Lord Hailsham of St. Marylebone (London: Butterworth, 1973-), vol. 11, §1,2.

17. Cf. R. A. Duff, *Punishment, Communication, and Community* (Oxford: Oxford University Press, 2001), p. 63, on "public wrongs": "They are wrongs against their direct victims as members of the community, and so also wrongs against the community."

18. In civil cases the law distinguishes *damages* — for wrong — from *compensation* — for loss — (see Halsbury, *Laws of England,* vol. 12, §1103), and recognizes the possibility that a victim might be wronged without being harmed (Halsbury, vol. 45, §1204).

19. Halbury, vol. 11, §3.

to the principle of proportion. But to what must force be proportionate? Not to the suspect's guilt, for of this we know nothing until a court has heard the case. Arrest is not punishment; its purpose is to bring the unjudged to judgment. If a suspect is killed without due process, it does not serve the cause of public judgment at all, however much he may have deserved it. The force is proportioned, rather, to the *apparent danger to the public or particular individuals posed by the failure of the arrest.* Violence against the person should only be used to avert the likelihood of comparable injury should the suspect escape. The prospective judgment is a judgment of circumstance. Such judgment is, of course, relative to the possibilities for alternative means of arrest; for a well-resourced and well-trained police unit the failure to arrest one day may not be a great concern, since a secure arrest is likely to follow on the next; an under-resourced unit, on the other hand, may judge that failure to arrest now means failure for ever. The under-resourced unit will therefore be more likely to use force; and rightly, since its own poor equipment restricts the range of alternatives. The price we pay for under-equipping and under-manning the police is to lower the threshold for legitimate use of force.

* * *

The truth of the doctrine of the three powers is that the act of judgment on which political authority is founded is not an instantaneous or unarticulated act. It has its own unfolding shape, which includes provision, adjudication, and legislation. Correspondingly, this doctrine qualifies the somewhat mythical monarchism of representation with a realistic account of the dialectical and cooperative arrangements that must, in fact, sustain any government.

Nevertheless, the doctrine of the powers of government cannot complete an account of just constitution. The first reason for this is that even in the best administered states emergencies arise which suspend the distinct operation of the three powers, and if that had the effect of illegitimizing the government, there would be no stable government anywhere. Consider the case where the police have to use lethal force in making an arrest. For reasons that will be immediately apparent, this cannot be justified within the ordinary scope of the provisionary power of government, for the purpose of that power is to make the arrest safely and bring the suspect to court. But an emergency may supervene in the course of an arrest that imposes a more urgent need than safe arrest: that is, to protect an innocent person whose safety is immediately threatened. In that case a judgment has to be made on the spot and given immediate effect, in favor of the innocent and against the guilty — not "innocent" and "guilty" with respect to the original offense for which the arrest was intended (that case has still not been judged), but innocent and guilty with respect to the *new* threat now urgently presented. This is no longer simply a judgment of circumstance, bringing the unjudged to judgment, but an act of a judiciary character carried through to execution upon the wrongdoer.

This extension of police powers into the judiciary sphere occurs by the principle of *iudicium cessans,* "failure of judgment." Where the appropriate judicial authority is unavailable or unable to function, authority for judgment reverts to the holder of the provisionary power, the "first power" of government. The emergency does not allow the ordinary differentiation of the first and second powers to take effect, because communication between them is impossible in the time available for effective action; and so the whole authority to judge devolves upon the agent of the first power on the spot, who becomes, as it were, a primitive monarch until communication can be established again, exercising all the powers of judgment necessary for the emergency.

The principle of *iudicium cessans* rests on the supposition there can never be a vacuum of judgment; when ordinary organs of judgment cannot function, extraordinary ones must be devised. This principle permits even a private citizen to exercise political authority in risking an assailant's life to save a victim's. The whole apparatus of government failing to be on hand when needed, the private citizen improvises it, rushing to his neighbor's defense with full authority until the ordinary authority can arrive and take over. Yet since it is clearly pernicious to civil order that the most extreme powers of government should be assumed in this occasional fashion, the first power of government is responsible for providing for emergencies in advance, to the extent that they may be foreseen. So Grotius argued that governments should issue licenses to captains of ships to use force in repelling piracy on the high seas, since it "is perilous for a Christian in a private capacity to assume responsibility, in his own or in the public interest, for the punishment, especially the capital punishment, of a criminal."[20] The tri-polar structure of assailant, victim, and vindicator is fundamental to the public ownership of an act of force, which is to say that there is no such thing as legitimate self-defense. This was St. Augustine's understanding of the crucial passage in the Sermon on the Mount (Matt. 5:39ff.), in which private self-defense is prohibited: it takes *love of neighbor* to authorize an act of vindication by force.

We may be tempted to object to Augustine's doctrine that it is likely to save the appearances of the Sermon on the Mount without saving anything of substance. Can we not argue, after all, that self-defense is never a purely private concern, since there is always a public interest in preventing crime? So is not the prohibited *private* self-defense so abstract that we would never perform it anyway? This objection will not hold up. There is certainly a public interest in preventing crime, but the public interest does not require the prevention of crime by *any* means. It is in the public interest that I should not be murdered, but it is not in the public interest that I should anticipate the murderer's assault by killing him. It is for the common good that we rush to the defense of our neighbor, but it is not for the common good that we rush to our own defense, for in a bi-polar confrontation the community is not represented.

St. Thomas, seeking to reconcile the Augustinian doctrine on the subject with the traditions of Roman law, appealed to the principle of double effect in support of a qualified notion of self-defense.[21] The intention of saving one's life is legitimate, Thomas argued; indeed, one has a greater obligation to save one's own life than to save another's. Such force as is required to save one's own life, then, may be used, but without intending the death of the assailant, for only political authority has the right to intend the death of anyone. That last observation is quite restrictive if we take the word "intend" with full seriousness. We would have to conclude that not even to save our own life should we seek an assailant's death, but at most should seek to disable him. On this strict interpretation Thomas was still deferential to the Augustinian doctrine, though his later interpreters, like the civil law, simply assumed that killing in self-defense was a natural right. On any interpretation Thomas permits acts that may foreseeably kill the assailant — on

---

20. *De iure belli ac pacis* 2.20.14; *IG*, p. 814.
21. *Summa Theologiae* II-2.64.7.

the presumption that we have a greater responsibility to save our own life than our assailant's. This presumption is dubious. True, our own lives are the more familiar responsibility, since we dutifully eat and drink and take precautions against illness every day, while saving another's life is a rare occurrence. Yet when another's life does fall into our hands to risk or to preserve, our primary business is with it, not with ourselves, even if that life happens to belong to our enemy. We are not at that moment in the position of arbitrators, weighing up the claims of one life impartially against another; we are simply entrusted with our enemy's life, to value it or not to value it. That said, the ban on unintended but foreseeable killing should not be allowed to expand indefinitely to rule out any possible risk to the assailant. There are moments at which one should be prepared to give one's life away, others when one ought to be reluctant to do so, if only out of care for one's dependents. A good general policy is for private citizens to carry no weapons of self-defense and to keep no such weapons in their homes. A defense improvised with whatever comes to hand may perhaps be lethal to the assailant, but is certainly not calculated to be so.

The situation is different when the imperiled victim is an officer seeking to make an arrest, for the officer's safety must as such be seen as a matter of public interest. An officer in pursuance of duty may justifiably act to defend not only the life of a third person, but his or her own — and, indeed, may be *required* so to act, as the agent of political authority on the spot, in order to defend the common good. The officer is a politically authorized representative.

The execution of a suspect in the course of arrest is an event that ought to rouse great anxiety in a civilized society, since it demonstrates the fragility of the governing institutions. It is always, in an important sense, a failure. Judgment is given, but summarily and without consideration. Yet fraught with anxiety as such events are, we recognize that they may occasionally be necessary, i.e., not merely inevitable but the right thing to do in the circumstances. Though the pursuit of *ordered* judgment has failed, they are not instances of *not giving* judgment. Improvised judgment is the means by which government discharges its responsibilities, however unsatisfactorily, in extreme circumstances. When all the apparatus for considered judgment is rendered temporarily useless, agents of government may and must still judge.

International Judgment

In confining its account of just constitution to the internal function of one state in isolation, the doctrine of the three powers is easily accommodated to the the Lockean and Kantian idea of the state as a moral universe in itself, and of international relations as a morally and legally vacant state of nature, qualified only by particular treaties and conventions. Here theology as well as moral coherence must take a different path, preferring the Grotian conception that the international sphere is already law-governed of itself, being regulated by the law of God, natural and revealed, as well as by customary *ius gentium,* prior to any treaty and convention. We need, then, to add a third strand in an account of the just constitution of government, relating the authority of any given state to that of international principles and institutions.

The kingdom of God is a unified world community under God's rule. In making it the center of his proclamation, Jesus took up the expectations of ancient Israel, the hopes that Zion cherished not merely for its own peace in isolation, but for a peaceful international community. In Psalm 87:4-6, on one version of the text, men of every race were to call Zion their mother. Occasionally this hope had been envisaged in terms of an absorption of other nations into Israel, as when Deutero-Zechariah said of the coastal city-states, "they will be like a clan in Judah" (9:7). But this was the exception, and anyway it concerned cities that had historically acknowledged the throne of David. It was much more common to think of Jerusalem as a spiritual and liturgical center for the independent peoples of the world. Thus Trito-Zechariah suggested that the nations "will go up year by year to worship the king, and to keep the pilgrim feast of Tabernacles" (14:16).

From these sources Christians learned to hope for a unified world. The climax of St. John's Gospel occurs when some "Greeks" visiting Jerusalem wish to be presented to Jesus, who exclaims in reply that "the hour has come for the Son of Man to be glorified" (12:20-23). It is this hope for a universal realm that explains a certain tendency in Christian thinkers to sound an anti-political note when "politics" is associated, as it often is, with faction and division. So Tertullian, taking up the Socratic claim to be a world citizen, declares his contempt for party and status: "We are cool towards the blaze of glory and dignity, and have no need of political combinations. Nothing is more foreign to us than the *res publica.* One *res publica* we know, of which all are citizens — the universe."[1]

Faction and division are connected with pride and glory, which in turn belong to the formation of community identities. The suspicion of separate and divisive political identities is echoed throughout the patristic period. Augustine thought that no community could have an interest in whether it was self-governed or ruled by others: "Have done with the vaunting, and what are all men but men?"[2] The Romans did no wrong to the nations they ruled in ruling them, since they governed them by the same laws that they governed themselves. The wrong of the Roman empire lay in the violent conquest, driven by unbridled ambition and lust for glory, through which it was achieved. But it could be conceived, Augustine thought, that a plurality of nations would agree to place themselves voluntarily under one government. Here the greatest ancient critic of the Roman imperial project opens the door as wide as he can to the hypothetical possibility of a benign world-empire. Elsewhere he is equally ready to speculate on the hypothesis of a plurality of nations coexisting independently like so many households in a city — but this, too, is only a hypothetical possibility.[3]

Many of Augustine's contemporaries, however, did not hesitate to conclude that a unified world-empire, overcoming divisions once and for all, was the appropriate political expression for the coming of the

1. *Apologeticus* 38.
2. *City of God* 5.17.
3. *City of God* 4.15.

kingdom of God in Christ. In a fateful turn of thought early Christian apologists had found significance in the historical coincidence of the Incarnation with the Augustan settlement in Rome. What today is called (in none too friendly a tone) "Constantinianism," grew from a seed-thought on the part of Christians who still had grave moral difficulties about serving in the army or in government: the fruit of the Incarnation would be a world at peace united under a single empire. This paved the way for a very vigorous line of apologetic when the Christian empire arose. "The manifold forms of government, the tyrannies and republics, the siege of cities and devastation of countries caused thereby, were now no more, and one God was proclaimed to all mankind. At the same time one universal power, the Roman empire, arose and flourished, while the enduring and implacable hatred of nation against nation was now removed; and as the knowledge of one God and one way of religion and salvation, even the doctrine of Christ, was made known to all mankind; so at the self-same period the entire dominion of the Roman empire being vested in a single sovereign, profound peace reigned throughout the world."[4]

We are so well attuned to finding in the association of empire and peace merely the legitimation of power interests, that we can overlook too easily its appeal to the religious mind: "only concord knows God."[5] This appeal was not peculiar to the East, where Roman rule, however shaken, continued for a millennium after Constantine, but also inspired the attempts of Charlemagne and his successors. Serious advocates of voluntary world government, indeed, have not been lacking in our own era. The moral logic of their aspiration, though not its universality, has strengthened the fervor of those who have attempted to

---

4. Eusebius of Caesarea, *Speech on the Dedication of Holy Sepulchre Church (Laus Constantini)* 16; *IG,* p. 58. Cf. Prudentius, *Contra Oriationem Symmachi* 2.586-91: *discordes linguis populos et dissona cultu regna volens sociare Deus subiungier uni imperio, quidquid tractabile moribus esset, concordique iugo retinacula mollia ferre constituit, quo corda hominum coniuncta teneret religionis amor; nec enim fit copula Christo digna, nisi implicitas societ mens unica gentes.* ["God, wishing to bring into partnership peoples of different speech and realms of discordant manners, determined that all the civilized world should be harnessed to one ruling power and bear gentle bonds in harmony under the yoke, so that love of their religion should hold men's hearts in union; for no bond is made that is worthy of Christ unless unity of spirit leaves together the nations it associates."] Trans. H. J. Thomson (Cambridge, MA: Harvard University Press [Loeb Classical Library], 1949).

5. Prudentius, *Contra Oriationem Symmachi* 2.593: *sola Deum novit concordia.*

forge a political unity out of the European nations. The ideal of world government, however, has proved impossible to disentangle from the realities of the imperial-colonial enterprise. For a very short period the British empire became the nearest approximation to universal rule that the modern era had seen. Its motives, however mixed, included a heady moral idealism. But the world (and the British) repudiated this enterprise, so that today the word "colonialism" has acquired a sense almost synonymous with "tyranny." This was due to a conceptual and a practical difficulty.

Setting aside all the moral ambiguities surrounding the acquisition of colonial possessions and all the perils to world peace aroused by envy of them, the idea itself, even at its most successful and conscientious, was seen to run into a conceptual contradiction. World government is an abstract idea: the government of a people with no internal relations of mutual recognition. A people with no relations has no identity, and the government of those with no identity has no legitimacy. Whatever their claims to universality, in practice all empires need strong boundaries, which define their identity by excluding peoples who live beyond them. The practical difficulty is a direct implication of this. The more imperial rule encourages the confidence and freedom of its subjects, the more it finds its unitary governing structures under strain. To be a single political society is to act together in certain ways, to have a unitary sense of identity in certain common undertakings. When initiatives and endeavors lead in different directions, it becomes more difficult to hold them within a single decision-making structure. The more cultural pursuits flourish in an empire, then, the more oppressive the regulatory authority comes to feel. The Roman empire found that it had to function as two parallel structures, one for each of its two dominant language-groups. This points to the inevitable reality of all empire: it must recreate the "I-Thou" structure it has attempted to suppress. Practicalities have changed since it took weeks for messengers to reach Rome from Byzantium, but the need of competent communities for space to frame their own social identities and initiatives has not changed.

Properly understood, the idea of a world-people is a theological and eschatological one: it envisages mankind set free from sin to attend in worship to the ultimate "Thou," who is God. The kingdom of God can have no concrete representation upon earth except the indirect one afforded by the church. We cannot simply extend the proximate universality of a people onto the worldwide scale. Universal fellowship is a paradoxical relation, a "xenophilia," love of the foreigner, that reaches out for engagement beyond the boundaries of settled community. Richard Hooker wrote sympathetically of "the wonderful delight men have, some to visit foreign countries, some to discover nations not heard of in former ages, we all to know the affairs and dealings of other people, yea to be in league of amity with them."[6] The foreigner is a messenger from outside our world, a horizon that opens us up to the provisionality of our identities and leads us to hope for a kingdom not of this world. Love for the foreigner has an erotic character, different from the complacent affinities that bind us to our neighbors in a single political community.

From this it might seem possible to draw a conclusion directly opposed to the imperial one: since international relations transcend political identities, they can have no form except a religious and moral one; there can be no international politics. But this negative conclusion would be no less a mistake than the positive conclusion of imperialism. Our membership in the kingdom of God may be transcendent, but it can be gestured towards in the way we do our earthly justice. In the Middle Ages Christians conceived of an alternative form of witness to world order, one that lay within the "spiritual" realm, vested in the papacy. "Spiritual" authority on this account was to include the understanding of justice.[7] The law by which they sought to govern the relations of kings did not simply have to be invented; it was given to the world in the order of nature, and revealed in new clarity by the Gospel. The popes were conceived as constituting a kind of international tribunal that could pronounce authoritatively on matters of right between sovereigns where no domestic right prevailed. Controversially, this could include a

---

6. *Laws of Ecclesiastical Polity* 1.10.12.

7. Cf. Giles of Rome, *On Ecclesiastical Power* 3.5: "A temporal thing is said to be spiritual not only if it is annexed to spiritual things, but also if spiritual things are annexed to it. And since, in a sense, all crimes and all mortal sins can be called spiritual in that they slay our spirit and our soul, it follows that the spiritual power will be able to intervene in disputes involving any temporal question whatsoever if those disputes are brought forward together with an allegation of crime; for it rests with the spiritual power to judge every mortal sin and to rebuke every Christian for it." Trans. R. W. Dyson, in *IG,* p. 373.

claim to pronounce on constitutional right, the power to depose rulers whose possession of rule was radically defective.[8]

The clash between empire and papacy, whatever else it may have meant, was a clash between two forms of Christian witness to world peace, one through the forging of a single political community, the other through the association of many political communities in respect for international law. The success of the popes lay in the fact that their authority, though limited, could reach further, approximating more closely to universal rule. The claims of papalism at their best anticipate those which have driven the search for international authority in later times, and, indeed, were the original inspiration for them. When the New World opened up before the astonished gaze of Europe, it seemed as natural to say that the pope should have the responsibility for ordering it as it seems to us to say that the United Nations should have the responsibility for ordering Iraq.

On reflection the wiser heads of Vitoria and the Second Scholastic forced a reconsideration of this assumption. "Temporal" authority over the new world rested with the indigenous communities that already occupied it. "The barbarians undoubtedly possessed as true dominion, both public and private, as any Christians."[9] And except for some crime that merited war, their authority could not justly be taken from them. And although the popes' spiritual authority to depose princes was recognized in Christendom, the pagan communities of the Americas could not be expected to recognize it short of conversion to Christianity. "The reason why the barbarians cannot be compelled by force to accept Christ and his faith is that these are things for which they cannot be furnished with evident proof by natural reasonings. But much less can the dominion of the pope be so proved. Therefore they cannot be compelled by force to recognize the papal dominion."[10] The important

8. Gregory VII, *Letter* 8.21: "They have agreed as with one spirit and one voice that all major cases, all especially important affairs, and the judgments of all churches ought to be referred to her (*sc.* the Roman church) as to their head and mother, that from her there shall be no appeal, that her judgments may not and cannot be reviewed or reversed by anyone." Trans. E. Emerton, in *IG*, p. 244. *Dictatus Papae* 12: "That he may depose emperors." Trans. S. Z. Ehler and J. B. Morrall, in *IG*, p. 242.

9. Francesco di Vitoria, *De Indis* 1.6.23. Trans. A. Pagden and J. Lawrance (Cambridge: Cambridge University Press, 1991).

10. Di Vitoria, *De Indis* 2.2.31.

step taken here was to distinguish the authority of international justice, to which Vitoria never doubts that the Native Americans' right of self-government is subject, from the authority of the given institution of justice, the papacy, which could only be intelligible within the premises of Christianity.

When, however, after the high-tide of European nationalism, the West came to revisit the question of international authority, the model that found favor was a more papal than imperial one. What was needed was not world government, but a seat of judgment that could declare international right with sufficient authority to strengthen the aspirations for peace among independent political communities. "This public authority," as John XXIII put it, "having world-wide power and endowed with the proper means for the efficacious pursuit of its objective, which is the universal common good in concrete form, must be set up by common accord and not imposed by force."[11] The search for adequate institutions in the wake of the World Wars produced the United Nations organization with its General Assembly, Security Council, and dependent agencies. These differed from the papal model at two points. In the first place its function was conceived to lie in the secular, not in the spiritual realm. The division between spiritual and secular cannot correspond to a division between justice and material well-being. Justice is the business of secular government, and to give judgment is the way in which secular authority enacts justice. In the second place it does not claim to pronounce on the legitimacy of the states that comprise it.

The problem of envisaging international authority correctly is that of positing authority where there is no government. The United Nations cannot relate to the states that comprise it "federally," as a government to the subordinate social groupings within a people. It is not itself a sovereign actor in the international sphere, and exercises no representative authority on behalf of any political community — for "the international community" is not a real community, but an abstract universal. And so the UN cannot prescribe to a state with the authority that a government may use to prescribe to its subjects. Nor does it have power of its own to enforce the judgments it delivers, which are purely declarative. The UN exercises its authority wholly on suffrance of the

11. *Pacem in Terris* (1963) 138.

common will of states to act in concert. That authority can easily be brought to nothing when the common will falters.

On the other hand, it is real political authority that the UN exercises, and not merely moral or spiritual authority. Since the sphere of the international inevitably invokes a certain transcendence, it is not uncommon to attempt to sacralize the UN, to view it as a temple enclosed in its sacred *temenos*, kept apart from the profane compromise of political action in order to give voice to a claim that transcends human politics in a permanently critical posture. Of such a UN we can only say that it would be superfluous to requirements. The word of God is abroad on the earth; the community of God tastes of the life of heaven on earth. There is no vacancy for a substitute for these, and if there were, it would not take the form of a politically constituted organ with juridical, parliamentary, and administrative organization. The United Nations is important precisely as an agent of earthly politics, introducing an international point of reference that is to frame the decisions of national governments. As such it commands action, and its judgments are as much human compromises, sometimes good ones, sometimes bad ones, as all other judgments that command action. The almost audible sigh of disappointment that arose when, after the fall of the iron curtain, the UN showed signs of becoming politically active, was an indication of how little that truth was understood. It is the function of human judgment in international affairs not to freeze action into a state of permanent inaction, but to create a framework of lawfulness within which action may be responsible and coordinated.

The role of international authority is an ancillary one, though not for that reason of less importance: it is to provide a way in which states that exercise their own judgments within their own jurisdictions may combine to articulate a common judgment, when the threat of international strife makes such combination necessary. The UN offers assistance to its members, it does not supplant them. Its judgments, we may say, are not its own, but the judgments of those who sent it — and that, not in the corporate sense that political representatives act for us when they rule us, but in a more immediate sense: the judgments belong to the assembled states, because they have reached them together. What, then, is the authority of these judgments over dissentients? It is the authority of the law that is prior to any international institution and prior to any international convention, the "law of nations," an aspect of the natural right of God within creation, confirmed as such by the time-honored customs and usages of states in their dealings with one another. The whole realm of international authority is unintelligible without the supposition of such a law. The role of international institutions is to help the peoples shape their common inheritance of customary practice and universal moral conviction into a functioning international practice. It ministers to the lawfulness of states, determines the height and depth and breadth of the lawfulness to which judgments on international affairs must be formed, providing a common judgment that they can enact within their own spheres of legitimate authority.

Here we are pointing to a double asymmetry in the role of international institutions. On the one hand, there is an asymmetry between international institutions and *ius gentium,* radically understood as *ius naturale,* an aspect of the law of God. The latter is necessarily universal; the former only approximate more or less closely to universal authority, since their authority is derived from it by means of conventions. (This applies also to positive international law, which is essentially a law of custom and convention.) On the other hand, there is an asymmetry between international institutions and national. The authority of the "international community" over the political societies that constitute it, derived from their agreement to act together, is not like that of a political community over its citizens — hence the importance of the quotation marks, which are not intended to deny the importance of such a community, merely to warn against a false ontologization. In both its aspects this double asymmetry is necessitated by the rejection of contractarianism. For if we think of the political society itself as constituted by a rational agreement of citizens to act together, the formation of international institutions simply repeats the formation of political society itself, as the Kantian federal tradition supposed, with appropriate adjustments and on a larger scale. In the words of its most distinguished recent representative, it is a matter of "the extension of liberal ideas of social contract to the Law of Peoples." But the logical outcome of the contractarian proposal must be a world government. The difficulties that stand in the way of such a notion need not deflect a theory that has never acknowledged the role of political identity. So the idea of a Society of Peoples that relates symmetrically to its constituent political societies as they relate to their citizens, wobbles dangerously upon a windy edge: it is liable to topple over into asymmetry, on the one hand, and it is liable to lead to world government on the other. We must suppose that it was mere conservatism on Rawls's part that he did not make the latter move.[12] To conceive a reason why world government is not realistic is at the same time to conceive the reason why the relation between international and national cannot be symmetrical, namely, the representative identity of peoples.

International authority assists national governments in exercising each of the three powers of government, judicial, legislative, and provisionary, though without assuming the full exercise of any of them.

(i) It is initially surprising, perhaps, that courts comprise so small a part of the United Nations system. The reason is that courts require a sphere of jurisdiction in which a common legal tradition can be developed. Courts set apart from the general implementation of law within a society need to be justified by the largely self-contained character of the law which they administer. A clash of jurisdictions between one court system and another is a recipe for political instability. International courts, then, have been slow to develop because of the threat they could pose to the unified administration of law. It is generally preferable that international law should be administered by national courts. Yet there are matters for which an international court is more obvious recourse. The trial of war crimes is one such point, not only because the law of war is so relatively self-contained, comprised essentially in the Geneva Conventions and Protocols (the most important civilizational landmarks of the twentieth century) and a series of related conventions, but because the states most likely to try war crimes are also likely to be *parti pris* as combatants. It did not add to the authority of the war-crimes tribunals after the Second World War that they were mounted by the victorious allies to try the crimes of the defeated Axis. The development of a permanent and universal international war-crimes authority would seem to be one of the major international goals that remains to be achieved.

---

12. John Rawls, *The Law of Peoples* (Cambridge, MA: Harvard University Press, 2002), p. 30. Cf. p. 55: "The Law of Peoples is an extension of a liberal conception of justice for a domestic regime to a Society of Peoples." Rawls's resistance to what he calls the "cosmopolitan view" (pp. 82f.) treats it as a synthesis of incompatible ideas: global justice for individuals on the one hand, a plural system of peoples on the other. With the case against a plural system of peoples he does not, so far as I can see, engage.

What can go wrong is illustrated clearly enough by international courts outside the United Nations system. The European Court of Human Rights, one of the landmarks of the internationalism of the post-war twentieth century, has increasingly displayed a tendency to generate conflict. This conflict is not with *governments* alone, which might be forgivable, even welcome in some circumstances, but with *local expectations of justice.* The Court has acquired an unenviable reputation for making nonsense of predictable and serviceable legal arrangements in the interests of one or two determined individual plaintiffs. The fault is not simply that the Court is international (though that raises the question of how responsive it can be to local expectations), for similar problems have arisen with Bills of Rights in national jurisdictions, most notably in Canada. The fault lies in the way the Court's task was conceived, as taking individual human rights out of the fabric of law and treating them in isolation, which is incoherent. The characteristic methodology of a judgment from Strasbourg is to set aside most of the questions that would seem materially important, in order to concentrate exclusively on what it takes to be the human-rights features. But whatever a human right is — and this is not the moment to wrestle with the conceptual difficulties of that notion — it cannot be something detachable from justice. The only right worth defending is a right conferred within the operative justice of a society; and the only justice worth having is one that confers the appropriate rights. Natural right is the foundation of the positive laws of a society; it comprises not only personal inviolabilities, but also obligations of sociability. The attempt to separate the two will always tend to the fantastic — like a medicine that has become so specialized that those who treat lung complaints have no interest in the functioning of their patients' hearts. The usefulness of Britain's Human Rights Act, which has aimed to bring judgments under the Rights Convention into British courts, will be shown by whether it succeeds in reuniting the two concepts of "rights" and "law," which have become so absurdly separated.

(ii) International law, founded on custom and codified in convention, contains no statute-law, since there is no government to act "in parliament," i.e., in consultation with the people for which it legislates. Consultation among governments is not at all the same thing as consultation between government and people. What it yields is conventions, agreements to recognize the same obligations in law as other states. Conventions typically require the ratification of national parliaments, but are not in other ways open for national parliaments to shape, so they command less *prima facie* procedural legitimacy than statute-law. When a convention reinforces a universal moral perception and builds on a generally accepted practice, however, it has a crucial role in bringing to the national courts widely held moral convictions that would otherwise have been unjusticiable. The striking impact of the Convention on Torture upon the extradition laws of Western states is a positive example of how international law can function well as a framework for cooperation among jurisdictions.

It is essential, however, that law promoted by international agencies be recognizable as natural justice. International law must be solemn; it must also be rather limited in scope. The courts that are to implement it have responsibilities to their own societies and their laws. In international as in national affairs there can be too much enthusiasm for legislation. International legislation may run ahead of the capacity of national courts to enforce it and of the deliberations of peoples to ratify it. Idealistic legislation, in fact, is the curse of the international order. It is fuelled by energy from the expansive bureaucratic surplus in modern government. Ministries entrusted with affairs that lie too low in their government's priorities make common cause with their opposite numbers in other governments to promote international legislation that will force their governments to act. But the authority of international law is not well served by making it the vehicle for broadly defined practical goals for which it is difficult to secure cooperation, however worthy they are in themselves. We may well shake our heads in disbelief when we are told that a "right to development" has found its way into international law through UN mediation.

(iii) In the intense debate about the role of the Security Council in the Iraq conflict of 2003 there was frequent evidence of a misunderstanding, namely that the authorizations of that body were juridical, making given actions "legal" or "illegal" as such. But the Council's role is to coordinate the provisionary response to dangerous events, rather than to enunciate and apply accepted law. In the exercise of this authority it may and can condemn certain actions and authorize others, with an authority that imposes a legal obligation on states to desist from some actions and to support others. These condemnations and authorizations need to be consistent with existing international law, but may well not be implied by it. At the time of the Kosovo crisis such a weighty authority as Professor Ian Brownlie declared that there was no basis in international law for humanitarian intervention. But the political reality of asking any people to stand idly by and watch its neighbors be slaughtered would simply be to bring international law itself into disrepute. In such circumstances, it is for the provisionary branches of government, acting by international consensus, to go beyond codified law and authorize one another to do what God's law has clearly imprinted on the conscience of mankind.

Questions of international right may be codified generically as law, and this can dictate our handling of them to a certain degree. The law can state in universal terms that a nation that has occupied adjunct territories in a legitimate war of self-defense is entitled to found such settlements there as are necessary to protect its security. But whether Israel is justified in founding settlements in occupied Palestinian territories, and if so how many, requires a judgment not only on the legalities of the situation (which a court could make) but also on the threat that it presents to peace, which must be for agents of the provisionary power of governments to decide. It is of these that the General Assembly and the Security Council are comprised.

This accounts for a large part of the work of the United Nations: not only for the crisis-management of the Security Council, but also for the many agencies that promote policy priorities articulated in the General Assembly. But the defining feature of the provisionary work of the United Nations lies in what it does not have: a standing army answerable only to itself. This lack is not an accident or an oversight, but essential to its international character as a body that can only act when its member states act through it. If a United Nations army (as opposed to "blue beret" forces put together for the occasion by member states) were always waiting in the wings to enforce each judgment of the Security Council irrespective of national commitments, the organization would itself have become an imperial government. Yet precisely its status of dependence exposes it to risk. For the judgments that nations reach in common deliberation do not always command such overwhelming motivation as to prompt those same nations to expand their military budgets and order their troops out of barracks to support them. And perhaps that is for the best. It is no bad thing that the hard question of "what it's worth" should be before the nations of the world when they consider cooperating in a course of action that could include military conflict.

The lack of a standing military resource goes some way to explain one puzzling aspect of the current world order, the emergence of a sin-

gle superpower. When the Soviet Union collapsed in 1991, it was reasonable to think that the superpower system was at an end. Hunger for the
"peace dividend" and the lack of a serious enemy would prompt the
United States to scale back on its military investment. But this has not
happened. There are, no doubt, many reasons, but one very serious reason is that the United Nations had need of it. The Gulf War of 1991 demonstrated that it was possible to exert international authority with new
decisiveness if a powerful military partner was ready to act as the core
around which a coalition of states could group itself. The single superpower system is required by the ambitions the world has for an effective
international body. This partnership, however, began to sour almost as
soon as it was forged. (As with other currently troubling features of US
external affairs, the ominous trends were developing throughout the
nineties.) The partner wanted an international authority more account-
able for its spending and its decision-making; the authority wanted a
partner more tactful in promoting its own views on international order.
The recent descent of the partnership into mutual recrimination is the
worst possible omen for the future of international authority.

*   *   *

Such discussions invite the predictable question: is it not, after all, the
function of international authority to prevent war, rather than to fight
it? The answer has two aspects. On the one hand, the UN has been
made the focus of chiliastic aspirations for an earthly peace, often cherished before and as often disappointed. Such hopes are the prerogative
of saints and sluggards, those who can dare to believe in the coming of
God, on the one hand, and those who cannot dare to believe in the reality of human finitude and sin on the other. On the other hand, the UN
can impose a moral discipline and restraint upon war such as to transform its character.[13]

The Indo-European words for war (Lat. *bellum,* Fr. *guerre,* Engl. *war*)
point to its bilateralism. *Bellum* is *duellum,* a conflict between two parties without a third to mediate. This is the formal distinction between
what is undertaken in war and what is undertaken in domestic justice.

13. For a fuller treatment of what follows see my essay, *The Just War Revisited* (Cambridge: Cambridge University Press, 2003).

It does not matter whether the two parties are distinct peoples, or factions within the same people, or even individuals; or whether one of them, or both, or neither is a government. The unmediated pitting of one party against another is what constitutes war and merits the disapprobation of war as lawless anarchy. Yet this formal description does not account for all the moral possibilities of war. For we may recognize that such moments of apparently unmediated conflict are, in fact, not unmediated at all. They are mediated by the law of God that governs all relations among humankind. The first step in transforming war is to bring bilateral conflict under the control of this recognition.

The project in Christendom which now goes by the not wholly enlightening name of "just war theory" — it is not a theory, and is not about just wars! — understands war as the paradigm case of *iudicium cessans*. "The only reason for it," as Suárez wrote, "is that an act of punitive justice is indispensable to mankind, and that no more fitting means for it is forthcoming within the limits of nature and human action."[14] Vitoria, in the powerful peroration of his *Relectio* on the law of war, urges the victor to "think of himself as a judge sitting in judgment between two commonwealths, one the injured party and the other the offender."[15] The anarchic logic of self-defense is thus replaced by the ordered logic of judgment. *Iudicium cessans* affirms a right and duty to act in judgment when institutions that ought to act are unavailable. For there can be no vacuum of judgment. At the same time, it affirms the logic of judgment by which such improvised action is disciplined. In a state of war we face a threat which it falls outside the competence of any judiciary to control; the responsibility for improvising judgment falls back upon the first power of government. As in an emergency when a police officer confronts an armed and dangerous criminal, the situation is formally a duel, yet morally the triangular relation of judge to victim and assailant dictates the permissions that govern the proceedings. *Iudicium cessans*, the "judgment unavailable," is still *iudicium intelligibile*, a judgment that is thinkable. In the light of God's judgment we can and must conceive what judgment requires, and conceiving it, we can freely bind ourselves to it as a moral discipline of action.

14. *De triplici virtute theologica* 3.13.4.7; *IG*, p. 739.
15. *De iure belli relectio* 3.9.60. Trans. A. Pagden and J. Lawrance (Cambridge: Cambridge University Press, 1991).

This was how the moral logic of the just war theory gave rise to the political realities of international authority. The thinkable judgment could be made actual by founding a seat of judgment. Yet one does not escape from the logic of *iudicium cessans* merely by founding institutions. *Iudicium cessans* is the limiting condition of the United Nations, as of all political institutions: the UN has authority only for as long as it continues to fashion and carry through policy for dealing with unfolding events. When it loses its grip, its authority to command lapses. We recall from the crisis of January 2003 that it was the threat of the use of the veto that caused the initiative to fall from the hands of the Security Council. For the veto functions like an electrical circuitbreaker, switching the power off when there is danger of an overload. The power on which the Security Council depends is the cooperation of its members, without which it can command no authority. It cannot be used to serve a strategy of denial. The Security Council may command authoritatively that something shall be done in a crisis; but it cannot command authoritatively that nothing shall be done in a crisis.

Fragile as the authority of the UN is, the effect of its operations is of very great importance. In late 2002, when the world argued passionately over whether it could be right for the UN to authorize war against Iraq, there lay behind this debate another debate on a question of even greater significance, about which the two principal military allies disagreed. On what grounds could it be right to go to war? Would grounds of preventive self-defense be sufficient, or would the only sufficient ground be the need to vindicate international authority? This was a debate about all wars, or more precisely, about the role of international authority in authorizing any war. When there is an effective international authority, the presenting cause for armed conflict will always be that its attempts to regulate a dangerous situation have been defied, and must be upheld. This does not abolish armed conflict, which is a Utopian dream, but it does two important things: it brings conflict under the political discipline of third-party arbitration, and it prevents the rush to war ahead of serious conciliatory efforts.

In the course of the past three chapters we have explored three contributory strands in an answer to the question of the just constitution of a representative structure: one in terms of an entitlement derived from a historic act of popular legitimation; one in terms of an internal form that gives proper scope to the articulation of judgment; and one in terms of an international system of cooperation and respect for the authority of international law. These criteria govern our prospective judgments about how we may set up a government, and they govern our retrospective judgments on how well an act of constitution has been performed. But our judgments do not determine the authority of the political community that has been constituted. Political authority arises from the co-incidence of judgment and representation, not from judgment alone. Neither separately nor together do these criteria provide a definition of a representative structure that could be used to validate or invalidate a state. And so they do not entitle us to rule out ill-constituted states as nullities. For representation is a relation not reducible to other relations; its occurrence is demonstrated ostensively, by recognition.

This was the point overlooked in the Hildebrandine claim to an authority to depose ill-constituted governments. It rested on the assumption that international authority was derived immediately from God, and that national authority was derived from it. The truth is the opposite: while the kingdom of God is not present on earth, such international authorities as there are must rest on a foundation of peoples below them. Ill-constituted states may sometimes need to be punished for their crimes or prevented from committing them, but they cannot simply be set aside for failing to reach a formal threshold of constitutional adequacy. This was the point that the thinkers of the Second Scholastic made against the claim that papal authority could ignore the indigenous American societies and confront the New World as a clean sheet — persuasively, but alas! too late.

Christians, if they are wise, will understand upholding international authority as a duty of practical political reason in obedience to the hope of the Gospel. But this will have nothing to do with secular millenarian hopes, whether for the superseding of the nation-state or for the abolition of war. International authority is not itself an object of faith nor a matter of prophecy, for it is not itself the rule of God over the world. It is a simple assistance in ordering the agreements and conflicts of peoples, the disasters, the fears and the achievements, the wars and rumors of wars, within a framework of human lawfulness. Those to whom that does not seem a great gain must be reminded that to demand everything is to get nothing. We must make those gains for peace that are open to us to make. "For God is not a God of disorder, but of peace" (1 Cor. 14:33).

PART III

Life Beyond Judgment: Communication

13

Judge Not!

In opposition to every politics of identity and self-complacency God has set the cross of Jesus Christ, before which, as the prophet said, "kings shall shut their mouths" (Isa. 52:15). In Christ's cross he "has disarmed the rules and authorities, and made a triumphant public display of them" (Col. 2:15). It is a *royal* cross, challenging the conditions of earthly political authority with the coming of the kingdom of God. "Now is the judgment of this world; now shall the ruler of this world be cast out" (John 12:31). "The world" is a concretized spiritual possibility, an identity asserted apart from God's gift. In refusing divine judgment, the world refuses reality, and in refusing reality, "the form of the world," as St. Paul says, "passes away" (1 Cor. 7:31). At every point in history passing identities with every appearance of solidity are confronted with the solidity of the cross, which has the appearance of passing away.

New Testament writers often refer to "rules and authorities," or "rulers of this world," subdued before Christ who is exalted "above every rule and power and lordship" (Eph. 1:21f.) It is correct to understand these as political entities; yet in that they are conceived as supramundane and angelic beings, it is their *spiritual* character that is singled out, their capacity to shape the identity of all who serve them. Thus in the book of Daniel we find angels representing the powers of the Near East, fighting out the region's fate among themselves. The political rulers of the world are angelic and spiritual precisely because they are representative; and they are political rulers precisely because they are angelic and spiritual. In the cross they meet the final representative identity of mankind. "And I, when I am lifted up from the earth, will draw all men to myself" (John 12:32).

The cross challenges the *aesthetic* basis of representative rules and authorities. The ugliest of sights, the humiliated and tortured figure with "no form or comeliness" (Isa. 53:2), has, in a decisive reversal of visual-aesthetic value, become the object of profoundest attraction. The public aesthetic of the cross has revealed new possibilities for political action, evoking compassion as a politically uniting force and empowering the martyr and the oppressed.[1] "This beauteous form assures a pitious minde."[2] True followers and false imitators of the cross have between them changed the shape of earthly politics: Ambrose's "tyranny of impotence" has many victories to its score.[3] As a visible emblem the cross has drawn men, women, and children into a universal community of attention, overreaching the bounds of their national, tribal, and family identities. Buildings that display it have become the focus of cities and the landmarks of rural communities. Its representations in high visual art command continual astonishment. A roomful of tourists in Ghent Cathedral, standing and staring with intense stillness at the Van Eycks' *Adoration of the Lamb*, reenact unconsciously the very scene depicted there: pilgrims who stand and gaze at the sight of the sacrificed lamb, the goal and satisfaction of their journeys. And with the pilgrims and the hermits standing before the heavenly city we find judges and soldiers, looking on the true object of their exertions in our earthly cities. Here, indeed, is something to be seen, a sight which, for as long as it is in the world, will organize the world around itself, never eclipsed by the leering faces on election posters and television screens. The *sweet cross (dulce lignum)* has outshone the glamor and attraction that binds us to our political leaders; it has shown their appeal to be shallow and moody, by calling out the deepest springs of our loyalty and love. In the cross God has pronounced his "Ichabod!" upon the limelight of human importance.

The cross challenges the *covenant with death* which the rules and au-

---

1. Cf. J. G. Hamann's remarks about "the aesthetic conformity to the cross" that "disarms the tyranny of prevailing usages of speech," quoted in Oswald Bayer, *Freiheit als Antwort* (Tübingen: Mohr-Siebeck, 1995), p. 295.

2. John Donne, "Holy Sonnets" 9 (1633).

3. *Epistle* 75.23: *Habemus tyrannidem nostram. Tyrannis sacerdotum infirmitas est.*

thorities have made. For the inexorable rule of human tradition is that societies flourish only on the manure of their dead members' flesh. Our civilizations are all whitewashed tombs, their culture made available to each new generation by the dying of the previous one. Every self-conscious culture knows what it owes to death, that debt of "room" within the time-space framework that can neither be paid for by gratitude nor even regretted. This knowledge is its guilty nostalgia, the "haunting sense of loss" of which the hymn speaks, willing the past deeds and thoughts of former generations as the support of present deeds and thoughts, while still willing them past and gone. Our predecessors are our human sacrifice. But through the *cross of life* God has taken his place alongside the dead, our victims. He has exposed our melancholy collusion with death by revealing the resurrection of the dead, and by calling to existence a communion of the dead with the living.

The cross challenges the *exclusion* by which the rules and authorities define their identities. Representative political authorities include only by excluding. They exclude those who do not belong to them, and they exclude those who, while belonging, incur their condemnation. Restrictive immigration on the one hand, penal exclusion from society on the other, are not occasional illiberal lapses, but brute conditions of political order. From within the logic of political community these two categories of exclusion appear different; from outside they appear very much the same. Whether for "trespasses" or for "uncircumcision of the flesh," the "bond with its legal requirements" stands over against them (Col. 2:13, 14). But in the *reconciling cross* God has taken upon himself the "reproach" of the political authorities, "outside the gate" (Heb. 13:12f.). He has exposed the limits of their just order; he has shown up the restrictions of their sympathies, asserting in their place a kingdom truly universal in its scope.

It is the decisive test of a political theology, whether and how clearly it can articulate this counter-political moment in the New Testament proclamation of the cross, with its moral implication: "Judge not, that you be not judged!" (Matt. 7:1). Political theology has set its face from the beginning against an *a*-political theology — that is to say, a theology that simply disinterests itself in the order of social life and the practice of judgment, and presents the Gospel wholly as a realm of the spirit available to solitary individuals. It is a matter of debate as to whether such an apolitical theology has ever been propounded in a pure form, and by whom, or whether we merely have to guard against tendencies that could, if uncorrected, lead to it. However that may be, recent political theology has countered such tendencies by referring not to the more positive accounts of politics that may be found in the New Testament, but to these fundamental *counter*-political claims. For the counter-political is not apolitical. It is not indifferent, but takes its stand within the sphere of political claims. The overthrowing of the rules and authorities on God's part is a political act.

Given this starting point, however, another false trail offers itself, which, though setting off in another direction, ends up in very much the same place. That is the totalizing of politics within the framework of the counter-political. The overthrowing of the rules and authorities is the matrix within which a "critical" politics is formed. This politics has as its goal the formless dispersal of political power to all worthwhile human enterprises. But that is an incoherent goal; for the power of politics is a socially formed power that operates to maintain social form. Loss of form means depoliticization, and depoliticization means loss of power — absolutely, and not merely by redistribution. Political theology that follows this route often ends up paradoxically banishing politics as a theme of discussion, since every conceivable human enterprise, from biblical criticism to blowing our noses, is hailed as a "political" gesture — meaning no more than that it is undertaken in a self-assertive and anti-authoritarian spirit.

Political power taken out of the formal disciplines of judgment evaporates into the unrealized and unrealizable. Because judgment is, from the beginning, an act and not an institution, the power to judge can be improvised and seized hold of. The Gospel warning against the pretensions of government, "Judge not!" may evoke a false echo: a hundred thousand voices call to their neighbors, "Judge not!," and then . . . judge! The history of modernity since the seventeenth century has been the history of demoticized judgment, in which a people determined to be free has failed to understand that freedom is the fruit of *not*-judging. Kierkegaard, writing in 1846, described as well as anyone could the character of the society that judges demotically. "The public" is an abstract power, a "phantom," that has devised the press as its public expression, a substitute for a real and passionate crowd. Never assembled, never making policy, never following through on any lead that it itself gives, it is inconsistent in its judgments and knows no principle of action except envy — the strategy of denial that "stifles and impedes."[4] One can only wonder at how many, otherwise observant of the world around them, continue to conduct themselves as in a world of despots, guarding against the dangers posed to freedom by the judgments of governments and failing to guard against the unaccountable judgments of "the public"! We may notice John Rawls's astonishing opinion that a "well ordered society," i.e., a liberal democracy, can only engage in expansionist and aggressive policies when the people are deceived by their political leaders.[5] Perhaps it is not wholly innocent, this failure to observe the modern condition. For it would require of us a severe honesty about where we get our judgments from, and how we deploy them.[6]

Kierkegaard can be of help, too, in understanding the psychological character of this totalized politics. It suffers from an excess of possibility over necessity; it is an infinity that lacks the finitude to become actual. The totalized politics embraces everything, so that we become nothing in respect of it, with no way to define our social agency in relation to it. The vis-à-vis of our multiple ends-of-action and the protection afforded them by the political act collapses. We have no way of distinguishing what our lives are really about from the measures we take to defend them. So a well-conceived political theology begins from the point of transition between the political and the counter-political, the defining limit where closure is imposed upon the act of judgment, an opening made for that free activity of *not judging.* That point is marked by the command to obey. This command has sometimes, of course, been the one and only political command remembered by an apolitical theology, and is therefore, understandably, suspect in political theology. It has too often been the door by which the form of the political has been expelled from theological consideration. But it can also be the door by which the political re-enters. The "power to obey," as Kierkegaard said, is the power to submit to the necessity in ourselves, to accept ourselves as a "perfectly definite something."[7] So it was that

4. *A Literary Review,* trans. Alistair Hannay (Harmondsworth: Penguin Books, 2001), pp. 67-86.

5. *The Law of Peoples* (Cambridge: Harvard University Press, 2002), pp. 51-54.

6. See my *Common Objects of Love* (Grand Rapids: Eerdmans, 2002), pp. 69f.

7. *The Sickness Unto Death,* trans. Walter Lowrie (Princeton: Princeton University Press, 1941), p. 169.

the suffering servant fulfilled his vocation — not apolitically! — by "opening not his mouth" before "oppression and judgment" (Isa. 53:7f.) By obedience we determine ourselves not to judge at the point where judgment *has* been given, not to perpetuate the act of judgment, but to allow it to be overtaken by the goal it was intended to serve, that of free social engagement. This act of not-judging is an end of judgment in a positive as well as a negative sense. Judgment cannot reach its completion without it, and so it is in its own way an act of judgment upon an act of judgment. It is what Jesus calls "judging for yourselves."

When we judge for ourselves, we judge that the good that God by his own judgment has set before us to do is now open for us to do. When we persist in judging when judgment should have been given closure, we impose a division between evil and good that no longer corresponds to God's own division, and so fails to put before us the good that God has willed for us to do. We assert our own knowledge of the good at variance with his.[8] That means that we place our common action on a false footing: we form our political solidarities arbitrarily — in terms, as Carl Schmitt implacably put it, of "friend and enemy."[9] But even friendships formed in this way are, of course, little more than truces between enemies.

False politicization is a temptation to philosophy as well as to theology. Plato's unhappy attempt to turn Dionysius of Syracuse into a philosopher-king is the perennial reminder of philosophy's limitations in this respect. "Back from Syracuse?" asked a witty colleague of Heidegger, when he returned to teaching after his equally disastrous foray into Nazi politics as University Rector.[10] The too-easy inference of policy from world-description produces an idealist politics that corrupts the practice it hoped to perfect. Plato and Heidegger were both

---

8. On this see, famously, the section of Dietrich Bonhoeffer's *Ethik* entitled "Die Liebe Gottes und der Zerfall der Welt," ed. I. and H. E. Tödt, E. Feil, and C. Green (Gutersloh: Kaiser, 1998), pp. 301-41. English trans. N. Horton-Smith (London: Collins, 1964), pp. 17-54.

9. "The specific political distinction to which political actions and motives can be reduced is that between friend and enemy." *The Concept of the Political,* trans. G. Schwab (Chicago: University of Chicago Press, 1996). I owe the quotation to Mark Lilla, *The Reckless Mind: Intellectuals in Politics* (New York: New York Review Books, 2001), p. 56.

10. Lilla, *Reckless Mind,* p. 43. In what follows I am further indebted to Lilla's chapter on Heidegger.

fortunate to get away with a bad fright; it would have been much worse if they had been successful. And among theologians, how should we not recall the admirably principled Savonarola, who suffered something worse than a bad fright? Nearer our own time there have been many who found Marxism a convenient conduit to guide the streams of Christian reformist passion into the water-pots of a political program, and they, too, have been exposed to humiliating results. There was, for instance, the sad case of the high-minded church-based organization devoted to "fair trade": importing goods on a non-profit basis from producers whose treatment of their labor-force could be vouched for, it found it did not have enough goods of this kind to fill a handsome sales-catalogue; so it embraced the policy of importing freely from selected countries where labor policies seemed beneficently anti-capitalist. Thus it became a channel for imports from the People's Republic of China, heavily dependent at the time, as later became notorious, on slave-labor.

It was the need for a fence against this error that gave currency to the secularist dogmas of our time. I use the term "dogmas" here not as a term of abuse, but quite strictly, to indicate the role of secularism as an operative rule of intellectual procedure meant to govern the possibilities of thought *a priori*. If there has been a tentative renewal of political theology in the West in recent decades (of which this essay and its predecessor are one attempt among others), it has been prompted by the recognition that a *cordon sanitaire* between politics and theology, or between politics and philosophy, cannot claim intelligibly to be a *pre-condition* for thought, but only an *imposition* on it, and therefore has within itself the character of tyranny. There could undoubtedly be worse tyrannies than that of the regnant liberal secularism, so sensitively averse to overt physical suffering. That much must always be said in its favor. But what cannot be said for it is that it fosters freedom. For in attempting to dictate what is true on the basis of what is convenient, it shuts down the human calling to the knowledge of the truth.

Politics may honestly insist on practicality, and refuse to be asked — by anyone, and for any reason — to attempt what cannot be done. Yet the demand for practical politics may all too easily be a dishonest ruse to evade a more searching demand, which is to re-conceive the possibilities of politics within a transcendent horizon. Politics, however practical, may not forbid the philosopher or theologian to think in public about a practice-transcending practice. Thought must not be denied its "realistic Utopia." It must not be forced to choose between abstract speculation with no practical import and a close-up deliberative casuistry imprisoned by immediate practicalities. At this point, surely, a rejection of ideological politics must offer something better than Hannah Arendt's boast, fortunately empty, to view politics "with eyes unclouded by philosophy." Thinking may be led horribly astray, but the only corrective for thinking gone astray is thinking better.

Political theology is in a position to make the corrective move. It can speak not only of the ways of judgment, but of the ways to and from judgment. It has heard Jesus say, "Judge not!" and it has heard him say, "Why do you not judge for yourselves?"; and it can trace the line of thought by which judging for ourselves becomes the first step towards not judging. The society that refrains from judging is not a society *without* judgment, persisting in primal innocence before the knowledge of wrong. Not-judging is not detachment from judgment, nor a bewildered shrug of the shoulders in the face of its imponderable demands. On the contrary, it is a society that has felt the need for judgment, has cried to God for judgment, and has seen it revealed in Christ; and believing what it has seen, it has judged for itself. A society that refrains from judgment does so because it has the judgment of God to defer to. Living under God's judgment, then, and embracing it as the law of its life, it is free not to judge, since all human judgment is merely interim, waiting for the judgment that is to come. Such an earthly society is "unpolitical" in a helpful sense, because its politics of expectancy has gone to the heart of the political and emerged into life beyond judgment. Through the lens of this post-political society, political theology can view as in a mirror the pre-political society of God's creation, and can understand political judgment as a moment in parentheses between the two, an interim service that is a "definite something," with its defined beginning and its defined end.[11] In political theology — for the first time, we may say, in the light of the proclamation of the kingdom of God — the vis-à-vis of the political act and the social life comes clearly into view.

Sometimes political theology is presented as the *whole* of theology:

---

11. Cf. John Ponet, *A Short Treatise of Political Power* 50; *IG,* p. 700: "Civil power is a power and ordinance of God appointed to certain things, but no general minister over all things."

its goal is then taken to be a (more or less reconstructed) set of theological beliefs on the presupposition of a (more or less unargued) set of political postures.[12] A hybrid of Catholic and Protestant apologetics, this mode of political theology brings the Protestant interest in doctrinal reconstruction into contact with the Catholic interest in verifying doctrine by the authority of the church. In such an exercise the political positions never become an object of interrogation in their own right. Yet neither are the Christian beliefs given scope to validate themselves on their own terms, but are forced to show themselves amenable to the political positions established on the page before the book began. To build theological belief on public doctrine (*doxa* in Plato's sense) always carries a high degree of risk, for public doctrine generated out of local tradition may acquire a patina of self-evidence as short-lived as it is, for the moment, overwhelming. Public doctrine about political morality is especially subject to the vagaries of tradition, since the dissenter is exposed not only to disagreement but to opprobrium, and conformity imposes itself with even greater force.

Political theology, rather, is an intellectual enquiry located on the horizon of the theology of the church. Every aspect of theology is a pursuit *of* the church; but theology also has a self-descriptive moment when it speaks *about* the church, "ecclesiology." The self-descriptive moment then leads out to a missionary horizon, where the church encounters the "other" that is summoned into the church, the world that God is redeeming. It is on this missionary horizon that political theology arises. Political theology is not ecclesial self-description directly, but a description of the world as it appears on this horizon, prepared for the church's mission by the Holy Spirit that runs ahead of the church. As ecclesiology belongs within the doctrine of the Holy Spirit, so does political theology; but since the Holy Spirit always attests the Father and the Son, so political theology, too, properly has a trinitarian shape. That is the reason for setting its content out, as we have done in the three parts of this work, as judgment, representation, and communication. Under each of these considerations the world is seen from the church's horizon as vis-à-vis to the church. In the first place we speak of the God-given right of judgment within the world, and of the

12. To cite one recent example of this program, we may mention Kathryn Tanner, *The Politics of God* (Minneapolis: Fortress Press, 1992).

church's deference to that right, not usurping the privileged sphere of secular judgment. In the second place we speak of the God-given representative of mankind, and of the church's challenge to all other political representations. And in the third place we speak of the eschatological summons to social communication, and of the church's modeling of communication as life beyond judgment.

As the model for the communication of the Spirit in the world, the church is defined as the community that "judges not," but bears witness to a final judgment. To speak of the church as a "counterpolitical" society is in constructive tension with speaking of it as a "political society."[13] It is the bearer of a discourse that defers judgment, seeking further reflection and a discourse "between the times" in the moment of God's patience. This discourse is its life, both as an announcement and as a lived display. For the church is the community within which the Spirit is "given," representing the eschatological identity of humankind, and embodying it provisionally for all to see and enter. Ultimately the church will judge, for God has given judgment to the twelve apostles who are seated on the twelve thrones of the patriarchs of Israel. But the revelation of the church as *polis*, living immediately under the rule of God, coincides with the revelation of the church as *bride*, in marital fellowship with God. The completion and finalization of political order under the free and worshipping embrace of God's rule coincides with the completion and finalization of social order in complete and uncoerced fellowship with God. Precisely because this is its true political nature, we may speak of the church as "postpolitical," revealing the final form of human society. In face of the church all previous identities are shown to be merely provisional, waiting to be brought under that final universal identity and subordinated to it.

The third aspect of political theology, then, we might call "pure social theory." It is an account of what it means for human beings to live together without judging, an account, prescinding from political authority and judgment, of the social humanity that the world is summoned by the Spirit of God to become. To that extent it is also implicitly a description of the church, though, again, an abstract description, prescinding from the missionary vis-à-vis, the historically necessary

13. Cf. *Desire of the Nations* (Cambridge: Cambridge University Press, 1996), pp. 158-74.

confrontation of church and world. In understanding the church, like Israel, as the "chosen people" and the "sanctified race" (1 Pet. 2:9), the apostles understood it as the paradigm society; which means not that the church conforms to some general conception of society, but that society anticipates in some measure, and in some measure falls short of, the sociality modelled in the church. This is not, of course, to be misunderstood as an exclusivist suggestion — which would be self-defeating, and frankly incredible — that only within the church do we find social coexistence. Social coexistence is wherever human existence is. But the church is the locus of social renewal and recovery. It summons created fellowship back from judging to acting, back to open sociability from hardened political identities. The church as the "end" of political community is the matrix within which the created shape of human sociality emerges into view.

For sociality itself is not a bare empirical *datum,* but a historical and eschatological destiny. It is something we cannot pretend to get behind, as though there were a pre-social individual human nature with "basic needs" that generated society as an instrument for its own protection. When God said, "It is not good for man to be alone," that was not an afterthought, but the determining moment in the creation of the human race. On the other hand, society is elaborated in history towards a *plerôma,* its full coming-to-expression. The church displays the necessary character of social coexistence, but displays it as a divine summons to human freedom, not as a closed and coercive system, as it can too easily appear when observed only from outside, sociologically. In the church we look forward to the sociality of the human race gathered around the throne of God and of the Lamb, and we look back upon the given sociality of the race in its creation, apart from sin and the necessity of human rule.

14

Communication

How, then, are we to describe in general terms the active social life that exists before and after judgment, and apart from it? What categories shall "pure social theory" call upon? In conceiving society as "communication," we draw primarily on a favorite expression of St. Paul, *koinōnia*, which has inspired ecumenical approaches to the theology of the church in the last generation.[1] The scope of this word is shown by the English nouns that may be needed to translate it: concrete "community" on the one hand, dynamic "communion" or "communication" on the other. Its active sense is kept alive by the closely associated words *koinōnein*, "to communicate," and *koinōnos*, "one who communicates," and it continues to be felt in the medieval Latin of the scholastics, who could refer even to a concrete community as a *communicatio*, a "sphere of communication." To "communicate" is to hold some thing as common, to make it a common possession, to treat it as "ours," rather than "yours" or "mine." The partners to a communication form a community, a "we," in relation to the object in which they participate. The object may be material goods, and *koinōnia* may stand for charitable giving, or alms (Rom. 15:26).[2] But the church is also

1. The work of the late Jean-Marie Tillard OP is a landmark of this development. See his *Church of Churches,* trans R. de Peaux (Collegeville, MN: Liturgical Press, 1992). See also Walter Kasper, "*Communio:* The Guiding Concept of Catholic Ecumenical Theology," in *That They May All Be One* (London and New York: Burns & Oates, 2004), pp. 50-74.

2. Using a different verb, St. Luke tells us that the first word of John the Baptist to the crowds who asked him what they should do, was: "share" (Luke 3:11).

and supremely the "communication of the Holy Spirit" (2 Cor. 13:14). It is the Spirit which the church shares; yet the Spirit is also the ground for sharing everything else "*in* the Spirit." In holding the Spirit as common possession, the church is possessed as a community by the Spirit. There may also, unhappily, be *koinōnia* in demons (1 Cor. 10:20). But in the *koinōnia* of the Spirit the church's unity is assured, for it is characteristic only of the "dumb" spirits of pagan worship that they lead spirit-possessed individuals off "in all directions" (1 Cor. 12:2). Within the church the spiritual endowments and contributions of individual members converge upon a common life and a common confession, "Jesus is Lord" (1 Cor. 12:3), and individual communications of various kinds are "distributions" (*diaireseis*, 12:4-6), particular performances within the divine operation of a single organic whole.[3]

But we also have in mind that this term had an important function for John Wyclif, who used it to elaborate his distinctive conception of a "lordship" *(dominium)* that did not depend on property. "Lordship" he defines as "the disposition of a rational being by which it is assigned control over someone or something who serves it."[4] Communication "is not inconsistent with true lordship, neither does lordship necessarily imply property."[5] Property means "lordship without communication on equal terms," i.e., what we might call "absolute" property, allowing no obligation to anyone else in respect of what is one's own.[6] God's own lordship is exercised not by keeping his own to himself, but by "communication." Nothing is more characteristic of him than "lending" — not giving outright, since God cannot alienate from himself the lordship of any created thing, but he can and does bring human beings into fellowship with him in the disposition of all that he

---

3. In the earliest and longest of his three discussions of the "gifts" in 1 Cor. 12, Paul places his emphasis wholly upon unity, though this is obscured by modern English translations, which like to render διαιρέσεις as "varieties." It is true that in illustration he makes some use of the principle of diversity of complementary functions, but the concern of the argument does not lie with the convergence of *generic* differences of function but with *individual* contributions: "*to each* is given the manifestation (φανέρωσις) of the Spirit for the common good" (12:7). The theme is differently angled in the discussion in Romans 12, and differently again, with an emphasis on church office, in Ephesians 4.

4. *De divino dominio* 1.1.1d.

5. *De divino dominio* 3.1.70c. English translation, *IG*, p. 487.

6. *De civili dominio* 1.18.40c, *IG*, p. 495.

has made.[7] That God has done this universally, i.e., shared creation as a whole with mankind as a whole, is the ground on which we have a communicative interest in anything whatever. But that interest depends on our responsiveness to God's communication. So, in Wyclif's most famously controversial thesis, "any and every righteous man is lord of the whole sense-perceptible world," and in receiving any thing we receive the whole world with it.[8] In communicating the goods of creation with one another we discover a radical equality with one another in relation to God. For none of us is the *source* of a communication that he makes with another, since we all hold whatever we communicate directly from Christ.[9]

To communicate something is to hold it as a common possession. We may summarize the logic in the formula: *This "mine" is "ours."* "The full number of those who believed were of one heart and soul, and no one said that any of the things that belonged to him was his own, but they had everything in common," reports St. Luke (Acts 4:32). This is a composite statement of what it means to call the early church a "community," *koinōnia:* there was unity of "heart and soul" and communication of material goods. The unity of heart and soul was expressed in the conviction with which they declared the apostles' message (4:31). The material communication was essentially a way of understanding the meaning of property: Christians had "things that belonged" to them, *huparkhonta,* but they did not see them as *idia,* "their own," but as *koina,* "common," not "mine," but "ours."

(i) This logic must be distinguished, in the first place, from: *This "mine" is "yours."* Communication is not an act of *absolute bestowal.* The "mine" is not cancelled, but taken up into the larger "ours." In human society there is no bestowal in which the donor merely negates his or her relation to the object. The exception, perhaps, is a bequest to take effect upon our death. A gift that implies our disappearance can be made only as we leave the human community altogether; but since "all live to God," perhaps even that is only an apparent exception. The transmission of any good from one person to another creates a relation through which we enjoy the object in a new way together. When I give a

---

7. *De divino dominio* 3.4.78a, *IG,* pp. 487f.
8. *De civili dominio* 1.7.15d, 16d, *IG,* p. 488.
9. *De civili dominio* 3.13.93d, *IG,* p. 491.

present to my son, I deprive myself of something, yet I am satisfied when I see him making use of it; the link between myself and my son completes my interest in the gift. If he subsequently refers to "your gift," the use of the possessive pronoun "your" is not in the least strained. But what if there is no conscious link? Suppose I give anonymously to a charity for refugees, and the refugees never know from whom the gift came? My gift is still a factor in my continuing interest in the refugees; and if I have *no* continuing interest, that, so far from proving my gift sincere, puts it in a rather dubious light. My sincerity as a giver is proved by the satisfaction I take in their welfare.

The idea of absolute and unmotivated bestowal has been held in high admiration in some Christian circles, and has often been said to be the true meaning of Christian love, *agapē*. This moral misunderstanding is due to two theological misunderstandings. On the one hand, it arises from a deist conception of creation, by which God, in conferring being on the creation, removes himself from it. In Jewish and orthodox Christian doctrine creation is a covenant, grounding a *coexistence* of God and his creatures. The Garden of Eden is the first communication, the space where God and humankind are to be at home together. On the other hand, it arises from a negative conception of salvation, by which perfection is conceived as the annihilation of desire. But the teaching of Jesus on selfless giving is not that we should desire nothing, but that we should desire *one* thing, the eschatological community of the kingdom of heaven.[10]

(ii) In the second place, the logic of communication is not the logic of exchange. If we describe the logic of communication as, *This "mine" is "ours,"* exchange may be characterized as, *This "mine" is yours, this "yours" mine.* The "mine" returns to me as "mine" in another form, the "yours" to you as "yours" in another form. Exchange is the project of enhancing existing relations of distinct subjects to objects, the "mine" and the "yours," by causing the two subject-object relations to interact — but only as a means to the development of each on its own terms. The project of exchange terminates in the enhanced return of the mine and the yours to their original owners.

---

10. Cf. Matt. 6:1-5, "They have their reward." On the *locus classicus* for this issue, the 17th-century dispute about Quietism between Bossuet and Fénélon, see further Chapter 16, below.

John Milbank, who has been to the fore in criticizing the idea of love as self-sacrifice, has advocated an alternative that "rejects any one-sided 'personalism,'" that of "gift-exchange."[11] The full scope of his account of gift-exchange has yet to be expounded; but while awaiting further developments, we may venture a comment on Milbank's programmatic statement that "gift is an exchange . . . because it is asymmetrical reciprocity and non-identical repetition." "Exchange" is not synonymous with "reciprocity" or "repetition"; still less is it synonymous with "participation," another term that Milbank places in close connection with it. "Exchange" imports the idea of closure to a transaction, restoring the parties to the independence of the *status quo ante*, each strengthened by the return of value in a different form. The chiasmus symbolized in the letter X depicts not only a meeting of the ways but a parting. Much of profound significance may be said by way of the chiasmus about the engagement of God with mankind: how could we overlook, for example, the role of chiasmic motifs in J. S. Bach's musical meditations on the cross? But exchange can be no more than a moment in some more ultimate settlement. The chiasmus must find rest in a cadence that brings its polyphonic voices to a final harmony. The substitutionary moment of the cross must issue in the union of resurrection.[12]

The concept of exchange is not fundamental to community. It is a device, abstract and formal, created together with the institution of trade, the market. To trade is to effect an exchange of goods between two otherwise equal and unrelated agents. By entering the exchange, each converts the form of his possessions: from consumables to durables, from raw materials to artifacts, or however his projects require. It is therefore only a preliminary to actually doing something with the pos-

11. On self-sacrifice see especially his "Grace: The Midwinter Sacrifice," in *Being Reconciled: Ontology and Pardon* (London and New York: Routledge, 2003), pp. 138-61. We are promised more extensive work on gift-exchange (p. x), but we already have a preliminary sketch in "Can a Gift Be Given? Prolegomena to a Future Trinitarian Metaphysic," *Modern Theology* 11, no. 1 (1995). The "gift-exchange" is distinguished from pure exchange by the manner in which the return is made: delayed, non-identical and, as is sometimes added, indirect, involving the recipience of a third party. For another gesture in a similar direction see Stephen H. Webb, *The Gifting God: a Trinitarian Ethics of Excess* (New York: Oxford University Press, 1996).

12. Milbank may not perhaps be resistant to such thoughts, to judge from the opaque hint, that "forgiveness . . . perfects gift-exchange as fusion." *Being Reconciled*, p. 70.

sessions — having a meal, reading a book, building a house, or whatever. It positions each party effectively for the serious business of communication. The abstract character of exchange appears as soon as we recognize that market-transactions, too, are also communications. The market itself, the community of transaction, belongs to neither party alone but to the two parties together; it is not exchanged between them, but held in common. In order to exchange our exclusive property, we must participate in what is not anyone's exclusive property. Even the goods exchanged are, in a certain sense, held in common by the parties. Only *exchange-value* returns where it began. Furthermore, as medieval economic theorists recognized, precise exchange of value is thinkable only as a point of exact equilibrium, unattainable in reality. Every actual exchange falls to one side or other of the point; it is therefore either a true act of communication, in which the participant who does less well cheerfully releases his grip on his own for the sake of the common good, or it is an act of coercion, in which one side, by fraud or force, deprives the other of what is his own.[13]

Aristotle distinguished "forcible" and "voluntary" exchange.[14] It is easy to see why forcible exchange does not constitute community. The maintenance of a slave, whose work is treated instrumentally as a

---

13. Odd Langholm draws attention to the awareness in medieval thinkers of the relation between exchange and communication (*The Legacy of Scholasticism in Economic Thought: Antecedents of Choice and Power* [Cambridge: Cambridge University Press, 1998], pp. 101-2). Thus Albertus Magnus (*Ethica* 5.2.9: 356, on Aristotle, *Ethica Nicomachea* 1132b33-1133a5) describes the contract of exchange as a *fluxus et refluxus gratiarum*, while Duns Scotus (*Quaestiones in IV Sententiarum, Opus Oxoniense*, 4.15.2 [*Opera Omnia* 18 (Paris, 1894), pp. 283-84]) argues from the unattainability of exact exchange-equivalence that all exchange presupposes a readiness in either partner to make a gift. Exchange-value is determined only imprecisely, because it depends on what is to be expected in normal market conditions, and these conditions cannot be described precisely. This would be an insuperable barrier to the effecting of any exchange, were it not that the party that does less well is ready to remit whatever disadvantage he or she may suffer to the other as a token of good will. But this, as Duns indicates, requires generosity on *both* sides, since the obscurity of true market values means that there is no objective clarity as to *which* side is getting the better of the other. In other words, exchange cannot arise in social isolation, because no given participant can be assured of benefiting from it. It requires something prior: a context of communication within which the parties to exchange are already engaged, so that the whole weight of justifying the exchange does not fall on the exchange itself, but on the context that it serves.

14. *Ethica Nicomachea* 1131a2.

means to the owner's advantage, constitutes no communication between the two. But when the slave's work is perceived by either party or by both as a contribution to a common weal, then the transmission of maintenance in return for labor forms a communicative relation, the germ of a community. In the end, we may predict, this perception *must* supervene in any such relation between human beings. Divine providence never allows two human beings to work together without discovering some kind of community. That is why we can confidently describe the neglect of slaves' or day-laborers' welfare as *cruelty*, a description presupposing a fully social relation between the parties. You can be cruel by neglect only because there is a community of right against which your cruelty offends. The idea that a slave's capacity to labor is someone else's property, is just one aspect of the suggestion — false from the ground up — that a relation can be constituted solely out of the self-interest of one or both parties; for no such purely proprietorial relation could ever subsist between human beings. The question posed by slavery, then, is whether we will persist in maintaining this false account of what must, in reality, either be a cooperative relation or an abusive one. The early church, often criticized for failing to demand the "abolition" of slavery, dealt with the institution in the most direct way: it treated the proprietorial idea as fraudulent mystification; it taught its slave-members to regard their "masters" as brothers who depended on their help. When a true description of the relation was in place, the legal construct could only lose its credibility.[15]

But the same is true of a voluntary exchange-relation, bilaterally undertaken, where either party supposedly seeks only the enhanced return of his or her own. The question for our times is whether we can do as well with the voluntary exchange-contract as the early church did with the forcible exchange of slavery. Our relations with others may include commercial exchange-transactions; but exchange cannot be the whole truth of the relations and obligations formed around them. "This is a purely commercial transaction" can never be more than a specious explanation of social engagements that are either community-building or

15. Lactantius, *Inst. div.* 5.15 (*IG*, p. 53); Ambrose, *Ep.* 7 (*IG*, pp. 79-82); *Tract. in Luc* 9.29; Gregory of Nyssa, *Hom. in Eccl.* 4. See my remarks in *The Desire of the Nations* (Cambridge: Cambridge University Press, 1996), pp. 263-66, and in the article "Liberté B: théologie morale" in *Dictionnaire Critique de Théologie*, dir. Jean-Yves Lacoste (Paris: Presses Universitaires de France, 1998), pp. 654-56.

exploitative. No undertaking is "purely" commercial. Every engagement in which exchange takes place implies a social context of things held in common; our exchange-transaction either upholds the justice of that community, or it flouts it.

(iii) Yet there is a place for speaking of *our own*. The logic of communication sets the idea of "mine" alongside that of "ours." One who communicates lays claim to the goods as his own, in order to make them another's, too. Without the possessory moment there could be no communication, and so no community. Without it we could have no satisfaction, no fulfillment in our communication; there could be no image of God, no going forth of the self into the other. We possess what we transmit, and we possess what has been transmitted to us. That affords the basis for the contribution we make to the common good. It is not a mistake, then, to speak of private interests pursued and satisfied in communications. The mistake lies in thinking of private interest either as the *foundation* or as the *goal* of communication. Private interest is the median point, the moment of rest between communications, the communication that gave rise to it on the one hand, and the communication that gives expression to it, on the other.

The social use of goods cannot be constructed *out of* individual interests in things, so that something is originally "mine" *before* it becomes "ours," the conception influentially christened "possessive individualism."[16] This is just one more version of the attempt to conjure society out of individuality, laying hold of the self-sufficiency of God and the ungrounded character of creation and claiming them for human existence and self-foundation. Human community is not a product of human foundation; it is a condition of being human, a gift of God. God alone, who in creation covenanted himself as our God, has posited community groundlessly, and no repetition of that act is thinkable. In making an "ours" out of "mine," we actually elaborate a preexisting "ours" that is already latent within the "mine." But neither, on the other hand, does the social use of goods merely *promote* individual interests, interests which, extracted from society and located apart from it, could amount to no more than interests in consumption. Our private interests do not lie in consumption, but in accomplishing pub-

16. C. B. Macpherson, *The Political Theory of Possessive Individualism* (Oxford: Clarendon, 1962).

lic communications. No more truly "private" interest could be imagined, indeed, than our interest in contributing to a community, which is to say, an interest in work.

*   *   *

In its earliest sense "communication" was a broad enough term to encompass every kind of good that might be held in common by two or more people: "things, services, and common rights *(iura),* by which the numerous and various needs of each and every symbiote are supplied, the self-sufficiency and mutuality of life and human society are achieved, and social life is established and conserved."[17] Yet behind our modern habit of restricting the term to the transmission of information there lies a true perception. To communicate anything, material or spiritual, is to give it a meaning. The paradigm object of communication, transmitted in common between two or more people, is the word. Words underlie every form of human communication. The sharing of food may constitute a shared meal, a sign of fellowship; as a sign of fellowship, the meal may be an affirmation of common understanding or purpose; as an affirmation of purpose, it may be a pledge of loyalty, and so on.[18] Which meanings are appropriate to any given sharing of food will be indicated by the words that connect and comment on the material features of the performance.

To communicate goods, then, is to invest them with layers of social significance. They are enhanced as they are communicated. This may be by physical transformation, as when a craftsman shapes raw material to make an artifact; it may be by reinterpretation, as when a composer takes the familiar C-major triad and places it in a fascinating melodic and harmonic context; or it may simply be by redistribution, as when a merchant conveys a container-load of avocados from the place of their growth to the northern supermarkets. "Work" is the most general term for every human activity that enhances the material of communication, developing its social meaning, converting material goods into spiritual

---

17. Johannes Althusius, *Politica methodice digesta* (1614) 1.7, trans. F. S. Carney (Indianapolis: Liberty Fund, 1995), p. 19. Cf. *IG,* p. 760.

18. On which see Leon Kass's memorable book, *The Hungry Soul* (New York: Free Press, 1994); also the brief but penetrating discussion by Robert Spaemann, *Glück und Wohlwollen* (Munich: Klett-Cotta, 1988), pp. 214ff.

forces by the alchemy of communication. Work is the human vocation within the world, serving the human vocation beyond the world; it is the *usus mundi* that prepares for the *fruitio Dei*. As material goods are transmitted, so they are worn out and used up, but it is not the moment of consumption that generates the social meaning of the goods. Consumption is significant only as the accompaniment of work; but work invests goods with a meaning that is not consumed, but simply recedes into the caverns of memory. (Every librarian knows that books are threatened with consumption *as material objects,* which is the cause of their first headache, conservation; but they are never consumed *as titles,* which is the cause of their second headache, ever-expanding demand for stack-space.) All acts of high culture — the reading of a book, the making of a piece of furniture — are acts of work, primarily; only secondarily and incidentally are they acts of consumption.

And if work is the essence of social communication, unemployment is the paradigm of social breakdown. It arises when a society fails to afford its members appropriate opportunities and conditions for communicating with one another, so that each may add his or her contribution to the meaning-structure of the activity of the whole. "Work" and "unemployment" here are clearly not meant in a way that is confined to activities dealt with in the formal employment market. The work of the traditional housewife, on the one hand, and of the traditional rural landowner on the other, have generally been seen as socially useful, though they have never fitted comfortably into the framework of the market. The idea that the one was a kind of slave and the other a kind of drone arose from the purely theoretical mistake of totalizing the paradigm of wage-employment. Yet such a wide accounting for all kinds of work by no means leaves "unemployment," which must include underemployment and misemployment, as an empty category.

Around the communication of the various kinds of good there form specialist communities, of learning, industry, commerce, homebuilding, and so on, each with its own appropriate structure defining the roles of its participants and sustaining its patterns of communication over time. A school is run differently from a hospital, because communicating learning and communicating health care are different. (Of the general science of "management," the less said the better!) Yet these differing institutions are designed not merely to communicate *one thing,* but to communicate that one thing *in the context of other* communications. Any one of these specialist communities must form part of a larger communicative whole. I know no better way of describing this than Herman Dooyeweerd's useful concept of the "organizing function" of an institution and its "enkaptic relations."[19] A business organization is organized around our need to distribute material goods, but cannot function without a moral and intellectual context to determine such matters as the rules of fair trade and information on availability of materials and markets. A family is organized around our need for emotional community, but pursues this goal in a context of economic and intellectual activities: setting food on the table and teaching the young how to speak. And so on. What this leads to is that overlapping spheres of communication are not radically opposed, encountering one another's laws only on the boundaries where their jurisdictions meet. They invite a unifying conception, a word that draws them together, relating the rationale of each to the rationale of the others. This comprehensive word presents us with the whole that we call a "society."

A given society contains many different spheres of communication. The idea of an undifferentiated society — the self-contained subsistence-farming household that consumes what it produces, constructs the buildings it occupies, educates its own children, and conducts its own worship — is, in the end, only a thought experiment. True, some cultures have differentiated less, and maintained household self-sufficiency more, than others; but none can resist the pull towards specialized communications. We may think of a town with its churches, its sports clubs, its chamber of commerce, its philharmonic society, its school, and its hospital. Each of these is a focus of communication in a different sphere, drawing on the same broadly identical pool of participants. Defining that pool of participants is the town itself, the "society," not one more specialist sphere, but a sphere of spheres. Among the various titles given it by Althusius, we may single out two: it is a *societas mixta*, as opposed to the *societas simplex* that communicates one thing; and it is a *universitas*, or "whole." Not a *composite* whole of *constituent* parts, as though each sphere occupied a territory and encountered other spheres at the edge of its do-

---

19. Among the many places where this conception is explained, see initially *A Christian Theory of Social Institutions*, trans. Magnus Verbrugge (La Jolla, CA: Herman Dooyeweerd Foundation, 1986), especially pp. 64-69.

main. Recalling the original sense of "spheres" as circles existing within one another, we may think of them as meeting not at an edge but at a center, like a multitude of leaves finding a common source in a single stem. A society has no "business"; it exists simply as the *coherence* in which the spheres of communication flourish in relation to each other.

To describe the different spheres of communication, then, and their interdependence on one another, is the first task of an account of society. Such an account faces two opposing temptations, both characteristic of theoretical enterprises in general. On the one hand it may take a short cut to simplicity by describing society wholly in terms of one feature. The unifying word of the society reflects the complexities of the created order itself. The various categories of goods within society are incommensurable, and the loss of one kind can never be compensated for by others. Aristotle's hint that "everything must be measured by some one measure" has proved a perennial temptation, inviting us to suppose that there is a simple scale on which all social achievements may be aggregated. Inevitably it turns out to be a material scale, since only material goods are susceptible to accurate measurement. By this scale we presume to think of whole societies as "prosperous," "deprived," as "backwaters," and so on.[20] In fact there is no simple scale; communities can enjoy startling wealth in one respect while being startlingly deprived in others. The other temptation is for theory to overreach itself and become lost in a jungle of complexity, attempting to identify all the possible things there are to communicate, all the possible significative relations among them, and so to enumerate all possible forms of organization corresponding to them. What we should look for in an account of society is no more than a broadly heuristic classification of kinds of communication, sufficient to indicate the ways in which one kind of communication acts as a vehicle for others.

But there is a second task to be performed alongside the first. This is to give an account of the social whole that keeps the spheres of communication together — and especially an account of what makes them concrete, particular and plural, in contrast to the *universal* fellowship of

20. *Ethica Nicomachea* 1133a25. He continues: "In reality, this measure is need, which holds everything together; for if people needed nothing, or needed things to different extents, there would be either no exchange or not the same exchange. And currency has become a sort of pledge of need, by convention." Trans. Terence Irwin (Indianapolis: Hackett, 1999), p. 75.

the human race. Why, after all, is there more than one society? It is one of the oldest questions of political reflection, as the answer given to it in Genesis 11:1-9 may suggest. And since there is more than one, how can we believe in the unity of the human race? It is at this point that ecclesiology becomes critically important to social theory; for the church differs from all societies that we know otherwise in representing the kingdom of heaven, the universal humankind subject to God's rule. Apart from "one holy catholic and apostolic church" the posit of universal human fellowship is irreconcilably in contradiction to the concrete and bounded spheres of communication that we actually live in; and this thrusts on the latter a weight of universal significance that they cannot bear.

A well-established pattern of social theory in Protestant theology identifies three or four key spheres of communication: church, state, household, and sometimes industry. Luther had his doctrine of the three "estates," *oeconomia, politia, ecclesia,* from which Bonhoeffer drew his four "mandates," *Arbeit, Ehe, Obrigkeit,* and *Kirche.*[21] The Puritans promoted similar schemata: Baxter's *Christian Directory* (1673) is organized into "Christian Ethicks" (on private duties), "Christian Oeconomicks," "Christian Ecclesiasticks," and "Christian Politicks." This pattern has a superficially evident weakness, that it appears to be based on nothing stronger than intuition, with no exegetical or doctrinal argument to support it; but this is true of many great insights, and is not fatal. In this case there is a deeper weakness, which is that it ranges the church among a number of elementary social forms. The difficulty can be approached from either of two points of view. From the point of view of the church, this seems to undermine ecclesiology by ignoring both the *historical* identity of the church as the church of Jesus and the *eschatological* identity of the church as the heavenly city. Assimilated to other generalizable spheres of society, the church ceases to be the universal community, the "catholic church," and becomes instead merely the "particular church" that rises and falls with the social unit that em-

---

21. Dietrich Bonhoeffer, *Ethik,* ed. I. and H. E. Tödt, E. Feil, and C. Green (Gutersloh: Kaiser, 1998), pp. 54-61. English trans. N. Horton-Smith (London: Collins, 1964), pp. 207-13. For Luther's doctrine see Oswald Bayer, "Natur und Institution," *Freiheit als Antwort* (Tübingen: Mohr-Siebeck, 1995), pp. 116-46. Barth's critique of this type of thesis in Brunner, Althaus, and Bonhoeffer (*Church Dogmatics* III/4, §52.1 [Eng. trans. Edinburgh: T & T Clark, 1961], pp. 3-31) still rewards attention.

braces it. From the point of view of the social spheres, government, household, etc., they are not envisaged concretely, as *this* government or *this* household. They are therefore liable to assume improper universal overtones. "The" nation has induced men and women to commit crimes that would never have been perpetrated in the name of "this" nation, i.e., one nation among others before the horizon of a catholic humanity.

How are we to understand the concreteness of particular societies? By identifying them in terms of the *place* in which they are situated. Place is the social communication of space. A saying of Gregory the Great preserved in Bede declares, "Things should not be loved for the sake of places, but places for the sake of good things."[22] Places are the precondition for social communication in material and intellectual goods.

The primary institution of society, through which it maintains the differentiation of spheres, is the market and its ruling principle, exchange. The market is driven by cultural growth, not, as Aristotle thought, by the need to consume. But market-exchange is a purely instrumental device. The fundamental social reality that underlies it is not exchange, but the sharing of a common space to move around in, a neighborhood. We "go out" to market, for there can be markets only where people meet. They are the sign of a local society. "If someone that wanted a physician or a carpenter or any other craftsman had to set off on a long foreign journey, the whole of society would have come to nothing. Here, then, is why God founded cities, and brought a multitude together in one place."[23] But then, again, only when we go out can we come home. Our local adventures carry us into meetings, crossings of paths, interactions; they also allow us back in to the withdrawn existence that we conduct alone or with our intimates. Homing, as well as exploring, is an aspect of our topical relations. The household, too, to be distinguished as a sphere of communication, must have a locality. Place, the determinant of society, enables the division of our concerns into *public* and *private*.

---

22. Bede, *Historia ecclesiastica gentis Anglorum* 1.27.2. I owe the quotation to Henry Mayr-Harting, *The Coming of Christianity to Anglo-Saxon England* (University Park, PA: Pennsylvania State Press, 1991), p. 178.

23. Chrysostom, *Homily on 1 Corinthians* 34.

Place is an abstract concept, but precisely in its abstractness lies its importance. It stands for a totality of diverse communications that cannot be defined by any material description. It is posited in the reflective awareness of our participation in many communications that somehow, despite their diversity, cohere. Our place is not the space we presently occupy, where our bodies happen at this moment to displace the air; it is a function of our social communications, extending as far as they extend.

It is a high achievement to define society in terms of place, rather than blood-relationship, language, economic practice, or whatever, and so conceive it as a concrete universal, embracing all the forms of society that arise within a formally defined area of spatial contiguity. It is not, as Maritain suggested, a merely "physical or external" definition, for only *communications* determine local boundaries.²⁴ Space has no boundaries of its own. It is true, of course, that geographical features such as seas, deserts, and mountain ranges shape the social possibilities that arise among them, and this is what we refer to by the term "natural boundaries." But they do so only in the context of given types of communication; as these types change, so does the meaning of the geographical features. Civilizations that found navigation easier than land-transport grew up around a sea rather than on one shore; mountain ranges and deserts, which divide agricultural and manufacturing civilizations, embrace and protect communities of hunters and herders. The fact that a sea is the boundary of an island realm is a function of the communications of its inhabitants, not of the physical properties of the sea.

Two broad lines of mistaken assumption about place can be traced through Western culture, and have a certain philosophical affinity with each other. One is the attempt to abolish or escape from it into placelessness, the characteristic Platonist temptation; the other is the attempt to make it comprehensible as property. The latter is the tendency of the Enlightenment, a tendency that has left its mark all over

---

24. Cf. Jacques Maritain, *Man and the State* (Chicago: University of Chicago Press, 1951), p. 207: "Living together does not mean occupying the same place in space. It does not mean, either, being subjected to the same physical or external conditions or pressures, or the same pattern of life. . . . Living together means sharing as men, not as beasts, that is, with a basic free acceptance, in certain common sufferings and in a certain human task."

the landscape of North America. It was thought that place, like property, could be common only in its wild state, and that civilizing it meant privatizing it. The whole of civilized place thus came to be perceived as an extension of that very proper privacy which attaches to domestic habitations. The assumption that land not in private ownership was "unexploited" was a terrible engine of colonial conquest in the sixteenth and seventeenth centuries. It confused place with space, which really does need occupying. And it also confused occupation with privatization and exclusive possession.[25]

Commons, i.e., places with unrestricted access, are actually as much the creation of a civilization as private places are. One might venture to think that the more completely the two interpenetrate each other, the more successfully a civilization flourishes. A public park is more humane if it can support private undertakings. In Oxford's Christ Church Meadow the visiting public likes to see a herd of cattle grazing peacefully in the service of some local farmer, and when the cattle disappear, there are anxious inquiries about their fate. A private estate is more humane if there are public rights of way across it. Once space becomes inhabited as "place," it is assigned to various social uses, public, private, and a blend of the two; every one of these uses depends on the others. Only some uses, some of them individual (such as habitation), some undertaken by communities (such as storage, or organized technical work), require total privacy or exclusion; many uses may be compatible both with public access and with private employment. The private exploitation of a meadow, for example, may be sufficiently protected by a prohibition of picking flowers or letting dogs worry the sheep.

In sealing the identity of a society, place protects it against totalitarian pretensions. By identifying itself with a place name, a society acknowledges itself to be one among many societies. For a society is a "whole" only in a local sense. It is *the* society in a given place, but it is not "society"; no one society can be *the whole*. Localities have boundaries that also form horizons. If bounded locality fosters neighborly responsibility within the society's compass, horizoned locality makes the society itself into a neighbor.

There is nothing ominous, therefore, about the diversification and

---

25. See "The Loss of a Sense of Place," in Oliver O'Donovan and Joan Lockwood O'Donovan, *Bonds of Imperfection* (Grand Rapids: Eerdmans, 2004), pp. 296-320.

differentiation of communications, when these are controlled by the mutual responsibility of those who live in neighborly proximity to one another. In the simplest model of differentiated society, where the artisan produces tools for the farmer, who produces food for the priest, who offers prayers for the soldier, who fights battles for the artisan, they all belong to a common locality. The society in that place diversifies itself as the result of a moral enquiry into the needs of neighbors. That enquiry may be well or badly directed, but it is certainly not uniform from place to place; there are as many answers to the question about what special spheres are needed, as their are neighborhoods in which to ask it. How, then, do the more complex societies that we confront in real life differ from this model? They extend locality to the limits of imagined cooperation, including not only the immediate relations of mutual support but the mediated ones. Locality becomes a layered concept, reaching from the most proximate contiguity to the broadest regionality, depending on what the various communications require of it. The "people," as we have said, is the largest collective agency that we can practically conceive, embracing all the smaller local communities with their various specialist communities. Yet even at this widest political level society is local; which means that it is one concrete society among a plurality. A plural international system is implied in the essential interrelation of societies and places.

If we ignore the role of place, the idea of society can hardly fail to become threatening to freedom. One route to this begins with the attempt to make society look like just another *special* sphere of communication: as we belong to specialist communities of interest in learning and in health care, so we belong to this community with its own special interests in mutual respect and sociality.[26] It is a short step from thinking that this is what society *is,* to thinking dictatorially that this is what society must *be made to be.* And since there is nothing to explain why there should be more than *one* society of this kind, to which all belong by virtue of sharing the same interest in mutual respect and sociality, it

---

26. See, e.g., R. A. Duff, *Punishment, Communication, and Community* (Oxford: Oxford University Press, 2001), p. 47, attempting to define a political community by analogy with an academic community: "They [fellow-citizens] constitute a community insofar as they aspire, and know that they aspire, to share the community-defining values of autonomy, freedom, and privacy . . . and insofar as they aspire, and know that they aspire, to an appropriate mutual concern for one another in the light of those values."

is a short further step to thinking that no local society can ever be fully socialized until it is subordinated to an all-encompassing ideologically-formed worldwide community. This was the nakedly imperial idealism of Kant's demand for universal federation. It is still present in the agenda of imperial democratization.

A similar dénouement can be reached from the opposite starting-point by insisting on the wrong kind of universality. If we think of the relation of society to the special spheres of communication as that of a whole to its parts, then the whole will seem to be a preeminent organizational sphere governing and unifying its subordinates like a federal government its provinces. We will then need to establish some kind of "provincial rights" to protect the integrity of the subordinate parts. This is the idea expressed in the concept of "subsidiarity," so often invoked in political and theological circles.[27] But the conception is a mistake. Distinct spheres of communication do not relate to each other as separate and bounded parts of a single whole: the business enterprise, the family, and the school are not like Ontario, Manitoba, and Quebec. Nor does "society" relate to these spheres as Canada relates to Ontario, Manitoba, and Quebec, having a writ that simply runs over the interprovincial boundaries. When society is understood as a total system, it assumes the claims of overriding necessity. By the operation of constant laws it propels the differentiation and diversification of spheres, and integrates the process into an all-embracing unity, "taking the place," as Bernd Wannenwetsch perceptively puts it, "of evolution."[28] This conception is irresistibly totalitarian.

It is not surprising, then, that the sudden expansion of the place-surmounting communications of cyberspace have aroused such a widespread sense of the ominous. It is as difficult not to ask as it is impossible to answer the question, what implications the growth of the "virtual market" may have. Hyperbolic claims are easily swapped for doom-laden predictions, which simply puts us in a position too familiar to technological society, that of having achieved something that we do not know how to describe responsibly. Yet there is something poten-

27. See Joan Lockwood O'Donovan, "Subsidiarity and Political Authority in Theological Perspective," in Oliver O'Donovan and Joan Lockwood O'Donovan, *Bonds of Imperfection*, pp. 225-45.

28. *Political Worship: Ethics for Christian Citizens,* trans. Margaret Kohl (Oxford: Oxford University Press, 2004), p. 213, commenting on the program of Niklas Luhmann.

tially and actually ominous in our infatuation with non-local communication. Commanding at a distance has long been the sign of power, and the enthusiasm for it is obviously power-oriented. We need at least to be aware of the temptations that accompany such power. When I have entered my credit card number and double-clicked on the "confirm" box, some packer somewhere has to act on my order, some driver struggle through the traffic on the motorway, some postman find my front door. For me, as for the slave-owners of the early modern colonies, it is all too easy to overlook those on whom the gratifying of my desires depends, and to succumb to the illusion that the tips of my fingers on keyboard and mouse have freed *them* from the constraints of place, too!

15

Household and City

"Pure" social theory is abstract. To explore society in terms of its communications is to strip away its forms of representation and judgment and to view its members as eschatologically equal under the rule of God. Actually to project an ideal of eschatological equality onto the political order of secular society produces a tyrannous idealism, for social reality as we encounter it is always shaped by representation and judgment one way or the other. Eschatological equality belongs to the "not yet" of the kingdom. But the counter-political witness of the church, too, is constrained by that "not yet." It points to the future appearing of the one representative, and to the decisive judgment he will give. It models the eschatological community. But it is not simply identical with the eschatological community that will live without structure or form other than the immediate presence of God and the Lamb in its midst. The church can say, "our *koinōnia* is with the Father and with his Son Jesus Christ"; but it also bears historical witness to God's judgments past and future: "what we have seen and heard we tell you, that you may have communion with us" (1 John 1:3). It is taught to shun worldly titles of authority in its midst, such as Rabbi, Father, Doctor (Matt. 23:8-11); and yet there is a structured authority in the church that safeguards its witness, an authority grounded in the testimony of the apostles and the eyewitness generation. The counter-political community has its own forms of representation, different in kind from those prevailing in a political community.[1] "You know that those who are supposed to rule over the Gentiles lord it over them, and their great men exercise authority over them. But it shall not be so among you; but whoever would be great among you must be your servant" (*diakonos* — Mark 10:42f.).[2] Ecclesiology must speak of what tradition calls the church's "services," or "ministries" *(diakoniai).*

There are reasons to shy away from a theology of ministry, persuasive reasons, perhaps, given the history of controversy surrounding it, which ecumenical instincts may well prefer to leave to one side. The difficulty has been to determine up to what point the actual forms of ministry prevailing in the church are theologically required, and from what point they can be attributed to contingent circumstance. There have been many proposals for marking this boundary, lying on a spectrum between a maximalist pole, which might attempt to defend Pope, bishops, priests, deacons, archdeacons, acolytes, choirboys, and whatever other ministry there may be or may ever have been, as all essential to the church's life, and a minimalist pole that would relegate such questions wholesale to history and circumstance, leaving them to the discretion of the "particular church" of any time and place. Since neither of these two extreme ideal-types are plausible, the boundary between the necessary and the contingent has to be drawn with discrimination. When discrimination fails, we end up taking the essential marks of the church for traditions, and the traditions for essential marks.

Well-established traditions may, of course, be sufficient for many practical purposes. In order to prove that something is worth having or doing, it is not necessary to show that it never could be, and never could have been, otherwise. So when Cranmer prefaced his Ordinal with the famous claim that "it is evident unto all men diligently reading holy Scripture and ancient Authors, that from the Apostles' time there have been these Orders of Ministers in Christ's Church: Bishops, Priests, and Deacons," he clearly thought the appeal to unbroken tradition quite enough to warrant the preservation of these orders in the reformed

1. The traditional expression has been that ecclesiastical office is, of its nature, "without jurisdiction."

2. Even though, as Jesus points out in St. Luke's version of the saying, 22:25f., there are some designations of secular authority that pretend to obscure the difference.

Church of England. And when, more recently, the First Anglican–
Roman Catholic International Commission argued that "the only see
which makes any claim to universal primacy and which has exercised
and still exercises such *episcope* is the see of Rome . . . ," it thought this
purely historical fact strong enough to support the practical conclusion: "it seems appropriate that in any future union a universal primacy
. . . should be held by that see." To embrace this conclusion it was not
necessary to think that Jesus' words to Peter founded a universal primacy for all time. It was enough to see in the traditional institution
God's providential means for reconciling the churches at this juncture
of history.[3]

Failure to draw the necessary line risks compromising theological
integrity by an insistence on the *de facto:* bishops, priests, deacons, and
perhaps Pope, are necessary because they are there, regardless of the coherence of the tradition that has put them there. By this move theology
loses its critical function as the judge of tradition, and with it loses its
doxological tone of voice, for we cannot hymn the saving works of God
if we cannot, or will not, distinguish what God has done from what human ingenuity has come up with. Some over-insistence on the Holy
See, like some over-insistence on the historic episcopate, has had exactly the same effect as under-insistence: it establishes the forms of
ministry on the brute fact of how it has always been done, not on what
the redemption of the world in Christ requires.

How, then, may we approach this contentious tract of theological
discussion? Three preliminary observations may be made:

---

3. *Authority in the Church I* §23, in *The Final Report* (London: CTS/SPCK, 1982), p. 64.
Under pressure of subsequent objections the Commission held, broadly speaking, to the
line it first struck. Though insisting that its argument was "more than historical," it
conceded the possibility of conceiving of a universal primacy located elsewhere than in
Rome, and said that the claim for Rome was "an affirmation at a different level from the
assertion of the necessity of a universal primacy," one related to the "providential action
of the Holy Spirit" ("Elucidation" §8, p. 76). In *Authority II* the claim for the papacy's *ius
divinum* was read simply as a denial that the Pope derives authority from Councils (§15,
p. 88). Both documents avoided equating the worldwide primacy that Rome has historically claimed and exercised with that (truly) universal primacy which "will be needed in
a reunited church" (§9, p. 85). Unhappily, the successor Commission was by no means so
precise in its claims, nor even careful in reading its predecessor's work (see *The Gift of Authority* §§45-48).

(a) Patterns of ministry given by God the Holy Spirit must be discerned, first of all, in relation to the visible life of the universal church. A tradition going back to Augustine distinguished the church "invisible" from the church as "visible" in the course of history. Because the secrets of the heart are known only to God, and because the dead who belong to the church are hidden in Christ, we cannot see this body of Christ, this bride that God has designated for his Son, as it really is. What we can see are the outward things, the performances and institutions, the offices and responsibilities, the ceremonies and acts of worship, that constitute the appearance of the church, solid, plain, and evident things that present themselves to our eyes and conceal the mystery that can only be the object of our hope and longing. An important Calvinist qualification to this thesis distinguished within the visible church between the "particular" church and the church universal, or "catholic."[4] The significance of this lay in the recognition that not only *institutions* — official leadership, appointed synods, geographically located places of worship, etc. — are evident to our eyes as we look out for the church visible in the world. Less precisely located, but still apparent if we look out appropriately, is the worldwide community of Christian believers, associated by the word and sacraments. The institutional structures, when they are true to themselves, serve this visible society. "Visible" does not imply "obvious." If we wish to see a "particular" church, we may find one, perhaps, in the Yellow Pages under "Religious Organizations," but if we wish to see the church catholic, we shall have to pray for discernment: "Show me, dear Christ, thy spouse so bright and clear!"[5]

Confessing the one holy catholic and apostolic church, like confessing God the Father, Son, and Holy Spirit, begins with the verb, *credo.* The visibility of what God has done in the world is a visibility for faith — faith not as opposed to sight, but as enabling it. Without faith we do not know where to look. And it also requires faith to discern the church's ministries. It is a matter of recognizing the services God has given to his church in all times and places, whether or not these services are generally acknowledged for what they are, whether or not they are named correctly, whether or not they are preserved in the same form in

---

4. See my *On the Thirty Nine Articles: A Conversation with Tudor Christianity* (Carlisle: Paternoster Press, 1993), pp. 88-96.

5. John Donne, "Holy Sonnets" 18.

unbroken tradition, whether or not they are broken by disobedience or disunity. The theological standing of a ministry called "episcopacy" is not determined by whether all or most communions acknowledge it, or whether those with the better claim to unbroken continuity have officials designated by the title "bishop." It is a matter of what the Holy Spirit has always done, and still does. There is an entertaining and edifying story that Otto Dibelius founded the line of "bishops" of the Evangelical Church of Berlin-Brandenburg in 1945, because when dealing with the Allied Occupying Powers, whose sense for local ecclesiastical order was not highly nuanced, he found it easier to say "I am the bishop" than to explain what a *Vorsitzender* was. But the question of whether and how episcopacy was exercised in Berlin-Brandenburg cannot be determined by which item of vocabulary Professor Dibelius found most convenient. It is determined by what the Holy Spirit did in that place "to equip the saints for the work of ministry" (Eph. 4:12). (We need hardly remark on the extraordinary disparity between the title "deacon" and the practice of diaconal ministry within the institutional tradition!) It is, at any rate, a good ecumenical rule to approach the structures of any church assuming we shall find in them, even if only implicitly, the forms of ministry which God has given to the church.

That is why it was a breakthrough of the very greatest moment when the Second Vatican Council acknowledged the "truly Christian endowments for our common heritage . . . the riches of Christ and virtuous works" to be found in churches outside the Roman communion — an observation which immediately, and fittingly, prompted a doxology: "God is always wonderful in his works and worthy of all praise." Here Catholic ecclesiology asserted its authentic theological voice, and witnessed a moment of grace in the history of the twentieth century church for which we can never be too thankful. And precisely because this recognition of other Christian ministries was not juridical but wholly theological, the complaint that followed it carried not only juridical but theological weight: "Nevertheless, the divisions among Christians prevent the Catholic church from reaching the fullness of catholicity proper to her." Faith may discern not only the graces of the *catholica,* but also its shortcomings and sins.[6]

---

6. *Unitatis Redintegratio* 4, in *Vatican Council II: The Conciliar and Post-conciliar Documents,* ed. Austin Flannery, rev. ed. (Dublin: Dominican Publications, 1988), p. 458.

*(b) Patterns of ministry given by God the Holy Spirit must be discerned in rela-
tion to the essential communications of the church.* A similar point has been
usefully made by Stanley Hauerwas and others who represent the Aristotelian turn in Protestant theology, in speaking of the church's "practices." This lays entirely justified stress on the fact that the church's authority does not reside in its verbal proclamation alone, but in its form
of life as a community of the Holy Spirit. Yet "practices" is a problematic term, which has been used too heterogeneously, conflating the Aristotelian theory of the virtues with such distinctly ecclesiastical ceremonies as the celebration of the sacraments. We ought at least to
separate the general "practices" of the church from the formal "church
signs" of baptism and eucharist.[7] These are the primary authorizing
marks of the church, defining rituals of participation in Christ's incarnation, death, and resurrection, which draw their intelligibility directly
from the Christ-event itself.[8]

At a second level of authority are the pastoral, didactic, and missionary practices constituting the Christian life of the church. These
are best understood as patterns of communication. To assign them a
secondary level of authority is not to belittle their importance. Their
authority is secondary in the same sense that the work of the Holy
Spirit is secondary to the work of Christ, not implying ontological difference, merely a proper sequence in the economy of salvation, where
the once-for-all event that saved the world leads on to its manifestation
in the church. The sacraments are Christologically determined, the

7. In *Desire of the Nations* (Cambridge: Cambridge University Press, 1996), pp. 169-92, I
argued that these two universally acknowledged sacraments of the Gospel should be
classed together with the observance of the Lord's Day and the laying-on of hands as
church-signs.

8. When I wrote *The Desire of the Nations* I hoped that the sacraments might provide a
basis for a theology of ministry, and in a passage of small print on p. 174 I suggested
"tentatively" how this might unfold. In general terms, of course, this path had been
beaten hard before I took it: an ordained ministry has often been seen as a provision for
the due performance of the sacraments and especially the eucharist. Traditionally this
yielded a single undifferentiated "priesthood," distinguished by *sacerdotium* from lay
membership of the church, rather than the differentiated ministry of bishops, priests,
and deacons. I hoped to overcome this difficulty by making the tetrad of church-signs
the ground for a tetrad of corresponding ministries, somewhat awkwardly including lay
charisms among them. This had more ingenuity than strength, and I now regard this
route to a theology of ministry as closed.

church's communications and ministries are Pneumatologically determined. There is more flexibility, more historical change in patterns of ministry than in the sacraments; yet there is consistency in the divine mission of the Spirit, and there is consistency, too, in the ministries the Spirit bestows.

(c) Patterns of ministry given by God the Holy Spirit must be discerned in relation to the testimony of the apostolic church, the church of the New Testament. The experience of the apostolic church was historically of its time and setting, which is quite enough to warn us off restorationist attempts to recreate in modern conditions the precise apostolic forms for ruling the church. Even if this could be done convincingly on the evidence available, there is no reason to think that the Holy Spirit intends us to venture on such reconstructions rather than shape our ministries to the missionary and pastoral challenges we face. Yet this does not entitle us to slam the Acts of the Apostles and the Pastoral Epistles shut. For the shape of the early church's ministry is a testament not only to historical circumstances, but to the character of the church and its mission. We are in no position to do much improvising until we have learned from the apostolic models what the shape of a faithful ministry in a faithful church must be. We have evidence enough from history of the distortions that ensue when the church responds to challenges circumstantially, without thought to its own character and mission: bureaucratic or parliamentary inflation in church government, managerialism in pastoral ministry — and to these deformations of our own day we can easily add a list from the past: the medieval "clerk" with his monopoly on learning and teaching, the diversion of pastoral benefices to support intellectual pursuits, the military and grandee bishops of feudal and early modern society, and so on. *What* the church is and does essentially, must determine the forms in which it does it, and for that, as for all aspects of the church's life, the post-Pentecostal church of the apostolic age is an irreplaceable model.

*   *   *

It is commonly enough said that the ancient world separated *polis* and *oikos,* city and household, the sphere of the public and the sphere of the private. As a generalization it will serve, and we may accept it without underwriting everything that has been made of it. It is commonly enough said, too, that Christianity allowed the two spheres to mingle in a single type of community that married the political authority of the city with the mutual affection of the household. This claim, put forward by Hannah Arendt as a reproach to the familiarized *civitas* of Christianity, has sometimes been worn as a badge of pride by her Christian respondents, who have seen it as a way to overcome the traditional standoff between institutionalized Roman Catholicism and privatized Liberal Protestantism. But this is doubtful. A church that is at once household and city will always tend to be one of the two literally, the other metaphorically: either a family-like city or a city-like household.[9] The antithesis of household and city needs to be taken forward in a dialectical account of how each impacts on the other when ruled by the Spirit of Christ, and each becomes turned towards the other without losing their polarity.

The line that demarcated the two was drawn differently in the ancient world from that separating "family" and "society" today. The "household" was more broadly circumscribed than the family now is: though built around relationships of kin and marriage, it included household servants, and functioned as an economic unit not only in consumption but in production, as a small business. Within its domestic space were performed the tasks of making and selling, as well as those of eating, sleeping, and child-rearing. In the period when the church arose within the Mediterranean culture the household was the sphere in which innovative and expansive energies could flourish. The collapse of antique republicanism under the weight of empire and international trade had frozen political life into bureaucratic administration. But the household was adaptable. It was anything but "private" in the modern sense of a space withdrawn, subjective and quiet. It was the social space where the aspirations of ordinary people to develop their engagements could find expression, sometimes experimentally. At one end of the Mediterranean the communal living of the Essenes, at the other end the expansion of the great Roman aristocratic families through adoption, clientage, and skilled slavery, demonstrated in different ways the amenability of the ancient household to cultural complexification.

---

9. See Bernd Wannenwetsch, *Political Worship*, trans. M. Kohl (Oxford: Oxford University Press, 2004), pp. 133-59, 170-75.

The earliest descriptions of the young Christian community indicate the two poles around which it formed: "day by day, attending the temple together and breaking bread in their homes" (Acts 2:46). Two kinds of meeting, each in its own location, corresponded to two kinds of activity, "breaking of bread" and prayers (2:42). The temple provided the central meeting place; believers' homes were many. From the beginning, then, the church took form as a city and as households. It had its *res publica* and its *res privata,* constituted by the two objects of its sharing, the bread of common life that human beings eat and the speech that human beings address to God. The households were independent centers of *koinōnia.* "They sold possessions and belongings," we are told, "and distributed the proceeds to all, as any had need" (2:45), and there is no suggestion at this early stage of a central organization. Proprietors distributed the proceeds of their sale themselves. It was a matter of free communication of goods in mutual solicitude, initiated from multiple domestic centers of real wealth. The expanding household extends to domestic organization the established Jewish practice of almsgiving. No material object is more significantly shared than a loaf broken at the meal table; in this sharing all the resources for life are represented.

We are reminded that in Jesus' teaching the kingdom of God is presented in terms of a wedding feast, or, more generally, of a banquet. Yet this image of domestic celebration is often placed in a political context: "The kingdom of heaven may be compared to a *king* who gave a marriage feast for his son" (Matt. 22:2), and the story then proceeds with all the drama of political conflict: acts of violent resistance and violent suppression, the supplanting of old nobilities by new ones, spies infiltrated into the royal household and detected, and so on. It is not the domestic alone or the political alone that displays the kingdom of God socially, but that conjunction of the public and the private that may be suggested by the amphibious households of royalty. Domestic *koinōnia* could not give form to the church on its own. Its material communicativeness — "they had all things in common" — had to lead out into liturgical all-inclusiveness — "they were together in one place" (Acts 2:43). The church was not merely the sum of its households, but had its political center. The circumscribed communication of food and shelter is linked with the communication of a common word, uncircumscribed and without limit.

St. Luke's account of the earliest church approaches from Peter's sermon at Pentecost and the resulting conversion of large numbers. In this way the subject of the next sentence, Acts 2:42, is given: it is the Pentecostal believers who "devoted themselves to the apostles' teaching and fellowship, to the breaking of bread and the prayers." The church is first encountered at its Pentecostal moment, living in the power of the Spirit. The primary emphasis, then, falls on the *didachē* of the apostles as the common object of belief. To this there is at once added the emphasis on *koinōnia*. Teaching and communication together display the social form of the power of the Spirit; the grace of God is declared, and as it is declared, shared.

Sharing then takes effect in a further pair of activities, "the breaking of bread and prayers." Both are subsumed under *koinōnia*, so that the structure of the four items, "the apostles' teaching and *koinōnia*, the breaking of bread and prayers," is not strictly chiastic. Yet the *koinōnia* of prayers participates directly and centrally in the apostles' word (for it is a word of invocation as well as a word of proclamation: at 6:4 the apostles' ministry of the word includes prayer as well as preaching), while the common meals extend *koinōnia* to the material necessities of life. If the sharing of the word is the distinctly Pentecostal gift, the sharing of material welfare is an outflowing of the grace of the Resurrection, in which the risen Jesus ate with his disciples. We are not yet looking specifically at the Eucharist, though that is implied, but simply at the concrete sharing of community in the material gifts of God.

The narrative then (2:43) steps back from the Pentecostal event to trace in more general terms the emergence of *koinōnia* out of *didachē:* "And awe came upon every soul, and many wonders and signs were done through the apostles. And all who believed were together, and had all things in common." Fear is the immediate experience of each witness of the Pentecostal community. Fear generates faith, and from faith there arises *convergence in place* ("were together") and *sharing of life* ("had all things in common"). In these two movements the essential form of a community is described.

What impact, then, did the presence of the Holy Spirit make upon the underlying bipolar social organization of city and household?

(i) The *city,* in the first place, was defined by divine word and responsive speech. The classical city was memorably described by Arendt as a place of mutual "appearance," in which each citizen won a public presence by appearing before the gaze of others. But to whom was this mutual appearance answerable? What was appearance *about,* in the last resort? What made it mutually affirming and not mutually terrifying? What could evoke unforced and unforcing communication? Instead of "appearing before" one another, these Christian citizens appeared before God. In its central meeting the sovereignty of God's word was celebrated, attended to, and responded to. The city became a liturgy of praise.

We note, however, that the liturgical word defined the city in two ways: there is, on the one hand, the "apostles' teaching," and on the other there is the responsive speech of prayer. As defined by the apostolic *teaching*, the city is a universal community; but as defined by given acts of *speech*, it is a limited, non-universal community, tied to the material conditions in which it is possible for one person to hear and respond to what another says.

A community defined by reference to a word is in principle universal; it enforces no closure and posts no boundaries. It is immediately different from the city bounded materially by territory. The great point of contrast between material and spiritual goods is that the latter may be communicated indefinitely, without restriction. We do not limit others' possession of spiritual or intellectual goods by possessing them ourselves. When one mathematician communicates a proof he has discovered to a second mathematician, two mathematicians know the proof; the first mathematician does not know it any differently, or any less, than when he was the only one to know it. Intellectual communication multiplies without dividing. Material communication, on the other hand, restricts the possession of the object as it extends it. Appropriated to the symbolic meaning it bears, the object becomes unavailable for other meanings. And as with their physical structure, so with their power of signification, material objects are not inexhaustible. They cannot bear indefinitely multiple meanings. In excluding an infinite number of meanings, material communication excludes also an infinite number of communicators: by appropriating some material good as "ours," we rule out some conceivable further "his" or "hers." A material thing cannot be "ours" and everybody's indifferently. With the sharing of material goods there has to be a "right of disposition," a determination, to the exclusion of other determinations, of how the goods are to be put to common service; and this is the essence of "private ownership," or "property."

That is why the central gathering of the church day by day at the Jerusalem temple is not yet the universal city which it anticipates. The truly universal Jerusalem is yet to be revealed, as a later prophet will say, "from heaven." Only the word itself is universal, and its universality is emphasized in Luke's account by the very phenomenon that will result in his picture of the early church soon becoming obsolete: mission. Not for long will the gathering in the temple contain the swelling numbers of believers, or form a center for their geographical dispersion. The temple meeting points to the universality of the church, but is itself only a "particular church," a local community. Other such meetings in other places will come into being. Yet the apostles' teaching, in the form of Holy Scripture and the sacraments of the Gospel, will still be the universal point of reference, holding all these particular churches together as one holy, catholic, and apostolic church.

From the point of view of the nervous modern liberal this doctrinal catholicity makes the Christian city an "ideological" construction. At one level that observation is irresistible, and should be regarded as no reproach. To the extent that politics aspires to rationality, it must accept its high destiny of being word-governed, not merely in an instrumental way, but because it is subservient to the truth. Threatening ideological implications are removed if we recognize that "apostles' doctrine" is neither uncomplicatedly the apostles' *own* doctrine, nor is it uncomplicatedly *doctrine*. It is the speech of God about his Son and the speech of Jesus Christ about his Father. Though mediated through the testimony of an eyewitness generation, it is of universal validity, an unrivalled criterion by which all our responding speech, our "liturgy," must be judged. The word of God is universal as the daily prayers in the temple are not; it transcends the limits of their testimony through the prophetic and missionary presence of the Holy Spirit. Ideology, in the sense that we properly fear it and reject it, is the fate of a society that has learned from the church to be word-governed but has rejected the transcendent critical authority of *that* word, making the "dogma" of some received orthodoxy the final test instead of Scripture. The apostles' teaching is an elect testimony, a word from God that must be closed, precisely in order that under the authority of its criticism the conditions of free speech may arise. These conditions are not those of debate, but of worship.

(ii) The *household*, in the second place, was expanded by its task of material sharing. The division of its personnel into family members and family possessions was done away with, so that it became a sphere of social formation and mutual service open to participation. This forced a reevaluation especially of the place of the domestic slave. As we see from the repeated prescriptions for household roles in the New Testament epistles, slaves were bound into the moral community of the household by a network of reciprocal responsibilities, part of a domestic "brotherhood" that counts them in. Thus for Augustine, adapting the ancient wisdom that the household is the building block of the city, the most important aspects of the political demeanor of Christians were modelled by the relationships of the household.[10] These were by no means egalitarian, for great authority rests with the household head, the *paterfamilias*. Yet, in a tradition of Christian household-interpretation running back to Clement of Alexandria, Augustine sees the headship of the household as a position of burdensome responsibility for the material needs of the whole community: "heads of households should have more to put up with in their task than their servants have in theirs." The point of difference in the Christian household is that the servants have a dignity equal to "children," i.e., members by birth. It was always so, Augustine thought, even in the days of the Jewish patriarchs, with respect to the religious formation due equally to children and servants; but in pre-Christian times members by birth still had a privileged position in the assignment of material goods. In the Christian household, on the other hand, economic management is practiced in the interests of *all* the household members. "Though they [the heads of households] appear to command, their commands do not issue from a craving to dominate, but from a readiness for responsibility, not from a pride that asserts mastery, but from a compassionate care for material wellbeing."

It is clear enough that the expansion of the household put a new pressure upon the "family" in the narrower sense, that more restricted network of consanguine and affine relations. In this the early Christians were led by the recorded words of Jesus: "Who are my mother and my brothers? . . . Whoever does the will of my Father in heaven is my brother or sister or mother" (Matt. 12:48-50). Yet since the enlarged household still had the responsibility of nurture and education, it carried the family, in the narrower sense, along within it. Only with the modern extrication of economy, and to a lesser extent of education, *from* the household did the status of the family become questionable in itself. The twentieth-century determination of Christians to defend

10. *City of God* 19.14-17; *IG*, pp. 157-60.

the family can be seen as the response to a crisis caused by the dilution of the household's economic and educational roles.[11] Economic production having become separated from the household, and education remaining tied (inevitably) to economic production, there is much less for the household to manage: with its business reduced to consumption and the early nurture of children, it has become more focussed than ever upon the moment of biological reproduction and the relations surrounding it. Our modern concern with the defense of the family, then, is only apparently at odds with family-critical elements in the teaching of Jesus; for the weakness from which the family suffers in late modernity is precisely that to which Jesus' teaching is addressed: a self-enclosed narrowness of scope and a focus upon consumption.

It is central to the early Christian conception of the household that it was concerned with opportunities for *work*. Work formed the central theme of early Christian "communism," and this provides the clue to the early church's attitude to wealth: "As for the rich in this world, charge them . . . to do good, to be rich in good deeds" (1 Tim. 6:17f.).[12] "Disorder" *(ataktia)* is the term by which the New Testament church discussed a preoccupation with consumption: "accepting bread *dōrean*," i.e., giving nothing back (2 Thess. 3:8). A word from Jesus instructed missionaries, who, as Christians agreed, had a right to be supported: "*Dōrean* you have received, *dōrean* give!" (Matt. 10:8). The whole point of a sharing community is that together with material resources it shares an opportunity to contribute. It makes workers out of those who formerly had no work to do. In this context the apostolic

---

11. Hannah Arendt's influential description of the "rise of society" as the extrapolation into the political realm of the household's preoccupation with economic necessity (*The Human Condition* [Garden City, NY: Doubleday, 1959], pp. 38-49) attributed too exclusive an economic interest to the ancient household. This failed to observe how the process not only undermined the city but the household, too, subverting its integration of economic with traditioning functions, and so dehumanizing the economic realm. The most prominent twentieth-century Christian initiatives in relation to the family have been Roman Catholic: the Second Vatican Council's *Gaudium et Spes* 47-52; John Paul II's *Familiaris Consortio* and *Letter to Families;* the *Catechism of the Catholic Church*, 2197-2233.

12. To which the apostle adds two characteristic adjectives, which set the exhortation in its proper household context: εὐμεταδότους, κοινωνίκους, "good at sharing, ready to communicate."

catechesis could appeal to the classical value of self-sufficiency, *autarkeia,* as in quoting the proverb, "whoever does not want to work, shall not eat," and urging Christians to "get on quietly with their work and eat their own bread" (2 Thess. 3:10ff.). Yet this virtue was understood in an unclassical sense in the Christian household. It no longer represented the independence of the individual who can turn a profit and make his own way in life, but the discipline and modesty of those who contribute to the community as much as, or more than, they take out. In an early acknowledgment of what will later be a cornerstone of Christian civilization, the First Letter to Timothy admits that the life of common sharing is economically successful. It allows for the generation of a surplus, and this presents a temptation to those who "desire to be wealthy": they think there is profit to be made from the common life of the worshipping community. Indeed there is a profit, the letter declares, but it depends on a practice of *autarkeia* that is content to take no more than necessary from the common stock. The essence of self-sufficiency is not a drive to accumulate resources, but a recognition that one's personal material needs are quite limited, given the limited span of bodily life (1 Tim. 6:5-9).

It is a measure of the collapse of the household ideal that this positive teaching about *koinōnia* was later refocussed towards a negative judgment about property. In the second and third centuries Christian writers still understood what the New Testament teaching had been about; both Clement of Alexandria and Lactantius understood private property as the necessary condition for sharing.[13] But fourth-century preachers (most notably, Ambrose in the West and Chrysostom in the East) combined the Christian understanding of communication with a

---

13. Clement, *Paidagogos* 2.3: "What we acquire without difficulty, and use with ease, we praise, keep easily, and communicate freely." 2.13: "All things, therefore, are common, and not for the rich to appropriate an undue share. That expression, therefore, 'I possess, and possess in abundance; why should I not enjoy?' is suitable neither to man nor society. It is more loveable to say: 'I have; why should I not give to those in need?'" *Quis dives saluetur* 11: "It is not . . . a command to fling away the substance that belongs to him and to part with his riches, but to banish from the soul its . . . attachment to them." 13: "How much more useful is [it] . . . when by possessing a sufficiency a man is himself in no distress about moneymaking and also helps those he ought? For what sharing would be left among men, if nobody had anything?" Lactantius, *Institutes* 5.6: "Property had previously been a matter of one person contributing his labor for the use of all."

Stoic antithesis of common possession and private property, producing an impassioned line of argument against accumulated wealth and acquisitiveness, which conceived of private property as a kind of Fall. Property-right, as they came to understand it under the influence of Roman law, implied an irremediably private claim to solitary possession, and so was a form of sin.[14] Thus the negative side of the New Testament's teaching was preserved, but without household communication. Apart from that context property could only appear as an end in itself, an isolation from others and their needs.[15] The implication was that almsgiving, too, must be valued for negative reasons, as the means to disembarrass oneself of ungodly wealth. Alms thus became a uniquely privileged form of communication, the sole means of vindicating the principle of common possession. What appears, then, to be a radicalization of the Christian view of wealth conceals, in effect, the loss of its most important element and the incorporation of an individualist idea of proprietorship.

The Fathers argued (1) by analogy with animal life, which does not know any kind of property; (2) by extrapolation from natural goods, such as air and water, that are not susceptible of accumulation;[16] (3) on the basis of natural human equality in birth and death.[17] To give property away to the poor was conceived: (1) as an avowal that animal life needs nothing beyond immediate bodily requirements and that material wealth is irrelevant to the spiritual life; (2) as reparation for primitive crimes of usurpation;[18] (3) as an act of distributive justice, asserting the community of goods and the importance of circulation;[19] (4) as an assertion of mastery over material goods.[20] *Only* the poor were a proper object of such gifts, since the purpose of the gift was essentially negative, i.e., to ensure the minimum necessary accumulation of wealth in any hands whatever. Investment was confined to "lending to God"; one

14. For a general statement see Ambrose, *De officiis* 1.28.132-36; *IG*, pp. 84f.

15. Ambrose, *Naboth* 12; *IG*, p. 77.

16. Chrysostom, *Homilia 12 in 1 Tim.; IG*, p. 102.

17. Ambrose, *Naboth* 2f.; *IG*, p. 76.

18. Chrysostom, *Homilia 12 in 1 Tim.*

19. Ambrose, *De officiis* 1.11.38: . . . *ut communes iudices partus naturae, quae omnibus ad usum generat fructus terrarum, ut quod habes largiaris pauperi.* . . . Also Ambrose, *Naboth* 52; *IG*, p. 78.

20. Ambrose, *Naboth* 63; *IG*, p. 79.

did not use wealth to support a promising undertaking or someone else's talent.[21]

The conception of property as a Fall made little concession to the role of divine providence in human wealth. We find, however, a variety of attempts to make good this lack. A conservative attempt presented the inequity of private property as existing by God's permission in order to give greater scope to virtue: to justice on the part of the rich, and to patience on the part of the poor. A more ambitious conception was advanced by Augustine, pointing the way to a more extensive reevaluation. Extrapolating from the exceptional legal position in the province of Africa, where all land was theoretically vested in the *SPQR* and held *precario* or "leasehold" (a situation similar to that obtaining today in Hong Kong), Augustine argued that private property belonged to the sphere of *ius humanum,* falling under the dispositions of political authority for the restraint of sin. Like punishment, it was a beneficially coercive restraint on man's natural injustice.

Magnificent as the fourth-century invective against accumulation is, its critique of property is wrongly focussed. The conception of human material life as like that of animals (though ignoring the elements of territoriality and basic culture in many animal communities) treats the relationship of man to material resources solely as one of consumption, and does not acknowledge the human capacity for work. Its conception of material resources, treating the elements as paradigms, ignores the openness of natural goods to cultural development. Its conception of human equality, too, is asocial, since birth and death are hardly typical examples of human relations: the nakedness of birth is an extraordinary condition, in which the infant is cast on the world without protection, while death is even more problematic, since it is questionable whether it is "natural" at all.[22] And "the poor" are understood purely negatively, not as human beings or societies deprived in certain concrete ways and in need of extra assistance, but simply as the reverse-image of the over-resourced rich. In Chrysostom's famous parable of the City of the Rich and the City of the Poor, the poor are "phi-

21. Ambrose, *Naboth* 36f.; *IG,* pp. 77f.

22. 1 Tim. 6:7 makes the rather different point that birth and death bound the lifespan within which we participate in culture, so that cultural ambitions should be tailored to a realistic awareness of their temporal limits.

losophers with no superflous wants," free of luxury goods but able to command raw materials and skills, "in need of nothing."[23]

The notion that property is essentially individual goes with the thought that it follows from the biological need to consume. But the biological need cannot be the source or goal of any social relation on its own, and is certainly not the source and goal of the social and cultural right of property. Exclusion of the public from material goods is itself a *social* relation between people and things, a practice that may be dictated by the exhaustibility of the goods, but is not to be confused with it. Something is not private simply by virtue of being exhaustible. The pebbles that lie on the beach are exhaustible, but being involved in no prior social meaning may be picked up, taken home if they are pretty enough, or bounced across the waves if they are flat enough. Property is not a primitive relation of consuming individual to consumed thing, but a system of social appropriations of things to meanings, and as such capable of political development. So we have all kinds of property: individual property, corporate property, state property, property absolute, property with easements, and so on, as the law in any community may devise.

Correspondingly, the notion of a primitive common possession without particular property is underdetermined, lacking in any social principle of assignment. Even if common possession is interpreted practically as giving to the poor, it is still underdetermined. By determining what a gift is to mean in any case — providing allotments for indigent farmers, for example, or building orphanages — anyone who gives to the poor exercises existing property rights and founds new ones. In deciding what the gift is for, one excludes other possible uses of it, and prevents others from deciding differently. In directing to whom the gift is given, one invests with property someone who has not had that property hitherto. This was well understood later by St. Thomas, who maintained that property derives from common possession as a simple administrative implication. All goods are destined for the common good; but the common good is not cared for adequately without particular agents to assume their own particular responsibilities. Only in the limit-case of irresponsible use, the famous instance of the starving thief to whom the competent proprietor has refused help,

23. *Homily on 1 Corinthians* 34.

does the claim of common possession override the claim of property right.[24]

The source of property is the act of communication. Property is a moment arising within the act of communication, in which something that is ours becomes mine in order to become ours again. The exclusiveness of property arises from the need to shape the inclusiveness of communication. The moment at which I say "mine" in relation to any material possession is the moment at which I exercise the creative disposition as to *how* it will be taken into the common life as "ours." It is the moment at which my work for the common good assumes a definite form.

This reverses the order of work and property propounded by John Locke, for whom work was connected with property not as its goal but as its condition.[25] By acting on an object in certain ways, he thought, we establish our property in it — which is to say, simply, that what "property" *means* is the relation between self and object which results from my acting on it. I have a proprietorial relation to a virus that I have genetically modified, but not to a virus that merely makes me ill. I have a proprietorial relation to fruit I have picked, but not to fruit I leave to rot upon the ground. What this doctrine fails to allow is that both work and property acquire meaning only as part of a wider social communication. Locke makes no distinction between work and mere labor, and so fails to see that labor becomes work, and the fruits of labor become property, only through communication with others. Consider as an illustration the status of Robinson Crusoe's island before Man Friday arrives: those parts of the island in which Crusoe has labored are cultivated and domesticated, other parts are still wild. But it

24. *Summa Theologiae* II-2.66.7. Thomas's account, in stressing the need for assignment, fails to allow for *persisting* common rights, such as we find in common law: rights of passage, for example, the right to drink flowing water, the rights of squatters, etc. On these cf. Grotius, *De iure belli ac pacis* 2.2.6-17.

25. *Two Treatises of Government* 5.27: "Though the Earth, and all inferior Creatures, be common to all Men, yet every Man has a *Property* in his own *Person*. This no Body has any Right to but himself. The *Labour* of his Body, and the *Work* of his Hands, we may say, are properly his. Whatsoever then he removes out of the State that Nature hath provided, and left it in, he hath mixed his *Labour* with, and joyned to it something that is his own, and thereby makes it his *Property*. It being by him removed from the common state Nature placed it in, it hath by this *labour* something annexed to it, that excludes the common right of other Men."

makes no sense to say that the domesticated parts are Crusoe's *property*. To introduce the category of property is to raise the question of how he will share the exploitation of the island with others. There is no other context in which it can make sense.

Only as it confers the power to work may property also imply a power to consume. To consume, as the Franciscans saw more clearly than Locke, we do not need a right of property. If it is only a matter of eating and drinking, the meal may just as well be the donor's property until it is extinguished by disappearing into the friar's belly.[26] The scholastic distinction between the two rights of property, the "right of disposition" *(ius disponendi)* and the "right of consumption" *(ius fruendi),* was at fault in mentioning a right of consumption at all. The right of property is simply and solely the right to make dispositions for the common good; it is the command on resources which allows us to be participating agents in social communication. This right is shaped and ordered by the underlying truth that the material wealth of the earth is the common possession of all mankind. That truth orders our use of property to the common good. The special significance of almsgiving as a form of communication is that it manifests this ordering by being immediately responsive to need. It highlights the communicative responsibility which all property, corporate or individual, carries with it.

The church renews society by renewing possibilities for work. It is possible to regret the fact that the expanded household was a comparatively short-lived experiment. But it matters less how long it continued in its expanded form, than how this experience of expanded domestic community continued to shape the Christian moral imagination in construing property as communication. Other forms of wider domestic care replaced the expanded household. Monastic communities were among its heirs; after them, initiatives in town- or village-wide charitable provision; and, in our own days, international aid agencies. There is in principle no limit to the forms in which Christians may discover opportunities to use their material resources as a medium of communication that opens up a sphere of work for them to do. And, in the default

---

26. The confusion of work with biological assimilation is startlingly evident in Locke's implausible claim (5.26) that "the Fruit, or Venison, that nourishes wild *Indian* . . . must be his, and so his, i.e., a part of him, that another can have no right to it, before it can do him any good for the support of his Life."

position, "always with you," there is the original Jewish model of almsgiving, which Christian *koinōnia* built upon. It is a kind of inchoate communication, for the giving of alms to a beggar cannot be socially completed unless the beggar is put in a position to work, i.e., enabled to proceed to an act of communication of his or her own. Yet almsgiving has its own importance as a placeholder for communication when full communication is not yet possible. It is a recognition that the task of sharing is never done, and a sign of hope that God will complete what we cannot. The difficulty that every society has in facing its beggars — even Ambrose could exclaim, "The greed of beggars today is quite without precedent; they come in the pink of health, for no reason but vagrancy!" — is in inverse proportion to its hope in the transforming judgment of God.[27]

*   *   *

In the fourth chapter of the Acts of the Apostles (4:34f.) a new departure is described: "as many as were owners of lands or houses sold them and brought the proceeds of what was sold and laid it at the apostles' feet, and it was distributed to each as any had need." The liquidation of real property, already mentioned in 2:45, now gives rise to a central administrative arrangement. Proprietors no longer exploit the realized value of their property within their own households, but put it at the disposal of the apostles.

The narrative of Ananias and Sapphira, commenting on this innovation, implies that the proprietor had discretion not only as to whether the value of his property should be realized in the first place, but whether, once realized, it should be administered by himself or centrally. "While it remained unsold, did it not remain your own? And after it was sold, was it not at your disposal?" (Acts 5:4). It also implies something more surprising, that the gesture of renunciation, if made, was to be total. To attempt to combine the roles of proprietor and donor to the apostolic chest was to "lie to the Holy Spirit." This was an either-or decision: either one exercised the powers of private household-charity, or one renounced them. In making a single gift of all his resources, the donor made himself propertiless, like someone in later generations who

27. Ambrose, *De officiis* 2.16; *IG*, p. 88.

joined a religious community. In renouncing the use of his property, the donor also renounced the burden of household-responsibility that went with it. He bought himself a freedom to respond to other opportunities for service, not only without the cares of domestic economy but without the ties to the central meetings of the church. He could pursue a life of service to the Gospel in mission, free to travel and found new local centers of Christian worship. It is no accident that Barnabas, chief among wealthy donors of the early church, took a leading role among its early missionaries.

But while freeing the individual, the donation imposed new burdens on the central church. The city now begins to assume some of the tasks of the household, and the first steps are taken which will eventually lead to the disappearance of the household as a unit of *koinōnia*. The effect of voluntary renunciation of property is thus, paradoxically, to create new structures of property ownership. Private wealth, having been poured into the household first, ends up in the city-church, the first of the many corporate proprietors of Christendom. Strengthening the role of the city-church as corporate owner and provider is a subtext of the fourth-century polemic against private acquisitiveness. When in the high Middle Ages corporate wealth itself became a focus of criticism, the successor to the corporate proprietor was the universal proprietor, the Pope, whose imagined role as the primary owner of all wealth anticipated the function assigned to the state centuries later by socialism.

In this necessary paradox we find the root of the Minor Friars' doctrine of "simple use." In its original Franciscan simplicity this looked as though it would amount to the claim that the only relation we may have to material goods is that of consumption: "use" without "disposition" means simply using *up*, which is why Friar Tuck, like other friars in hostile caricature, is fat, for he has nothing to do with what comes his way but eat and drink it. In reality, however, the Friars had a constructive preaching mission to fulfil, and to fulfil it they needed to dispose exclusively of movable and immovable possessions (houses, books, etc.). If they were to deny their own property in such things, they had to assert the property of others: the original donors, on the one hand, whose proprietorship in their gifts was thought to persist, and the Pope on the other. "Non-proprietary" or "evangelical" possession could only be conceived as a privileged vocation, not as a universal demand. In attempting to recover from the patristic tradition the position of almsgiving as the uniquely privileged form of communication, the mendicant friars conceived themselves as "the poor," a class that could never hold property but must always appeal to the charity of others. Their "perfect" way of life could benefit from the moral claim of common possession, but without challenging the institution of property as such. A similar paradox arises, curiously, in relation to modern capitalism, to the extent that theoretically it consecrates individual consumption as the horizon of all economic activity. In practice, however, it recognizes all kinds of strategies this side of the horizon for corporate survival and growth.

The renunciation of wealth cannot be understood apart from another kind of renunciation that was characteristic of ancient Christianity, the renunciation of marriage. The sexual and the economic, which together formed the framework of the household, were closely tied together in the ascetic imagination of Christian antiquity. They were both part of the material world, on which we must be prepared to turn our backs for the sake of the heavenly and spiritual. Rich though this conception was in opportunities for misunderstandings of a dualistic kind, its underlying inspiration was eschatological rather than world-refusing. The informal authority of the ascetics, a sometimes disturbing feature in church polity of the patristic era, arose from the vividness with which they represented in their privations and their prayers the presence of God active in the world. So it was that the logic of renunciation was to lead in the end to a new, more radically conceived type of household, "monasticism" as we paradoxically call it, meaning the religious community where unmarried Christians live and work together, not leaving the world but penetrating it with new patterns of sharing resources and life. The impact of monasticism upon the evangelization of Northern Europe was decisive, not least because of the sheerly economic gains reaped by communities of adults free of the tasks of child-rearing and able to devote surplus energy to other civilized arts — notably those of literature and learning. The much-criticized "worldliness" of the later monastic tradition was born of its missionary success in occupying and serving the world; it was the reverse side of the Benedictine devotion to work.

For the earliest church, however, the immediate impact of renunciation was the conversion of the household-city dialectic into two forms of ministry, both centered in the local church, a ministry of the word and a ministry of "tables" — an expression that hovers with nice ambiguity between a reference to food and a reference to financial organization. The householders' work of distribution began to fall to the apostles, a daily responsibility as we are told at Acts 6:1, demanding something more than goodwill to accomplish. St. Luke advanced large claims for the economic effectiveness of this development: "there was not a needy person among them" (4:34). The complaints which open the narrative of the institution of the Seven tend to confirm this boast; it is when there is enough to go round that questions of equitable distribution raise their heads most sharply. A central distributive system made the church more conscious of the sub-communities of which it was composed, sub-communities constituted by pre-existing identities, "Hebrew" and "Hellenist," probably to be understood as linguistic communities. That such subordinate identities would arise in the church was an obvious implication of its household structure, for households are inevitably reinforced by bonds of consanguinity, affinity, and proximity. The response of the apostles is not to challenge the right of these identities to any presence or notice in the church. However universal its fellowship (more truly universal than a political community can ever be), the church must embrace rather than reject existing bonds of identification, and these can make claims of mutual equity on one another.

The apostles' response is administrative: the community is summoned to make arrangements to ensure that wrong is not perpetuated. The apostles' words (6:2f.) introduce two important terms, *diakonia,* "ministry," and *episkopē,* "oversight": "It is not right that we should . . . minister — *diakonein* — at tables. . . . Look out — *episkepsasthe* — seven accredited men." What do these terms mean? *Diakonia* has a very wide semantic field in the New Testament and related documents. Every Christian is a *diakonos,* a servant of others as Jesus himself came "not to be served but to serve *(diakonēsai)*" (Mark 10:45). Ministry is the essence of the church's mutual relations in communication. It is not a special task confined to the Seven, even though later tradition will call them "deacons." Oversight, on the other hand, is a reflexive role, a special task that will protect the practice of ministry. What is lacking, the apostles suggest, is a class of specially responsible persons "set over" *(katastēsomen epi)* the ministry of household sharing that is everybody's primary business. They are to manage the sharing, to protect it against distortion and corruption, to safeguard the form of the church. Not, of course, that this oversight is *independent* of the church; it is precisely as an expression of the community's own oversight of its affairs that it will select the Seven as overseers.

Not one, but two "ministries" are mentioned in the apostles' reply, not only the ministry of tables, but the ministry of the word (including prayer), corresponding to the original foci of church life in the households and the temple. With the separation and definition of the oversight of ministry of tables, it becomes clear that the ministry of the word, too, must have its *episkopē:* "As for us, we will devote ourselves to prayer and the ministry of the word" (6:4). No more is this ministry the apostles' prerogative than the ministry of tables is the prerogative of the Seven. The communication of the Gospel and the discerning of God's will in its light are tasks committed to the whole church. So we find one apostle addressing a church vexed by schism, recalling the essentials of teaching that they received with their baptism: "I have not written because you do not know the truth, but because you do know it. . . . The anointing you received remains in you, and you have no need of anyone to teach you, since the anointing teaches you everything, and is true and does not lie" (1 John 2:21, 27). Yet there is still scope for the apostle to write to the church, since "this is the promise which he delivered to us." The historic fact of the apostolic commission gives that group of primary witnesses a decisive role in helping those who already know the distinction in practice between truth and falsehood.

This raised the question of how the oversight of the word was to be extended beyond the scope of the original local church, Jerusalem. The Acts of the Apostles chronicles a series of steps: initially, the Twelve divide their labor between Jerusalem and Samaria (8:14); then they send an emissary to Antioch (11:22); then in new missionary foundations the missionaries appoint "elders" *(presbyteroi)* in each congregation (14:23). The relation between these missionary foundations and the Jerusalem apostles was at the heart of Paul's struggles to vindicate his own authority. The oversight of Jerusalem, Paul insisted, was not executive but doctrinal. It was an oversight of *word,* not of *policy.* His own Gentile mission was founded independently by direct initiative of the Holy Spirit. The essential continuity with Jerusalem was simply that "the

Gospel that I preach among the gentiles" should have been admitted by James, Peter, and John to be in need of no supplement, "lest I should run, or have run, in vain" (Gal. 2:2-10). The function of this increasingly devolved responsibility was to secure the normativity of the apostolic Gospel for each place, mediating between the universality of the word and the contingency of localities. It was to defend the effectiveness of the new communities that the preaching of the Gospel established, to defend the integrity of the local church as a community living in the truth.

The order of responsibility which came to be known as the "presbyterate," then, was charged with protecting the evangelical discourse in the local church. What the church enacts in the world through its *koinōnia,* it expounds by the ministry of the word. It is a ministry of teaching, not only about the kingdom of God established in Christ and yet to be revealed, and not only about the church which foreshadows the coming revelation, but also about the powers of the kingdom in the world at large. The word of God rules the church and directs its mission; but to ensure that its authority is effectively supreme within the local church requires attention to the demands and challenges of the place.

But there was another means by which the apostolic group exercised oversight more widely than the city of Jerusalem. As the Johannine literature repeatedly reminds us, the apostles *wrote.* In the Acts of the Apostles, too, the authority of the decision reached in Jerusalem about Gentile converts was sealed by a general letter (15:23-29). By this means the apostles drew a line between the historically unrepeatable authority of their own eyewitness testimony to Christ and the subsequent evolution of a ministry of oversight. They ensured that the future shape of an oversight of the word should be exegetical, governed by the texts in which their own witness was preserved. Familiar with the character of an exegetical ministry in rabbinic Judaism, they shaped the ministry of their successors — though not their own, which was a testimony to "what we have heard and seen with our eyes . . . and our hands have touched" (1 John 1:1) — to conform to it. To that extent it is correct to say that they conceived their writings as Holy Scripture.

The two terms, "ministry" and "oversight," were thus applied equally to the pastoral and doctrinal spheres: there was a ministry of tables and there was a ministry of the word; there was an oversight of the one ministry and an oversight of the other. Shortly, however, we find them applied separately to the two spheres, referring simply to oversight: there are *diakonoi,* and there are *episkopoi,* "deacons" and "bishops." Nothing at all depends, as is apparent, on an exclusive claim for the historical normativity of this pair of terms.[28] Responsibility for oversight of the word was especially stratified and varied in its nomenclature: we find references to "teachers," and, frequently already in the New Testament, to "elders" *(presbyteroi).*[29] The point is simply that the foundational structure of the local ministry is twofold, reflecting the original distribution of pastoral and doctrinal functions between household and church.

One subsequent elaboration of the pattern, however, seemed so deeply implied in its logic that theologians were hesitant to regard it simply as a contingent historical fact, though forced to admit that it was not explicitly witnessed in the New Testament. That was the emergence of a single local bishop out of a collective episcopate or presbyterate. To state the logic of this development needs some care. It is not sufficient, on the one hand, to speak, as classical Protestantism has done, of a principle of presidency or eminence necessarily present within any collective, a "chiefty" among presbyters. That imposes a secular principle of the unity of government where it does not belong, and so makes the bishop a functional rather than a theological figure.[30] The argument for the episcopate — I shall use "episcopate," "episcopacy," and "bishop" in our usual restricted sense, not with the width of *episkopē* — must be a theological one: the single bishop ensures the rela-

28. Phil. 1:1 and 1 Tim. 3:1-13 afford the only explicit examples of this pair of terms, together and exclusively, in the New Testament; it is also found in Didache 15:1. With the list enlarged to include "teachers" there is also Hermas, *Vision* 3.5.1.

29. To add to this we find a generalized use of the term *apostoloi,* "missionaries," not assimilable to any of the categories of responsibility within the local church.

30. Hooker, *Laws of Ecclesiastical Polity* 7.2.2; Grotius, *De imperio summarum potestatum circa sacra* 11.3. In Ignatius of Antioch, it is true, there was an attempt to justify the monarchical principle theologically by making the single bishop an image of God among his presbyters, an unfortunate move to iconic significance, which does nothing to explain why a bishop needs to be a human being rather than a statue (which Ignatius's bishop frequently resembles!). Once we grasp the functional significance of the bishop as a guarantee of catholic unity, it will be seen that nothing depends on the literal unity of the figure, provided that there are procedures to secure agreement among those who share the office with each other and with the world church.

tion of those who exercise the collective episcopate to the preaching and teaching of the universal church.

But to argue this, it is not sufficient to refer to a local succession. An argument that owes its parentage to Irenaeus of Lyon traces each metropolitan bishopric back to a founding apostle. In Irenaeus's hands the point of this claim, which he thought unimpugnable historically, was to assure the canon of the New Testament Scriptures and so facilitate the proving of tradition by the apostolic writings, which were for him the essential canon of apostolicity.[31] Once a uniform canon of Scripture was agreed, this circumstantial reinforcement for it, of which the historical soundness anyway ceased to be apparent, was hardly necessary. Even if it could be historically confirmed in every (every!) instance, succession could establish nothing beyond a limited right of tradition that must bow before apostolic doctrine. And continuity of local tradition cannot be made a justification in itself without paganizing Christianity. Both these attempts to explain the episcopate end up with the same problem: the single bishop reinforces "bounded locality." Sometimes he reinforces the development of a larger locality aggregated out of smaller ones, the "diocese," but that is a bounded locality, too, defined by what it contains and not by its relations to what lies outside it. The bishop thus becomes a typical local representative, identified with a local community and speaking out of it to the world, and so is essentially a secular, not an evangelical, figure.

Ecclesial catholicity is not constructed from below, as secular universality is, by treaties and conventions made among local communities through their representatives. Universal fellowship is the *original* gift of the church, the presence of the kingdom of heaven, only subsequently distributed into locally particular manifestations.[32] An explanation of the episcopal office depends, then, on an adequate dialectics of place. A place must be understood not only in terms of its boundaries, which limit the local society to what lies geographically within them, but in terms of its horizons, which relate the local society to all that lies geographically beyond them. An ecclesial ministry constituted

31. Irenaeus, *Adversus Haereses* 3.1-4.

32. Cf. John Paul II, quoted at *Some Aspects of the Church Understood as Communion* (Rome: Congregation for the Doctrine of the Faith, 1992), 9: "The universal Church cannot be conceived as the sum of the particular Churches, or as a federation of particular Churches."

locally must have two aspects, bounded and horizoned, one turned inward, the other outward, one focussed on the integrity of *koinōnia* within the place, the other on the integrity of *koinōnia* with the universal church. The authenticity of the church's local witness to the truth must be protected from the two sides, against a deracinated failure to relate it to the actual conditions of the place, and against a parochial isolation and immured self-sufficiency. The two facets of the oversight of the word look in these two directions. The distinctive function of the bishop among the presbyters is to ensure the opening of the local to the universal church on the only possible terms: agreement in the universal truth of the Gospel.

The question of universal primacy can be approached only from within the logic of the episcopal order. If it is possible to think of a central figure among local bishops, acting as St. Peter may be held to have acted among the apostles, it is an *episcopal* role that is thought of, a role existing precisely for the ends that the episcopate exists to serve. We do not require a Petrine office to introduce universal and catholic responsibility, for universal and catholic responsibility is already expressed in the episcopate. But we may require such a role to support and facilitate what is already there.

So much an Anglican theologian can responsibly say about a possible Petrine office within a possible united church. Unhappily, that still leaves a certain distance, which it is important to measure carefully, from the official Roman Catholic view. This distance is not that between late-medieval conciliarism and papalism, the one approach deriving the universal church from the particular, the other the particular from the universal. Once we concede a universal ministry, the suggestion that a council is superior to it is sufficiently answered by what *Lumen Gentium* says of the college of bishops: "together with their head, the Supreme Pontiff, and never apart from him."[33] The office of a universal pastor and the work of a universal council would necessarily be complementary, and there could be no formal theological principle to decide which took precedence in case of conflict. If God did not spare the church the humiliation of such a conflict, he would certainly not spare it the wholesome responsibility of discerning the substantive points at issue and judging them on their merits.

The 1992 document of the Congregation for the Doctrine of the Faith, *On Certain Aspects of the Church as Communion,* enables us to identify the key prob-

---

33. *Lumen Gentium* 22, in *Vatican Council II: The Conciliar and Post-conciliar Documents,* ed. Austin Flannery (Dublin: Dominican Publications, 1988), p. 375.

lem clearly. It begins with a series of fine statements that ought to command strong general assent: communion has a double dimension, vertical and horizontal (3); it is at once visible and invisible, and thus mission-oriented (4); the eucharist is its focal point (5 — may we add baptism?); it includes the glorified as well as the pilgrim saints. The Congregation then elaborates the relation between the universal and particular church (7-10), urging correctly that the universal is not just a federal association of the particular: the church is both in and of the churches, and the churches in and of the church. In keeping with this we are then warned (11) that the churchly character of a particular church is not complete by virtue of the fact that it celebrates the eucharist, for "from the eucharistic centre arises the necessary openness of every celebrating community, of every particular Church; by allowing itself to be drawn into the open arms of the Lord, it achieves insertion into his one and undivided Body."

These words are immediately followed by a startling change of gear: "For this reason too, the existence of the Petrine ministry, which is a foundation of the unity of the Episcopate and of the universal Church, bears a profound correspondence to the eucharistic character of the Church." The relation of this last sentence of paragraph 11 to what has gone before, is entirely opaque, the application of the term "foundation" to the Petrine ministry quite unprepared for. Given the way the argument has proceeded from communion as the fundamental reality of the church, how can a specialized ministry be a "foundation," rather than a service or a safeguard? And how can the Petrine ministry be a foundation "of the unity of the episcopate," since the episcopate is anyway the ministry of unity? ("The episcopate is one," we shall be told, "just as the eucharist is one" [14].) A thunderstorm of ministerial foundationalism seems to have burst unannounced upon the balmy summer breezes of communion-ecclesiology. The foundationalist gale rages more fiercely: the unity of the church is now said to be "rooted in the unity of the Episcopate" (12), and the bishop to be the "source and foundation of the unity of the particular Church" (13). It begins to blow itself out when "the primacy of the Bishop of Rome and the episcopal college" are said simply to be "proper elements" of the universal church; and after that last puff the sun comes out again.

Two comments suffice: (1) To embark on ecclesiology from the reality of *universal communion* does not authorize a seamless transition to *universal ministry*. The step from universal fellowship to universal ministry must be taken self-consciously and argued for. Universal fellowship is a gift and a task of the Gospel; universal ministry is a service to confirm the gift and assist the task. We must not on any account allow ourselves to think of the ministry (in any of its forms) as a *root*, or *foundation*, of the universal fellowship. (2) Tradition has identified the universal ministry as the *episcopate as a whole*. To argue that a single universal office must assist the bishops requires a further step, to be taken self-consciously and argued for. We must not on any account allow ourselves to think of the Petrine office as the foundation of the episcopate.

The ministries are known by their effects; when we see the effects we may discern that the Spirit is giving the church its authentic shape. What impact, then, will these effects have on the political society in which the church lives? If a political society has in its midst a church that is taught by an episcopate not to confine its deliberations to the local, national, linguistic, or racial spheres, but to explore contested issues in a catholic manner, not only attending to Christians from every present source, but also from every past age, it must have a profound effect. A society influenced by such a church will be restrained from universalizing its own local experiences and perspectives. The narrow and culture-bound spirit that affects every society, especially those that are most triumphant, the spirit which expects to export its local assumptions and values *en masse* and makes no effort to learn from others', meets a roadblock when it comes face to face with a church supported by a functioning episcopal ministry.[34]

If a political society has in its midst a church taught by a presbyterate to confess the authority of God's word in the context of its place, it has a continual stimulus to reflect on the meaning of its local traditions. Such reflection does not permit blind endorsement of traditions, not even traditions of criticism of traditions: it takes tradition seriously precisely as those aspects of its common life for which it is immediately responsible, where the judgments of God's kingdom are to be revealed. Its sense of local identity will be self-questioning, expressed in well-focussed attention to prevailing local forms of idolatrous and worldly communications. Debates fostered within such a church will not, as political judgment is bound to, wait on the threat of actual damage and harm, but will warn and counsel of future judgment, which Marsiglio of Padua understood to be the role of the priesthood.

If a political society has in its midst a church taught by a diaconate to sustain communities of material *koinōnia,* this challenges it to ques-

---

34. Of the international crisis threatening the Anglican Communion as I write it is enough to say that it is only ostensibly about the ordination and marriage of homosexuals. In reality it is about the catholic responsibility and function of the episcopate.

tion the prevailing patterns of social standing and honor. It will be more ready to redirect its resources counter to popular social valuations, to break down walls that limit the flow of material assistance. This response by no means always tends in one direction. A society of aristocratic structure may learn to promote individual opportunity and to encourage lowborn talent, while a competitive meritocratic society may learn to care for the naturally under-endowed, and to reinforce the importance of family community.

An effective church with an effective ministry, in holding out the word of life, than which there is no other human good within the world or outside it, will render assistance to the political functions in society by forwarding the social good which they exist to defend. But that is to take the very longest view of the relationship. In holding out the word of life, an effective church with an effective ministry issues the call, "Repent, for the kingdom of God is at hand!" And so in the short, the medium, and even the penultimate term the presence of the church in political society can be a disturbing factor, as those who first thought Christianity worth persecuting understood quite well. It presents a counter-political moment in social existence; it restrains the thirst for judgment; it points beyond the boundaries of political identity; it undermines received traditions of representation; it utters truths that question unchallenged public doctrines. It does all these things because it represents God's kingdom, before which the authorities and powers of this world must cast down their crowns, never to pick them up again.

16

The Longest Part

The counter-political moment takes effect as the church takes form as a *koinōnia* of the Holy Spirit in the midst of society's communications. But there is another way of approaching the counter-political moment. It takes effect, too, when individual believers, as subjects of two political realms, present and future, judge for themselves.

"Why do you not judge for yourselves what is right?" asked Jesus, and told the parable of the litigants on the road to show what he meant (Luke 12:57-59). The phrase translated "for yourselves" *(aph' heautōn)* is an ambiguous one, and we may perhaps catch its nuances better if we say, "of yourselves." In the first place, there is a judgment that arises *from* ourselves; it is the result of reflection, won from the knowledge of our hearts rather than from outside. We may form a private judgment without prompting, without the prior exercise of judgment in the public realm. The word "judgment" is used in this context in a secondary sense. It has to do with private reflection and not with public enactment. Yet it is not mere opinion, a mental exercise with no practical relevance. By anticipating privately the judgments of those authorized to make them publicly, we contribute to a social comprehension of the work of government, the condition for authority to have effect. Reflective judgment therefore supports political judgment, anticipating its labored conclusions while, as the parable puts it, the parties are still on the way to court. But this judgment must be *aph' heautōn* in another sense. It is judgment *on* ourselves, judgment that has to do with our own case, our own controversy with our adversary. Reflecting on the conditions of judgment, we know we cannot get to the bottom of each case of each litigant; we know that the meaning of particular events is given contextually, and that understanding of them is gained only as we investigate the context. But in this one case we can know that we have sufficient knowledge, because what we know of ourselves is decisive. In this one case, then, we may act as judge, and pronounce on what we owe our adversary. Here is a startling reversal of the practical rule that no one may judge in his or her own cause; it is precisely our own cause that we will judge most clearly, if we have once been liberated from self-defensiveness to assume the reflective position that judges "of" ourselves. And then we may act as decisively as any judge to give our adversary his right.

A judgment on ourselves anticipates by internal witness a judgment soon to be pronounced publicly. But each human being finds him- or herself in that position before God's judgment. The resolution of the litigant on the road to court is not merely a model of self-knowledge; it is a parable for faith itself. To judge of oneself is the very heart of faith in God. And with this act the individual emerges decisively as the primary agent. The church believes, to be sure; but only as each believing member of the church believes. The faith of the church is not prior to the faith of its members, but presupposes it. "The church with psalms must shout," wrote Herbert, "No doore can keep them out:/But above all the heart/Must bear the longest part."[1] It is not obvious, of course, that this must necessarily be so. We may reasonably think that our beliefs are, for the most part, shaped by the society to which we belong; they are the very point at which we are least on our own. The belief that the moon goes round the earth is a communal belief, which few of us have had occasion to check out for ourselves; even fewer have wagered any serious interest of their own on its being true. But faith in the crucified and risen Christ involves conformity to his cross; it means sharing his isolation and rejection. The summons to it, then, is addressed to the individual: "If anyone would come after me, let him deny himself and take up his cross and follow me" (Mark 8:34).

From the patristic period Christian thinkers maintained that "conversion," by which they meant not simply the point of initiation into

---

1. "Antiphon (1)," *The Works of George Herbert,* ed. F. E. Hutchinson (Oxford: Clarendon Press, 1941), p. 53.

the Christian community but its ongoing moral discipline, lay by way of a reflexive turn to the self, a discovery of what lay "within." "God and the soul" were linked together as the content of true wisdom. In this way Christians took up the challenge of the ancient Delphic counsel, "Know thyself!" The Platonic influence upon how the turn to the self was described has been often and well documented. Yet the patristic account of the theme follows rather the moral shape of Jesus' teaching on conversion: "Give for alms what is within . . ." (Luke 11:41), which gave them the sense that reflection was morally indeterminate. "Turn inward to yourself," Augustine counseled, "but do not remain there!"[2] The "selfing" of the soul, which clothed it with moral dignity as a center upon which the world and everything in it converged, proceeded to a moment of "unselfing" in which the "I" was displaced through a moment of transformation wrought by God. So the Delphic counsel was qualified in the sense of Romans 12:2: "Do not be conformed to this world, but be transformed by the renewal of your mind." This dynamic was explored in many ways, including the reading of the Song of Songs in terms of the soul's erotic pursuit of God. Augustine articulated the ambiguity of the inward movement in speaking of "self-love," a term which courts a deliberate polyvalence: on the one hand, there is a self-love in which the subject finds its good in God and in the restoration of his trinitarian image in the soul; on the other, there is a self-love in which the subject is content with itself, complacent *(sibi placere)* in its own powers. With this radical parting of the ways within the practice of reflection, there opens up a similarly radical division in society. For both ways of self-love create a social existence of a kind: the two loves made two cities, the one based on the fragile and deceptive community of self-interest, the other on the rediscovery of others as neighbors "in" God.[3]

From these patristic roots there grew a tradition of teaching and speculation that acquired the awkward epithet, "spiritual." From the scholastic period, which conceived the ambition to systematize and objectivize the study of theology, the tradition of spiritual teaching has been in an uncomfortable relation to the systematic theological main-

2. *Sermon* 330.3.

3. *City of God* 14.28. On this subject see my *The Problem of Self-love in Saint Augustine* (New Haven: Yale University Press, 1980).

stream. The divergence in the tradition has been accounted for institutionally, as a separation between monastery and school; it has been accounted for functionally, as a separation between the exercise of prayer and the instruction of the pulpit; it has even been accounted for as a separation between a spiritual elite and common believers. It was, no doubt, encouraged by the esotericism of the newly influential texts of Dionysius the Areopagite, though it would be a mistake to limit the spiritual tradition to the type of apophatic mysticism that owed its paternity to him. The root of the matter was that the spiritual tradition took up a distinctive subject matter, the forms of consciousness that correspond to the working of God within the individual soul. In principle, then, spiritual theology needs to be integrated into the body of theology as a necessary *topic,* though perhaps a rather speculative topic that needs to be kept well pruned back. Its point of departure lies in the properly theological assertion that the individual believer, filled with the Holy Spirit, participates directly and subjectively in the life of God. The believer does not participate in God at one remove, through the life of the church. The saving history of Jesus Christ is not mediated to the believer uniquely through participating in the sacraments, but it takes its own reflected form in the hidden interior struggle for moral and spiritual integrity. The cross and resurrection of Christ is the matrix within which the saving experience of conversion, of the death and rebirth of the self, can be grasped subjectively. "O be thou nail'd unto my heart, and crucified againe!"[4] This "again" is not the recrucifying of Christ that is done, according to the apostle, when we persist in sin (Heb. 6:6); it is a further moment in the triumph of the Paschal event when it is applied to the soul of the believer.

The spiritual approach to theology flourished most strongly precisely within the most important Christian experiment in household community, monasticism. It is hard to overestimate the significance to Western culture of that simple architectural feature, the monk's *cella.* When we look with modern eyes at the archeological remains of early medieval cells, we see them as tiny, enclosed, and bare; they speak to us of the austerity and self-affliction we associate with the period. But to those who inhabited such small spaces they spoke quite differently: they were a kingdom, a place that guaranteed solitude, designed to

4. John Donne, "Litanie" 2.

meet the needs of their own spiritual integrity. "If you wish to achieve a compunction that touches the heart," à Kempis wrote, "go back to your room, and keep the tumult of the world locked out. . . . In your cell you will find what you most often lose outside."[5] The power of medieval monasticism to draw recruits of the highest capability away from the lures of political power and marriage must have had much to do with the promise of the private room, the scope for personal development and self-discovery.

*   *   *

Talk of the individual's reflective judgment has to resist a current of opinion in contemporary moral thought, Christian and secular, which reckons to have emancipated itself from the delusive individualism of modernity. A critique of modern individualism, however, must distinguish two quite different ways in which the individual has been conceived in modern thought since the seventeenth century. On the one hand there has been the pre-political individual of contractarian theory, the individual of Hobbes, Locke, and Rousseau, revived in recent times by Rawls, who is an underdetermined atom from which the molecular structures of society are constructed by processes of negotiation and compromise. Of that individual we have said a great deal already, and do not need to say much more. Bearer of no personality, no social identity, no aspirations above those of fulfilling the most basic needs, he encounters us simply as the bearer of "human rights," that tide of undifferentiated demands that relentlessly erodes the coasts of our social institutions. Though at the height of his political power today, his critical fate is already sealed, like that of the atom itself. Just as the indivisible atom has turned out to be a function of electro-magnetic charges, so the atomic individual is a function of social forces. The powers of negotiation and compromise this individual was supposed to command were never *individual* powers in the first place.

But there is another kind of individual to be met with in modernity, the post-political individual who has risen by reflective self-consciousness above the constraints of society. The "Individual" of Hegel, Kierkegaard, or Sartre was not the atomic unit of Hobbes or

5. *De imitatione Christi* 1.20.5.

Locke, but a subject who *achieved* individuality by developing a reflective relation to him or herself and to the community. This individual, the modern devotee of the Delphic "Know thyself!," cannot be dismissed so easily. For we can detect a strong resemblance, and in the case of a Christian writer like Kierkegaard more than a resemblance, to the Christian "soul," the believer who has found in Jesus' death and resurrection a matrix for the reformation and reappropriation of his or her own identity. Modernity has capitalized heavily on the Christian soul, and a critique of modern individualism has to study the balance sheet. For the sense in which the modern subject is post-political will correspond, with or without fidelity, to the sense in which the church and the Christian soul are post-political.

Modernity, that great carcass around which a shoal of shark-toothed narratives forever wheels and hovers, traces its origins in part to the fate of the spiritual tradition. When we speak of the "turn to the subject" as a key element in the formation of modernity, it is not that there was never any idea of reflection before. What happened, rather, was the emergence of the reflective subject as a center of *public* interest. Why did early-modern philosophy find it necessary to re-trace and re-describe a journey of introspection that since late antiquity had been the prerogative of the devout? What brought the imperative, "Know thyself!" to the top of its critical agenda? To ask this question is to invite an enlargement of the popular but too-tenuous narrative of the "Cartesian soul," a narrative that takes modernity back to Descartes's speculative search for certainty in response to skepticism. The genesis and character of modernity has to do at least as much and perhaps more with a distinctive approach to practical reason. Affective rather than epistemological skepticism provoked the modern elaboration of the self.

When the spiritual writers asked themselves why they should presume to commit the inner experiences of the saints to writing, they replied that it was to encourage the aspirations of other saints in the making.[6] They did not write in order to interrogate what introspection

---

6. Jean Gerson, *De mystica theologia* i.prol.ii: *si de te loquendum est . . . exultemus cum tremore et doceamus cum humilitate, querendo unicam gloriam nominis tui per servos tuos, dominos et fratres meos, quibus ideo de secretis sapientie tue loqui velle michi videor ut, dimissis interim sterilioribus studiis divaricantibus animum ad multa, inflammet eos verbum spiritus tui querere te in simplicitate cordis. . . .*

found. They never doubted that the soul was a site of both godward and selfward motions, and that the penitential purifying of the godward and purging of the selfward led progressively towards a climax of the soul, where reflection became redundant in the simplicity of the soul's view of God. Only with the sixteenth century's radical perspectives on the sinfulness of the heart did these assumptions about the content of the soul become doubtful. The term "skepticism" was first applied to a new kind of reflective introspection, quizzical, uncertain, and distanced, which viewed the affective impulses of the soul with no conviction of their moral coherence. Montaigne's essay "On Repentance" famously expresses the new mood: "I cannot fix my subject. . . . I catch him here, as he is at the moment when I turn my attention to him. I do not portray his being; I portray his passage; not a passage from one age to another . . . but from day to day, from minute to minute."[7]

Such a view of the inner life raised alarming questions about the stability and intelligibility of the public realm. If we cannot speak clearly of the motives that make us act, how can we say what our public actions mean? One response to this dilemma was to re-found society on the worst possible assumption, viewing human motivation as reducible to an interest in self-preservation. An alternative response was to make a move in some sense parallel to Descartes's claim to a necessary and unshakable truth within self-consciousness: to search within the soul for an attitude that was necessarily free of moral ambiguity, which would serve as a new foundation. By stripping away equivocal rationalizations they believed they could uncover an affective disposition wholly free of self-reference, beyond the reach of reflection and skeptical doubt, a simple and undialectical embrace of the good. The good itself and the soul which sought it converged upon the simplicity of a mathematical point. "Nothing can possibly be conceived in the world, or even out of it, which can be called good without qualification, except a *good will*," proclaimed Kant at the start of his "foundation-laying" for moral metaphysics.[8] We may label this disposition "affective independence."

7. Michel de Montaigne, *Essays* 3.2, trans. J. M. Cohen (Harmondsworth: Penguin Books, 1958).

8. *Grundlegung der Metaphysik der Sitten* 393: "Er ist überall nichts in der Welt, ja überhaupt auch außer derselben zu denken möglich, was ohne Einschränkung für gut könnte gehalten werden, als allein ein *guter Wille*."

If François de Salignac de la Mothe-Fénélon serves as a paradigmatic figure for the conception, it is not that he was more adventurous or original than those who cultivated *les voies intérieurs* before him, nor that he had more influence on those who came after him. But the impassioned controversy about "quietism" that opposed him to the traditionally Augustinian Jean-Bénigne Bossuet in the last decade of the seventeenth century brought out certain features of the development with striking clarity, so that we can see how the older esoteric tradition fed into the modern reconstruction of the conscientious self. In his programmatic essay, *Explication des Maximes des Saints sur la Vie Intérieur* (1697), Fénélon defended the ideal, represented by Francis de Sales, of a "pure" or "disinterested" love of God as the highest achievement of Christian perfection, open only to a few specially gifted saints who, under pressure of a special testing, are led to renounce salvation for themselves in order to conform themselves wholly to the will of God. This ideal displays to the full the paradox of reflection as a spiritual means. Reflection, Fénélon assumes, is coterminous with *amour propre,* and to be perfect is to be freed from it into immediate apprehension of God. Yet assuming the point of view of a "director of souls," that ambiguous invention of the Counter-Reformation which boasted its own pastoral science of counsel and interpretation, Fénélon's defense of the unreflective leads him deeper and deeper into an objectified reflection, an extensive psychology of religious states based wholly on literary testimony. If his work is a milestone on the road to modernity, it is partly because he writes of exalted spiritual states without admitting to any interest in experiencing them. He is like a scientific explorer, seeking to trace back the streams of mediated and rational consciousness to a source in some moment of immediacy.

What affective independence seemed to promise was a state of immediate responsiveness to God's will, free of self-orientation or calculation such as inevitably characterized interactions among human beings. In a curious way it reflected aspirations of the theopolitical tradition for the monarch: responsible to God and answerable to no one besides, he was a self without private interest or initiative, wholly engaged in regulating the interests and initiatives of his subjects. It was not a coincidence that Fénélon's most renowned work was devoted to instructing the Duc de Bourgogne on how to be king: "to know men . . . try them . . . deliver yourself to no one." The state of indifference afforded a similarly sovereign regulative control. It was a "positive and formal will," which became "the principle of all disinterested desires which the written law commands."[9] The object of the will could only be God as he is essentially in himself. Confronted by Bossuet's reminder of the Johannine principle that we love because God first loved us, Fénélon retorted with another startling anticipation of Kant: God's "amiability" was necessarily a matter of his essence, quite independent of his actual love for us, which, as a free decree, was no more than an accident.[10] Of the many objections of varying persuasiveness marshaled by Bossuet against this idea, one seems especially telling: affective independence was a cover for despair.[11] To this charge there was a reply: the saint continued to hope, simply because hope was commanded by God. But Bossuet was right to be suspicious of this. It drained hope of its existential authenticity. The saint's withdrawal of the will from the self's own future was the very move most characteristic of true despair, protecting against disappointment by denying a place for hope. And so, if "pure love" had no place for hope, it was no longer self-commitment. The saint flamboyantly laid his own salvation on the line in the encounter with God, but only after he had withdrawn his interest from it.

At this point affective independence converges with a parallel development sprung originally from the same source, that of the modern "conscience." The transformation of the reflective conscience, drained

9. *Les Aventures de Télémaque* 18, *Oeuvres* II, ed. Jacques Le Brun (Paris: Gallimard, 1997), p. 315. *Explication des Maximes des Saints sur la Vie Intérieure, Oeuvres* I, ed. Jacques Le Brun (Paris: Gallimard, 1983), pp. 1023-26: "C'est une volonté positive et formelle, qui nous fait vouloir réellement toute volonté de Dieu" (5, p. 1023f.). "La sainte indifférence . . . est le principe réel et positif de tous les désirs désintéressés que la loi écrite nous commande . . ." (6, p. 1026).

10. *Lettre à M. l'Évêque de Meaux sur la Charité* 1, in *Oeuvres Complets* III, ed. M. Gosselin (Paris, 1851): "Ainsi un décret libre et gratuit, qui est une chose accidentelle, est la seule chose qui nous rend Dieu aimable! Sans ce décret libre et accidentel, il ne le seroit point par son essence infiniment parfaite." Cf. Kant, *Critique of Practical Reason* 22, 27, trans. Mary J. Gregor (Cambridge: Cambridge University Press, 1996): "All material practical principles . . . come under the general principle of self-love. . . . If a rational being is to think of his maxims as practical universal laws, he can think of them only as principles which contain the determining grounds of the will not by their matter but only by their form."

11. In the "Avertissement" of his *Divers Écrits sur le Livre des Maximes des Saints, Oeuvres de Bossuet,* vol. 28 (Versailles: Lebel, 1817), Bossuet identifies four principal questions in the controversy, of which the first is: Is it permitted deliberately to despair?

of Christ-centered formation and cut off from the discursive content of practical reason, into an immediate and peremptory awareness of obligation, is a very similar early-modern phenomenon to the stripping of reflection from the love of God. As the mystic, denied the knowledge of grace, was left only with the knowledge of God's commands, so the conscientious individual is stripped even of the knowledge of God himself, leaving only the bare imperative encountering him in abstraction. The idea of monarchical sovereignty attached itself quite especially to conscience, as we can see in a rather conventional passage from Kierkegaard, which could speak for the aspirations of the whole nineteenth century: "Take the most insignificant, the most looked-down-upon servant, imagine someone we call a poor, simple, impoverished scrub-woman who earns her living by the most lowly labor — she has, Christianly understood, the right . . . to say, 'I am doing this work for my daily bread, but that I do it as carefully as I do, that I do for conscience's sake.' In a secular sense there is only one man, only one single man who recognizes no other duty than the duty of conscience — that is the king. And yet this poor woman, Christianly understood, has the right to say regally to herself before God, 'I am doing this for the sake of conscience!'"[12]

Conscience in the Christian tradition had been a consistently *discursive* self-consciousness, a roomy mental space for reflection and deliberation, where every kind of information was at home, and above all information about the redemptive goodness of God. Conscience was memory in responsibility, the workshop of practical reason, a formal rather than an efficient or final cause. Insofar as it laid claim to authority, it was simply the believer's authority to reach decisions reflectively rather than accept decisions made for him by others — an authority conceived dialectically in response to that of the church to give moral counsel. But the sovereignty of conscience imported a kind of peremptory immediacy, cutting short deliberation and negotiation. The modern conscience, in Butler's well-known phrase, "magisterially exerts itself."[13] And with this it changed from a guarantee of freedom into a tyrant. The rational agent was left helpless before the voice that came from nowhere and could be mediated by no rational argument.

12. *Works of Love*, trans. H. and E. Hong (New York: Harper, 1962), p. 137.

13. Joseph Butler, *Sermons* 2.10, in *The Works of Joseph Butler*, ed. W. E. Gladstone, vol. 2 (Oxford: Clarendon Press, 1896), p. 59.

The peremptory conscience was a mythical embodiment of inarticulate and terrifying certainties buried in the depths of the psyche.

It is apparent that the term "conscience" *(suneidēsis,* sometimes in a verbal form, *sunoida)* enters the New Testament through Paul. Its occurrence is preponderantly in the Pauline letters and literature from Paul's sphere of influence — not overlooking the careful use of the noun by Luke in speeches assigned to Paul. It has been suggested plausibly that Paul took the term up from his Corinthian correspondents, though it should not be overlooked that both verb and noun occur occasionally in the Septuagint.

First and most simply, conscience is used as a *noun of action,* meaning "awareness," with an object such as "God" (1 Pet. 2:19), "sins" (Heb. 10:2), "the idol" (1 Cor. 8:7), an incident of public concern (Lev. 5:1 LXX), and on one possible understanding of the difficult 1 Cor. 10:29a, "oneself" and "another." Often it has the overtone of a knowledge shared between one person and another, as when Sapphira was complicit with Ananias (Acts 5:2), or when others know of one's acts and character (2 Cor. 4:2; 5:11). Secondly, we meet a reflexive sense, still as a verbal noun, "self-awareness," and especially moral self-awareness. It is used for the awareness of guilt (1 Cor. 4:4, quoting Job 27:6 LXX), an experience that may be portrayed, as in the classical tradition, as having a witness to one's acts, as in Rom. 2:15, 9:1, 2 Cor. 1:12, or of being reproved (John 8:9), or judged (1 Cor. 10:29b).

In the third place conscience is conceived not simply as an occasional state but as a settled moral relation to oneself, a moral character. So we have the "evil" conscience (Heb. 10:22), the "good" (Heb. 13:18; 1 Pet. 3:16; 1 Tim. 1:19) or "pure" conscience (1 Tim. 3:9; 2 Tim. 1:3), the conscience free from blame (Acts 23:1; 24:16). These are all more than states of mind; they are moral states of the self. Connected with them is the phrase, "for conscience's sake" (Rom. 13:5; 1 Cor. 10:25, 27f.), which can be paraphrased, "as a moral issue." Finally, this moral character is identified with the "inner self" in its transformation through God's saving work: not perfected by sacrifice but purified by the blood of Christ (Heb. 9:9, 14), in baptism and through Christ's resurrection (1 Pet. 3:21).

At no point in the New Testament, as Peirce pointed out long ago, does the conscience have a *directive* role, instructing us how to act.[14] This changes in the Greek patristic literature, which very frequently speaks of the conscience as an "instructor," *didaskalos.*[15] What is the content of its instruction? A passage

---

14. C. A. Peirce, *Conscience in the New Testament* (London: SCM, 1955), p. 109.

15. The range of illustrations marshalled under συνείδησις in G. W. H. Lampe's *Patristic Greek Lexicon* (Oxford: Clarendon Press, 1961) undermined Peirce's claim, which has, however, continued to enjoy some currency, that it was translation into the Latin

from John Chrysostom, on which a more famous passage in Kant was modeled, speaks of two instructors, creation without and conscience within, the latter murmuring suggestions as to "all that is to be done."[16] The implication is usually that the conscience gives general moral instruction, rather than particular. Occasionally, conscience says "do this!" in particular, but only as the last point on a train of moral reasoning, for conscience is "a warmer and a brighter reasoning."[17] Conscience and reason can be treated more or less as equivalent.[18] Its content is in fact nothing else than the "natural law" — repeatedly referred to in this connection.[19]

The introduction of a directive function does not, however, lessen the reflective function of conscience. It opens the mind and its reasons to examination, makes us clear to ourselves; by it the soul is "laid bare" (Clement of Alexandria); it "illuminates" secret proceedings.[20] It is the repository where our records are kept, our *secretarium*.[21] Inaccessible to other humans, it is represented as the "wilderness" where the psalmist of Psalm 55:7 longs to flee and be at rest.[22] Its deliveries about ourselves afford security against the hostile or uncomprehending judgments of others.[23] Above all, conscience is the "natural tribunal of judgment."[24] It reproves us, and indeed can be seen as the adversary in Jesus' parable, "come to an agreement with your adversary while you are on the road."[25] It is where we judge ourselves before judging another, the site at which we receive reward and punishment, and find assurance of true penitence and pardon.[26]

Sometimes, especially in the Greek tradition, conscience is conceived as an addition to our human rational capacities, "something divine" placed in our minds by God. In that case the conscience is always good, and the danger lies simply in stopping it up, as the Philistines did to Jacob's well.[27] More normally,

---

conscientia that gave the notion a significantly wider sense. In what follows Lampe may be consulted for Greek references not attributed in full.

16. *Sermones de Anna* 1.3.

17. Dorotheos of Gaza, *Didaskaliai* 3.40

18. Chrysostom, *Hom. in Rom.* 5 ad 2:16.

19. Cf. Origen, *Comm. Rom.* 6: *Aperte hic naturalem legem dicit tamdiu ignorari a nobis, quamdiu aetatis processu noverimus inter bonum et malum discernere et a conscientia nostra audierimus. Loquitur enim nobis intra conscientiam et dicit 'non concupisces'.*

20. Dorotheos of Gaza, *Didaskaliai* 3.40.

21. Augustine, *De Genesi contra Manichaeos* 2.5.6.

22. Augustine, *Enarr. Ps.* 54.9; *Sermo* 47.11, 23.

23. Tertullian, *De carne Christi* 3; Ambrose, *De officiis* 1.5.18; Cassian, *Collationes* 21.22.

24. Basil, *Hom. in princ. Prov.* 9.

25. Dorotheos of Gaza, *Didaskaliai* 3.41.

26. Augustine, *Sermo* 13.6.7; Ambrose, *De officiis* 3.4.24; Cassian, *Collationes* 20.5.

27. Dorotheos of Gaza, *Didaskaliai* 3.40.

however, and especially in the West, conscience is a human faculty within the mind, or sometimes a synonym for the mind itself. An influential passage of Jerome introduces it (under the name *synteresis*) as the fourth and most authoritative part of the soul, which corrects the rational, appetitive, and passionate parts when they go wrong.[28] Reflection is "return to our conscience"; it is the bedroom to which we retire for rest; the stomach of the inner man.[29] In this line of thought the conscience may be either good or bad. We pray to be found with it "unstained" in the last judgment.[30] The bad conscience "pursues itself," and there is no further inward space to which we can flee to escape its torments.[31] On the last day it will act as our executioner.[32] Either way, conscience involves awareness not only of ourselves, but of God (Clement of Alexandria). Its abyss is exposed to God, and God sets his throne in the conscience of the just.[33] And so it is frequently associated with prayer. It fortifies our confidence in petition for forgiveness, and speaks in a voice that God hears.[34] It ferries the intentions of our prayers straight to God.[35]

In summary, the patristic idea of "conscience" was that of an inner space created within the seat of human agency, the heart. It is captured by Ambrose's observation that "David the prophet taught us that we should go about in our heart as though in a large house; that we should converse with it as with some trusted companion."[36] Conscience is our self-opening to the probing interrogation and challenge of an encounter with God. The difficulty with the patristic conscience is the absence of reflection on the relation of this inner discourse to the Paschal mystery. The application to the conscience of the death and resurrection of Christ, as in Hebrews and 1 Peter, drops out of sight, so that the encounter with God often seems to be removed from the trinitarian field of vision that characterizes patristic theology otherwise.

A considerable change occurs in the scholastic discussions. As Potts noted, they are only remotely attached to Scripture; to which we may add that they have a very narrow base in patristic tradition, too.[37] Absent now is all mention of encounter with God. Conscience is discussed as a human function, exclu-

---

28. *Comm. in Ez.* 1.1.

29. Augustine, *Ep.* 106.4; *Enarr. Ps.* 33.8, 35.5; *Tract in Ioh.* 32.4.

30. Basil, *Hom. Ps.* 33.4.

31. Augustine, *Tract in Ioh.* 41.4; *Enarr. Ps.* 30.1.8.

32. Gregory of Nyssa, *De beatitudinibus* 5.

33. Augustine, *Confessions* 10.2.2; *Enarr. Ps.* 45.9.

34. Gregory of Nyssa, *De oratione dominica* 4; *De vita Moysis* 2.118.

35. Clement of Alexandria, *Stromateis* 7.7.

36. *De officiis* 3.1.

37. Timothy C. Potts, *Conscience in Medieval Philosophy* (Cambridge: Cambridge University Press, 1980), p. 61.

sively moral and primarily directive, by which the mind grasps and applies moral principles. Divided into two correlated aspects called *synderesis* and *conscientia*, the relation between which is variously explained, conscience is a discursive process of thought starting in universal principle and concluding in actual judgment. It is, as such, both fallible and corrigible. Behind the famous discussions of whether the mistaken conscience "binds" are the radical claims of Abelard for the invincible ignorance that removes the character of sin.[38] The elusive scholastic conclusion that the mistaken conscience binds without excusing, amounts simply to this: to exercise the faculty of moral judgment implies being subject to moral obligation, but a sense of moral obligation does not always correspond to objective right. The reason that a mistaken conscience binds is that conscience binds; that is what the exercise of conscience is, and if it did not lay us under obligation, it would not be conscience. The phenomenon of the mistaken conscience is to generate a subjective obligation at odds with the real relations of right and wrong; that is what an erroneous conscience does, and if it did not lead us to do wrong, it would not be erroneous. If this appears to place the moral agent in a no-win situation, that creates a dilemma, but it is not a logical contradiction; for the conclusions of conscience are not a once-for-all matter, and they may and must be conscientiously reviewed. Changing one's mind, too, can be an obligation of conscience. Precisely because our conscience is a persisting power or disposition of the mind, the first obligation under which it lays us is the obligation to go on using it, to keep on asking the moral question.[39]

The problematic element in the legacy of scholasticism was the separation of the moral conscience from the devotional heart. And there was a further move that was to prove ambiguous: to credit its *a priori* grasp of moral first principles with a necessity like that of the reason's acceptance of logical first principles. Error, they were inclined to think, arises only in secondary, contingent judgments about what is good *in fact*. Yet even so our fundamental moral apperceptions can be faulty in the way that the appetitive power, as opposed to the intellective power, can be faulty: by being too weak, by holding back "in suspense," rather than committing itself.[40]

---

38. *Scito te ipsum*, 1.110-31. The actual use of the word *conscientia* occurs only once in the work, in a section-title which, attested by only one family of manuscripts, may not be original.

39. Thomas Aquinas, *Summa Theologiae* II-1.19.5f. For other early scholastic texts see Potts, *Conscience in Medieval Philosophy*.

40. Cf. J. Gerson, *De mystica theologia* 1.13: *simplex intelligentia sicut non potest dissentire talibus veritatibus agnitione habita quid termini significent, ita non potest synderesis nolle positive principia prima moralium, dum sibi per intelligentiam monstrata sunt. Utrum vero possit ea non velle, hoc est in suspenso tenere se, communis oppinio affirmativam partem tenet.*

With Luther interest in the conscience swung back from the prospective exercise of practical reason to the retrospective experience of guilt, which afforded an opportunity for a striking recovery of its theological and soteriological content. The deliveries of the conscience were now the judgments of God. What Baylor calls "the new object of conscience" is God's "simultaneous condemnation and justification of the person as he stands before God." In this there are two features to notice: on the one hand, the conscience has extended its focus once again to include the encounter with God; on the other, the self to which the conscience turns, and with which it identifies itself, is an eschatologically unified self, a "spirit" that transcends the body and the mind in an immediacy of non-discursive worship.[41] With God and salvation restored to it, conscience now goes beyond reflection; it dissolves into the immediacy of faith. In sixteenth-century Protestantism, then, the conscience resumed its place in Christian language about salvation; biblical language about the conscience washed in Christ's blood and raised from death in his resurrection became current again. When William Perkins wrote a book on "the case" of conscience, he did not mean to discuss what Robert Sanderson would discuss under the title "cases of conscience" a century later, i.e., moral dilemmas. The proper concern of the believer's conscience was, for him as for Calvin, the assurance of salvation.[42]

However, the primarily theological use of the concept of conscience did not persist. The scholastic limitation of conscience to the objects of practical reason was soon reasserted, but with a perilous difference: immediacy, having attached itself while the conscience attended to the last things, clung to it when it returned to human practical concerns. Here, then, were the conditions under which the morally directive conscience became peremptory. In the second half of the seventeenth century we find Jeremy Taylor, a typical Renaissance assembler of Christian and classical quotations, joining the scholastic conception of the conscience with that of the immediate presence of God. The synthesis is achieved by describing the conscience as God's "deputy." Classical talk of conscience as "God unto us" is edifying, but not literal, Taylor thinks. The conscience is an aspect of God's providential government: "God is in our hearts by his laws; he rules in us by his substitute, the conscience." On the one hand, then, the conscience is an element of the created human mind, not the

---

41. Michael G. Baylor, *Action and Person* (Leiden: Brill, 1977), especially pp. 198-200, on the Holy of Holies in the 1521 *Sermon von dreierlei gutem Leben, das Gewissen zu unterrichten*.

42. Cf. Calvin, *Institutes* 3.19.2: "the consciences of believers, while seeking the assurance of their justification before God, must rise above the law, and think no more of obtaining justification by it."

Holy Spirit within it. It is we who speak to ourselves in the deliveries of our conscience, which is "our mind thus furnished with a holy rule and conducted by a divine guide." On the other hand, conscience is not, as in the scholastics, an ordinary human mental function like the others; it has an exalted intermediary status as "God's watchman and intelligencer" — the hint of angelology in this description should not be missed. Yet this mediatorial role is not related in any specific way to the mediation of Christ. Conscience is the image of God, and reflects the Trinity as compounded of memory, understanding, and will; but this is the immanent, not the economic Trinity. Conscience "is in God's stead to us to punish and to reward," but not to redeem or console. The scholastic parallelism of *ratio* and *synderesis* opens up here into a yawning gulf between conscience and faith: "faith tells us why, conscience tells us what we are to do."[43]

We are thus presented with a voice in the soul that immediately and simply, independently of reason, without appeal to the Gospel, commands us in the name of God, and sanctions its commands with torments of anxiety and fear. The discursive character of conscience, preserved in the patristic conception by the image of space and in the scholastic treatment by the discursive progression from *synderesis* to *conscientia,* has now disappeared. Instead, we hear that half-mythical voice whose authority the moral-sense philosophers would have us "enforce upon ourselves" in tribute to "that ancient precept, *Reverence thyself!*"[44]

Modern man is distinguished by sudden eruptions of raw moral certainty, moments of moralistic and ideological judgment which permit no reflective or deliberative interrogation. These moments aside, modern man is distinguished by a resolute and inexhaustible self-doubt. For moral certainty is located on the horizon of thought and action; it is a goal of perpetual approximation, an ideal indefinitely deferred. What we most commonly see when we look at "the modern subject," then, is not the absolute clarity of immediate knowledge, but labored detachment, the ascetic subjection of the self as an object of scientific description, the painstaking stripping-off of layers of decep-

43. *Ductor Dubitantium or The Rule of Conscience* 1.1.1-10.

44. Butler, *Sermons,* preface 19, ed. Gladstone, p. 14. The account of the development of conscience which I gave in *Resurrection and Moral Order* (Leicester: Apollos; Grand Rapids: Eerdmans, 1986), pp. 114-20, now seems to me too unsympathetic to the earlier phases of the tradition and too ready to dispense altogether with the task of reflective self-examination. The critical points made there, however, strike me as valid in relation to the early-modern conscience.

tion, the constant battle of wits to penetrate the smokescreens of the self by ever more resourceful self-censure. Modernity is known by its reflectivity, yet this is not the reflectivity that Christianity shaped. It is not formed by hopeful attention to the inner dialogue with God, but by the incessant and disappointing struggle to get to the core of things, to occupy a position of strategic command. Kierkegaard understood this very well: reflection, he thought, had turned into "reflective stagnation," and it was the essential form of despair.[45]

It is not the natural sciences that form the essence of modern knowing, but the human sciences: every woman her own psychologist, every man his neighbor's anthropologist. The natural sciences, indeed, have been threatened with incomprehensibility by the relentless drive to self-transcendence in the human sciences. In the natural sciences transcendence is given naturally; it is the relation of the human observer to the non-human object of observation. The scientific abstraction from teleology is at home in an interaction where observation, not cooperation, is the rule. Among the questions which natural science cannot answer, then, is that of its own value. That is a question for practical reason, and the confidence of natural science relies on the supposition that there is a secure answer to it. But with the preoccupation of practical reason in the systematic doubting of itself, the coherence of natural science as a human endeavor becomes obscure. The comically tortured posture of late-modern scientism is to find moral and intellectual dignity only in a posture that excludes the admission of all moral and intellectual dignity.

Driven by doubt, this reflectivity can never reach its point of rest. It oscillates between the exertion of "the will," which is what remains when love is drained of knowledge, and the speculations of "theory." (The change that overtook the word "theory" is eloquent: for Aristotle it spoke of contemplation, but in modernity it came to mean a purely provisional hypothesis.) Perpetually oriented to the elusive moment of immediacy, the modern subject stands aloof from his own kind, reflecting

---

45. *A Literary Review*, trans. A. Hannay (Harmondsworth: Penguin Books, 2001), p. 86: "Reflection is not the evil, but the reflective condition and stagnation in reflection are the abuse and the corruption that, by transforming the prerequisites into evasions, bring about regression." *Sickness unto Death*, trans. W. Lowrie (Princeton: Princeton University Press, 1941), p. 194: "Despair over the earthly . . . is really despair also about the eternal and over oneself. . . . this is the formula for all despair."

objectively upon it, subordinating it to the logic of affective detachment, holding back from participation. The modern subject does not, like the traditional Christian soul, withdraw from the world to be conformed to the image of a self-communicating God, and so become similarly self-communicative. For the God the modern subject seeks is a God reduced to absolute will. If we were to ask a thoughtful Christian of the Enlightenment, such a one, say, as John Bampton, Canon of Salisbury, in what respects the emergent "modernity" appeared to him in a threatening and dangerous light, we would probably be told that the peril lay in Deism or Unitarianism. And perhaps, after all, that provides the most revealing genealogy of modernity that there has yet been.

The subject thus in course of constant self-construction is "unsituated." As Robert Spaemann has expressed it, it "is defined by its consciousness. It has no face."[46] It cannot view itself as more than circumstantially party to any human relation, for the subject's relations, like everything else that surrounds it, are reduced to a hypothesis. Consider the plot of Da Ponte and Mozart's *Così Fan Tutte,* a light-hearted eighteenth-century manifesto for enlightenment by self-knowledge. Events unfold under the manipulative control of Don Alfonso, an older man who, scornfully observing the naïve infatuation of two young men, talks them into an experiment that will reveal the very plastic quality of their beloveds' affections, and incidentally of their own. Who is Don Alfonso? Not someone who has ever loved! He is simply the representation of an abstraction: he speaks for the ambition of the two young men for self-transcendence, their aspiration to be liberated from the first immediacy of erotic emotion. (The ambiguity of the aspiration is suggested by the cooperation between Alfonso and the debauched maid Despina, whose interests lie wholly in the hedonistic possibilities of temporary attachments.) The experiment works as planned; the young men's darlings are subjected to the test of absence and persuaded to fall for two romantic strangers, who are the same two men but the wrong way round. The youths gain their bitter insight, and learn that human emotions are neither infinite nor eternal. And then? The curtain falls, leaving us to imagine what kind of marriages could possibly follow such a courtship. We should not, of course, be so humorless as to take the plot as though it recommended emotional exploitation; but to take it

46. *Personen* (Stuttgart: Klett-Cotta, 1996), p. 144.

humorously is to appreciate the point of the puzzle it poses so neatly: how can mature self-knowledge as the Enlightenment conceives it be compatible with free and unforced loving relations?

For as long as the absoluteness of the Christian revelation was taken for granted, the lofty superiority of the subject from society hardly seemed to matter, since for conscience's sake, or for the will of God, the individual would perform everything and more that society expected of him. He was serviceable to society's political organs, too. Habits of self-direction and self-judgment relieved government of some of the weight of its ordinary burdens of passing judgment; but more importantly, the subjective capacity to conceive and respond to the will of God as a sufficient reason for doing right and a sufficient justification for suffering pain, relieved society of another burden, which it could never bear and was never meant to, that of justifying right action and patient suffering. A recurrent line of Protestant polemic used to boast that the greater success of Protestantism in cultivating the conscience accounted for the capacity of Protestant nations to develop economically and technologically. Half of this may be discounted as merely self-congratulatory. The other half has a measure of ambiguous truth, which lies in the Reformation's success in unlocking the introspective energy of monastic spirituality and giving it wider currency in piety outside the cloister. But the very means by which this was achieved tended to make it short-lived. How long could introspective prayer remain a social force once the protecting walls that had nurtured it were torn down?

The modern subject's service to society was at the cost of undermining the authority of society's institutions. Affective independence made all authorities irrelevant, as though the final redundancy of politics had come about already. Its serviceability was not on neighborly terms; it did not acknowledge the authority of the communicative tradition. The subject became, at best, the agent of God to recreate the world, at worst a surrogate god. Skepticism over social forms is endemic to the modern project, and as the lordly posture of the individual has grown steadily less disciplined by awe of the divine, the decay of earthly authority has been its inevitable fruit. But that is not the worst of it. Sovereignly abstracted from cosmic dependence upon God and fellowship with neighbors, the conscientious individual has also been cut off from the worldliness of moral order; and since the order of creation is the only point of reference to judge what it is good for created beings to do, he is left with no recourse to practical reason. In the naïve, categorical phase of modernity the effect was to heighten the separation of faith and reason: the commands of God were absolute, unrelated to the world in which they were given; they required obedience without making sense, sanctioned wholly by rewards and punishments.[47] In the later, historical phase of modernity the divine commands were dissolved into human constructs, and the subject was left with nothing but his own self-positing to guide him, a conscience without material content. To this debacle of the practical intelligence we give the name "moral relativism."

*   *   *

The conscientious individual as conceived by modernity is a distorted version of something genuinely redemptive, the evangelical summons to be judge of ourselves. The self-judging Christian is, of course, good for society and its organs of judgment. But this is not because political authority has, as it were, fashioned such an individual to its own preferred shape. On the contrary, the presence of the self-judging believer in its midst is a warning of its own ultimate redundancy, when all human judgment will be swallowed up in the glad assent of redeemed mankind to the judgments of God in the triumph of the Lamb, where the whole content of the human good is found and our existence justified to us. The self-judging believer, precisely for that reason, is not an isolated individual, but a social one. He, or she, is the "just man" of whom the prophet spoke, who "lives by faith" (Hab. 2:4): a believer in the self-communicating God, a citizen of the eschatological city, a member of the church of Jesus Christ, a situated individual, who transcends society only within the terms of the vis-à-vis of church and world. To restore the true form of the individual subject is to recover the proper relation in which the believer stands to the church.

Reinhard Hütter has offered a concise summary of the post-liberal

47. Cf. John Locke, "Of Ethick in General" 12: "To establish morality therefor upon its proper basis & such foundations as may carry an obligation with them we must first prove a law which always supposes a law maker one that has a superiority & right to ordeyne & also a power to reward & punish according to the tenor of the law establishd by him." *Writings on Religion,* ed. Victor Nuovo (Oxford: Oxford University Press, 2002), p. 14.

consensus on this relation: "It is not the subject that is the end of the church, but the church that is the end of the subject."[48] The noun "end" is meant teleologically; but carries the suggestion, too, that to each end there corresponds a means. In denying that the subject is the church's end, Hütter denies that the church's significance is exhausted as a means to the good of individual believers. Its communications do not reach their term in its members, in the way that, for example, the educational communications of a school reach their term in the students, or the care offered in a hospital reaches its term in the patients. This denial is certainly neither wrong nor unnecessary. It takes aim at what I have elsewhere called "angel ecclesiology," a conception that vaunts the authority of the church at the cost of making it a provisional instrument to the perfection of the individual.[49] The church, in that conception, is like the law in St. Paul, a nursemaid that nags and restrains, counsels and commands, until the child grows up. It is a hairsbreadth balance whether we think, as liberal Protestants think, that after all the child *has* grown up and can do without the nursemaid now, or, as conservative Catholics think, that the child still needs her. Either way, the conclusion is the same: the child is to grow up to act without the nursemaid, the believer is to achieve freedom from the church. This is not the ecclesiology of the New Testament.

What of the positive aspect of the thesis, that the church is the end of the subject? It is not intended to suggest that the church abolishes the subject; rather, that the subject is fully accounted for, its significance wholly satisfied, by the church. The subject is a "means," a contributory element, to the community. Whether we are satisfied with this depends on how we interpret the relation of means to end — for the apparent clarity of these terms is liable to break down into a spectrum of different ideas. We may interpret it here as a kind of socialization-thesis: the subject that begins in separate and isolated self-possession emerges as a situated subject, determined by relations within the community. There is a transition from abstract individuality to concrete sociality; the one state is left behind as the other is acquired.

But we should measure this conception against the practice of baptism, for baptism focuses, as nothing else can, the relation of the be-

48. *Bound to Be Free* (Grand Rapids: Eerdmans, 2004), pp. 43f.
49. *Resurrection and Moral Order,* pp. 164f.

lieving individual to the believing community. In baptism we see paradigmatically represented the encounter between the faith of the church and the faith of the individual who embraces and confesses it. The believer is fulfilled by incorporation in the church. But incorporation presupposes belief, not belief incorporation. If belief presupposed incorporation, what state of mind could we attribute to the baptismal candidate? There can surely be no neutral state, in which the individual is as though stripped bare of the social relations determined by sin but not yet clothed in the social relations determined by faith. For if that were the case, faith would be something subsequent to renouncing sin, a second stage, and the candidate who had renounced sin would be in the curious position of simply choosing whether to believe or not. From time to time the Western tradition has stumbled into such a conception, only to appreciate its impossibility in the light of God's grace; it is the essence, perhaps, of what came to be known as "Molinism." The individual is never abstracted from relations in that sense. It is *as* a believer that the individual is baptized, already conditioned by the faith which God has brought to birth in him or her as an individual. But that faith is not a different faith, distinct from and waiting to be added to the faith of the church. It is already the faith of the church. Being incorporated in the community does not mean changing from an individual to a corporate faith. The individual, *qua* believer, is already of the church when he is joined to the church in baptism. Nor does the believer within the church cease at any point to be the individual disciple who was first called to "take up his cross . . . daily" (Luke 9:23).

This leads us, then, to reformulate Hütter's positive thesis. Rather than say that the community is the end of the subject, we should say that *the subject is realized in the church, the church completed in the subject.* So Paul and his apostolic companions claim to address their instruction and counsel to "each individual," in order to present each individual "fully realized" in Christ. This includes attention to the inwardness of the individual, to the "inner man" that is to be mastered by the Spirit of God, that Christ "may dwell in your hearts by faith."[50] These

---

50. Col. 1:28: νουθετοῦντες πάντα ἄνθρωπον καὶ διδάσκοντες πάντα ἄνθρωπον . . . ἵνα παραστήσωμεν πάντα ἄνθρωπον τέλειον ἐν Χριστῷ. Eph. 3:16f.: κραταιωθῆναι διὰ τοῦ Πνεύματος αὐτοῦ εἰς τὸν ἔσω ἄνθρωπον, κατοικῆσαι τὸν Χριστὸν . . . ἐν ταῖς καρδίαις ὑμῶν.

are subjective experiences that form the goal of the apostolic ministry, but subjective experiences that draw the one affected into a new objective reality: "to be renewed in the spirit of your mind, to put on the new man which has been created in God's fashion in righteousness and holiness of truth" (Eph. 4:24). In correspondence to these forms of subjective progress, "the whole body grows with the growth of God" (Col. 2:19).

The incorporation of the believer into the church's faith, then, is an event of personal faith. The individual, governed by the inner control of the Holy Spirit, discovers that what is common to the church, the knowledge of mankind's salvation wrought in Christ, is acutely and precisely true for him or her. In loving and choosing mankind in Christ, God has loved and chosen me. I am the mankind Christ died for. In raising mankind to new life, God raised me to new life. The reiterated "for me" — "as though all that he did, or suffered, had been done, and suffered for my soule alone" — is the effect of participation in a body of which I am, in fact, by no means the only one.[51] What is the meaning of "as though"? It abstracts a moment in a process of the renewal of community — a real moment, not a fictive projection, but only a moment, which depends on the other moments preceding and following. In my incorporation into the community, the whole community flows into me. My experience of my salvation is determined at every point by the saving experience of the community, and the experience of the community extends at every point into my experience of salvation. My knowledge of myself is made new, as though I had not known myself before, stretched out to fill the dimensions of the new man in Christ, who is not distributed and divided among us in partial lots, but is wholly present in each, equally present in all.

Here we must recall the extended contrast developed by St. Paul between two kinds of "practical conception" *(phronēma)*, that of "the flesh" and that of "the spirit" (Rom. 8:4-16). The conception of the flesh is a kind of worldly immediacy, not the first immediacy of sense and instinct, but a reflective immediacy. It is practical reason consciously throwing itself upon the world as the senses and instincts deliver it, refusing the internal conditions of true reasoning, and so em-

51. John Donne, *The Sermons of John Donne*, ed. George R. Potter and Evelyn M. Simpson, vol. 2 (Berkeley: University of California Press, 1955), sermon 2.9, p. 211.

bracing death. The "conception of the spirit," on the other hand, is a practical disposition that has entered fully into the internal dialogue of the human spirit with the Spirit of God. The spiritual conception accepts direction from within, which is not, however, self-direction. Here is the dialogue of "conscience" in its true form: "the Spirit of God joining with our own spirit" in a discovery of our powers of agency, as "sons of God." This dialogue "adopts" us into the family-relations of the godhead in the economy of salvation: we call on God as Father, as his Son calls on him; we share the wealth of his presence together with the glorified Christ. And the experience of our own lives takes on a shape like his, that of suffering that leads to glorification. The alternative to the dialogue of spirit and Spirit, Paul tells us, is not an absence of spirit, but a spirit of dependent fear. Fear of what, and for what? It is the fear that accompanies the struggle of the fragile and unsupported self to exist alone, a fear for the self and a fear of everything and everyone, seeing the whole world, even God himself, as an enemy and predator.

St. Paul takes up his discussion of the alternative practical conceptions a little later (Rom. 12:3-16), speaking of a "sober conception" *(sōphronein)*, won by detachment from the conformist pressures of the world, which avoids an "inflated conception" *(huperphronein)*. The inflated conception is that of the solipsistic, frozen "I": the conception of the self's transcendence of others *(hupsēla phronein)* or of the self's apartness and self-sufficiency *(phronimoi par' heautois* 12:16). The sober conception is proportioned to a "measure of faith" that God gives to each. That is to say, the sense of self as agent is fully situated within a knowledge of God's redeeming work in one body which has many members. And so the sober conception opens into a practice of communication with others at every level: "rejoice with those who rejoice, weep with those who weep" (12:15). The sense of being "I," of being blessed with the benefits that God pours on mankind in Christ, leads straight into a sense of "we." The more I conceive myself correctly as an agent before God, the more I discern the path of my agency as intersecting and interweaving with other paths, as occupying a particular position in the world that does not belong to everybody else, with particular obligations that do not weigh on other people. Deliberation about my responsibilities makes me one of a multitude again; but not as if I had discovered the impracticability of my youthful heroic ideals and settled down to a conformist middle age, but because I conceive myself *within* the multitude as the site of a personally unique experience.[52]

The subject is realized in the church, the church completed in the subject. That is to say something more than that the believer needs the church and the church needs the believer. It is to say that the individual who judges of himself bears within himself the full self-consciousness of the church's communicative vocation, acquiring a moral identity conferred by the eternal *polis* to which he belongs. And in doing so, he completes the church, replicating its communications within the "heart," i.e., by reflection and self-consciousness before God. "Above all the heart must bear the longest part" — the longest part, that is, precisely *of* the church's psalm-shouting, and by bearing its part the heart prevents the psalms from being *mere* shouting. Psalms mediated through the heart bring back into the church a self-awareness and obedient will that belongs originally to the powers of the soul. The church is thus carried onward and inward in the vocation of the eschatological Bride. This is the sense in which we may speak properly of the church as "invisible." The visible form of community is impressed upon the invisible life of subjective inwardness, down into the depths of the heart, to be restored at the last to full visibility when the secrets of all hearts are disclosed.

A doctrine taught by William of Ockham, of importance in the period antecedent to the Reformation, was that the visible church could be present in just one member alone; and though she were wholly apostate otherwise, the gates of hell would not prevail against her.[53] We could say that Kierkegaard's insight — and perhaps his temptation — was to see how this doctrine, conceived to account for error in the official organs of the church, corresponded to a kind of necessary truth about practical reason. The believer must, in the logic of discipleship, behave "as though" he or she were alone, as though all the rest had fled as they fled from Christ in Gethsemane. Does this "as though" deliver us back to the affective independence of Fénelon's saint, who suffers as though God's saving will were in doubt? No: in the first place, the

52. Cf. C. S. Lewis, *Letters,* ed. W. H. Lewis (London: Geoffrey Bles, 1966), p. 242: "I would prefer to combat the 'I'm special' feeling not by the thought 'I'm no more special than anyone else', but by the feeling, 'Everyone is as special as me.'"

53. See A. S. McGrade, *The Political Thought of William of Ockham: Personal and Institutional Principles* (Cambridge: Cambridge University Press, 1974), pp. 47ff.

apostasy of the church is not an impossibility like the apostasy of God; in the second place, even this possible supposition can only be hypothetical, whereas for Fénélon the desolation of the saint under testing was "in some sense absolute."[54] In being open to the isolation of Elijah, the believer may never forget the prophet's rebuke at 1 Kings 19:18. Was this, perhaps, Kierkegaard's mistake at the end?

In taking up a posture of faithfulness before otherwise total apostasy, the believer accepts the task of the church in the world, and so continues the transmission of the church, mediating it and purifying it. Obedience to Christ requires this reflective discernment, the inward appropriation of the heart, "apart from" the supportive consolations of the visible community. Through the faithful individual, then, the church obeys the command, "Do not be conformed to this world, but be transformed by the renewal of your mind" (Rom. 12:2). St. Paul could write of "divisions" *(haireseis)* necessary for "the genuine" *(dokimoi)* to become evident (1 Cor. 11:19). That there should be times of testing in which Christians are divided against Christians, and in which the question of where true Christianity lies is thrown wholly upon the reflective individual to discern, serves the final disclosure of the church itself, which has its deepest continuity in a line of faithful apostolic transmission of belief from the heart, not in any other type of institutional succession. Such events do not bring the church to an end. On the contrary, they demonstrate the truth of the promise about the gates of hell.

In observing this we are helped to see how the church both is and is not a "political" society. The Holy Spirit in the church does what the rulers of the nations do in their societies: he judges between the genuine and the false, the *dokimoi* and the *adokimoi*. This is not something that any *episkopos* could do; for the work of oversight lies solely with the authentication and safeguarding of the transmission of word and fellowship. So the church "judges not," yet it is judged. It has no prince to judge for it, yet it consists of those who will "judge for themselves," each member passing judgment before the word of God on his or her own disobedience in repentance and faith. Here is the anonymous

---

54. *Explication des Maximes* 10, in *Oeuvres* I, ed. J. Le Brun (Paris: Gallimard, 1983), p. 1035: "Tous les sacrifices que les âmes les plus désintéressés font d'ordinaire sur leur béatitude éternelle sont conditionels. . . . Il n'y a que le cas des dernières épreuves où ce sacrifice devient en quelque manière absolu."

"conqueror" of the letters to the churches in the Apocalypse, a figure very much in the singular, alone and without the support of the community, but who turns out to have a social identity after all: "he who conquers, I will make him a pillar in the temple of my God. I will write on him the name of my God and the name of the city of my God, the new Jerusalem which comes down from my God out of heaven, and my own new name" (Rev. 3:12).

In the kingdom of heaven, when the rulers of the nations cast their crowns before the throne of the Lamb, the institutions of judgment will be redundant. And so will be the counter-political institutions of the church itself. There is no temple, we are told, in the new Jerusalem (Rev. 21:22). The sacraments themselves are to pass away in the fullness of sight. The lucid truth of self-knowledge in the light of the knowledge of God shows us the mutually enfolding love and justice of the kingdom of heaven, the heart of our social existence.

Index of Names and Titles of Anonymous Works

Index of Subjects

Index of Scriptural References